FAST COMPANY
Six Decades of Racers, Rascals and Rods

"Speedy" Bill Smith
with Dave Argabright

FAST COMPANY

By "Speedy" Bill Smith
with Dave Argabright

© 2009 Dave Argabright

ISBN-13: 978-0-9719639-6-2
ISBN-10: 0-9719639-6-7

Published by:
American Scene Press
P.O. Box 84
Fishers, IN 46038
www.americanscenepress.com

Front cover image of Speedy Bill by Doug Auld
All photos appear courtesy of the Smith Collection unless
otherwise noted

Printed with pride in the USA by Print Communications, Inc.
Indianapolis, Indiana

Acknowledgements

This book would not be possible without the generous help of a great number of people.

To begin, Joyce Smith was an indispensible help at every turn. She was a key proofreader, and assisted greatly as Bill and I recounted the many stories that comprise *Fast Company*. She showed remarkable organization and patience, and kept the project going through the early stages, always the most difficult period with an effort like this. Joyce is a first-class sweetheart, and working with her was a pleasure.

Ken Schrader and Dr. Dick Berggren kindly agreed to provide the Foreword and Introduction, respectively, and both were a delight to work with.

Several people at Speedway Motors helped with various elements, particularly Geri Braziel as she searched and coordinated the effort to provide the photos needed to illustrate the project. Despite her busy workload at Speedway, Geri was always there with quick turnaround of whatever was asked. Damon Lee was responsive and helpful as well.

A number of people helped with background information, most notably Bob Mays of Speedway Motors. Bob is a premier historian, and he helped with the clarification of several dates and places that were obscured slightly by the fog of time, and provided many photos as well. Bob Wilson and Bill Wright of Knoxville Raceway also helped with some important statistics. Good friend Steven Cole Smith, formerly of *Car and Driver* magazine, provided some most helpful background on the Dale car.

Doug Auld of *Sprint Car & Midget* magazine provided the photo of Speedy Bill that graces the cover of *Fast Company*. Doug is a good and loyal friend, and he offered support and encouragement throughout the many months this project spanned.

Corinne Economaki of *National Speed Sport News* once again served as an irreplaceable editor, providing steady guidance and keen insight at every turn.

Many people at Print Communications in Indianapolis, where *Fast Company* was proudly produced, were invaluable partners in the process. Kane Neese once again led the way, coordinating all aspects of the printing and binding operation. Linda Burchett contributed another creative cover design (that's six straight!) and was a delight throughout the process. Others at PCI who continue to be key friends and partners are Mike Herman, Lisa Martin-Spear, and of course the friendly Mary Ott and Laura Shepler who remain the distinctive voices on the telephone.

A number of people helped get the word out on this book, in particular Doug Auld of *Sprint Car and Midget* magazine and Lew Boyd and Cary Stratton of Coastal 181. And kudos to Jeff Walker and Kathie Collins of Jeff's Storage for their ongoing support.

My family was remarkably patient as this project consumed great blocks of time, particularly in the late stages. My wife Sherry and our children were very understanding as the stress and strain of producing this book mounted.

Finally, I wish to thank the loyal readers who continue to support these types of efforts. Producing a book is a scary and difficult proposition, but my readers and friends have steadfastly supported each project I have undertaken, giving me the confidence to continue. Without them, all of this is a moot point, and I continue to be both humbled and moved by their confidence and readership.

Dave Argabright
Fishers, Ind.

Contents

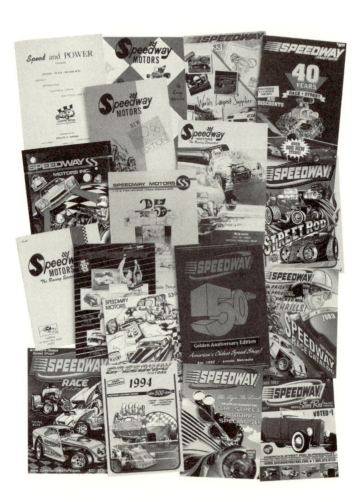

Foreword

It was 1978 or so, and I was a driving a sprint car for Ray Marler. My career was just beginning, and I hadn't wandered too far from home quite yet. We decided to race at Sedalia, Missouri, with NSCA, a Midwestern series that I think was some kind of spinoff from the IMCA.

Ray and I came wheeling into the pit area that night, and parked right next to Speedy Bill Smith and the Speedway Motors No. 4x. Doug Wolfgang was his driver, and I instantly looked over at their operation and said, "Oh, my gosh, this is big-time."

From that moment on, Speedy Bill was one of the guys I admired in our sport. He took a few minutes to talk with me that night at Sedalia, and since then I've always considered him a friend. That's a big deal, because when Bill is your friend, he's a longtime and loyal friend.

As a kid, I had known about the Speedway Motors catalog since, well, forever. It was something you'd see in just about every race shop or garage. I kind of viewed it like some big institutional thing, without a face, until I met Bill. That's when I discovered that behind the company name and the catalog was a guy who loved racing as much as anyone I've ever known.

That's probably the first thing I'd say to describe Speedy Bill. The guy is absolutely passionate about racing, about street rods, about cars. Maybe that's why we immediately hit it off so well; I love those things, too. If you're into racing or hot rods, you've got something in common with Bill whether you've met him or not.

However, Bill was different from most people in one important way: Early on, he figured out how to translate his passion for automobiles into a viable business. Building a business is tough, and Bill has worked hard at this. But I believe one reason he has succeeded is that he never lost sight of his passion for automotive performance. He goes about his business from a different perspective than most. It's not just, "How can I make a buck?" It's more like, "How can I make the industry better?"

You can't talk about Bill and his career without also mentioning his wife Joyce. She has been with Bill every step of the way. They definitely operate as a team, for sure. Like Bill, Joyce has a zest for life, and a great way with people. In fact, Joyce is even more of a people person than Bill. If you're in a room with Joyce and you're breathing, before the night is over she'll have talked to you and made a new friend. That's just how it is.

The second key thing about Bill is his drive, and his fierce determination. He's a very strong person. If he sets his mind out there to do something, he's going to get it done.

But, man, I wouldn't want to be in a position of trying to stop Bill from accomplishing something! He'd be a tough competitor in any arena. I'll bet it wasn't much fun racing against him in those early days, because he's an absolute hardcore guy when it comes to competition, and winning.

Growing up in the Midwest, I definitely knew about the No. 4x. I was aware they could go and win against USAC, and I knew enough to realize that it was really a special thing. It was BIG. That wasn't supposed to happen; he wasn't supposed to go into their backyard and beat them. But he did, and that was something special.

So don't ever try to tell Bill he can't do something. All you're doing is lighting a fire that is going to get awful hot before it's done.

At the same time, he goes about things in the right way, even in a competitive situation. Whether you're talking racing or business or whatever, he's going to get it done without using anybody up in the process. His ethics and his philosophy are a little different than what you see these days; I've seen him introduce a new product that is very reasonably priced, with the idea of making a little bit but not a huge amount, with the goal of taking care of people in the long run.

If I'm going to relate Bill to somebody I've been involved with, I've got to put him right there with Rick Hendrick. They are both hard-core racers who were also smart enough — and with enough foresight — to build a successful business, the right way.

Obviously, Speedway and Bill could have never survived for almost 60 years if he wasn't doing something right. This is a small circle, and people talk. Bill's reputation at Speedway is first class, and always has been.

We have a lot of good "racers." But not very many people are good racers/good businessmen/good family men, all the different categories that Speedy Bill has.

Another thing I find really cool is the fact that Bill's sons are all involved in the business with him. That's neat. Each of the boys ventured out to do other things, and they've all come back. Each one has a little different area of expertise, and it's a great fit. Plus, it looks like Speedy Bill and Joyce have built a foundation for the business to continue for many years to come.

If I'm anywhere and I find out that Bill is also there, I seek him out immediately. PRI show, SEMA, anything. And I don't exactly know why, but he's called me a few times to ask about this or that. Somehow he took a liking to us I can't explain. He put his arms around me and offered a little bit of guidance, and I was quite honored.

If Bill likes you and trusts you, he's a very loyal friend. It goes past business or racing or whatever; it's all about friendship.

Boy, what a museum he has built! I've visited three or four times in recent years, and I get excited just talking about it. It's like a window into a world I love: motorsports and automotive things, all tied together. I've tried to describe it to people, but I can't. It's just too...amazing, I guess, is the best word I can use. It's a massive collection of meaningful stuff, presented in a way that respects the people behind the items, and excites the passions of any of us who love motorsports and automotive performance. It really is first class in every way.

If I'm anywhere close to Lincoln, they can count on seeing me at Bill's place. Whether it's all day or just having lunch with Bill and Joyce for a couple of hours, I'm there. The museum by itself is fabulous, but if you can tour the place with Bill, that's even better.

I can't wait to read this book. I've heard lots of these stories directly from Bill, and they're great! I can sit and listen to those stories forever, I really can. It was a big-time honor to be asked to write this foreword and be a part of Bill's story.

So Bill and Joyce, thanks for being my friend, and congratulations on putting a lifetime of great experiences down on paper.

Ken Schrader
Championship racer
Concord, N.C.

Introduction

During the 41 years I've covered auto racing, I've met everyone in racing who is important and a lot of people who thought they were important, but weren't.

Lincoln, Nebraska's Speedy Bill Smith is damn important and he's been damn important for more than 50 years.

As he continues to work seven-day weeks, Speedy Bill is the living role model of racing entrepreneurship. His career began when he opened a modest 400-square-foot storefront from which he sold tire chains. His wife provided seed money for the store. Bill has become a one-of-a-kind businessman with his family playing an enormously important support role. His success goes well beyond auto-racing retailing and includes manufacturing, the preservation of the artifacts of several categories of history, real estate, race teams, governance of the sport, hot rods, and even pedal cars.

The sport's insiders look up to Speedy Bill Smith not just for his accomplishments, but because he has done it with his wife, Joyce, and his four sons, each of whom work in the business today. While many families are pleased to get through Thanksgiving dinner without someone hitting someone else with a turkey leg, every day the Smith family, with Bill as its leader, works together as they achieve shared goals.

Although nobody gets to the top of anything without facing hardship, Speedy Bill has been through so much that most people facing what he has faced would have given up long ago. A youthful year spent in a body cast was followed by another in the hospital. He was then badly injured when struck by an errant wheel-and-tire assembly in the pits. There have been recent significant health issues as well. His medical problems have caused Smith to face death several times. Each time, he has courageously fought back to triumphantly return to his many interests. So, the tenacity with which he has focused on his businesses did not come uninterrupted. Medical matters have pulled him away, sometimes when he's needed his health the most. But, he persevered and overcame seemingly insurmountable obstacles.

If all Bill Smith did was build Speedway Motors into America's biggest retailer of hard-core racing equipment, that would have been sufficient for him to have been inducted into several halls of fame. But he has done so much more.

Speedy Bill's is America's foremost a collector and curator of American racing history. He has acquired and restored the finest collection of racing engines in the world. His race car collection includes some of the most historically significant machines in the sport's history. But, there's also a massive pedal car collection, toy tin car collection, monkey wrench collection and even a collection of 33 1/3 rpm records with songs about racing. If all he had done in his life was to have built the collections, Speedy Bill would have been in multiple halls of fame.

There's also a significant real estate empire. It's said he owns half of Lincoln, Nebraska. Locals claim that the other half he doesn't want or he'd have bought it, too.

As a race car owner, Speedy Bill won all of the important races he wanted to win. From the Hulman Classic when it was the most important sprint-car race in the country to championships, Speedy Bill won everything he cared about. He won those races and championships by getting his hands dirty working on the cars himself. From Jan Opperman to Doug Wolfgang, Ron Shuman, and Lloyd Beckman, Speedy Bill's cars were the most desired rides of their day because they ran up front and didn't break. He personally built many of the chassis and engines that won big races.

For those suffering from medical misfortune, Bill Smith is the guiding light who proves there can be decades of health and happiness for those who battle injury and disease with steadfast determination.

Early in my career, I asked a very popular driver who had won multiple championships and hundreds of races to define his greatest accomplishment. I was stunned when he told me it was that he was still around, still competitive after a long career. Surely, I expected to hear about a race he'd won or a championship he'd earned. Time has proven that racer's analysis correct, that longevity trumps every other accomplishment.

Speedy Bill, after all these years, after all of his success, is not only still around, he's still at the top of his game as he has been for decades. He says he'll keep working "until they close the lid on the box," which we hope won't be for a long time. As he keeps working, Speedway Motors is already the oldest race car parts retailer in the world. From its massive catalogs, you can buy everything you need to build a street rod, gaskets for a high-end oval track engine, pedal cars and parts, fuel injection, springs, and technical books.

On the eve of this book going to press, as he blew out the candles on his 80th birthday cake, Bill bought a huge parts manufacturing operation and became involved in a major new racing trade show. He continues to be a visitor to races where features run well after midnight while others much younger than he had gone to bed many hours earlier.

He is a fierce competitor, just like he always was. He is as independent and outspoken today as when I first met him more than 30 years ago. His opinions are sought by many in the business as he is the most important player in each of his many chosen fields of activity.

You are about to have the good fortune to get to know Speedy Bill in this book. Read the book well and take to heart the lessons Speedy Bill's life offers. You won't turn many pages before you'll develop an enormous respect for him and for what he's done. That respect will grow with each chapter. Like me, as you read along, you'll wonder what he might do next.

Dick Berggren
Pit road reporter for NASCAR
on FOX and SPEED channel
Ipswich, Mass.

Good things come from good people. My parents, Mabel and Donald Smith were the best...THANKS!

To my lifelong companion, wife of 57 years, business partner and best friend Joyce, and my four sons: Carson, Craig, Clay and Jason.

It takes a team to make it happen!

1

Showdown

As soon as I drew that pill, I knew. We were being cheated, before we even got started.

Terre Haute, Ind., at the Action Track, May 1, 1976. I'm standing at the pit gate, signing in my race car — the Speedway Motors sprint car, driven by Jan Opperman — for the Tony Hulman Classic, a USAC sprint car race.

I had that sinking feeling in my gut, because I knew we weren't getting a fair shake. The stakes were high: This was the greatest, biggest, most important race in the history of sprint car racing. Am I exaggerating? No. That assessment of the race was made not by me, but by those who observe and study the history of the sport. And in the years following, events transpired to prove that it *was* the most important sprint car race in history.

But there I was, standing there holding a little "pill," which is a small piece of plastic with a number on it. The number determines your position in the qualifying order, which is a critical factor when you're racing on dirt, especially at a daytime race under the bright Indiana sun. The track would dry very quickly in those conditions, and sprint cars don't like a dry track. They like moisture, so they can dig their big tires in for traction.

My driver and I were both entering that race as an outsider. The event was sanctioned by the Indianapolis-based United States Auto Club (USAC), which at the time controlled much of open-wheel racing in America. It literally was organized as a club, and if you weren't a "member," you were not viewed as completely legitimate in the eyes of those who were members.

You even had to be "invited" to race with them. You needed a USAC license to compete; however, the club allowed two unlicensed "outsiders" to come in using what was known as a "Temporary Permit" or "TP." Well, we were one of the chosen two invited to the Terre Haute race. It was Opperman and our friend Bubby Jones, a racer from Illinois.

We were there because of the tremendous fan following Jan Opperman enjoyed. At that moment, he was a great racer, a man of extraordinary talent. He was also a hippie. In 1976, when America was still undergoing great social change, a hippie was quite the controversial figure. Good or bad? Depends on where you stood. Jan had long hair and wore moccasins and talked about Jesus, which certainly made him unique among race drivers. He was also a winner, and that's the factor that *really* led to his huge following of fans.

All of this made Jan a powerful draw at the front gate. That's why we were invited that day; the Terre Haute promoters realized that Opperman would sell lots of tickets. And the atmosphere was sensational, the stuff of Hollywood movies. There was a tremendous conflict in play, that of Opperman — the hippie, the free-spirited outsider — up against the best in USAC — the "establishment" — in a rare showdown on the same race track.

We were very confident we could win. Of course, we knew going in that USAC had some great competitors. Pancho Carter was a great racer, as well as Sheldon Kinser, Tom Bigelow, and Larry Dickson, among others. But I knew my driver was better than all of them. And as always, I was confident in our race car. The Speedway Motors 4x was a potent machine, and had won races throughout the country for many years.

See, that's another thing; I couldn't even use my number, "4x." Even though I had used that number since the late 1940s, USAC required us to renumber the car, because they didn't allow the use of letters. So that day we lettered our car as No. 64. It was just one more annoying issue with USAC and their silly rules.

Jan had been racing my car off-and-on since 1969. We had certainly had our moments, and I fired him more than once. He quit me more than once, too. But we always managed to reconcile because we had something in common. We liked winning. Well, I *loved* winning. Winning was what I was about, and it was as important to me as the blood running through my veins. Whenever I towed my car through a pit gate, I wasn't there to race; I was there to win!

That's why I was so angry when I drew our qualifying pill. We drew a very high number, which meant we would be going out at the tail end of the order. Our chances of cutting a good lap were very, very remote. In my gut, I knew our high number wasn't merely a matter of bad luck. I knew something was up. Sure, I'm cynical. Sure, I'm suspicious. When you've been around as long as I have, and seen all the things I have, it makes you that way. I've seen too many people use their authority and influence to protect their personal interests. And I knew the USAC officials didn't want Jan to win the biggest sprint car race of the season. So they jiggered the draw, and made sure we got a high number. How? They probably had us draw from a different container, which held only very high numbers.

As I headed for our pit, I was steaming. Now we were behind the 8-ball, and winning the race was going to be very difficult. But we weren't beaten quite yet.

Racing and automobiles have been a big part of my life since I was a young boy. I'm a competitive person, and I'm all about winning. Some people might say winning is an obsession with me, and that observation probably isn't too far off. Two things have been a driving force in my life: a passion for success, and a powerful fear of failure. Frankly, I'm not sure which was stronger. I was probably more frightened of failure than anything else.

In those early years, when I was still a teenager in Lincoln, Neb., I built my own race car and drove it myself. But my mother figured out what was going on, and she put her foot down. It was bad enough that her boy was constantly dragging junk cars home to repair, but he wasn't about to get his head torn off by some old race car. So that was final: I wasn't to drive any more.

I honored my mother's wishes, and instead became a car builder, owner, and mechanic. Chief cook and bottle washer, you might say. I worked on the car all week, and hired the best driver I could find to drive it. Sometimes that was for just one night; if the guy couldn't get the job done, you have to send him packing. If he's pretty good, maybe we can race together for a while. I had many drivers down through the years, many of whom had a nice, long tenure in my car.

Finding — and keeping — good drivers is never easy. Drivers are fickle, and I suppose car owners are fickle, too. If I thought another guy could do a better job, I certainly wasn't above firing my driver and hiring the next guy. And a few of my drivers weren't above quitting me to go drive for someone else.

I worked hard to provide the best car possible, and I wouldn't show up if I didn't believe my car could win the race. I wasn't interested in just having a driver; I wanted a *winner*.

Jan Opperman was a winner. From the first moment we met, I could see the intensity and desire in his eyes, and on the track I saw his natural talent. God, he had talent; of all the drivers I've watched through the years—and these old eyes have sure seen some race drivers—he had the most God-given ability. It was natural with Jan; he could do things with the race car and not even know he did them. He didn't have to use his mind; he used the rest of his senses, so much so that he was driving by instinct much of the time.

Despite our terrible draw, Jan came through on his qualifying lap. He qualified fifth, which was outstanding under the circumstances. We would be starting on the front row of the feature event. Now we were back on an even playing field.

I knew we had a good race car, although we had to change several things to be allowed to run with USAC. For example, we ran brakes on only three wheels; USAC required four. We also had to change to 9.5-inch wheels; I don't know how they settled on that number, but I suspect it had more to do with keeping their nucleus of racers different from everybody else than anything. They required me to show papers that the key parts on our car had been "magnafluxed"—that's an X-ray process to detect cracks—which again is another way to turn away "uninvited" cars.

But I jumped through all the hoops, and our car was 100-percent legal. Now it was up to Jan.

For those of us at Terre Haute, we could almost feel the glare of history upon us. Certainly, we felt the eyes of a national audience; the race was broadcast live on ABC's *Wide World of Sports*, which in 1976 was the most popular sports show in the world. These were the days before cable television changed the broadcasting landscape, and *Wide World of Sports* had an enormous audience each Saturday afternoon.

Not only that, but the race shared that day's broadcast with the Kentucky Derby! They opened the show with our heat races, then cut away to Churchill Downs for the Derby. As the Derby finished, the broadcast was back to Terre Haute and our feature event.

That's why this was the most important race in sprint car history. Never before or since has there been such a vast national audience for a sprint car race. Literally tens of millions of Americans were sitting in front of the TV that Saturday afternoon.

The purse was another reason the event was special. A USAC sprint car race in 1976 typically paid anywhere from $500 to $800 to the winner, but this race offered $12,500! It was off the charts in terms of payoff. That's part of the reason we were there; I like to race where the stakes are high, because it's more challenging, and more fun. If we could come in there and win the money, boy, what a feather in our cap!

They had a big gala party the night before, and it seemed like every banker and top businessman from Indianapolis to St. Louis was there. Country singer Charley Pride was at the track on Saturday afternoon to sing, and everything came together to create an atmosphere that was almost electric.

I love that setting. It puts pressure on you to perform, but I thrive under pressure. It's like a drug, and it's the stuff that has fueled racing people since the beginning of time.

There was something else in play that afternoon, something that over time proved to be more important than the money or the prestige of the Tony Hulman Classic.

Sprint car racing was in the midst of a monumental power shift, and this race would prove to be the pivotal moment of that shift. As long as anyone could remember, there had been two categories of racing: USAC, and "outlaw." Outlaws were the guys who raced outside of the USAC sanction, and for many years they were looked upon as inferior.

However, around the mid-1970s a new breed of racer was emerging, and Jan Opperman was far and away the most visible of that new breed. With his long hair and moccasins, and his free spirit personality, he was definitely an outlaw. No doubt about that! Jan, along with a lot of other racers, was finally earning the national respect he deserved, and it had sparked a very heated debate within the sport.

On one side of the debate were the traditionalists. They argued that Jan was overrated, and he couldn't cut it in USAC. Jan had won a lot of races by this time, but they said those wins were meaningless because they came against "weaker competition." (Which was bullshit, but that's another story.) They said guys like Pancho Carter would eat him alive if Jan had the courage to show up and race against him.

On the other side, a growing but fervent group argued that Jan was as good as anybody in USAC. They pointed to his enormous talent, and all those wins, as evidence that he was indeed the real McCoy.

For my part, I got plenty fired up when somebody made the remark that only USAC had the top cars. Oh, really? My cars had been winning around the country since before USAC was launched in 1956, and I took exception to the idea that we were somehow inferior because we didn't race with USAC. And it was guilt by association, because it was implied that not only was Jan Opperman an outlaw, but his car was, too!

The debate went round-and-round, and it all came to a head on that May afternoon at Terre Haute. We came to race against USAC, in its biggest race, at one of its most familiar tracks. In other words, we were now in USAC's back yard.

It was time to put up, or shut up. Well, I'll tell you this much: Speedy Bill Smith wasn't ready to shut up.

Pancho Carter was a young, tough racer in 1976, a talented guy who raced not just for fame and money, but pride. I don't know what was going through Pancho's mind on that day, but I'm sure he felt a lot of pressure. One thing that made Pancho so tough on the race track was that he hated losing. He was a fierce competitor. Plus, much of the talk wasn't just about USAC vs. outlaws, but Pancho Carter vs. Jan Opperman.

When the race started, Jan jumped out into the lead. Almost like a movie script, within two laps Pancho was right there on his tail, driving like an absolute madman. You could almost see the enormous desire on the part of both men. Jan really wanted to win that race, and so did Pancho. And it was more than just personal; both probably wanted to uphold the honor of their respective following.

Our Speedway Motors car had been having quite a season. We had won 34 of our past 46 starts, which in sprint car racing is a very successful average. Our crew—Terry Otero and John Singer—had really done the job getting our car ready for each race. John Larson was building our engines, and Don Maxwell was building our chassis in my shop back in Lincoln.

Jan drove a perfect race, just perfect. And our car performed flawlessly too. We had to be perfect, because Pancho was right there, ready to take advantage of the slightest bobble. Jan stayed right up in the fast groove on the outside, even though that's often a treacherous, rough ride.

There was a late caution flag, with just one lap remaining in the race. You're always nervous on the restart, because anything can happen. We were so close…could Jan hold on?

Pancho was all over him on the restart, but Jan didn't wilt. He made his last lap without a mistake, and crossed the finish line with Pancho right behind.

A moment or two before, things got rough down in turns one and two. Sheldon Kinser and Chuck Gurney got tangled up, and Gurney took a violent, end-over-end ride out of the place. Jan saw Gurney's wrecked car outside the track, and after taking the checkered flag he stopped our car on the track, jumped out, and ran to Gurney's aid.

Pancho drove his car, which was owned by Steve Stapp, back to their pit. He climbed out of the cockpit and literally stepped onto the hood and stomped the fuel injection stacks clear off the car. Seems he was frustrated that the car hadn't performed well enough.

Hey, they aren't out there playing patty-cake; winning consumes you, and when you fall short it's hard to describe just how rotten that feels.

Secretly, I loved seeing Pancho all upset. That's the stuff I thrive on, because I love it when my competitors show their emotions. That's when I know we've done something; we've beaten them in a race that means a lot.

When we stood there on the front straightaway for the victory photos, that was a good feeling. I've won a lot of races in my day, but that afternoon was one of the most satisfying.

From that moment on, sprint car racing was different.

Nobody would ever again question Jan's talent; he had beaten USAC's best. And our car performed perfectly, shooting holes in the theory that USAC had an exclusive on the best cars.

The outlaw element of sprint car racing had been validated. Less than two years later the World of Outlaws sprint car series was formed, holding its first race in Texas. I was at that race, too, with another exciting driver named Doug Wolfgang; but that's a story for another chapter.

Later that fall, Jan was critically injured at the Hoosier Hundred in Indianapolis, and his career was never the same. But his legacy was already set, because he truly was a driving force in changing the course of the sport.

Of course, I wasn't content with just winning the race. Remember the issue of us not getting a fair shake in the qualifying draw? I was still steamed about that, so I took out a full-page ad in *National Speed Sport News* calling out USAC on the topic. I feel that no matter who you are, when you come through the pit gate to race there should be a level playing field. They didn't provide a level playing field — that's the world according to Bill — and that wasn't right.

Like I said, Speedy Bill wasn't ready to shut up.

Deep down inside, adversity fires me up. It gets my blood pumping, and fuels a tremendous amount of desire.

How do you silence your critics? How do you respond when you've been wronged? How do you prove yourself as a competitor, regardless of the circumstances?

Win. That's how. Just win.

2

Early Years

The doctor propped my mouth open, leaning in close as he poked my throat with a small wooden tongue depressor. The smell of antiseptic hung in the air of his small office, located on the fifth floor of a building in downtown Lincoln, Neb. My throat was badly swollen, and it was painful to swallow.

It was 1934, and I was five years old. Our country was deep into the Great Depression, and much of America sat around the radio listening to reports of the FBI's relentless pursuit of gangsters such as John Dillinger and Ma Barker's gang. But I was oblivious to such national matters; all I knew is that I had a very sore throat.

Dr. Rider stepped back and nodded to my mother, standing nearby.

"Those tonsils will have to come out," he said in a matter-of-fact tone, like you'd mention that the sun is shining.

Dr. Rider had been a battlefield surgeon in Europe during World War I, and his way of thinking was that pain didn't matter very much. The concept of "patient comfort" probably never crossed his mind.

While my mom held me, Dr. Rider reached into a nearby drawer and retrieved a tool I'd describe today as a pair of side-cutters. He pried my mouth open and reached back into my throat, and started whacking away.

Anesthesia? Nothing doing. This was quick and dirty surgery, primitive style. In a few minutes he had my tonsils out, and sent me on my way with my mom, who was probably stunned and shaken from the experience.

Why did they take me to this particular doctor? I never asked them, but I assume it was because he was cheap. It wasn't because my folks wouldn't have given me the best; it's just that they didn't have the best to give me. They gave me what they had. They were like everybody else, scratching and clawing to survive the Depression.

My grandfather was staying with us at the time, and I remember getting home and my throat still hurting. My grandfather was something of a vagabond, and he'd come stay at our house when he was out of money. He'd stay a few days and enjoy my mother's cooking, borrow some money from my dad, and be on his way. He was an interesting guy, and he ultimately taught me how to play poker and shoot craps and all the other things a young man of five or six years old should know.

I told my granddad I was thirsty, so he poured me a big glass of orange juice. That's not a good idea for a kid who's just had his tonsils out; I don't think it could have been more painful if you'd poured fire down my throat.

That "battlefield" tonsillectomy had some long-lasting implications. From the time I was in kindergarten to 12th grade, we would have eye, ear, nose and throat examinations each year at school. In would come some sleepy kid who was training to be a doctor, maybe with a nurse helping him, and we'd all line up along the wall to wait our turn.

"All right...open up and say, 'Ahhhh...'"

The doctor and the nurse would gaze intently at someone's throat, then quickly move on to the next kid. But for me it was always the same: The guy would look into my throat, and say something in amazement to the nurse. They'd both look at me for a minute and one would say to me, "Who took your tonsils out?"

"Dr. Rider."

They just laughed and nodded in understanding, then moved on to the next kid.

It took many years for me to understand what they were talking about. When he removed my tonsils, Dr. Rider had also cut off the swinging tissue that hangs from the top of my palate. This controls the air going into your voice box, and it's difficult to speak properly without it. I guess when he was hacking away at those tonsils he cut out anything that got in the way.

That was my first medical adventure, but it wasn't my last. I'm a walking, talking exhibit of the medical profession, a man who has been chopped on and mangled on many occasions. Sometimes the doctors helped me; sometimes they gave me years of misery.

But I'm not complaining. Why complain? I've made it to 80 years old, so all things considered I don't have much to beef about.

I was born in Lincoln in 1929, on June 22. That's the longest day of the year, if you're wondering. I was the only child of Donald and Mabel Bower Smith. My dad worked for the Lincoln Telephone and Telegraph Company, and my mother was a housewife. That's the profession of nearly all women of the era: housewife. Of all the kids I knew, our moms all stayed home to raise their kids and keep the household going.

I had great parents, and I can easily see various traits I picked up from each. My father had an amazing work ethic, and he once worked 13 years straight without missing one minute of work. 13 *years*. Not for sickness, funerals, anything. He would go to work 30 minutes early each day, and he'd stay late if needed. His work ethic was like nobody I've ever known, and I've tried to apply that lesson throughout my working life. Although my work ethic might pale in comparison to my dad's, I've certainly never been afraid of work. My dad worked for 47 years at the same job, and I don't recall once hearing him complain about anything related to his job.

My father was the finest man I've ever known. Naturally, everybody thinks fondly of their father; but in my case, my dad really was a great person. In my lifetime, I never once heard him swear, nor did I ever once see him drunk. He was calm and steady, and he didn't raise his voice toward anyone. He was quite a sports fan, and we often traveled to sporting events together. I enjoyed spending time with my father, because he was such a pleasant person to be around.

Dad was the second-oldest in a family of two boys and two girls. His father sold tombstones via horse-and-buggy throughout the Nebraska territory. They lived in Harvard, Neb., in a big old house. But my grandfather died suddenly when my father was nine years old, and that turned the family's world upside-down.

My grandmother couldn't hold the family together, so she had to put my father to work on a nearby farm in exchange for his room and board. He took his meager belongings to live on the farm, where he was not treated like a member of the family. He lived in the barn, where he would take his meals each day, all alone. That made my father a very quiet person.

I suppose that's what I admire most about my father. He had a dreadful time late in his childhood, and was forced to grow up much earlier than he should have. But instead of becoming bitter and complaining, he quietly rose above his circumstances, and was an excellent student. He was a good athlete and was offered a football scholarship at the University of Nebraska. He declined, because he felt the need to get a job right away and make his way in life.

My father liked things to be in perfect order. Each day he came home from work and took a shower, then went outside to work in the yard, which was nicer than any park you'd ever see. He was very industrious; he'd paint our house and keep everything in tip-top shape. He couldn't trade a $10 bill for a five; he was not a businessman. But he didn't try to take on things he couldn't do. He stayed within his range.

He never once had a charge account, and they paid cash for anything they bought. He'd buy a new car every couple of years, maybe a Plymouth or a Dodge, of course without a radio or heater. He would purchase an aftermarket heater down at Sears, because that was less expensive than the factory option.

It's hard to explain how frugal my parents were. However, that wasn't uncommon among people of that time. I almost laugh when I contrast that to today's society; anything you want, you charge it, right now. No problem. Pay for it later! Or maybe not even pay for it at all.

I learned an awful lot from my dad. They played penny ante poker in our basement, my folks and their friends. I'd sit on a nearby chair, watching them play and listening to the conversation. I'd watch my father, and it was obvious he studied the game very carefully. There would be five guys sitting around the table, and everybody would ante. Then he'd drop out. He might ante and drop out of 10 pots before he'd stay.

I asked him once, "Why don't you stay and play?"

He just looked at me and smiled.

"Because you can't win that way, son," he said. "You have to have the cards to win the game."

And then he said something I'll never forget.

"If you want to win in a game, you'd better know the game, and you'd better know the players."

I've used that observation all my life, probably more than anything else. I didn't try to go to Wall Street to take on the Wall Street gang; I didn't try to go to the Indianapolis 500 and take on that gang. I played games where I knew the players, and I felt I could win the game. You don't win all the games, but you try. I was lucky to hear my father's words during such a formative period in my life.

"Know the game."

From my mother I got tenacity.

My mother was totally loving to me, but she was also a taskmaster. I always feared the wrath of my mother worse than anything. Later in my teenage years, if there was something I thought I might get by with, such as stealing a hubcap or something, everything was tempered by the thought of dealing with my mother if I got caught. God, that would be murder, facing my mother when I had done something wrong. That was the greatest deterrent a kid could ever have.

She was a tough, tough mother. She set very high standards, and insisted I live up to those standards. There were no compromises. Things were black-and-white, and nothing was left to interpretation. My grades in school, my behavior, all those things were highly scrutinized, and she let me know in no uncertain terms if I had fallen short.

My mother taught me that if you want to achieve things, you have to set the bar high and then work toward it. That has served me well, I think. The bar is set so high on anything today, business or otherwise, that if you want to achieve to that level and feel like you've accomplished something, you had better be more tenacious than the other guy.

One year at Christmas my mother took me with her to Sears. The salespeople at the store were demonstrating a little metal tractor. It was an intriguing little toy, with a key on the back which, when wound, would make it crawl across the floor. I was fascinated with this toy, and I pleaded with my mother to buy it for me. It was 89 cents.

"No, I can't buy that, but I'll make it so that you can earn the money to buy it yourself," she explained.

I was probably six years old, and I remember this vividly. We went home and my mother took a fruit jar from the cabinet and screwed on a lid that had a small slit into which coins could be dropped. If I would help her wash and dry the dishes, she'd put a penny in the jar. If I'd take the garbage out—which was a half-block away—I'd get a penny for that. Soon enough I was taking the jar down from the shelf, shaking it and trying to guess how many pennies I had.

I kept asking my mother, "Do we have enough?" Finally one day she smiled and said, "I think you have enough." We went down to Sears, and I proudly brought the toy tractor home.

Almost immediately I lost or broke one of the rubber tires on the thing, and that spoiled my playing with it a little bit. But the lesson stuck; if you want something badly enough, make it a goal and then work toward it. I realize that sounds terribly old-fashioned today, but I still believe it's the best way, particularly when you're talking about young children.

I've always made the statement to my sons — and later to my grandchildren — that the value of a dollar given is less than the value of a dollar earned. I still believe that's true. Even in today's society, it's very viable. Something given is not appreciated nearly as much as something worked for. A dollar, a material possession, an accomplishment, whatever, it's worth much more if you've earned it instead of someone giving it to you. If you have to scratch for it, it adds value.

My mother lived to be 99 years old, and throughout my life she rarely acknowledged any of my accomplishments. She knew I did something good, but she didn't want me to get the "big head." That's good, you know. Because you can get the big head more than you are warranted.

I built a successful business in my lifetime, and had some important racing accomplishments as well. But my fascination with automobiles was lost on my mother; she believed I was wasting my time.

"Why don't you quit fooling with those cars and get a real job?" I can hear her telling me that when I was 16 years old, completely enthralled with everything automotive.

Many years later, not long before my mother died, I stopped by to see her. Like I said earlier, she was 99 years old, but she was still very sharp and knew what was going on. She asked me where I had been the past few days. I explained that I had been to Tulsa, Okla., to see an important race called the Chili Bowl. You have to understand, this was just a few years ago, and I was 75 years old.

"How can you race in January?" she asked in amazement.

"It's an indoor race, mother."

"Hhrrrmph," she said, frowning. Then she said it again. "Why don't you quit fooling with those cars and get a real job?"

Quit fooling with those cars? I might as well try to quit breathing.

I wish I had the words to describe that feeling, that fascination with cars. If you share the passion, you instinctively understand me when I say I love everything about automobiles. Like thousands of my brethren, I can't adequately describe those feelings.

Where did it come from? I didn't get it from my mother or father, because neither was particularly interested. But at a very young age I discovered a boundless passion for cars, and it wasn't like a conscious decision. I just one day realized I loved cars more than anything, and couldn't stop thinking about them. That probably describes a lot of people on this planet. Of all the things modern humans have been fascinated with, the automobile probably leads the list. We've lived in them, we've died in them, had sex in them, customized them, written songs about them, and devoted nearly all of our waking hours to them. We can't get enough, and I've seen men devote their entire lives to automobiles and racing. Hell, I'm one of those men.

All I know is that in Lincoln, when I was not yet a teenager, I was wildly absorbed with automobiles. They wheezed, they coughed, they clanked, they stalled, and they cost money. But they were like wonderful pieces of art to me, either rattling down the street or sitting still.

My father built me a sandbox when I was three or four years old, and one of my earliest memories is playing with my toy cars in that sandbox. I was quite the thrill seeker at an early age; we had a steep lawn and driveway, and I was forever wanting to build a downhill racer to run down the driveway. My first venture came on my tricycle; I paused at the peak of the lawn, pushed off with my feet, and away I went. Unfortunately, I had a little too much guts, and it wasn't a happy ending.

I had a small bell on the handlebars of my tricycle, and I had taken it apart to see how it worked. When I hit the bottom of the hill, and the concrete driveway, I crashed and stuck the threaded end of the bell through the middle of my nose. From that point on, my nose was never actually attached to my skull. I always had a bad scar running across there, and as a teenager I thought that made me look tough. Funny thing, whenever I touched that scar with the end of my finger, I got a headache. There must have been some nerves attached to the headache trigger in my brain or something.

Sometimes I ran into mishaps that weren't of my own making. One day a neighbor girl was raking the clay road alongside her house, and I happened by. She was playing around with the rake and somehow hit me in the face, and one of the tongs pierced my right eye and hooked behind my skull. The girl got scared and took off, and I had to walk home carrying the rake still attached to my head. My mother was quite surprised at such a sight, I might add. She got to where she was downright paranoid about all the things that would happen to me.

My fascination with automobiles — really, all things mechanical — might have been because it was a distraction for me during a difficult period of my life.

When I was in third grade, I began to have leg aches and hip problems. I was limping around and had all kinds of difficulty. My parents took me to see the only orthopedic doctor in Lincoln, and he informed us that I had Perthes disease in both hips. We had no idea what that meant, because we had never heard of such a disease. We learned that it is an ailment related to a malfunction of the hip joints, caused by too much calcium in the socket. Instead of being like a bearing as is normal, a calcium buildup inhibited the joint from working properly.

That's why I couldn't spread my legs and do all the things other kids could do. I walked like a stick man.

This particular physician had written books and was known throughout the world, and had even taught in Europe. So he knew his stuff. Unfortunately, the treatment for this disease was quite unpleasant. They put me in a body cast, and made the lower half of my body completely immobile. The idea was to keep the hip joint exactly in place until the disease passed, or something like that. The body cast ran from the middle of my chest to the tips of my toes, with my knees spread by a bar fitted into the cast. In those days they began fitting the cast by putting me into a wool-type underwear. Wherever the cast was, I had this woolen underwear. Then they covered me with gauze webbing and plaster of Paris until the cast formed. When they were finished, the cast probably weighed as much as my entire body.

I wasn't able to attend school, and I missed the entire third grade and half of the fourth grade. A homebound teacher would come in and give me instruction at one o'clock each afternoon, three days a week. That was supposed to keep me up to speed with the other kids my age. I loved Buck Rogers, so she read to me from Buck Rogers comic books. And that was it. The sum of my education in third and fourth grade consisted of Buck Rogers comic books.

When I resumed my formal education, I successfully pleaded with the school to not set me back a grade. I was grateful for that, because to be set back a grade would have been devastating for me emotionally. However, the third and fourth grades are when you learn about vowels and consonants, and that's the foundation for your spelling. To this day, I am a horrible speller. Horrible! So much so that I later had to take remedial English in my senior year of college in order to graduate.

It was tough wearing that cast in the 1930s, because nobody had air conditioning. Imagine wearing wool underwear all summer long, topped off by a big, heavy cast. It wasn't so bad in the winter, but the summer was tough. When they changed the cast every three months, I would look at my legs to discover they were covered with dead skin. This created a stench that was beyond description. My mother would rub coconut oil on my legs, and I would look at them and say, "Move, legs, move!" But they wouldn't move at all. When the cast was removed for good, 18 months after my initial fitting, I had to learn to walk all over again.

Naturally, when you're in that cast some of your other bodily functions don't work very well. For example, my bowels. I had all sorts of difficulties, which often resulted in having to have an enema. This was done with a stainless steel nippled fixture, which was not very comfortable. At the time I only knew of the discomfort, and didn't realize the long-term implications. About a year later, several polyps formed at the edge of my bowel tract and rectum. I went back to Dr. Rider, and he cut 'em out. They didn't heal well; these are supposed to heal from the bottom up, and I had to go to the doctor every couple of days to make sure they weren't healing from the top up. If they were, he would insert his finger and break them loose to re-heal. That resulted in a lot of irritation in that part of my body.

Finally we visited the only rectal specialist in Lincoln. This guy eventually performed five surgeries on me over a period of several years. He finally cut the sphincter muscle, which is what is used to control your bowels. So that created a very real problem for me.

I suppose all of this is what caused my immune system to go out of whack. I became anemic, and they had me drinking a quart of milk each day. However, we later discovered that I'm allergic to milk. My immune system continued to be a problem, and I continued to lose weight. My bowels ran all the time, and I got to where I was skin and bones. When you lose that much weight, you become allergic to almost everything. They did an analysis of 150 different food items and found I was allergic to nearly all of them. Milk, peanuts, just about everything. To this day, I haven't had a glass of milk since I was 14 years old. I can get by with a tiny bit of ice cream, or milk in foods, but to drink a glass of milk would be a problem.

As you might imagine, it was a difficult period of my life, beginning with that body cast. Other kids my age were riding bikes, playing baseball, running, swinging. I couldn't do any of those things. If we wanted to leave the house, my dad would physically pick me up and stick me in the back seat of our car. In the winter and it was cold, they would pile blankets on me. My feet and ankles were exposed, so they'd tug some wool socks on my feet. Remember, cars didn't have much for heaters in those days.

Kids would come over to my house to play, and I got to where I could get down out of bed and, using my upper body, guide myself through a doorway. I wouldn't fit through a door normally because my legs were so wide, so I had to turn sideways.

Because of these things, I was different than the other kids. I suppose that was on my mind, but I don't remember thinking much about it. Kids are resilient, and able to deal with a lot more than we think they can. Plus, what could I do? There wasn't anything to be gained by feeling sorry for myself. I still had lots of energy and a strong desire to play and have fun.

At the time we lived at 4427 O Street in Lincoln. O Street is the longest straight street in the world, stretching far out from the Missouri River into the Nebraska countryside without making one turn, some 75 miles.

The only time I remember things being traumatic is when I had surgery. I was scared to death, which is probably natural for a child. Being in the hospital, you realize you are dependent on other people for everything. My parents, for example, provided their help and love, and that was very much the central foundation of my life. Their support got me through that difficult period of my life.

In fact, as I look back I think that's the reason I never left Lincoln. My home, and my parents, that was the only certainty I knew. That was my universe. That's the only thing I felt secure in, because I couldn't walk, or my health was a wreck, spending weeks in a hospital, and all that. But home, that was a wonderful place where a boy could feel that life was going to be all right after all. Later in my life, when I had an opportunity to leave, there was a strong sense that leaving Lincoln — and home — would mean leaving something I couldn't find anywhere else. Thoughts of pursuing my ambitions were strong, but not enough to offset the fears and uncertainties of leaving home. So I stayed.

It's kind of amazing, but in spite of all those health issues I look back and see a skinny kid who was actually a very normal child. I had plenty of friends and my passions were cars and Buck Rogers, in that order.

Through all the difficult times I had as a kid, I can also look back at some very fortunate things, as well. One good thing was meeting Milo.

Whether it was playing with cars in the sandbox or riding my wagon down the driveway, I was all about things with wheels. My dad bought my first wagon at the Goodwill store for a dollar, and he brought it home and cut up his garden hose to use for tires on the metal rims. Of course I immediately rolled the tires off the rim making sharp turns going down our driveway. Boy, those wild rides in the wagon really got my blood pumping.

A couple of blocks down the street lived a fellow who worked for the telephone company, where he was a switchboard repairman. The man's name was Milo Caslasky, and he was the first man I ever met whom I would classify as a mechanical genius. Throughout my life I've met some genuine craftsmen, men who had an ability to think beyond most others. Milo was such a man.

Of course, he was an *eccentric* genius. I was in my early teens when I got to know Milo, and his wife had left him a couple of years earlier and taken their children with her. Milo was living alone in this big four-bedroom home two blocks from our place.

I was prone to giving everybody a nickname, and Milo's nickname was "Scrounge." He had completely filled that big house with an incredible array of, well, junk. He'd prowl the local junkyards, keeping an eye out for broken things he could repair. These were scrap yards that bought paper, aluminum, all sorts of things. He'd also go to places like Goodwill and the Salvation Army. He'd spot a broken-down old bicycle, and he'd pick it up. A burned-out toaster, he'd pick it up. A broken iron, he'd pick it up. He had his entire house filled with stuff like that. His yard was filled with cast-iron fencing that he had dragged home from various scrap yards.

The many switchboards around Lincoln didn't need constant repair, so Milo simply had to call the phone company every 15 minutes to see if he was needed. Otherwise he had plenty of time to tinker with the infinite number of "projects" at his house. I started hanging around, watching him repair things, learning how things worked. It immediately aroused my natural curiosity of all things mechanical.

The best thing in Milo's house, however, wasn't all the junk needing fixing. It was a large stack of magazines such as *Popular*

Science, Popular Mechanics, and *Mechanix Illustrated* dating back to their first issues in the 1920s.

The discovery of those magazines literally changed the course of my life. I would devour the articles, learning about the principles of science and how they applied to making things work. I had read plenty of schoolbooks; but these books were different, because I could actually learn from them. Nothing else on the newsstand interested me. Remember, this was the days before *Hot Rod Magazine* or any other specialty automotive magazine. And there were certainly no racing magazines.

Every day when I got home from school I'd hurry to Milo's house. He'd pay me 15 cents an hour to help him, or 25 cents per hour if I'd take "products" instead of cash. To this day, I still have hundreds of those magazines I got from Milo in lieu of pay. I cherish them, because they were the center of my awakening to a new and wonderful world of mechanics.

Milo was a tremendous influence in my life, and he taught me how to fix almost anything. As you go through life, if you're lucky enough to have mentors like Milo, you can't trade that education for anything. You can't buy it. You can go to all the best colleges, and take all the training programs, but a mentor like Milo can have a much greater impact. He was a great guy to learn from. A kid has a mind like a sponge, and I eagerly soaked up that knowledge from Milo.

Aside from fixing all those toasters and bicycles, when I was 14 years old I was ready to take the next step. I studied my finances, and with my "job" at Milo's house I figured I could swing the deal. He had somehow acquired a 1917 Ford Model T pickup, and I immediately began imploring him to sell it to me.

Never mind that I was still two years away from getting a driver's license; and never mind that I was 14 and looked like I was 10. I was ready to hit the big time, and become the proud owner of my very own automobile.

Owning a car is the greatest moment possible for a kid who is completely nuts over cars. I can't even begin to tell you how excited I was. I had a car! My *very own* car!

I was ready to hit the streets. Look out, Lincoln!

3

A New World

The handlebars of the little 1947 BSA motorcycle quivered in my hands, and I squinted through the Nebraska dust. It was a half-mile fairgrounds dirt track, and I was getting my first real taste of competition as a motorcycle rider.

Perhaps it was Beatrice, or Fairbury, or Seward, or one of the 50-some such tracks in my area. It was 1948, and America was slowly getting back on her feet following World War II.

It was an exciting time to be an automotive nut. Racing was taking off like never before, fed by the nation's long-suppressed appetite for entertainment and excitement. Hot rodding was in the birthing process, making a wobbly entrance into the world.

There I was, 19 years old in the Nebraska heartland, taking it all in. I fancied myself quite the motorcycle rider, and the truth is I was pretty good. My desire to win was much greater than my fear of getting hurt or killed, so I didn't mind throwing that BSA into the corners with reckless abandon. We ran 'em with no brakes, so I fashioned myself a riding boot with a steel sole to help keep the thing under control. Who needed brakes? Not me...I was a big-time racer! Or so I imagined.

The BSA was an English bike, a single-cylinder with a hydraulic front fork. It was completely different than the Harley-Davidson and Indian motorcycles I raced against. They were big and bulky and not very sophisticated, while the BSA was nimble and light. At the time I weighed 115 pounds dripping wet, and on the straightaway those bigger bikes would blast past me with such speed that it would make my head spin. But when we got to the corner, as they wrestled the heavier machines to stay down in the groove, I'd slip past on the inside. Coming off the corner I'd see if any of those guys could eat the boards on the outside. In modern racing they call that a "slide job."

"The war" was something that happened far away, or so it seemed to me. I was 12 years old when Japan attacked Pearl Harbor, and over the next four years I probably didn't completely grasp what was happening. I went to a lot of movies at the theatres in downtown Lincoln, with a double feature and an RKO newsreel in between. Those newsreels were America's visual connection with the war. There was no television, or Internet through which to get news; our sources were the radio, the newsreels, and the newspaper. And the only thing I read in the newspaper was the comics page.

In shop class we built small wooden models of various airplanes to be sent to the coasts, where Civil Defense spotters were constantly on duty watching for enemy fighters and bombers. But all of that seemed very distant to a Nebraska kid in junior high school.

The things that brought the war home to me were the scrap drives and the rationing, particularly gasoline rationing. By this time Americans already had a love affair with their automobiles, and an insatiable desire for independence. You can do a lot of things to annoy Americans, but access to driving gets our attention quicker than anything else.

Gas rationing was my first real wake-up to how the world really works. Not the fairy-tale world, but the real world, the world of human nature.

The rationing program called for everybody to get three gallons per week. Coupons were issued, which could be redeemed at a filling station. My dad needed those three gallons to get back and forth to work, so we didn't dare drive anywhere else. But for many people, those coupons quickly became like currency, and a black market flourished.

In 1943 I got a job at the filling station next door to my house, the EN-AR-CO station at 44th and O Street. I'd work two hours each evening after school on Thursday and Friday. The EN-AR-CO stations all had signage out front with a small boy holding up a sign that listed the gasoline price. We sold two grades of gasoline, White Rose (regular) and Red Rose (ethyl). I was 14 years old, and green about how the world worked. However, I immediately noticed that we were always very busy, while other stations seemed much less so. I later realized that our station owner was buying ration coupons from farmers, then using them to acquire more gasoline, which he would sell on the black market for far above the normal retail price. It was so obvious, and so well known, that the station was soon known as "Blackie's." Gasoline was selling for about 20 cents a gallon at the time, but we were getting 50 cents a gallon. If you had money, you could get all the gasoline you wanted.

When I figured out what was going on, I immediately wondered if the authorities were going to come and arrest me. I knew Blackie could go to jail, but I figured they'd take me away, too, because I was pumping the gas. I was scared to death, and could hardly sleep at night with such worry. Deep down inside I knew I was doing something wrong. I kept waiting for the authorities to come to our front door to take me away, never to be seen again.

A couple of times Blackie ordered me to run the water hose into the gasoline storage tank at the station, "Just a little bit, kid, to raise the level." I knew this was wrong, because that water was going into somebody's tank. He was a chiseler, and I was helping him. But as a young kid I was too timid to speak out, and just did my job and kept quiet.

It was a good lesson, because it made me understand that it doesn't hurt to open your eyes and watch what goes on around you, because people are capable of dishonesty. A healthy skepticism, you might say. And through the years I've seen such things play out time and time again, when people do wrong things in business just because it's convenient or they want to get over on somebody.

I realized how rotten I felt inside, and I knew that feeling wasn't worth it. Just be honest, and treat people like you want to be treated, and let it go at that. Later on, as I matured and became more experienced in business, I learned that it's not only a matter of keeping a clear conscience; it's good business, too. When you stick to honest principles, your customers soon learn they can depend on you, over and over again.

Our station, incidentally, had to close each evening at 7 p.m. Almost all the area businesses closed each evening at that time, because the authorities wanted very few lights on after dark in case enemy bombers came that night. Now, if you're talking Nebraska, those bombers had better have a helluva range from Europe or Asia! But that was the mindset, because we were at war.

I mentioned Milo Caslasky earlier, and as the war years clicked away his influence on me couldn't be overstated. Reading those mechanical magazines and watching him repair things, I was absorbed in all things mechanical, learning how things worked.

But the element that most fascinated me was the piston engine, and the automobile. After some talking I made a deal with Milo to acquire his 1917 Ford Model T pickup, officially bringing me into the world of automobile ownership...and tinkering. I immediately began taking the car apart and putting it back together, my 14-year-old mind soaking up the details like a sponge.

Actually, I had already built a couple of "cars." In those days they made washing machines using a small 4-stroke gasoline engine with a kick-start you stepped on. These machines were a great improvement over a washboard, and soon became plentiful. I found one at a used furniture store, and then acquired some baby buggy wheels. I crafted a wooden cart, mounted the washing machine motor, and rigged a belt to drive the rear wheels. I didn't know anything about clutches, so I figured out how to tension the belt to engage the drive. Brakes? Well, just drag your feet on the ground.

One day I went roaring down O Street, which is also U.S. 34. A motorcycle cop pulled me over and came walking up with a fierce glare.

"Kid, what the hell do you think you're doing?"

"I'm driving my race car."

"Race car? That's what this thing is?"

"Sure! I built it myself!"

Keep in mind, I'm all of about 12 years old.

"Listen, kid," he growled. "First of all, race cars ain't allowed on the street. Second of all, you gotta be 16 years old to drive on the street, and have a driver's license. Are you 16? Do you have a driver's license?"

"Nope."

"Then get this thing off the street!" he screamed.

Live and learn. I was scared, and it was embarrassing, but one thing's for sure...those little Maytag carts were a lot more fun than a double-feature movie at a downtown theatre!

As the war drew to a close in 1945, I was 16 years old. Naturally, like just about any kid of that age, my mind wasn't on history, or the fact that America was on the cusp of a huge change, particularly in the world of racing and hot rodding. It was a tremendously exciting time, but of course I had no idea. I was just absorbed in buying and trading for broken-down cars, repairing them, and making a couple of bucks when I resold them.

In Nebraska, the most visible change brought about by the war was the great expansion of Air Force activity at Offutt Air Force Base near Omaha and the Lincoln Airfield. Both, I'm proud to say, played a major part in our war effort, and Offutt was a central part of U.S defense throughout the Cold War.

Offutt was the site of the Glenn L. Martin Bomber Plant, where B-29 and B-26 aircraft were built. Two particular planes manufactured there were of great historical consequence: The *Enola Gay* and *Bockscar*, which delivered the atomic bombs on Hiroshima and Nagasaki, respectively, ending WWII. Later, Offutt was headquarters of the U.S. Strategic Air Command.

Lincoln Airfield, which was only about seven miles from our house at 44th and O Street, was an important training school for aircraft mechanics, and later served as a training airfield for the crews of B-17, B-24, and B-29 Stratofortress bombers. Our bombers played a critical role in our victory over Germany and Japan; a lot of those crews came through Lincoln. Later, from about 1955 to 1966, Lincoln Airfield was commissioned as a U.S. Air Force base.

The growing presence of the Air Force in our area had an enormous impact on the local hot-rod scene. General Curtis LeMay, a prominent leader in the Air Force following the war, was an avid fan of sports car racing, and he saw to it that some of the best mechanical minds were stationed at Offutt and Lincoln. Most of those guys were into not just airplanes, but all things mechanical. As the hot-rod scene took off after the war, those boys embraced automobile performance and customizing in a big, big way.

This was happening at key pockets around the country. In southern California, for example, former and current G.I.'s were heavily into the hot-rod scene on the dry lakes such as Mirage, Muroc, and Rosamond. People such as Ak Miller, Howard Johansen, Wally Parks, and Bob Petersen were shaping the future of automobile performance, all the while not really knowing where it was going.

It's hard to explain today exactly how all of this came together at the same time. For almost five years, the war had deprived most of the country of entertainment and fun. A generation of young men was put through the harrowing experience of combat, while those of us at home lived through years of rationing and other inconveniences. Believe me, by early 1946 everybody was ready to have some fun.

For a lot of young men, fun meant cars. But the automobile situation in 1946 was not exactly good; all of the automobile manufacturers had shifted production to war materials, and no new models had been introduced since 1941. Tires had been awfully difficult to get during the war, and it took a while for manufacturing to catch up. Gasoline was of questionable quality, and very inconsistent.

But that made automotive performance all the more challenging, and enjoyable. Hot rodders figured out all sorts of ways to improve their cars.

Speed was the element on *everybody's* mind. Speed, speed, speed. Hot rodders were interested in anything that could make their car faster off the stop light, and faster on the top end. Whether it was side-by-side competition or just cruising around, we wanted a hot car that could dust off the next guy.

It had to be fast. And, by the way, if you could also make it look sharp, that's all the better.

The trick was, how do you make them faster?

If you don't know something, what do you do? You research the situation, and learn more. Read up on it, talk to people in the know, and experiment on your own.

However, in the late 1940s there was almost nobody you could turn to for advice or knowledge in terms of automotive performance. In a way, we were all working in a vacuum, stumbling here, succeeding there, with almost no technical information at our disposal.

Today, there is a great amount of information related to automotive performance and engineering. Data on metallurgy, data on lubricants, data on ignitions, data on fuel mixtures; there's a wealth of knowledge out there, right at your fingertips.

That was certainly not the case when I immersed myself in automotive work in the late 1940s. The concept of automotive performance was, relatively speaking, pretty new. Yes, people were building performance pieces before the war, but the explosion of interest in the subject following 1945 was just way beyond what anybody had done before.

There were plenty of auto mechanics at that time, but most mechanics were focused simply on repair. We were searching for something entirely different; we wanted to *improve*. In order to do this, you had to take the existing pieces and change them, or make new pieces. In doing so, you were venturing into territory that hadn't been traveled before, at least locally.

This is one of those things that's hard to describe to somebody younger. They have never lived in a world where you had an engine all apart in front of you, thinking of how to improve the thing, with literally not one shred of outside knowledge to help you. It seems impossible to someone today, because the world we live in is information-intensive.

So we learned on our own, all of us working on cars in the late 1940s. We tried different things; some ideas worked, and some didn't. The ideas that didn't work were sometimes pretty spectacular, I might add. When we had a success, we'd tell the next guy about it. When we had a failure, we shared that, too. You quickly built a mental database on what worked, and what didn't.

That, friends, was the genesis of the hot-rod culture that is still with us today. Even though it was competitive, we were in this together. We loved cars, we loved the hobby, and we felt a natural instinct to be around others who shared our passion.

Think about it: If you're looking to learn about hot rods, where is the best place to hang around? With the guys who are building and driving hot rods, right? They're the guys who have experimented and tried different things and they might have answers to some of your questions.

As my high school career drew to a close in 1947, I prepared to go to college. I was never a stellar student, but my parents both made it very clear at an early age that I would be attending college. Both of my parents had gone to secondary school, and were steadfast that college was in my future. I attended Lincoln High School, the largest high school in Nebraska. We had something like 1,900 students in three grades.

Going on to college was never my desire. By the time I got my driver's license I had already owned two or three cars, and within a year I was buying, selling and trading all kinds of cars, with a few motorcycles thrown in for good measure. I was hanging out with guys older than me by two or three years, so naturally I was copying their ways and ideas.

I had been running with older kids probably since I was 12 years old, when my mother began to wonder why my shoulders were always black-and-blue. It's because my bigger buddies were constantly punching my arm in friendly horseplay. I was the youngest, and they could hit lots harder than I could.

I became a pretty savvy car trader during this period. Sometimes I'd take an old Model T and remove the body, just leaving the seat and steering wheel on the chassis and driving it like that. It looked like a race car, which excited me to no end.

Of course, my parents were appalled to see me driving such a jalopy, and they insisted I park out back behind our garage. One day as I came rumbling home in my stripped-down Model T, I spotted my mother hanging the wash in our back yard on the clothesline. I figured I'd give her a scare by coming in the back way, where there was some open space.

I must have been carrying a little too much speed, because when my tires hit that wet grass I was out of control. In fact, I could have sworn that my car actually picked up speed.

Life lesson: Wet grass is not conducive to stopping a speeding car. Write it down.

As my car came roaring across the yard, my mother screamed and ran for her life, while the car knocked the clothesline down, scattering her clean wash. It was not a pretty sight. I was completely humiliated, and the wrath of mother, boy, was always damned tough.

My parents were believers in "tough love." Of course they had no idea what that phrase meant, but in today's world we hear family counselors talk about the solid mixture of love and discipline as "tough love." That's exactly what my parents believed in. They loved me, but they had no hesitation to tell me "no" if they thought I needed it.

I had put together a hot Model A roadster the winter of my senior year of high school, and the state basketball tournaments were held in March, about the time I was getting the car finished up. I was still working for Blackie at the gas station, and I'd get paid every Saturday night. One of the cheerleaders from Scottsbluff had caught my interest, and I told her I might bring my car to the game that coming Saturday night. You know, to show it off and impress her. She just smiled and giggled and thought that would be a great idea.

That absolutely lit my fire. However, I needed a set of ignition points, and a condenser, to get the car running. These parts were 89 cents at J&R Auto Parts. I didn't have 89 cents, and I wouldn't get paid until Saturday. I had a little bit of change in my pocket, but I was short the rest.

I asked my dad if he'd loan me a dollar until Saturday night. Now, this is the kindest man I've ever known, and the best man

I've ever known. He looked up at me and said, "Why don't you wait until Saturday night when you get paid?"

So I didn't get to drive my Model A that night. However, my dad did loan me his car to use, so I managed another way around the problem.

This was an important learning experience for me. Maybe you don't have to have something right now. Maybe it's best if you wait till you can afford it. I guess it was important, because I still remember it like it was yesterday.

I enrolled at the University of Nebraska in the fall of 1947, where I studied business. Nebraska had record enrollment that year, flooded by homecoming G.I.'s taking advantage of the G.I. Bill.

It didn't take long before a fraternity, Delta Tau Delta, asked me to pledge. I was shocked that the fraternity would recruit me so specifically, but then I quickly figured out why.

Stanley Stroh was one of my best friends in high school. A natural athlete, Stanley excelled at football, basketball, golf, anything he tried. He was the city and state champion in golf, and he was an all-state receiver in football. Although we came from different backgrounds and neighborhoods, Stanley and I became lifelong friends.

Of course Stanley was heavily recruited for athletics, particularly by various fraternities. At this time many fraternities fielded various sporting teams, and played against other fraternities. Believe it or not, some of those fraternity teams were better than the team fielded by the university. This became blood-and-guts competition, with bragging rights on the line.

I began to realize the fraternity's angle: If I joined their fraternity, I could probably talk Stanley into joining, too. As it turns out Stanley decided not to pledge, and the fraternity was stuck with me.

I was at Nebraska for about a year-and-a-half when my health issues returned. I was diagnosed with ulcerated colitis, which was a relatively new ailment in the medical field. Everyone was a bit mystified of what it is, and how to deal with it. Most of my difficulties stemmed from my prior medical issues, and of course no one dared discuss those sensitive topics.

Colitis killed 90 percent of those who contracted it in those days. My health steadily worsened, and I ultimately dropped out of school, figuring if I took a semester off I might get better.

While I was recovering, my dad and I decided to take a trip to see the 1948 Indianapolis 500, driving my brand-new '49

Chevrolet business coupe. I had sold both my Model A and my '34 roadster and bought the Chevy for $1,222.22. New cars were still difficult to get at that time, and I had to sign a document agreeing to keep the car for at least one year, because so many new cars were being diverted to the black market.

At this point in my life I had traveled very little. During the war my one and only out-of-state trip was to Cleveland to see the Great Lakes Exposition. So the idea of traveling to Indianapolis was very exciting to me.

We got to Indianapolis and found a gas station just a couple of blocks from the Indianapolis Motor Speedway, and the man allowed us to park the Chevy there. Dad and I slept in the back of the car, which was as nice as any motel setup you could ask for. On race day, we watched Mauri Rose drive through the corners with the sleeves on his T-shirt flapping in the wind! Exciting!

The race was four-and-a-half hours long, and when Mauri took the checkered flag everyone kept going. Each driver raced until they completed 500 miles, not just the leader. So some guys kept going until darkness finally ended the race.

The entire scene was quite the spectacle for this country boy from Nebraska. Not just the racing, but seeing the drunks laying on the ground, the race cars, the huge crowd, people panhandling, it was a fantastic scene.

After the race, my dad and I drove to Chicago to visit the Museum of Science and Industry. We encountered a traffic jam that was literally 30 miles long, and when we finally got to the head of the line we discovered it was only a four-way stop!

Visiting the museum was like being on another planet. Oh, God, I wanted to look at everything! I still have a picture of my dad and me at the museum. We also visited the Navy Pier, and several other sites around town. The entire visit was something very special that was burned into my young memory.

Some years later, I took my kids to Chicago but discovered that the town had been just about wrecked. The whole damn town. It looked like a completely different city, with graffiti, trash in the streets...the entire city had gone to hell, but the museum was still a very special place.

Eventually I began to regain my strength and get back to normal. My parents thought it was a good idea for me to enroll at Nebraska Wesleyan University in the autumn of 1949, because of the strong moral values the school supported. You actually had to sign a paper promising you wouldn't drink or smoke.

Some of the concerns of my parents might have been caused by all the rough-and-tumble former G.I.s who were still very prevalent on college campuses at that time.

I had lots of reservations about attending Nebraska Wesleyan. It was straight-and-narrow, and I was a bit of a cut-up. I couldn't imagine what it was going to be like, and I didn't know anyone attending the school. Luckily, I had gained enough credit hours in my 18 months at University of Nebraska to be considered a sophomore at NWU, so I wasn't starting completely from scratch.

Really, what I wanted to was forget about school and buy a gas station or a used car lot because I knew I could make money at those things. But my mother would hear none of that, and she insisted I stick with it and finish school.

It wasn't long at NWU before I was introduced to a pretty young freshman, Joyce Uphoff. I was immediately taken by her friendly, outgoing personality. Joyce is very much a people person, and it shows. When you walk into a crowd, she is instantly chatting with people, getting to know them, with no hesitation. She likes people, and, in turn, people like Joyce. I'm a lot slower to warm up to people, particularly in a crowd.

A funny story about when we met: Joyce came from North Platte, which is west of Lincoln. I arrived to pick her up for our first date wearing a new pair of shiny cowboy boots. She took one look at those shiny boots and laughed. "You look like a drug store cowboy," she said. Talk about putting me in my place...but I must not have minded too awful much, because it definitely wasn't our last date.

Joyce had a Christian upbringing as a Missouri Synod Lutheran, and had attended church school up until her high school years. She was elected president of her dormitory, a brand-new women's dorm, and was an Alpha Gamma Delta pledge. They were grooming her to be president of the local chapter, I think.

We spent a lot of time together, and we immediately clicked. She was very supportive of me, and we enjoyed working together. Throughout my college years I was still buying and selling cars, working off a small corner lot at 20th and P Street. She would help me wash cars at my lot, clean them up, things like that. Joyce didn't come from a wealthy background, so she had to work her way through school. She worked each afternoon as a secretary on campus for Rev. Mattingly, Dean Deal, and others.

I was prone to get mixed up in mischief during this period. Of course it wasn't me; it was all my friends, being a bad influence on me.

One night after I dropped Joyce off at her dorm, a couple of buddies and I decided to have some fun. The women's dorm had very strict hours, and ladies had to be in their rooms by 9:30. I had a gallon of bright red paint, so on the front of this women's dorm we wrote in large letters, "Cherry Factory."

Now, everybody knew I didn't spell worth a damn; I was immediately the prime suspect because "Cherry" was spelled wrong. So that one got me into a little bit of trouble.

Probably the best prank we pulled involved my Model T touring car. I had built the car that summer, and began driving it to school. My fraternity brothers wanted to buy it from me; their idea was to use it to drive out to the beer joint north of town in the afternoons after class. I sold them the car, but when the weather turned cold they couldn't get it started. It just sat outside the fraternity house and began to deteriorate.

On Halloween we began getting a little restless. Another fraternity down the way was known as kind of nerdy, and they had just placed new sod in the yard in front of their fraternity house.

Keep in mind, my fraternity was filled with tough guys, most of them former G.I.s who had seen extensive fighting in the war. One guy had a quart jar full of gold teeth he had "removed" from the mouths of dead Japanese soldiers with his rifle butt. This guy later became a doctor, by the way. So I was associated with some pretty tough characters.

We got the old Model T fired up, and decided we'd christen that new sod down the street. Boy, that Model T made a mess of their yard. I was at the wheel, with about 10 or 15 of my fraternity brothers urging me on. The guys from the other fraternity rushed outside and made a roadblock in the street, telling me I couldn't go any further. I stopped, because obviously I didn't want to run over these guys. But my brothers literally picked up the car and shoved it right through the crowd. Guys were flying every which way.

Somebody was taking photographs of all this, which was unfortunate. We took the car down to "Old Main," a building that had been a part of the school since before 1900. It had a great big walk in the front, leading to huge doors entering a foyer. Beyond that was a large stairway and a second-floor foyer.

The guys lifted the Model T, turned it on its side, and walked it through the front door. They carried it up the steps to the second-floor foyer, where they sat it upright and left it.

Boy, the school wasn't happy with a beat-up Model T parked on the second-floor foyer at Old Main. They really, really weren't happy. The car sat there for a month and a half, because they couldn't figure out how to get it out of there.

They knew who was responsible, but they couldn't prove it. They called all of us in for questioning, and threatened to expel us. I was just a few months short of graduating, and I didn't want any part of "expelled." My mother would have *really* not liked that.

We finally agreed that if they would drop all the charges, my fraternity brothers and I would see to it that the car was removed. So we worked it out to the satisfaction of all parties.

Was Joyce put off by these antics? Yes, and for a while I don't think she was very keen on me. She didn't want to be associated with Mr. Smith and his friends. But it was actually good clean fun. They'd probably put you in jail for these things today, because people in modern times have lost their sense of humor.

Despite the antics with my Theta Chi fraternity brothers, Joyce and I had a lot of fun together throughout our college years. I had acquired a "square 4" motorcycle that sounded just like an Offy, and we'd go riding. The first time she hopped on the back I told her, "Hold on!" and gave the throttle a squirt. I saw her feet go up each side of me, clear up in the air. Her thumbs were locked in the belt hoops of my pants, and she was laying upside down on the back of my seat, her feet in the air, holding onto my belt loops for dear life. Not a very dignified position and she didn't like that very much. But even in times like that, she had to admit we were having fun.

Joyce had been going with a guy who was planning to be a minister, so I was kind of a change of direction for her. You might even say I was out at the other end of the spectrum. In my mind I wasn't that bad, but I suppose if you'd been on the outside looking in it might have seemed that way.

In these years since, Joyce has often chuckled that she hasn't had a moments rest since she met me. In a way, that's true. My college days were winding down, and we were about to get very, very busy.

4

Hot Rod Roots

If I close my eyes, I can vividly picture the scene: 48th and O Street in Lincoln, around 1950. Cars rumble as they cruise past, some with good-looking paint jobs, some in dark primer. Roadsters, coupes, convertibles…stock, mildly souped-up, or really cooking. It's a buffet of color and horsepower, rolling past one by one.

It's Saturday night, and there is an electricity to the scene. Young guys, some with their girl friends, hanging out, studying everybody else's cars.

Your car was everything. Your car was *you*. Naturally, you wanted the fastest, best-looking car you could afford. Almost nobody was rich, but they funneled every spare cent into their hot rod. Like a rite of passage, you took great pride in making your car the best it could possibly be.

For many of us guys, we can trace our life's beginnings back to moments like that. Maybe it's Lincoln in 1950, or San Jose in 1960, or Jacksonville in 1970, or Indianapolis in 1980. The era or the exact location doesn't matter; if you're into cars, you understand. It's that time when, as a young man, you feel like you've stepped into a place in which you belong, a world you love. A world of cars, and noise, and performance.

Our world.

Mine, in my vivid, Technicolor memory, was in Lincoln. I was lucky to be born into a time when the hot rod world was being transformed into something huge and lasting, casting out a big net that captured almost my entire generation and millions of young males ever since.

The explosion of interest in hot rodding was in many ways going hand-in-hand with the boom in auto racing. Hot rodding and racing are different but similar; in their roots they are like siblings. Like children of common parents, or something like that.

In 1946 I began going with my buddies to the races at Council Bluffs, Iowa, where we'd watch Offy-powered midgets. There were very few televisions in America at that time, and the only race on the radio was the Indianapolis 500. In the immediate post-war years, midget racing drew from a very wide audience. Many of the people in the grandstands weren't really racing fans per se, but they just liked the noise and power and action. A lot of the young men looking on who were somewhat interested in racing got hooked on cars, period. Race cars, street cars, they liked both.

I was a guy who definitely liked both. Racing and hot rods were equally important to me. I pursued each passion in different ways: I built my own hot rods for the street, and worked on cars for other guys. I also became heavily involved in oval racing, first as a driver and later as a car owner.

I mentioned earlier Milo's 1917 Model T pickup. That car was the first of a long, long line of automobiles I owned. From that point on things got awfully busy for me. I learned how to repair and improve cars, and I was always buying a car that wasn't running, getting it going, and selling it for a few dollars profit.

I'd prowl around and find an old Model T sitting idle in an alleyway, where somebody had parked it as junk. I'd knock on a nearby door and find the owner, who might explain that the thing wasn't running. I'd offer the guy $5 to take it away, and oftentimes he'd accept my offer. I'd drag the thing home and try to figure out why it didn't run.

The big problem on those cars was the ignition, specifically the points. The Model T has an individual coil for each spark plug, and I figured out how to troubleshoot in a primitive way, and could quickly determine if the thing was within the scope of my limited mechanical knowledge.

Another common problem was a clogged fuel line. Gasoline back then was terrible compared to today. It was dirty, and the quality was very inconsistent. It was common to find water in your gas (remember Blackie?), along with the other dirt and junk that played hell with the carburetor. Sometimes I'd clean out the carburetor and that was enough to get the car going.

Once I got it running, I'd sell the car for maybe $10. Remember, this was a very old car at that time—vintage 1920s in 1944, '45—so the value wasn't that great. But I'd sell a few cars and make a couple of bucks. It was a struggle, and my profit margin was very slim.

All my buddies were also into cars, and we were forever trying to out-do each other. Whatever you can do, I can do better! I had to teach myself to weld because I realized that was something I'd do a lot while repairing cars. Again, it was mostly a matter of not knowing anyone who could teach me.

Somebody gave me a SOH HAL cylinder head for my '30 Model A roadster while I was still in high school. This was a single overhead cam design, and the lobes had all come loose on the steel shaft. HAL had made his own camshaft out of steel rod, stacking small metal plates in a fixture to drive the valves. I literally worked on that head for one year, trying to make it work. I'd put it on my car and my dad would tow me, and it would start, but as soon as he stopped it quit. I asked various people how to fix it, and they might say, "Check with the old guy working as a mechanic at so-and-so place, he raced back in the '30s..." So I'd go see him, and maybe he was familiar with the HAL and had a tidbit of information that could help.

To go to a typical shop mechanic and ask about a HAL head, he would look at you like you'd just asked him how to build a rocket to go to the moon. Speed parts, and how they worked, were completely foreign to nearly every mechanic at that time.

Talk about trial and error...it was a long, difficult struggle to learn about this stuff. It taught me that if I wanted to know about things, I'd have to learn it myself. Because often the outside expertise didn't help much.

The same applied to my brief stint as a racing driver. If there had been someone to mentor me as a driver, and teach me, maybe I could have been as good as anybody I ever hired. I was smart enough, and brave enough, but I didn't have anyone to teach me properly during my impressionable stage. But of course that didn't happen, so it wasn't supposed to be. Everything happens for a reason, I believe.

I did some really dumb things to my cars during the learning process. I would rebuild an engine, and made some key mistakes. Again, it was simply a lack of knowledge and experience. There were no books to turn to, so it was trial and error. In my case, a lot of error.

It's not fun to admit the dumb things I did. Dumb, dumb, dumb. However, I can tell you from talking to many of my fellow car nuts, they made the same mistakes. What seems elementary today was very murky and mysterious to a teenaged kid all those years ago.

I tore my Model T apart, and somehow acquired a set of .060-over pistons. I had no idea you had to bore the cylinders in order to fit the larger pistons. I somehow got 'em in the cylinders, buttoned up the engine, and that thing wouldn't budge. Wouldn't even move. So I took it all apart again, figuring out what the problem was. And I made a mental note: You can't put .060-over pistons in without boring the cylinders. Next time, I'd know.

There were so many times I'd be helplessly sitting there staring at some project, completely lost. I wished there was someone I could go to who could tell me what I needed to do. The learning curve seemed impossible. I had a powerful urge to learn, but my progress seemed to crawl along.

But I soldiered on, buying and selling those old cars. In fact, I got busy enough that I began to get nervous about being within the local rules. When you put a used car along the road with a for sale sign, the state referred to that as "curb-stoning." It was no big deal for the average individual, but if someone was doing it consistently the state demanded they get the proper license. I was always worried about getting into trouble, and I was afraid the state would come and arrest me for buying and selling all those cars. Finally, at age 18, I got my auto dealer's license.

To this day, 62 years later, I still maintain that license. I haven't sold cars for many years, but for sentimental reasons I keep my license current. I'll bet I've got the longest uninterrupted tenure as a dealer license-holder in Nebraska.

Besides, you never know when business might get tough, and I have to get out there and hustle some used Model Ts to put beans on the table!

My hangout was Elmer Hanson's Conoco station at 48th and O Street, where my hot rod buddies would congregate. We were all doing similar things: racing motorcycles, souping up our cars, just generally being car guys.

Each evening, guys were in and out, talking cars. It wasn't like everybody was there for hours at a time, and you might see one guy one night, and three the next night. Then you'd go out and test each other's cars.

I can vividly recall traveling down 10th Street in Lincoln, right in front of the county courthouse where our jail was located.

We roared past the place in my buddy's '34 Packard touring car with the top down, with me riding in the back seat. I was probably 17, 18 years old, and we were going something like 70 miles an hour.

Maybe that old Packard had been a police car in a prior life; that's what the cops used to chase the bank robbers of the 1930s. The boys from Kansas City, or maybe St. Paul, Minn., would send their hoods out into the farmlands of the Plains to rob banks, and bring the money back to the city. The crooks drove some pretty hot cars—literally and figuratively—and the cops had to use powerful cars like the Packard in order to keep up. It's hard to explain such a phenomenon today.

We were spending every minute working on our cars, trying to make them run faster. Economics was constantly a factor, because you always wanted more power than you could afford. As younger kids came along, too young for a driver's license, maybe they were hanging in the background, dreaming, hoping that someday they'd have a hot car.

Elmer's station was a classic old filling station with a two-bay service area, with a lube and wash on the side. It was on a big corner property, with lots of room. In those days it was kind of on the outskirts of town, but today it's almost the center of Lincoln, because of how the city has grown.

A lot of Friday and Saturday nights were spent downtown, parking in front of the department stores, hanging out. Gold and Company, Miller and Paine, those were the huge stores that anchored our downtown. You'd park along the street and here would come 15 or 20 guys in their cars. If it was summertime hot, you'd be sitting in your car with the doors propped open.

You'd sit and visit, talk cars, and maybe a couple of guys would go out on O Street to try each other out. Going east, 33rd and O was just about the last stoplight. My parents and I lived at 44th and O, so I had a ringside seat to some great street races. From 33rd to 44th was 10 blocks, where two large cemeteries were located. There was no egress in or out of the road there, so it naturally made a good place for side-by-side racing. If you could beat the guy from 33rd to 44th, you were the best.

Drive-in restaurants were also popular hangout spots. Many had been created during the war to serve the airmen from Lincoln air base. They had gravel lots, and anybody who spun their tires on the gravel, that was a big no-no. A lot of us had spent good money on our paint jobs, and you didn't want to spray gravel on other cars.

But it was Elmer's Conoco station where our car scene was really happening. Guys standing around talking, hoods up on the cars, crawling all over each other's machines, studying what they were doing, getting ideas. Somebody might say, "Next thing I want to get is a such-and-such…I saw a guy over in Omaha who had one, and it was neat!"

That was 100 percent how car ideas and product news was spread. There was no television, and very few magazines; it was all about studying other cars, particularly somebody from out of town who might have something new to us.

It was amazing the lengths we'd go to get something we wanted for our car. For example, one day I heard a set of Smitty mufflers, and I was absolutely enthralled. What was that sound? It was fantastic! Of course I wanted a set for my '40 Ford coupe, right away. When I learned what it was making the sound — the distinctive sound of a Smitty muffler — I set about locating a set for my '40. Unfortunately, the nearest set was Denver. No problem…I simply drove from Lincoln to Denver — about 500 miles each way — just to buy a set of Smitty mufflers. That's amazing when you think about it. But I did what I had to do, in order to get what I wanted for my car.

If you're a car guy, all of this probably sounds familiar to you. It was the same scene playing out in cities and towns all across America during this period, and it's still going on in a slightly different form. If you're a car guy, and you see a bunch of hot rods sitting around, you naturally gravitate to them. You want to see what they've got, what's going on.

Even if you're not looking for a race, you're interested in what other guys are doing with their cars. That's just part of who we are. It's inside of us. It's what the species is all about. You're drawn to it, and you're interested in it. If you have any background at all, even something as simple as changing the spark plugs, or changing the oil, you'll go and take a look at what somebody else has done to their car.

There are probably no two hot rods ever built that exactly parallel each other. Hot rodding should be named along the lines of, "I have made this car to fit *my* specifications." Even if you bought a brand-new car, you altered it to suit your tastes, to make it *your* car. Change the exhaust system, tint the windows, whatever, you leave your mark on the car. Drop the front end, change the wheels, whatever you want. It was that way in 1950, and it's still that way today.

It goes back a lot farther than 1950, of course. If you walk through my museum, you'll see plenty of pieces and parts that were built before 1950. People wanted to be unique, and have their car be able to start when another wouldn't, or stop better than anyone else, to turn better, accelerate faster, whatever. It was an extension of themselves, and their pride. Whitewall tires, bigger sun visors, and everything that's come down the pike is something that made a car unique and an extension of the individual.

By 1950, I began to realize that the entire car culture — everything from souped-up street cars to oval racing to drag racing to customizing — had consumed me. It was all I could think about, 24/7 (Well, Joyce was in that mix, too).

I was just about to finish college, working on my degree in Industrial Education. But I looked at my degree as nothing more than an insurance policy. My future wasn't in the classroom, teaching kids to weld. It was something much different. Things were just starting to come into focus, a little bit at a time.

5

Fateful Day At Hastings

By nature, I'm a very competitive person. In fact, I haven't met many people more competitive than me. Even as a small kid, I was fiercely competitive in almost everything I did. Marbles on the playground, whatever, I wanted to win.

But when I got very sick at eight years old, spending 18 months in a body cast, it made me different than all the other kids. Being different as an adult is not a big deal, but as a child it can be devastating. Teasing, taunting, it was all a part of being different.

I walked like a stick-man, and I was so skinny I looked like a twig. I couldn't possibly compete in things like basketball or football, because of my physical limitations. So I tried to think of things in which I could compete, and do the best I could.

That's probably why I was so drawn to mechanical things. If I could repair an old car and make a $5 profit, in my own little way, I've won. I've done something many other boys couldn't do. Then if I could repair and resell two cars, and make $10, I've won even more.

By the time I was 16 years old, that was my mindset. Making $5 was good, and making $10 was better. If one success was good, two were better.

When I began racing the BSA motorcycle, that was by far the most intense form of competition I had experienced. Boy, what a rush to compete in a race with other men: It was dangerous, it was exciting, and the satisfaction you got from winning was indescribable.

I suppose that's what hooked me on racing. In all these 80 years on earth, I haven't yet found anything that compares with the feeling you get when you win. As a driver, as a mechanic, as a car owner, even as a sponsor. It's a feeling I can't describe in words. It's like a rush of adrenaline, followed by a strong sense of accomplishment that nobody can take away what you just did.

It was only a matter of time before I began to think about racing cars instead of motorcycles. It didn't take a genius to see how dangerous the motorcycles were, and I had great respect for the bikes. I saw plenty of guys killed racing motorcycles, so I knew it was a dangerous hobby.

Some of my hot rod buddies had been drawn to auto racing in the area. This was when there was a big, broad gray area between street cars and racing cars. When you built a machine to excel on the street, a lot of the same principles applied to the cars you raced on the track. Naturally, there was crossover, both technically and culturally.

One of my buddies had a fenderless '32 Ford roadster. He had read in a magazine what the California guys were doing to their cars, and he used that knowledge on his car. About the same time, several area tracks began racing "hot rods" at county fairs in places like Hastings, Beatrice, Fairbury, and the like. These tracks — county fair half-mile dirt ovals — were all within 100 miles of Lincoln.

Guys began driving their street cars — unbeknownst to their parents — to these tracks on Sunday afternoon to compete in the hot rod events. After the race they'd drive 'em back home, provided they hadn't knocked the front end off by going through the fence, or worse yet, hurt themselves.

It wasn't long before those hot rod races got my attention. I had a '40 Ford I felt was the fastest car in town, with a top speed of over 80 mph. I'm talking 80 mph on a narrow, uneven, bumpy road. Nothing like the freeways or four-lane highways of today. On those old roads, 80 mph was quite hazardous to your health. My friend Woody Brinkman also had a '40 Ford coupe. The Fords were clearly the fastest cars of the day, although one of my friends was trying hard to build a '40 Chevrolet that could keep up with the Fords. He was a good machinist but he had his work cut out for him.

It was truly wide-open competition. Whatever you could dream up and apply to your car, give it a try. Multiple carburetors, bigger pistons, messing with the valves or ignition timing, exhaust systems, any of those things were on the table. Those were the hot rods of the day.

It's hard to pinpoint an exact starting point, because there really wasn't an exact date. In any case, the cars began to evolve almost immediately. And that's true of both drag racing and circle track racing. At first they were hot rods, exactly like a street car. Then came the roaring roadsters, which were a little different and slightly more specialized. Soon after came stock cars. The cars varied greatly by region, because everybody was learning and applying their knowledge at different rates in different areas.

Stock cars became jalopies; jalopies became modifieds; modifieds became supermodifieds; supermodifieds became sprint cars. This transition probably spanned something like 25, 30 years. Some of the modifieds — and I'm not referring to modern cars known as IMCA modifieds — were still being raced in pockets around the country as recently as 10 or 15 years ago.

The hot rods became roaring roadsters pretty quickly. These cars were built out of Model T bodies, with a flathead Ford engine. They were also being raced in other areas of the country, and we saw pictures of some of the California cars in magazines. It's amazing how things are so easily influenced, but from those photos we had some idea of what the cars were supposed to look like. You'd study the pictures, and begin trimming and hammering your car accordingly.

In late summer of 1948, I got the itch to try my hand at auto racing. I didn't want to race my '40 coupe, because it was too nice. So I bought a '30 Model A roadster, and dragged it home. The car had been sitting outside for so long, the interior reeked of mouse piss. I had no idea at the time, of course, but that '30 Model A was quite a memorable purchase: My very first race car.

We had a single-bay garage at our house that was built for a Model T, so narrow it could barely fit my dad's '36 Dodge. I parked my cars outside, in back. However, my dad kept our lawn perfect, and I had to tip my car over into the side yard to work on it. It was messy, and my mom and dad both disliked my hobby. If I had brothers and sisters I probably never would have gotten by with it, but being an only child probably gave me some leeway.

I bought a '32 Packard limousine for a tow car. When I finally had my race car finished, I got the kid down the street — he was 13, I think — to steer my race car while I drove the tow car. I later wondered, if you are just guiding a car down the street, do you need a driver's license?

We headed for Hastings, Neb., and my first race-driving experience. I didn't know a soul at the track that day, and there were 13 or 14 cars in the field. I'm fairly sure this was the first race ever held in Hastings. We got there pretty early, and I thought surely I'd know somebody in the pit area, but I didn't. We drove through the pit gate, and the crowd was behind the backstretch, standing on railroad flat cars on the tracks there because it offered a better view of the track. The admission was one dollar.

To collect admission, they sent drivers into the crowd with their helmets. They did this because the drivers were to get a percentage of the gate, and it was always a little dicey because the promoter had a great opportunity to cheat you.

How about this: Of the 13 or 14 drivers at Hastings that day, two eventually won the Daytona 500: Johnny Beauchamp (who won the first Daytona 500 but was denied the win in a scoring dispute) and Tiny Lund, both from Harlan, Iowa. I didn't know either man that day, but later got to know both very well.

Tiny had broken his arm in a motorcycle crash, and his arm was in a crooked cast. The promoter was skittish about Tiny driving with a broken arm, but Tiny wasn't bothered in the least. He drove for Dale Swanson, the man who later got a factory Chevrolet deal with Beauchamp.

Beauchamp won the race that day, and made $200. My debut as a racer was inauspicious, and I don't remember where I finished. But something else happened that day, something very important: I made $22.

I was still working for Blackie at the gas station, making 25 cents an hour. Think how many hours I'd have to work at the station to make $22! You'd work all day long, eight hours, to make two bucks.

I've often wondered: If I hadn't made any money that day, would racing have been as attractive to me? Probably not. It was the greed that got me, most likely. I recognized immediately that the racing deal could supplement my regular earnings, and that got me fired up. Such an idea would keep me fired up over the next three decades.

That day at Hastings hooked me, although I didn't drive very long, maybe a couple dozen times. I liked the racing part a lot, but the idea of getting hurt was on my mind. I wasn't afraid of an injury; I could deal with that stuff because I wanted so badly to race. But it was the idea of how my mother would react that was on my mind.

When I raced the motorcycle, I always prided myself that I never once went down. I always knew that if I went down, I might break my arm or something, and there was no way to hide such a thing from my mother. Whatever happened on the race track couldn't have been any worse that what I knew I faced from her.

I hadn't yet confided in her that I was racing the motorcycle myself. She knew I was forever building stuff, but she didn't know about the racing.

A couple of times she asked me, "You're not racing, are you?"

"Oh, no, I'm not racing."

I wasn't being truthful with her, of course. And that bothered me, very much. Some of it was my conscience; I knew it was wrong to lie, especially to your mother. In fact, I've often observed that the racing addiction is so powerful it would lead you to lie to your own mother. I know, because I did it.

I also knew that denying my driving to my mother wouldn't last forever anyway. If I busted my ass in the race car and came dragging home, there was no way to hide that from her. And I knew that if I kept racing — whether it was cars or motorcycles — sooner or later I'd bust my ass.

As a driver, I was out of control. Nobody had yet told me about slowing down to go faster. It's ironic, I've told that to more guys than probably anybody on the planet: Slow down to go faster. But I didn't know it myself at that stage. I just thought it took big gonads to go fast, and I figured mine were as big as anybody's. Whatever it took, I knew I wanted to do it. So I went out and raced wide open.

Pretty soon I drove my roadster through the fence and knocked the front end off it. This was a problem, because how was I going to get the car home, some 100 miles away, with the front end busted? I had to leave the car there that day, and it got me to thinking: I'm the chief cook, bottle washer, mechanic, driver, sign painter, I did it all. Now that I'm tearing it up, guess who's got to fix it? I began to figure on getting somebody else to drive it.

87 drivers later…

Right from the start, I wanted my race cars to be better than average. In fact, I wanted them to be the best. I didn't know yet how to make them the best, but that's what I wanted.

My '30 Model A roadster was okay, but I had better ideas. I began working on a '25 Model T body, because I saw a photo of such a car from California. Boy, I thought that was the ultimate. I found a '25 body, and took all the wood out of the body — the bodies of those old cars were lined and structured using wood — and the damn thing just laid flat in the yard. I thought, "Now, how do I keep it formed?"

Somebody suggested I build a structure of steel pipe or tubing inside the body panels, but that was beyond my abilities. So while the '25 body was laying flat in our yard, I spotted a Dodge roadster, and I was inspired. You know how it goes: "Man, I gotta have one of those!"

I rushed right out and got a Dodge roadster body. The metal was twice as thick in the Dodge, and I felt it was much better looking.

All of this was junkyard stuff, by the way. You didn't buy anything new. You could cruise the alleys in those days and buy broken-down cars for a song. My cars had not one piece of "speed" equipment, not one piece. Nothing. Zero. Stock junk. You'd take the stock pieces and try to use little bits of information to make them work better. For example, you'd take the distributor off and lock it into fully advanced; a guy showed me how to do that. That was my first "speed secret."

Beyond that, you didn't do much to 'em. You didn't mess with the crankshaft or the oiling system, any of those things. Usually you were simply trying to keep the engine together, and keep the car in one piece. It was a challenge, because these pieces weren't engineered or manufactured for the track. You'd break axles because they weren't made for a racing application. A stock Ford rear end isn't full floating, not the passenger car version. They don't have a bearing out on the end of the housing, so you'd put in a heavy axle key and tighten it up, because the key actually drove the wheel. You kept everything as tight as you knew how, but it was a challenge.

Two blocks from our home at 44th and O lived a kid named Neil Schuppaugh. We attended school together and became great friends, and when the time came to hire my first race driver, Neil was the man.

Neil was a big, strong kid, and his father was a cop. Neil was one of my hot rod buddies, hanging out at Elmer Hanson's Conoco station. His first car was a two-door Model A, and every minute Neil spent in that car, the throttle was wide open. It didn't matter if we were going one block or 100 miles, it was wide open. When I sat in the death seat (front passenger seat), I'd prop my feet on the dashboard because I had this fear of getting pitched through the windshield if he hit something.

Somebody told Neil he should have an oil pressure gauge in his Model A. We thought that was a fine idea, and figured it would be a cinch to install one. Well, you know how it is with kids; sometimes they're dumb as a box of rocks. We got out the electric drill, and drilled into the dash. However, we didn't realize that's where the fuel tank was located. We drilled right through the dash and into the fuel tank, and we're lucky it didn't blow us clear to Omaha. It's amazing to think about such engineering today; locating the fuel tank in the passenger compartment.

So now we had this hole in his dash, where gasoline would leak out if you filled the tank all the way up. To fix it properly we should have removed the dash and installed a new tank; however, that was beyond our technical abilities. We decided to make a wooden peg slightly larger than the hole, and pound the peg into the hole. When the peg worked loose over time, we'd just put another coat of shellac on the peg and knock it back into place.

In 1948 I decided to buy a new Chevrolet business coupe, and I placed my order with the local dealer. They said it would take six months to come in, so I continued to drive my beloved '34 Ford roadster. This was really quite a car, and I had spent a lot of time building it up. But the new Chevy came in much earlier than expected, so I was scrambling to sell my coupe.

Neil was interested, but I had reservations. This was a very fast car, one of the fastest in Lincoln. I had installed a rebuilt short block from Montgomery Ward, and when I was getting ready to put the heads on I noticed a ".000" stamping on the top of the pistons.

I was curious; by this time I knew you had to bore the cylinder slightly to do a rebuild job (I'd figured this out from the time I'd tried to put .060-over pistons into a standard bore cylinder). Then I looked at the pistons more closely, and realized that a zero was stamped over a nine. So it was actually .090 over bore.

The cylinder heads had been ground to straighten them up, which probably shaved quite a bit of metal. With that shaved head and the .090-over bore, along with a set of 4:11 gears, that thing was *fast*. There weren't many cars in Lincoln that could run over 70 mph, but this thing could do close to 90. It was an absolute flyer.

Neil came by Blackie's station to buy the car, and handed me the cash. He hopped into the '34 and started the engine, and went screaming out of the lot onto O Street in a complete broadslide. He was quickly out of sight, foot to the floor, engine wailing.

I can still see myself standing there in horror, saying to myself, "I just sold my best friend his coffin!"

Luckily Neil never crashed the car, or got hurt, but it wasn't for lack of trying. He was hell on wheels. On several occasions he outran the cops in their '37 Chevrolets, top speed 65 mph. They were no match for that '34. It helped that his dad was a local policeman, because now and then the police would come to Neil's house and lecture him, you know, "Don't do that any more!"

Lots of my buddies had run-ins with the police for speeding and street racing. Almost everybody I knew was a little bit wild, a little bit ornery, a little bit out-of-control. I was right in the thick of things, too, but I never once got a speeding ticket. In fact, not only have I never had a ticket, but I've never been arrested and I've never been fingerprinted. Not sure how that happened, I guess I was just lucky.

My pal Woody Brinkman, who later became an official with IMCA, wasn't so lucky. One day our local paper, the *Journal-Star*, put Woody's picture on the front page, because he had been cited for speeding 78 times.

Boy, I had some wild friends…

6

Dusty Sundays

Once I hired Neil Schuppaugh to drive my race car, it wasn't difficult to make the transition from driver to car owner. I liked Neil, and had known him nearly all my life. He was a certified wild man, and I'm not sure if the guy feared anything in the world.

Eventually the wild man was in my race car. First was my roaring roadster, but soon I built a jalopy—a 1936 Ford coupe—and Neil drove that as well.

It wasn't long before I experienced my first lesson as a car owner. We were racing at the Beatrice half-mile and in the midst of the action Neil crashed and stuck his arm through the windshield and got a very nasty cut. He was unable to drive that next weekend, so I was faced with trying to find a new driver.

I quickly realized that this was a never-ending quest for a car owner. Plus, I realized something else: The time I spent repairing my car after an accident was that much time I couldn't spend making it faster. In other words, if I was continually fixing and replacing broken parts, I didn't have the time to focus on how to improve my car. When you're constantly repairing, it's like you're running in place. Sure, there's lot of effort, but it's not focused on the things that make you go faster.

If you're not getting faster, you're not winning. If you're not winning, you're not making any money. That concept got my attention very quickly.

That's when I became a grumpy car owner. If you could win in my car, I liked you. But if you bent my car, buddy, I didn't like you. Not one bit. It wasn't long before I had a bad reputation as a guy who was very picky about whom he hired to drive his car. I didn't care if you were Jesus Christ himself; if you had a reputation as a crasher I wasn't interested in putting you in my car.

Racing was very informal in those years, the late 1940s and early '50s. It seemed like every county fairgrounds in Nebraska had a race track of some sort, certainly every county in the eastern part of the state. The local American Legion or VFW promoted many tracks, because as auto racing blossomed during this period they saw an opportunity to make money from ticket sales.

The purse was typically paid at the post following the races. Nebraska was a dry state at this time, but you could purchase beer at the Legion or VFW because they were members-only clubs.

The clubs would promote the races, collect the admission, and pay the purse. Most of the time we'd hang around the bar at the post after collecting our purse, then spend our winnings on beer. You'd always spend a couple of hours at the club afterward, drinking beer and having a good time with your racing friends and enemies. I'm fairly certain most of these clubs got all their money back that same night.

Some tracks later began running at night, although not many had lights. It was always very late when the races were over. They didn't have curfews to worry about or anything like that, and you might not see the feature start until 2:30 a.m. Then you'd go to the bar after, where there was no curfew, either. They'd stay open till the sun came up.

The race cars were constantly changing during this time. We began with the roaring roadsters, but soon after came the jalopies. The jalopies were kind of a different direction, a different philosophy. They were more affordable, and consequently there were more of 'em. These were more of an entry-level car. The fenders were cut out so they wouldn't rub the tire if they got pushed in, and the interior was gutted. But the windshield was still in place.

As the cars evolved, promoters would often run the two classes of cars together. I'd run my jalopy — a '34 Ford coupe — against roaring roadsters, because there weren't enough roadsters to run as a stand-alone class. The roadsters were more of an open-wheel car, but with a body.

Everything was home built. A jalopy was considered something of a stock car, because in our part of the country they had to have a closed roof. You could close it with a basic piece of aluminum the thickness of a beer can, but it had to be closed. But we saw photos from California where they ran cars with an open roof.

I think the reasoning for the closed roofs was safety, but that was kind of ironic. All of the cars of this era were terribly, terribly dangerous. You used a stock seat, and no safety belt. You might have been wearing your brother's leather football helmet, or maybe a more modern leather Cromwell. Of course there were few roll bars, because these were *stock* cars. Real stock cars. But they turned into jalopies after they got all beat up.

They didn't run the jalopies and roadsters together for very long. There came to be a lot more jalopies on the scene, and the roadsters fell out of favor. They declined just about as rapidly as midgets did. See, the midgets were extremely popular, but by the early 1950s it seemed they had peaked and people moved on to other forms of the sport.

The problem with the midgets was the same that we've seen repeated many times. They didn't get the car counts, and they didn't put on a good enough show. Not enough passing.

And there was always the problem of either the cars being too equal, and therefore very little passing, or the opposite: somebody with such a dominant piece it made the races boring. That was true with every type or race car, because somebody could think of a way to gain an advantage.

For example, you had Bob Rager in his Ranger-powered sprint car that he had "redefined" with a '27 Model T body, racing against podunk stock cars at our county fair half-mile tracks.

Now, remember, most of these races were held on Sunday afternoon, and it might be 115 degrees. Literally. The Ranger (which was actually a WWI-era airplane engine) was air-cooled, racing against Ford flathead V8s. If you've ever driven a flathead on a 115-degree day, you quickly discover the biggest problem is getting enough water to feed that pig. Because she's gonna be puking water everyplace, running hotter than the hubs of hell.

So Bob had a tremendous advantage with the Ranger, and he basically won all the races for a while. Later on, Bob's son Roger became a helluva race driver in his own right. Roger, in fact, led the Indianapolis 500 in 1980 with a stock-block Chevrolet engine.

But nobody stayed on top forever, not Bob or anybody. I think that was part of what motivated me for so many years: I saw guys come on strong then fade; I was determined I would never fade. That's what kept me motivated, and successful, for more than 30 years in a highly competitive sport.

We were typically racing once or twice a week, almost exclusively on weekends. We visited many different tracks, most of which aren't around today.

I did some historic things back then, stuff I laugh about now. I took my '34 Ford coupe to the very first race at Beatrice, Neb., to run the new quarter-mile dirt track there. The original track in Beatrice was located nearly downtown along the Blue River, but along this time they relocated the track outside of town at the county fairgrounds. This was the very first race held at the new location.

I hired Dutch Buettgenback to drive my car. Dutch was a brick mason and he had arms about the size of my waist; he was a very tough guy. (I always wanted tough guys around me, just in case one of our competitors paid us a visit in the pits afterward.)

He was hot-lapping my car, and he brought it in and said the steering was all bound up.

"I can't turn it," he said.

In my infinite wisdom, I said, "Get the hell out, I'll drive it."

I drove onto the track and was hot lapping, and somehow I flipped it down the front straightaway. The very first flip at the brand new race track. Some feat, 'eh?

I'm lying in the car, upside down, cussing like a parrot. A good buddy of mine, Gordy Shuck, came running over. Gordy and I raced against each other nearly all our lives, and he was one of the very few guys to call me, "Billy." Everybody called me Bill, or Speedy, or son-of-a-bitch, or whatever. But nobody called me "Billy," except Gordy and maybe a couple others.

I'm lying in that upside-down car in front of the packed grandstand, and Gordy sticks his head in my window.

"You okay, Billy?"

"Aw, this goddam thing…" So I wore it that day.

The first jalopy I built, the one Neil drove, was a '35 Ford coupe. Then I had a '32 Ford sedan, and later a '34 Ford coupe. All three were over a fairly short time. By the time I took my '34 to Playland Park, Woody Brinkman was driving for me.

Woody was an outstanding midget driver after the war. He outran Bill Vukovich and some of the stars of the day at Dallas and Oklahoma City. He was good, and he didn't crash, and that's why I liked him in my race car. I knew with Woody behind the wheel we wouldn't be bringing the car home in a basket. After his driving career had ended, Woody became a longtime flagman and official with IMCA, and later was part owner of the historic organization.

That day at Playland Park, my rear main seal was leaking so badly it coated the clutch in oil, and it wouldn't engage. The car wouldn't move. Woody and I hurried over to a local drugstore and bought a pound of alum. We took the inspection plate off the bell housing and blew the alum into the clutch area, and got it to where it would hold, and raced 'er.

Another memory I have of Woody is at Neligh, Neb., in probably 1949 or '50. They had never raced anything but horses at Neligh, but they decided to hold a roaring roadster race with their county fair. The roadsters were having a hard time getting enough cars for an event. You needed at least 12, 14 cars to put on a race in those days. A typical program was a couple of heat races, an Australian Pursuit race, and the feature race.

A lot of people today don't know about an Australian Pursuit race, but they were very common back then. You'd invert the field, and if you are passed, you have to pull in. The race goes a set number of laps and whoever is leading at the finish is the winner.

I had somebody else in my car that day at Neligh, and Woody drove up in his '40 Ford street car, he didn't have a car to drive and was just attending the race as a spectator. His '40 was a very fast street car, and Woody knew how to handle it.

We got to the track and grass was growing in the corner, and they didn't know if they should leave it there or not. They were also having trouble getting the water wagon from downtown to the track, because without watering the track all the spectators would turn to chocolate from the dust and sweat. They would at least sprinkle the straightaways.

Lots of our tracks were dusty like that. The backstretch and corners were as dusty as a tornado. From the grandstand, the only car you saw was the leader. The rest of it was a roar, obscured by the dust. As a driver you had to learn to drive by Braille; listen carefully, and when the guy ahead of you lifted, you had to lift and turn left.

They also had a baseball game going on that day at Neligh in the infield, so the people who didn't want to watch the race could watch the baseball game. A lady watching the race was hit in the head by a foul ball, and it knocked her cold. Knocked her clear out of the grandstand!

Once everybody got to the track, we realized we were short of cars. We only had maybe seven or eight entries for this wonderful event at the county fair. The officials were pleading for more cars, so Woody went out and got his '40 Ford coupe, completely street legal, and raced against the roaring roadsters. He ran third or so, which I thought was damned impressive.

Another of my early drivers was Rex Jordan, from right here in Lincoln. Rex and I had become longtime friends because of our mutual interests in hot rods and racing. He was known as "The Fox," partly because he had a very long nose. I've seen that nose get broken two or three times. He'd rough up the competitors on the track and they'd take a poke at him after the races, just reaching through the window and smacking him.

I helped Rex build one of the first roaring roadsters in our area. His dad was a machinist, so he knew a little more about machining than most young guys. Rex later became a terrific machinist himself. He built his own steering gear out of an old Chevy box, and he went to race at Beatrice and of course guess what happened? The steering gear failed and he launched over the edge of the track into a deep ravine, breaking his nose when it hit the steering wheel.

After helping Rex on his own car, he later drove my jalopy.

Thinking about all this really brings back memories. I'll never forget seeing my first auto race. It was 1941, just before WWII, and I was 12 years old. It was a midget race at Landis Field, a baseball park.

My dad took me out to the field and dropped me off, and I sat in the stands by myself. But that didn't matter. Wow, did I like racing! It was like you unleashed a drug in my bloodstream.

The hook was set, from that moment on.

The midgets had a distinct rise and fall during those early years. I attended lots of midget races, and they really were the inspiration for my passion for auto racing. We went to Council Bluffs on Friday or Saturday night. They also had midget races in Lincoln, they built a track at the airport and I went there often.

I never owned a midget, because for some reason I never had an allure to go midget racing, and I couldn't afford what it took to be competitive. I caught some heat a couple of years ago for a comment I made in a magazine where I said I never owned a midget because, "midget owners have midget minds."

Some people were apparently put off by that, but they took the comment too seriously. That was a common expression in the early 1950s, more as a joke than anything else. Of course different times have different perceptions, and mine was justified at the time. I'll defend them, always. I laugh when I think about this, because this debate was always in good fun between various segments of racers.

7

A New Adventure

By the early part of 1952, my life was incredibly busy and hectic. I was finishing my last semester at Nebraska Wesleyan, Joyce and I were planning an October wedding, I was still selling used cars at Wally's at 20th and P, and my racing addiction was in full bloom. I spent plenty of hours either working on my race cars or going to the races.

I was also very busy working on street cars for my buddies, making them run faster or sound better or both. I was working at home in my dad's garage at 44th and O Street in Lincoln, doing the work as a hobby. Yes, the guys paid me for working on their cars, but it wasn't truly a business. Not yet. I was experimenting with engine conversions, things like that. All of my "business" came through word of mouth; I'd put a dual exhaust system on my buddy's car, and somebody else would hear it and come to me, "Can you make my car sound like that?" That's how it got started.

I'll always remember 1952, however, not just for being busy, but because of the very significant events that came about at the same time, all of them life changing. Plus, I met two men who were very important mentors to me, teaching me things I use to this day, nearly 60 years later. The first was Wally Smith (no relation), and Henry "Hynie" Hompes.

Wally had a car lot at 1719 N Street in Lincoln, and was a very flamboyant, flashy guy who wore diamond rings on almost every finger. He was the typical car salesman of the day. If he needed to wipe his nose, he'd whip out a handkerchief that had a diamond ring tied on each corner. He also bought and sold guns, and was probably the busiest gun dealer in the area.

Wally was the best horse trader I ever knew. If you came in with an old shotgun and were looking for a fine rifle, he could figure a way to trade and he never lost money. I was fascinated with his knowledge, and the way he could think on his feet. Boy, was he sharp. It was a tough business but he was good enough at it to survive.

The concept of owning and operating a business was very different then. If you went in to borrow money to buy a commercial lot, the theory of the property appreciating wasn't even a factor. Real estate simply didn't increase in value like it did in later years. You'd sweat all those payments — after purchasing the lot on contract from the owner, without a bank loan — and hope like hell that one day you could sell it and get your money back. There were no guarantees and very few people had the capital to invest in real estate. A handful of people held most of the property. Land barons, I guess you'd say, in the city.

It was a period when it was very difficult to get a loan. The men at the bank could think of 20 reasons why they didn't want to lend to you. The focus was on the risk, and banks were very conservative. That made it tough if you were starting a business, because it was hard to get the capital together to get the thing going. That's why so many businesses failed; you simply ran out of money. You couldn't make it back fast enough to survive.

After meeting Wally in the late 1940s, I approached him about renting some space on his lot. It made sense to me, because I had a used car license, and I was still very busy buying and selling cars. I thought it was time to have a business location, because I was busy enough that I began to earn a reputation from people who had bought cars from me before.

Wally was open to the idea, and his son Chick said he'd help sell my cars when I wasn't around. This was important, because I was a full-time college student at the time. I couldn't be at the lot much, because I was in class. But both Wally and Chick did right by me, and sold a few of my cars. I was encouraged.

I started selling cars with an early form of "tote the note." A customer could buy a car with $5 down, making $5 weekly payments till it was paid off. The payments were due each Saturday morning. If they didn't show up with the money, that night I'd go looking for them, and I'd repossess the car.

I'd get shot at, chased, threatened, cussed, whatever, but I had no choice. If they stiffed me I'd go broke, sooner rather than later.

It might sound silly, buying a car with $5 down. But remember, $5 was a week's wages for many people in 1950. If you made $50 per week, that was considered a pretty decent salary. So $5 still meant quite a lot at that time. If I lost enough

$5 payments, it's obvious the impact it would have on my finances.

I was learning a lot about people, and business, and life. Remember what my dad told me: "If you want to win in a game, you'd better know the game, and you'd better know the players." That proved to be sound advice, and I can give you a good example.

My friend Bob Lundberg, who later was my announcer when I promoted some auto races, would often come by the lot on Wednesday and ask to borrow some money. The routine was the same for several weeks: He'd borrow $5, promising to pay me $10 that weekend. This went on for a while when one day he came in on a Saturday and said, "Well, Bill, I don't have your money."

I looked at him and he said, "I'll tell you what: Let's make a bet. I'll bet you the $10 I owe you that I can drink a half-pint of whiskey in seven seconds. If I can't, I'll owe you another $10."

Immediately my mind was calculating...the opening on a half-pint bottle of whiskey is only about as big as your little finger, and you can't make the whiskey flow out of the bottle in seven seconds. I figured there was no way he could do it.

"I'll take that bet."

The next few moments were a very, very important lesson for me. Bob reached over and got a glass, poured the whiskey into the glass, and drank it from the glass in just one swallow.

I hadn't known the game. I *thought* I knew, but I didn't. I didn't ask the right questions about the rules. It was a $10 lesson, one that I carry with me to this day.

Don't assume you know something. If you're at stake to wager, you damned well better have an absolute understanding of the process, and all the variables.

Thinking back, I was dumb and naïve to think about our wager in only one context. When he poured that whiskey into a glass, the entire equation changed. And I never considered that. I was too busy thinking about what I *thought* I knew.

Know the game, and know the players. Always.

I graduated from Nebraska Wesleyan in 1952 with a degree in Industrial Education, and immediately had an offer for a teaching position at a small school in the middle of Nebraska. The salary was $2,750 per year.

I was 23 years old, and my life was at a crossroads. I had been involved in racing in some form since I was 16, and had progressed to the role of car owner. My car had earned about

$4,500 the previous summer, with the driver getting 40 percent. Plus, I had made a few bucks with my car business.

I knew I could be successful and make a living at my business and racing. I was confident of that. It was what you might call a "no brainer," at least from my perspective.

I built my own engines and built many of my competitor's engines, too. Flathead Fords ruled, and I knew those engines. You kept close watch over your tires on the race car, because you could run a tire forever. If you crashed, you usually tore up a wheel and tire, at least, and that was bad. But I only hired drivers who would take care of my race car, and we both made money.

We were winning pretty frequently. In fact, there were times — particularly a few years later — when I watched my driver, Lloyd Beckman, against the rest of the field and thought, "I wonder why the rest of these guys showed up tonight?"

Sure, I was cocky. But you need some of that to be successful. If you're not a little bit cocky, you should probably find another game to play.

But I do know this: Every night we raced, I believed we could win. That was a very fun time. We actually got to the point where I'd come home and Joyce would say, "Did you win it?"

"No, we finished second."

"*Second!!??* What happened?"

She began thinking that every time we ran, we should win. And we did win a lot, but if you sit at the poker table for a while, you don't win every hand.

Sometime in early 1952 I hatched an idea I couldn't stop thinking about. What if I opened a speed shop, selling and installing performance parts?

Could such a business work in Lincoln? Yes, the hot-rod hobby was starting to take off, but it was still a very limited market. But I had the idea, and I couldn't stop thinking about it.

In the early 1950s a guy in town came up with the idea of a hobby shop, where you could rent space to work on your car. He rented a building, and guys brought their cars in and started working on them. I was still in college, and I'd swing by to take a look. It was actually pretty interesting, because guys were working on all kinds of stuff in there. Everything from radical "dream" creations to more traditional restorations of a Model A, for example.

You might see somebody trying to put a Continental kit on a car, or make up something they had seen in a magazine. The typical hot rodder wasn't in there; the hobby-shop crowd was more artistic. The guys installing hopped-up camshafts in their '32 roadsters, they weren't in the hobby shop. They were in garages around town, at their homes.

The fellow who owned the hobby shop probably figured on getting plenty of support from the many Air Force servicemen from Lincoln and Omaha, many of who were avid car guys. But what he didn't figure was that most of the airmen worked on their cars right there on the base.

It wasn't long before the hobby shop closed. Even though the car hobby was growing, Lincoln still wasn't a big enough market to make it work.

I wasn't discouraged, though. The more I thought about the idea of a speed shop the more I thought it was a good idea, particularly if I could install the parts for the customers.

Remember the story of me driving all the way to Denver just to buy a set of Smitty mufflers? That's how car guys are: hardcore. I figured there were enough hardcore guys in my region to make it work.

There was already a speed shop in Omaha, and one evening I drove up to take a look. The guy had already closed for the day, so I stood outside and looked in the windows. The man who owned the shop had been a midget driver, and had been hurt in the race car. I think he was in a wheelchair, which was a common injury in that era. If you were bold, you weren't gonna get old, not in those days.

I stood outside the man's shop, and dreamed. "If only I had a shop like this...I could make it in this business!"

Finally I decided I'd give the idea a try. I knew lots of hot rodders, and I knew lots of racers. Those guys all had the same issues I had: Where can I get quality parts for my race car, or my hot rod? That was the essence of it.

I've always found it's easier to sell your plan to yourself than anybody else. Most of the time, if I talked to people about what I wanted to do, they'd throw a wet blanket over me. "Gee, that's dumb, you shouldn't do that." "Why would you want to do that?"

Those people didn't have the same interests as me, the same passion. Whether you have enough guts to do it, or drive, or whatever—maybe the right word is foolishness—you're the easiest one to convince that your idea is sound.

I have that same issue today with my four sons, all of whom are in the business with me. I say I'm going to do something, and they say, "Nah, that doesn't sound like a good idea." I already think it's a great idea, but they usually need some convincing.

At the time, I don't think I told anyone about my idea, except Wally and Chick Smith. I told them I wanted to move out of their space and open my own shop. They were both very supportive, and encouraged me to give it a try.

I knew I needed a place with lots of visibility, and in Lincoln that meant O Street. It's the main thoroughfare from east to west, with plenty of traffic coming in and out of town each day. If I could get a place on O Street, where people could see me, it could work. I was sure of it. With all that visibility, I wouldn't have to spend as much money on advertising.

I didn't have enough money on my own to get the shop opened, so I borrowed $300 from Joyce. We weren't married yet, but were engaged.

Once I got the $300, I really got busy. I located a place at 2232 O Street, a 400-square-foot location that was 20' by 20', with a small lot outside to sell a few cars. I nailed down the details and paid the first month's rent, and got the phone hooked up. I found a sign painter to make me up a nice sign, and got that hung. We painted the place, trimmed the wood around the windows, and we were set. Purple was the color of my race cars, but I didn't dare paint the building purple. Even I wouldn't go that far.

Speedway Motors officially opened the doors in April 1952. I had my very own speed shop!

Where did I get the name? Actually, that's the name I had been using for three or four years on my motor vehicle dealer's license.

I had planned on saving my first dollar, but I needed it! I actually had it on the wall for a while, but one day I took it down and used it. That sounds stupid, but if you've ever had a business you know what I'm talking about. Especially when I needed a $300 loan from my fiancée to start the business in the first place.

I didn't have much room in my little pop stand. When you use that phrase today—pop stand—many people don't know what a pop stand is. "Let's blow this pop stand!" was a popular phrase in those days, essentially saying you were ready to leave someplace. A pop stand was a little business back in the day where they sold cold drinks, candy, etc. Usually a very small concern. So when I joke about my first shop being a pop stand, what I'm saying is that it wasn't very big.

I can't recall exactly how much I paid in rent, but I think it was $20 or $25 per month. It was a small amount of money, but those first few months when it came due, it didn't seem small. I quickly came to understand the constant challenge of cash flow, and just how vulnerable a business is to what I call "outside forces."

There are many elements *you* control: How you budget your money, hiring the right people, making the right advertising and purchasing decisions, things like that. But there are also an overwhelming number of things you don't control which absolutely affect your business.

For example, I remember that the horse races came to the state fair track two weeks before the fair, which was always held over Labor Day. Lincoln probably had a population of 75,000 at that time, and those two events—the horse races and then the fair—took just about every dollar out of our local economy. I mean, took every penny that wasn't earmarked for essentials such as food and rent.

Suddenly, my customers were broke for a few weeks. Think that affects your business? And there wasn't a thing I could do about it. You can't change the times, you can't change what's happening, so you just deal with it like a bump in the road and try to keep going. Work through it. Do your job the best you can, stand behind what you say, and do what you can do.

Earlier I mentioned Hynie Hompes, and what an important mentor he was to me. Hynie operated a Hudson automobile dealership next door to my shop at 1719 N, and he was willing to give me sound, solid advice on many occasions. Not long, drawn-out lectures, but straight advice with very few words.

Maybe somebody came in wanting to write me a check for a rear end. I wasn't sure if I should take a check from the out-of-town customer. So I'd tell the guy, "Give me just a minute, and I'll be right back."

I'd slip out my back door and hurry over to Hynie's office. "Hynie, this guy from out of town wants to give me a check for a rear end. What should I do?" He'd look at me and think for a minute, and say, "Kid, leave it on the shelf, or send him to the bank." Then he'd look back at his paperwork. Lesson was over. In other words, tell the guy no. Leave the part on the shelf.

I never questioned him, or debated with him. I didn't say, "Well, gee, Hynie, I could sure use the money…" I figured he knew what he was talking about. So I'd go back to the guy and say, "Sorry, buddy, you'll have to go to the bank, I can't take your out-of-town check."

Hynie knew what he was talking about. Later on, I got stiffed by so many of my customers — most of them were my fellow racers — that I put up a big neon sign that said, "NO CHECKS." That was an important lesson in the performance business. You never, ever sell race parts on credit. Because the guy puts the part on his car, and maybe he wipes out the entire car a week later. Or maybe be breaks something else and has to come up with more cash to replace that part, which he'll buy from somebody else because he still owes you money. Then when the season's over he looks at you and says, "Gee, Bill, sorry, but I'm broke!"

I damn near went broke learning that lesson.

Hynie was an interesting guy. He did well at his Hudson dealership, selling a type of car that didn't appeal to everybody. Hudson automobiles were flashy, often painted in exotic colors such as aqua or pink. He'd sell a car to a local hairdresser, or somebody real high-profile. He'd finance the cars himself, which at the time was unusual for a high-end *new* car.

Sometimes you'd see a brand new car in his showroom that was actually two or three years old. For example, in 1955 he might have a '52 Hudson sitting there that had never been sold. To have a model lingering there for three years, and then one day somebody would walk in and buy it, that just amazed me. I'd ask Hynie how he came out, and he always said, very enthusiastically, "I did okay!"

At the time I started the speed shop, almost everybody in the automotive parts business in Lincoln was Jewish. The hard parts stores — things like brakes and batteries and spark plugs — and the salvage yards, everything. It seemed like I was the only gentile trying to get into this business. That made it more difficult, because from the beginning I was an outsider. Not just because I was new, but because of cultural issues. The industry people in the area didn't have a lot of fondness for me, because I was different.

I guess that's why I appreciated Hynie so much. We were of different faiths, but that was never an issue. He was helpful and supportive, and was always encouraging me. There were lots of days I was overwhelmed, or just beat up from the rigors of business, but he'd offer an upbeat word or smile, and tell me to stick with it. Looking back, I realize now how much that meant to me. He really was a good friend.

One of the major problems I faced was that I couldn't buy inventory at wholesale. Most suppliers — remember, the performance industry was in its infancy — couldn't produce parts very fast, so even though it was a niche market, demand almost always exceeded supply.

Plus, sometimes the manufacturer would grant an exclusive wholesale deal through one of my competitors, and the only way I could buy the product was through him, and I had to pay full retail price. That was a tough proposition.

One of the solutions I came up with was to manufacture as many specialty pieces as I could. For example, one part of the business that kept growing was our engine swapping service. Guys would bring their Ford in, and ask us to pull out their flathead engine and drop in an overhead-valve Buick, Cadillac, or Oldsmobile engine because they had more power. We would figure out the conversion pieces needed, and we'd do the swap. Most of the time the conversion pieces didn't exist on the market, so I'd make 'em myself. That way, I could control more of the supply and process.

We also did a lot of engine rebuilding, and in time I bought a Stewart Warner engine balancer, which allowed us to build racing engines. When you turn an engine at a much higher rpm, it has a tendency to shake itself to pieces. But balancing made all the difference in the world.

Joyce never forgot the story regarding the engine balancer. She had saved funds to remodel our kitchen, but guess what...the funds were "diverted" to purchase the engine balancer. After they had built the room at our shop to house the balancer, Joyce proceeded to go back to the shop and ask what color her new kitchen was to be painted. Icebox white!

John Marsh was the balancing man. He later graduated from the University of Nebraska with a Masters degree, and still later became the Dean at the Milford Trade School. The story of the "icebox white" engine balancer has been told and retold many times, as we have remained friends all these years.

We did a lot of exhaust work. Dual exhausts were becoming very popular, and that was typically the first thing a hot rodder did to his car. It wasn't a difficult project, but most guys didn't weld or have access to the proper parts. That's where Speedway Motors came in, and we had a steady stream of customers asking for dual exhaust installation.

A fellow from the West Coast, Aaron Fenton, had developed a new line of exhaust products. Aaron was originally from

Lincoln, and he began offering things ranging from manifolds to a complete dual exhaust kit that became fairly popular. I made a deal with Aaron to buy some of his kits and pretty soon I was selling a few.

The products weren't great, and they took some time to install because they weren't exactly consistent. Again, the process of manufacturing was very crude compared to today, and standards were quite loose. You might get two sets side by side, but one needed a lot of bending and tweaking to fit the same application.

After some trial and error we figured it out and could get them on the customer's car pretty consistently.

Down the street from me was a guy named Benny Finkelstein, who sold hard parts from his shop, Ben's Auto Parts. I knew this, of course. What I did not know was that Aaron Fenton was actually Aaron Finkelstein, Benny's brother. Anti-Semitism was very pronounced during this era, and Aaron apparently felt he had a better chance of succeeding in southern California with a last name that didn't arouse such hostility. It's hard to imagine today, but at the time it was a very real problem for those of the Jewish faith.

Benny called Aaron and said, "This kid down the street is selling a few of your exhaust systems. Why don't you send us a boxcar load, because obviously the demand is pretty good."

Next thing you know, Benny is selling these exhaust systems for 40 percent less than I could *buy* 'em for. That was brutal. But we hung in there, and we'd still sell a few because nobody else knew how to install them like we did.

Pretty soon, guys were coming back to Benny's shop, telling them they were having trouble getting the things to fit. Benny just told them, "Go see that kid down at the speed shop, he knows what to do!" So here they'd come. I'd help 'em out, mostly because I hoped it would turn them into a customer.

About a year-and-a-half later, I got a call from Aaron.

"Benny doesn't want to sell my exhaust systems anymore," he said. "I've got a bunch of them sitting down there. Thought you'd be interested in buying them."

I said yes, I might be interested.

"What will you give me for 'em?" he asked.

I thought for a moment.

"Ten cents on the dollar."

"God, you're trying to kill me!" Aaron groaned.

"Aaron, for a year and a half you guys have been trying to kill *me*."

He paused for a moment.

"Well, take your truck down there and pick them up. Send me a check when you can."

Sometimes you just have to outlast 'em.

I figured I scored a real breakthrough as autumn came in 1952. I was scratching and clawing to find some margin, hoping somebody would sell me parts at wholesale.

A slick, fast-talking factory rep from Kansas City stopped by my store, and he said the magic words: "Dealer discount." He was selling tire chains, and he offered me a "deal" on this pallet of chains.

I figured this was a "can't miss" deal. It always snows in the winter here in Lincoln, and the streets aren't cleared like they are today. Tire chains were a hot commodity during a big Nebraska snowstorm.

End of the story...we had no snow during the winter of 1952-53. The weight of those damned chains on the pallet almost fell through the wooden floor of my speed shop! Spring came, and I sold them for scrap iron at the local salvage yard.

In business for yourself? Those learning curves are tough!

The first year was kind of tough for Speedway Motors, but I got through. Particularly the winter; when the snow flies, guys have their race cars put up, and aren't as busy with their hot rods. Plus, it was damned cold in my shop. I had a little gas heater, about the size of a small chest cooler, and during the winter I'd sit on the heater to keep warm.

I also picked up some showcases at an auction from a hardware store. These cases were very old, probably dating back to the 1920s or earlier. They were used to sell Keen pocketknives, and had "Keen Cutter" etched in the glass. They weren't really appropriate for selling speed parts, but it's all I could afford. I was so happy when somebody accidentally broke those panes of glass in the cases, and I could replace them with clear glass. But they stayed in there until somebody broke 'em; no need to spend the money until I had to.

One of the tricks of the trade was our inventory. Whenever I got a part in—particularly in my very early days—I'd put the part in the window, and put the empty box up on the shelf, making it look like I had two of them. I wanted to create the image that I had things in stock.

When a guy is looking for a part, it's very important you have it when he's looking for it. You don't want him going somewhere else.

I'll tell you a funny story about an exhaust-bending machine I bought.

A fellow out in California had a very busy muffler operation, and he built a machine that made it much easier to bend tubing. The tools of the day were very primitive, and bending tubing was a difficult process. But the guy combined a hydraulic press, a big steel I-beam, and a series of dies to create a very neat bending machine. It really was a breakthrough.

The guy had a brother who was quite the free spirit, and he apparently didn't think it was a good idea to have the wild-and-wooly brother hanging around the business all the time. So he offered the brother the opportunity to hit the road with one of his machines, telling him to go out into the world to sell this latest wonder of the world.

The brother got a new Cadillac convertible, put the machine on a trailer, and headed east. His first stop was Las Vegas, where he apparently had a good time at the casinos and somehow hooked up with a Vegas showgirl.

With his new girl on his arm, they hit the road. Their next stop was Salt Lake City, but his image didn't quite mesh with the Mormon culture, and he had no takers on the machine. Next was Denver, where he still didn't find a buyer.

He continued to wander east, where he rolled into Lincoln on a Saturday afternoon. By then the Vegas showgirl was looking a little tired and droopy.

The guy walked through my front door, and told me he had a machine that was going to change my life. Actually, I was interested. I told him that if he had a machine that could easily bend tubing, he was my new best friend. I could see the machine sitting on the trailer behind the Cadillac, and next thing you know he's backed up to our shop.

We plugged in the machine, and he's giving us a full demonstration. Boy, that was the slickest thing I'd ever seen.

I told him to sit tight, and I'd be right back. I hurried home. Joyce had been saving up money, and she had put back $2,500. I raided the savings and ran back to the shop, where I paid the guy and was the proud new owner of a tube bending machine.

The brother and the showgirl waved as they drove off into the sunset, and I never saw them again. Sometime later the brother back in California sold the business to one of the big chains, and as far as I know everybody lived happily ever after. As for me, I had that machine for many years until we finally just plumb wore it out. After using it to build countless exhaust systems, we later used it to bend moly tubing, and finally had the I-beam all crooked from the strain.

Kind of makes me wonder...I'll bet my machine lasted a lot longer than the Vegas showgirl, don't you suppose?

8

Motivated by Fear

Just between you and me, I have a confession to make: The one thing that motivates me more than anything else, from my first day opening the doors at Speedway Motors to yet today, is fear.

Most guys don't like to admit they have fear. It's not the macho thing to do. But I'll tell you, fear has been a powerful, powerful force in my lifetime. In my case I think it's been a positive, but it's still a painful truth.

What did I fear most? Failure. The fear of failure was the most powerful element I could have ever known, and it has stuck with me almost every minute of my life.

In racing, losing meant failure. So I didn't want to lose, I wanted to win. In business, closing my doors or going bankrupt would have been failure, and I wasn't prepared to live with that idea.

I guess I'm a proud individual, because the thought of having to face the world knowing I failed at something would be so painful I can't even imagine it. It goes back to me pleading with the elementary school not to set me back a grade when I missed 18 months of classroom time. Even though I would have had a perfectly legitimate reason to be set back, I was terrified of the thought of being considered a failure.

If my race cars couldn't win, everybody might snicker and say what a failure Bill Smith is. That thought motivated me to work harder than almost anybody, trying to make my cars faster and more durable than the other cars.

If my business couldn't make it, everybody might snicker again, and say what a terrible businessman I am. That thought motivated me to work long hours, put every dime back into the business, and ask my family to live a very austere lifestyle for many years to ensure my business could survive.

Fear of failure has been with me every step of the way. I've tried to keep it at bay, and not let it completely rule my life. As the years passed it's been a little easier because I feel more confident that my business won't fail, but the very thought of failure still gives me a cold shiver.

But in late 1952, my business was tenuous at best. The fact is, the deck was stacked against me. Failure was a very real possibility.

First of all, Speedway Motors was brand new. That's the most critical period for any business, particularly for small business. The rate of failure in first year is a very large percentage.

Second of all, I was working in a brand new field. The performance industry was still in its infancy, and most people on the street didn't have any idea what the concept was. In fact, there was really no "performance industry" yet; it was a scattered bunch of tiny businesses with hardcore guys at the helm, building and selling stuff to fellow enthusiasts. To say we were a niche is a large understatement.

Third, you don't exactly look at Lincoln as the cradle of the hot rod or racing hobby. It isn't southern California, or Indianapolis. If my business could sell stuff to cows and pigs, that would have made more sense. Within my tiny circle, there were only a handful of prospective hot rod and racing customers.

That's why, if you walked into our 400-square-foot shop at 2232 O Street in Lincoln sometime in 1952 or '53, you'd have seen a slender, hyperactive guy hustling behind the counter, going at top speed. If you'd have hung around till the evening, you would have seen that guy shift gears and begin working on race cars, getting ready for the upcoming weekend.

That was me, and my way of life. I was trying to survive, devoting all my energy to Speedway Motors, and to my race cars. I had a young family—Joyce and I were married on Oct. 26, 1952, and our first son Carson was born in 1954—but I also had a very understanding and supportive wife. Joyce kept everything together, never complained, and kept me from losing my mind.

If I were to study those early years and come up with some kind of analysis, I'd have to say my racing success came much more quickly than my business success. Speedway Motors grew slowly and steadily, but it was many years before it really took off. But on the racing side, by the mid-1950s we were winning frequently and had established ourselves as a pretty good force in our region.

In 1952, before my days as a race promoter, I hired my old friend Bob Lundberg to drive my '34 Ford coupe at the Ord, Neb., races. Bob and I had gone to high school together, and he was a highly intelligent man. Bob would come to school the first two weeks of the semester, and then skip the rest of the term, riding the rails to California, then hopping a banana boat to South America, or some other great adventure. After all this he would return to school in time to ace the semester exam and pass the course. His IQ was amazing, and it used to piss me off because I'd work hard the entire term just to get a decent grade, while he skipped nearly all the classes and did as well or better.

When we got to Ord, we saw that all the guys from Harlan, Iowa, were there, including Johnny Beauchamp and Tiny Lund. They were running their '39 and '40 Ford coupes. Dale Swanson operated a repair shop in Harlan, and he had built their cars. Dale was a genius when it came to building race cars, and boy, they were tough.

In those days it was illegal to run a locked rear end, which means the engine drove *both* rear wheels. The standard rear end drove only one wheel at a time, and that's what we were supposed to be running. If somebody suspected you were running a locked rear end, you could easily check it by jacking up one wheel and start the car with the transmission in gear. If the rear end was locked, the car would drive right off the jack.

During the race at Ord, one of the Iowa guys lost a rear wheel, yet he drove back to the pit area. In order to do that, the rear end had to be locked. Had to be!

But when the officials looked it over, it looked perfectly stock. It was like an optical illusion, because I saw with my own eyes the car driving with one rear wheel. But since it looked stock, nobody was disqualified.

It rained that night, and we were delayed for a little while. I was able to let some air out of Lundberg's tires to gain some traction, and when it stopped raining he could really drive forward. I loaded our spare tires, our jack, everything with some weight into the back of the coupe to help him get traction. We won the race, through sheer trickery and skullduggery.

It was probably 40 years later when I was sitting at a banquet table having an enjoyable conversation with Dale Swanson, who had built those Iowa cars. He really was an interesting guy, with some fascinating stories. I mentioned that night at Ord, and how I was sure those rear ends were locked.

Dale laughed, and nodded. He told me how he had discovered a very clever way of locking the rear ends without welding the spider gears. It was really an inspired bit of engineering; he installed the gears in such a way that when they got hot and expanded they locked together, yet by the time they were inspected they had cooled and everything looked perfectly normal. It was one of the most ingenious things I'd ever seen in all my years of mechanical experience.

I was glad he told me, because for years I had wondered how in the hell that car was able to drive back to the pits with only one rear wheel.

In 1953 I had my old friend Woody Brinkman driving my car, a '34 Ford coupe. We were racing every Sunday night at a new track in Lincoln called Capitol Beach. The track was located near an amusement park, not far from downtown. Woody had been married not long before, and was racing under the name "Bud Graves" so his wife wouldn't find out. They lived in an apartment house right next door to my speed shop.

Woody is about six years older than I, and had served in the Navy during the war. Like me, he started racing motorcycles, and after he returned from the war he got into midgets and was very good. He raced quite a bit at Playland Park in the Council Bluffs area, and traveled down into Oklahoma and Texas after the post-war midget boom down there.

Woody was a good driver, and although he was plenty wild, he rarely bent my race car. Otherwise, I would have fired him, friend or no friend. But he didn't tear much of my stuff up at all.

One Saturday afternoon, after I had spent several evenings getting my car ready for Sunday night, Woody stopped by my shop. Boy, was his tail dragging. I could tell he was really down.

"What's wrong?" I asked.

"Betty found my helmet in the trunk, and knew I'd been racing," he said. "I promised her when we got married I'd quit driving…there's hell to pay, Bill. She says she'll divorce me if I drive your car again. I've got to quit."

I sympathized with Woody, but I was in a jam. I needed to hire another driver, with very little time before tomorrow night.

"Well, who am I gonna get?" I asked him, kind of exasperated.

He looked up at me.

"Let me get you Lloyd Beckman," he said.

I had heard of Lloyd, but he was mostly a motorcycle racer who hadn't done much auto racing. Lloyd had primarily been racing over in Iowa, and I had raced in Nebraska and Kansas, so our paths hadn't really crossed.

Lloyd, in my mind, was too wild. He had a gold tooth in the front where he had gone through a fence and knocked it out. I immediately told Woody I wasn't interested in some wild-ass motorcycle racer who was going to tear up my car.

"No, Lloyd's a good race driver," Woody insisted. "He'll do you a good job."

I was in a bad spot. Under the duress of the situation, with nobody else to hire, I consented. I nodded my head to Woody, and he left to go find Beckman and ask him to drive my car.

And the life-long romance between Lloyd Beckman and Bill Smith was officially underway.

Of all of my drivers, all 87 or so, many were very good racers. Some, such as Jan Opperman and Doug Wolfgang, were sensational. But Lloyd was probably the best short-track racer I ever saw. Yeah, I know, that's saying something. But I mean it. The best.

Lloyd had a lot of natural, God-given talent. He was quick like a cat. If you've ever watched a cat jump from the floor to the table, you almost don't see them jump because they're so quick. Lloyd had those kind of reflexes.

I always said Lloyd had a gyro built into his tailbone. His balance, his reflexes, were amazing. In his prime, I've seen him touch the tip of his toe to his nose and you wouldn't even see it. I don't know how else to describe it other than to say he was simply cat quick.

Lloyd was ultimately married three times, and his first wife was a very short gal whose legs were about 15 inches long. They were champion roller skaters, she and Lloyd. To watch Lloyd roller skate or dance, it was fluid motion.

He was also a very tough cookie, physically. He had a mean scowl and a difficult disposition most of the time. Some of it was an act he used to encourage people to keep their distance, but he could and would fight when needed.

Lloyd was also tenacious, and he didn't like to lose. We made a lot of money together with our race car. In fact, Lloyd became a racer very quickly; he didn't want to have a regular job during the week, so he was extra motivated to win on the weekends so he could support himself. Isn't that the typical racer mindset?

Somewhere along the line during this period I got the bright idea that I wanted to start promoting races. I'm not exactly sure where such a hare-brained idea came from, but I got it in my head that promoting races was going to be my destiny, bigger than owning a race car, bigger than the speed shop.

I did some investigating, and figured out how the business worked. Much of the racing in this era took place at half-mile county fair tracks; there weren't many purpose-built auto racing facilities. Most of these county tracks were owned by a fair board, and they would hire a promoter to organize the racing events.

Each year in early January all the county fair managers in the region would come to the Cornhusker Hotel in Lincoln for a week-long session of booking carnival events, thrill-shows, racing events, all the things that made their county fairs viable. In addition to the livestock judging and pie contests, these were the events that took place in front of the grandstand.

I went to these meetings and pitched the idea that I could promote a race at your county fair. I would guarantee the cars, bring the announcer and officials, and handle the running of the event. Everything needed to put on the race, I would take care of. They provided the facility — the track, the lights, and so forth — and I'd help prepare the track and do the things needed to have the race.

One of the tracks that took me up on my offer was the Valley County Fairgrounds in Ord. I made the deal for three or four races there in the summer of 1953.

Along about this time a fellow from the South named Bill France was slowly gaining a foothold with a new group called NASCAR. France had expanded his reach clear up into our region, and was sanctioning weekly races at North Platte and some other Nebraska tracks.

Eddie O'Boyle was the NASCAR representative in our area, organizing what was called sportsman modified stock car races. Eddie and I talked about my desire to promote races, so we agreed to make our June 20 event a NASCAR race at Ord. This date was a "still" date, which means it took place without a fair being held on the adjoining fairgrounds.

Eddie created an organization called International Stock Car Ass'n to give us an identity, and off I flew into the wild blue yonder of promoting auto races.

Ord was a high-banked half-mile dirt track, a very fast place. At one time, along with Belleville, Kan., those were the two fastest high-banked half-mile dirt tracks in the country. They had quite a rivalry going, although Belleville eventually endured and won out, while Ord closed some years later.

I had raced at Ord in a roaring roadster in the late 1940s, and again as a car owner with Bob Lundberg driving in 1952, so I was very familiar with the track. It was Ord where I first met Bill France, and found him to be a pretty good guy.

NASCAR had a rule that the race promoter can't field a car in the race. In fact, I believe such a rule is still in place. But I figured if my car won the top money in the race, that made the promotion a lot easier. I couldn't let anyone know I had entered a car, of course, so instead of my normal color of purple we painted the car white. Beckman was my driver, and in 1953 he hadn't yet established himself, and nobody at Ord had ever heard of him before.

The other cars that showed that weekend looked terrible. Terrible! Junk, through and through. Several had hung a heavy transmission on the left running board to keep the car from rolling so badly through the turns, and others had ugly rollover bars welded on the outside of the roof. You couldn't help but wince when you looked at these hideous things.

Our '34 Ford coupe truly had them outclassed. We were lighter, we had more horsepower, and Beckman just romped. Drove away and left 'em. But nobody knew yet it was actually my car that won the race.

The race was finished in the afternoon, and later that night we were getting the payoff ready. There came a dispute among myself, NASCAR, and the racers, based on the payoff in the heat races. NASCAR required a specific posted payoff for each race, even though I was offering a percentage of the gate. However, I ruled that if you didn't finish your heat, you didn't get paid. My thinking was that if you ran two laps and quit, you didn't really finish in that position.

That riled them up, because they felt like if you started, you should get money, even if you dropped out on the first lap. That inspired a loud, long bitch session that we eventually resolved when I agreed to pay everybody who started the race.

By this time everybody was pretty well liquored up, and the racers were getting rowdy. Somehow, somebody figured out I owned the winning car. Boy, were they pissed! They immediately were up in arms, and they wanted to kill me.

Naturally, they were bigger and tougher than me, not to mention that I was seriously outnumbered. I suddenly remembered an important engagement back in Lincoln, so Joyce and I hurried out the door and got into our truck.

Last I saw of those boys, they were fading off of our rear bumper. Luckily, our truck had some speed parts installed, and we were able to make a quick getaway. After a few minutes there was nothing behind us but the darkness of the Nebraska night, and we breathed a sigh of relief.

My arrangement to promote the races at Ord also included a non-sanctioned race during the Valley County Fair, which was traditionally a very big event. For this one, I hired Bob Lundberg as my announcer. Bob had an incredible voice, and during the in-between times when he wasn't off chasing some adventure, he worked as a radio announcer.

Bob and I also co-promoted a race in October in southern Nebraska at Pawnee City, when the weather turned cold and we got a grand total of seven cars for the event. I think there were about seven people in the grandstands, too. It was literally well below freezing, and some of the cars coming from Iowa had their radiators freeze on the way over.

The only issue with Bob was his drinking. There was a bar in Lincoln, the Diamond Bar and Grille, located about two blocks from the University of Nebraska campus. Lots of football players from the university hung out at the Diamond, and these were some very tough characters. Big, mean, ornery mothers. They were always looking to prove how tough they were.

The Diamond offered a beer mug the size of a five-gallon bucket, and they had an ongoing contest to see who could drink this mug of beer the fastest. Bob heard about the contest, and he wanted to set a new track record, which was 45 minutes. Well, he went over there and lowered the record. By half. Later I asked him how he did it.

"Easy," he said. Remember, he's a very smart guy who figured out how to do many things I can't talk about in this book. "After I drank a little bit I went into the bathroom and stuck my finger down my throat and up-chucked all the beer. That emptied my stomach, so I could get right back at it and go again."

Unfortunately for me, the budding promoter, the town of Ord had a bar with a similar mug, and a similar contest. Bob had learned of a guy named Gordy Shuck—a racer who had been my friend from the roaring roadster days and remained my friend for many, many years—who was apparently pretty good at draining the mug as well. Bob wanted to meet Gordy and see who could drink the mug of beer the fastest.

The trouble was, this was the day of our race at Ord. I didn't know anything about Bob's plans, of course, because I'm out at the race track on the water truck, preparing for the race. Hot laps were scheduled for 7 p.m., with racing at 8.

I had hired another man as our flagman and pit director, but unfortunately he went with Bob to the bar. They both showed up at the track around 5:30 that evening, drunker than hoot owls. They couldn't even spell their name or hit their ass with both hands.

I thought, "Oh, man, what am I gonna do now? My announcer and flagman are both drunk!" But the show must go on.

The announcing stand was an elevated building up in a paddock in the infield. You could stand up there and see all directions around the track, and into the pit area. I told Bob to go ahead and get on the microphone, because the crowd was beginning to file in. Joyce was already up there, ready to begin her work as lap counter and scorekeeper.

The announcer was the most important element of your show in those days. Many times a guy who came to the county fair had never seen auto racing. So the announcer was critical, because it led the perception of that guy, and told him what was going on. You could have a wheel-to-wheel duel being described—and I've seen this happen many times in the old days of the IMCA—with everyone in the grandstand on their feet, cheering this great race. In reality one car was going down the backstretch while one car was on the frontstretch. But the announcer made it so exciting, it got the crowd into it. Believe me, the announcer is *still* a big factor in making the race exciting.

Bob got up into the announcer's stand, and locked the door behind him. He turned on the microphone, and with his words completely slurred, began telling the most awful, obscene dirty jokes you can imagine. Now, Ord is a nice farm community with a lot of church-going folks who were visiting the county fair to see if Grandma won the pie contest, and then go to the races. To say this was a shock to their sensibilities is an understatement.

In the meantime, my drunken pit steward began the driver's meeting. "All right, you dumb sons-a-bitches, here's how we're gonna run the race…"

So all the racers were mad at my official, and all the spectators were mad at the announcer. The people were seeking out the members of the fair board, complaining about this guy telling dirty jokes on the microphone. The fair board members were chasing me all over the infield, ready to string me up, and my flagman had wandered out onto the middle of the track during hot laps, with roaring cars passing him on both sides.

I was really in trouble. I had a lot of holes in the sieve to plug that night, and I guess we somehow got through it without anybody getting killed and me not getting strung up from a tree. It was one of those experiences that is funny now, but wasn't much fun at the time. And I don't recall if the monetary gain was enough to offset all the anxiety that came with it.

Even after a few such misadventures, it took a while to get the "promoter" urge out of my system. One thing was sure, though; no matter how badly things went, it seemed like it was always a big adventure.

Another of the fair boards to take me up on my offer of promoting their races was the group at Clay County, in Clay Center, Neb. This was a half-mile track, and the races would be during their fair.

I contacted all my racing buddies, competitors, everybody I knew with a race car, in hopes of getting enough cars. Among the drivers on hand were Bob Lundberg, Rex (The Fox) Jordan, and Gordy Shuck.

I was the promoter, pit steward, and flagman, and Joyce was our scorekeeper. It was a typical hot summer day, and we had a good crowd and enough cars to put on a good show.

To keep the crowd entertained, we added several unusual events, including an Australian Pursuit and a pig race. The pig race was fun; you took one lap around the track and stopped at the scorer's stand, where a pen with several piglets was set up. You'd jump from your race car and grab one of the pigs, jump back into the car, and take another lap, holding onto the pig while you drove the car. All of this was against the clock, with the best recorded time the winner.

This was all great fun, although I'm not sure if anyone asked the pigs if they were having a good time.

When Gordy came roaring up to grab his pig, he didn't get his car fully stopped. By the time he grabbed the pig and turned back around, his car was rolling on its own down the race track toward the first corner. What a show! There was Gordy, holding the pig by all fours, running after his race car. The crowd loved it, and it couldn't have been any better if we had planned it.

During the feature race Bob Lundberg's rear bumper came loose and was dragging on the track. This kicked up dust like a Texas tornado, and we had to black flag him. To his dying day, Bob looked back with great humor at that incident.

Rex Jordan was driving my '34 Ford sedan, and he was having a great day until he flew off the number one corner, getting himself tangled up with the barbed wire fence on the outside of the track (how about that for a great safety feature...barbed wire fence just outside the racing surface!). Rex came charging back onto the track, dragging portions of the fence. He made it all the way to turn three before the wire fence finally wrapped so tightly around the rear axle the car wouldn't move.

My mother and aunt Florence were on hand for this race, the first race they had ever attended. When they saw Rex's accident, they nearly fainted. From all the steam from his busted radiator, and that fence dragging along behind, they just knew the driver was on fire and we going to burn up right before their eyes! They both immediately left the track, and neither attended another race in my lifetime.

The middle part of the 1950s was a busy, exciting time in my life, but also very troubling. I was burning the candle at both ends, and that probably contributed to some serious health issues that nearly killed me.

On the flip side, Speedway Motors was taking a few wobbly steps toward growth, and my race cars were doing well. Also, my friendship with Tiny Lund blossomed into a project that gave me an opportunity to have one of my cars in the big-time world of NASCAR. It was fun, but it was a ton of work and worry.

But what the hell...if you're gonna live, you should try to live it out all the way, right? That was my theory back in the heady days of the '50s.

9

"How can I make my car go, Dr. Smith?"

In 1954, after two years of struggling at the "pop stand" at 2232 O Street, Speedway Motors was finally showing signs of growth. I needed more space, and I started thinking about how I could expand within my very limited financial resources.

I discussed it with my friend Wally Smith, and discovered he was thinking of downsizing his gun shop and used car business. We talked about it for a couple of months, and one day he said, "Let's trade spots!" So we did. Wally moved his business to my location on O Street, and I took over his 5,000-square-foot building at 1719 N Street. It would be the home of Speedway Motors for the next 24 years, where we would ultimately triple the square footage of our operation.

It was an easy move, because going from 400 square feet to 5,000 square feet is like going to heaven. I had all the space I needed, which was a great luxury. From the standpoint of paperwork and things, it was also very simple. Today, it would be much more complicated with leases, insurance papers, etc., but back then almost everybody rented commercial space on a month-to-month basis. There were very few long-term lease arrangements like is common today.

Business operations were a lot more fluid then. You might see somebody operating out of the same location for a couple of years, then get into a lean period and lose their location because they couldn't pay the rent. Pretty soon they'd resurface someplace else. It wasn't because they were fly-by-night; it's just that times were simpler, and more loosey-goosey than they are today.

The new building had once been home to a beer distributor, and there was still a huge overhead door in the front big enough to fit the trucks. The original parcel offered 100 feet of frontage, and was 150 feet deep. Later I expanded by buying neighboring property, but for the first several years I was pretty content with my location and setup.

I was doing a lot of muffler and exhaust work at that time, and I really needed a lift. However, a four-post lift was way outside my price range, so I had to think of another solution. I decided to dig a pit, like a grease pit. I knocked out the cement floor, then dug the hole, and my block-laying buddies came over to help set block each evening before they went to the bar. I had another friend who drove a cement truck, and he would swing by with leftover material that was going to be discarded, and that became my exhaust pit.

As it turned out, the pit was the best thing I could have done. It was far easier to install exhaust from a pit versus a lift, because you didn't have any fixtures getting in your way. Plus, if the car's gas tank was leaking a little bit, it didn't catch the whole place on fire. You always had to worry about stuff like that.

I continued to deal in used cars, and had a nice lot along with my speed shop. One challenge I had was that when somebody stopped by to look at a car, I had to lock up the speed shop because I didn't have any employees.

I was also selling new BSA and Triumph motorcycles. This wasn't a high-volume enterprise, and if you sold one every two or three months that was kind of a big deal. I'd park a motorcycle out front and every now and then somebody would stop by, wanting to know more. If the guy was serious, and had money, I might sell a motorcycle.

I was happy; but to be honest, things were awfully slim. Many times I thought about giving up, because I was second-guessing myself. I wondered if I was doing the right thing. Maybe I should go get a real job, like my mom always told me to do.

The first three years of our marriage, Joyce had a job at the Nebraska State Fair as a secretary. We lived on her salary, exclusively. Whatever profits the shop or the race car made, we put right back into the business. I mean, 100 percent, period. Sure, that made it tough in the short term, but in my mind it was the right thing to do. In retrospect, it was *absolutely* the right thing to do. The business would not have survived if I'd taken a salary. It took every penny it made — and then some — to keep it going in those early years.

We were also very busy starting a family. On July 4, 1954, we were to race at Topeka, Kan., with the IMCA late models. I had just bought Marv Copple's Olds 88, and I took Lloyd Beckman as my driver. Lloyd had not yet raced a late model. It was a hot, hot day, and because of the heat Lloyd lasted only a few laps. I had to replace him with the original owner-driver, Marv.

I hesitated to go to Topeka because Joyce was at home expecting our first child, due any day. Every time they made an announcement on the PA at Topeka, I just knew it was for me. But lucky me…we raced, dashed home, and our first son, Carson, was born on July 17. I remember because it was 105 degrees in Lincoln, and we raced that night at Capitol Beach. The side of my car normally said, "Owner – Bill Smith" but that night it said, "Owner – Bill Smith and Son."

Three more sons followed. Craig in 1956, Clay in '58, and Jason in '61. We were very blessed, and all four were healthy. This made for a busy household, of course. I guess we had our own mini racing team.

I was going to name Carson "Car Axle Smith," but Joyce wouldn't let me. I had discovered that "Bill Smith" is a very common name, so I wanted to give him something unique, something distinctive: Car Axle Smith. How about that? But it didn't happen.

I was working a lot of hours when the kids came along. Trying to make a living, trying to keep my race cars going, trying to promote a few races, trying to have babies, it was a cluster. Too much, probably. When we had two kids, we were living in a one-bedroom apartment over a garage in an alley. That wasn't too conducive to anything. Not a good family place. Craig's bedroom was actually a closet, and Carson's bed was located next to our beds. Talk about tight quarters!

Obviously, Joyce was the glue that held everything together. Plus, my mom and dad were active and involved with my family. My mother was a homemaker and didn't work, and you could set your clock on my dad's life. They were both the Rock of Gibraltar. Perfect parents, really. My dad took my sons fishing, hunting, things like that. Things I should have done myself but didn't take the time, because I was so absorbed in my business.

You didn't have to worry that maybe Grandpa was drinking too much, or chasing women, gambling, anything like that. If those kids had been with God they wouldn't have been in better hands.

I wish they could have come with me to the races, but you couldn't have kids — or women, for that matter — in the pits in those days.

To complicate matters, I almost died in 1955. My ulcerated colitis continued to plague me, and my health worsened. Doctors finally told me the only hope was a total colectomy, which was a very difficult surgery at that time. The doctors told me if — that's *if* — the surgery was successful, nobody had survived more than 10 years. I was 25 years old, and I thought, "Hmm, 10 years…that's 35 years old. The only people I know older than that are my folks.

Most of the people who had this surgery in 1955 — young and old alike — died within three days, many because they had lost the will to live. They didn't feel they could go on living in that condition.

In the days following my surgery, it was remarkable to watch others around me *will* themselves to die. I mean it literally: They willed themselves to die.

The desire to live was the key element to survival. I figured that out very quickly. It was a critical life lesson for me, as it turns out. Throughout the course of my life, I have been in "Code Blue" at least three times. "Code Blue" is the medical definition that means your condition is so critical that you will likely die within two minutes.

I vividly recall that moment, as the room was spinning around and things were getting foggy, when I said to myself, "I'm gonna beat this, because I'm going racing."

There was something inside me, something that wouldn't give up. Even though things were stacked against me, I was going to do what I set out to do. That's how powerful a force racing was with me. It drove me almost as much as the will to live, of life itself.

It was like, "I can't check out just yet, because there's more racing to do."

I'm sure many others have experienced this as well, because that's the way racing is. Especially when you're young, and you don't ever want to give up.

Nobody has yet discovered what the spark of life is. Doctors have figured out almost all other medical conditions, but they can't figure out what brings that mighty spark of life. All I know is that when you lose that spark, it's over. It's an intangible, but it's absolutely there.

I saw it play out right before my eyes in the days following my surgery. All around me, people who had undergone the same surgery would lose the will to live, and in an hour or two they were pulling the sheet over 'em.

Not me, brother. I want to live. I still had plenty of races to win, and cars to build.

Eventually, I was strong enough to be released from the hospital, and get back to work. I was still wobbly, and had lost enough weight that I was once again skin and bones. But the surgery was successful, because I lived through it.

Some of this stuff builds character, one way or another.

All through this trying time, Joyce was at Speedway, and my folks helped out with Carson.

One of the things I quickly realized was that a speed shop becomes a social gathering place for car guys and racers alike. They all had the fever, the interest.

At first it was mainly my buddies, and I always had three or four interesting cars around, so guys could look them over. A '46 Ford convertible, or a '37 Graham. Odd and unusual cars. And of course you were likely to see a '34, '35, or '36 roadster sitting around, and maybe a couple of coupes.

As my shop grew busier I began to realize the impact of all those car-crazy airmen from the Air Force bases in Omaha and Lincoln. They became immersed in our local hot-rod scene, and they brought a lot of hot-rodding knowledge from around the country. There were boys from all over, but I particularly remember strong contingents from California and the Carolinas.

The Carolina boys had what you could call an acute interest in performance enhancements for their vehicles. They needed big power to outrun the cops when they were hauling illegal whiskey. Those guys would come by the speed shop, and we had many great conversations about performance. It seemed we were all learning the same things, at about the same time.

I made lifelong friendships with some of those guys. Many, in fact, settled in Lincoln after their hitch was up. They were romantically involved, either with a local girl or with hot rods, and either romance is usually enough to change the course of a man's life.

One man I distinctly remember was Lee Warren Prout, a fellow from the Carolinas. He worked at my shop on a part-time basis; we hired several airmen through the years because they only had a morning muster, and were off the rest of the day. Remember, the war was over by then, and there wasn't that much for them to do. Lee went on to run a little company known as Petty Enterprises, and he built many of King Richard's cars. He hadn't raced before he went into the service, so it's easy to see the influence of Lincoln Air Base on the racing scene.

A typical afternoon at Speedway Motors saw all kinds of guys hanging out. It was almost like a pool hall, but instead of shooting pool a guy spent all his time talking about his fast car.

I probably made more money from the Coke machine than I did off parts. Decals, too. I sold lots of cheap decals.

Ford guys always loved decals; they didn't buy too many parts. They might put a dual exhaust on the car, but they sure soaked up those decals. They wouldn't buy a camshaft, or rocker arms, ignition, they wouldn't buy anything. Just decals and the Coke machine, that was their draw.

Chevrolet guys were the ones who would change everything on their car. Carburetor, cam, exhaust, distributor, gears, all those things. And of course I tried to make it easier by taking their used stuff on trade. If a guy went over to the Chevrolet store—located a block-and-a-half from my shop—on Saturday morning and bought a brand new '57 Chevrolet with fuel injection, he would drive the short distance to my shop and put two four-barrel carbs on the car. Because those injectors, nobody knew how to work on 'em, and nobody knew how to make 'em really run. Remember, fuel injection was a brand new unit at the time, and it was like a big mystery. Two four-barrels, however, would make that car really haul ass. Guaranteed.

So I'd pull the fuel injection unit off, and put it over on my "Used Parts" shelf, right in the front showroom. If you didn't like your wheels, I'd trade you for some new wheels. Or intake manifolds. Over time, I accumulated quite a selection of used parts.

Which was a good deal for everybody, because it kept the used parts in the marketplace and made it possible for the guy on a tight budget to improve his car. The people who couldn't afford to buy new, they bought used. Nothing wrong with that.

That made me a "one-stop" shop. If you couldn't buy new, come see me and look over the used shelf. Maybe there is something for you there. Many of the young studs in town, maybe 14, 15 years old, had to come to Speedway often to see what I had traded for.

It was all about me trying to stay alive, trying to make a living and keep my doors open.

In 1957 Pontiac also offered a fuel injection setup, but it was a dud. Lord knows, that thing would hardly pull itself, let alone race anybody. Naturally, I ended up with those things sitting on the shelf forever, because they got a bad name and nobody knew how to make 'em run. I'd probably still have 'em to this day if I hadn't managed to unload them somewhere along the line. However, they'd probably be worth something today, because some collector restoring a '57 Pontiac would love one.

The rascals and rodders hanging out at Speedway Motors during this time provided no end to the various adventures we'd get into. Don E., Bill F., Carl J., Bruce F., Neal S., to name just a few (we'll leave their last name out of it, because some local authorities might still have some outstanding things to discuss with these gentlemen).

Several of these guys worked for the Burlington Northern railroad, which had the best pay scale in town. Their hours were 4 p.m. to midnight, and they'd sleep a few hours and invade Speedway the next day.

The things they thought up were unreal. They were young and restless, made good money, were totally into cars, and they naturally evolved to drag racing. And street racing.

Many of them had old "work cars" from the railroad which sat outside in all kinds of weather. At some point it became fashionable for them to run their work cars into each other if they met on the street.

One morning a customer came rushing into my shop and said he just saw two cars side-swipe each other, and not even stop. "What's this country coming to??!!" the guy exclaimed.

I knew exactly who it was, and sure enough an hour or so later they both pulled into my parking lot—all torn up.

Another of the "brothers" was more careful with his work car, and never got involved in that stuff. So one night when he was busy the guys rolled his car into the alley and "center punched" it at about 25 mph.

Joe G., one of my more affluent customers, had a '32 Ford 3-window coupe with a big Buick engine and a 4-inch dropped axle we had installed. This car became the fastest street car in Lincoln for a period of time.

Joe said he wanted "the lowest car in town," so we installed a 6-inch dropped axle. As Joe was driving along O Street to cross the railroad at 20th Street, he caught the front axle on the tracks and tore the entire front end off the car. Today there is a law on the books in Lincoln mandating that front bumpers must be so many inches off the ground; we can thank Joe and Speedway Motors in part for that ordinance.

Later we built Joe a '50 Ford with a big Oldsmobile engine. He was winning races at many of the area drag strips in Lincoln, Omaha, Grand Island, Kearney, and others.

I built a '39 Chevy coupe with a small block Chevy V8 for a customer, and he skipped town without paying me. I managed to repossess the car, and boy, was this thing a runner. Joe bet me $100 he could beat the Chevy. I took the bet, knowing I couldn't lose because I built both cars! I won the race and the $100, and got lots of great publicity for Speedway.

There was quite a bit of drag racing going on at that time, and many of the local cars came from my shop. That was another Air Force "connection." The airstrips were perfectly suited for drag racing, and we used 'em.

Street racing was definitely outlawed, but it still happened. We would all get together on a Friday or Saturday night, and everything was planned in advance. We'd meet on a road where we could see the cops coming for a good distance, and it was typically a dead-end street with little traffic.

Today's NHRA has its roots in street racing, and in fact that was the reason the group was formed, to get kids off the streets onto a legitimate drag strip. Too many accidents were happening because of street racing. But it still went on, like it or not.

I was very involved in drag racing, because I was active in building hot rods at the time. Remember, this was still a time when if you had some basic skills, such as welding, you were unusual. In some ways, you were a valuable commodity. As our local drag racing scene grew, I built a lot of cars, a couple of which I drove myself. One of the cars I built and drove, an Oldsmobile with a Scotty Finn kit, ran 155 mph in the quarter-mile. This was in a rail dragster, so for the mid-'50s that was pretty fast.

Nearly all of the cars were still "street" cars. It was run-whatcha-brung, and nobody had the funds to build a specialized car for drag racing only. You'd drive your car to the strip on Sunday, change some things around for racing, then change them back when you were finished and drive the car all week long.

Later I bought a brand-new '56 Ford with a Police Interceptor package, which was supposed to be sold only to police departments, and were said to be the fastest things on the planet. I talked the local police chief in a little town south of Lincoln to pull strings and get me in line for one of these cars. We had to fudge just a little bit and say the car was for "Sheriff Bill."

This car would go! All black, 312-ci V8, two 4-barrel carbs, stick shift, with all the high-performance goodies of the day. It was a "factory hot rod," which everyone lusted for at that time. However, as fast as this car was, I couldn't beat most of the "engine conversion" cars I had built for many of my customers. Plus, the Chevrolet high-performance V8's that were beginning to appear were also just a tick faster.

I was drag racing the Ford around Lincoln, Kansas City, Kearney, and many towns throughout Nebraska and Kansas. Many area towns had seen the construction of airstrips to protect the Omaha SAC facility, and we used those strips for drag racing.

In retrospect it's easy to see now that our government spent more money on defense in that period than could ever be justified. If they ever add up everything we spent from 1941 to 1965, for example, it was a staggering, insane amount of money. Then again, that drove the economy, which made everybody feel good. A false economy, the way I perceive it. The world according to Bill.

It was fun traveling around during this period, getting to know the boys in Kansas City, Topeka, and elsewhere. This led to good things, because you learn from each other. And the camaraderie, that was enjoyable.

I don't think today's racers share the camaraderie like we did. Maybe it's because our sport was still very much viewed by the mainstream as something strange, and that made all of us something of an outcast. I think that draws a group of people together, when they recognize that we're kind of in this together, outcasts or not.

But those were fun, fun times, and I wouldn't trade any of those times for any of these times, no matter what the monetary differences would have been.

On one occasion several of us decided to drive our cars to the second NHRA meet in Kansas City, Mo. Bill F. was in his '40 Ford/Cadillac, Don E. was in his new Chrysler 300, Bruce F. was in his '56 Chevy high-performance V8, and Speedy Bill in his new '56 Ford Police Interceptor with Chuck Sears riding along.

This was a "road race" all the way, on two-lane highways, with no pit stops. We raced to Kansas City, attended the drag races, and raced home.

On the way down, Bruce F. was the winner. Bill F. was second, and Speedy Bill was third. Don E. had his brakes fail at a stop sign, and he ended up in the middle of a field.

We decided to take a different route home, because of possible safety patrols or police. It seemed that Bruce F. had been politely "requested" by the local authorities to leave Nebraska and never return because of his huge record of moving violations, so he thought it would be a good idea to avoid any further conversations with the authorities.

So we were trying to be a little more low-key on the return trip. This time there were only three of us, because Don's brake issues sort of eliminated him from competition. Bruce won again, Speedy was a close second, and Bill was third after losing control and ending up parked in a cow pasture.

On another trip I had a really close shave in my Police Interceptor. I had raced the car—which also served as our day-to-day family car—at Kearney and was headed home. It was 100 degrees that afternoon, and I'm rolling along Hwy. 34 with my "Bruce" re-cap drag slicks at about 115 mph.

The left rear tire blew and the cap wrapped over the traction master, locking the rear end. Solid. This jerked me from the right lane, across the highway into the ditch. As I'm sliding over a block-and-a-half, I just missed an oncoming car before I launched back across the highway and into the right-side ditch. I wasn't hurt, and the highway patrol thought there were two cars involved and never did quite figure out what had happened.

Boy, were the local guys crazy about drag racing! Don E. was one of the railroad boys with some disposable income, and we built him a '34 Ford 5-window coupe with a Cadillac V8 engine. We had everything pretty much finished late one afternoon when he came by the shop to pick up the car.

I explained that we had just a couple of small details to finish, but he really wanted to drive the car home that night. I said that would be fine, just bring the car by tomorrow and we'd finish up the remaining small items.

When he hadn't shown up by 11 a.m. the next morning, I called his house. His mother answered the phone and said, "Oh, Don isn't here...he left for California about six this morning..."

He was so eager to run his new car at some California drag strips, he just couldn't wait. I later found out that he drove the car all the way out west, straight through! Now, that's dedication.

Because of our geographical location, drag racing could never sustain itself here, and it began to gradually fade away. You need that magic number of people to make the racing commercially viable, and we didn't have that number. Over time, there just weren't enough people involved in drag racing in our part of the country.

California was a different story, of course. The scene there was much more robust, and that's why NHRA was formed out there, and the reason it ultimately took off. There were a significant number of people who were interested in drag racing.

Say, how about this: We actually had a dirt drag racing strip here in Nebraska. It was located on a farm out in Milford, about 20 miles west of Lincoln. I'll bet your town didn't have a dirt drag strip!

I think the only type of racing I never had much interest in was sports car racing, which is done almost exclusively on road courses.

My perception of a sports car racer was that they were a bunch of pussies. And I wasn't into hanging around with pussies; I wanted to hang around with tough guys. Hey, don't laugh; that was the common perception among hot rodders, drag racers, and circle track racers of the day. In fact, there remains today a lingering perception of that among many people.

That was my perception. A lot of my perceptions are wrong, by the way; I'll admit to that.

I was learning a lot about engines, and it really was an exciting time in that respect. I was building my own flathead Ford engines for my stock cars, and they always needed to be ported and relieved. That was the big phrase of the day, "ported and relieved." To do this, you had to take the block out of the car. There were no cookers to boil them, so you cleaned them up as well as you could, milled the heads, and ported and relieved them.

Dick Bloom was working for me at 2232 O Street, and he was also one of my early racing drivers. I had helped Dick build a '28 Model A roadster I sold him, and we converted it to a V8. We dropped a flathead Ford into the car, and he drove it on the street. It was full-fendered with side curtains and top, with 16-inch wheels in place of the stock 21-inch wheels. It was a nice car. We updated it with hydraulic brakes, because Fords all had mechanical brakes until '39 or '40.

That was another "retro-fit" we did a lot of, putting hydraulic brakes on pre-'40 Fords. The spindles and master cylinders from the later cars retrofit right onto the older models, and it was a nice conversion. It's funny to note that they're still doing those things, all these years later.

When I opened the speed shop in 1952, flathead engines were still dominant. But the tide was turning, because Cadillac made an overhead valve V8 beginning in 1949, as did Buick and Oldsmobile. Some of the guys with a little more money wanted an overhead valve engine in their car, and we'd do an engine conversion to Cadillac, Buick, or Oldsmobile. We offered a package deal, which included the engine, special motor mounts, a transmission adapter and shifter, and a complete exhaust system. Installed, of course.

These were factory-built engines, and we'd soup them up from there. Dual exhaust, ignition, stuff like that. The McCullough supercharger came into play a few years later, probably around 1955. I installed a lot of McCullough superchargers in my shop, and these were cars to be driven on the street.

Most of the people involved in hot rodding were relatively young and didn't have a lot of money. There were a few guys who got help from their parents, but most everybody else had a job and were paying their own way.

I was almost like a doctor, because every day guys would come into my shop and ask my advice. "What's going to sound really good on my Oldsmobile?" Or maybe, "How can we pep up my Chevy?" It was like going to the doctor or pharmacist and asking what you should take for a headache.

We were quickly figuring out ways to soup up the existing street engines. Valve jobs, boring the block, putting in a different camshaft, every day brought more knowledge. You could tweak the rocker arms by changing the lift ratio, and that was another modification we were soon offering.

There isn't a week that goes by where I'm out in some public setting here in Lincoln, and somebody will come up and say, "You put a dual exhaust on my car back in '58, and boy, it really sounded good!"

This is what made an impression on people, and it illustrates the power of hot-rod emotions. The idea of making a car sound nice still resonates in a guy's head, 50 years later!

In 1955 Chevrolet came out with a new overhead valve 265-ci V8 engine. Frankly, it was pretty much a dud in the beginning. Now, I don't mean to say the small block Chevy engine was a dud; it proved to be the engine that changed the course of hot rodding, racing, and almost everything else.

But in the early form, it was a long, long way from being a performance engine. By this time the world had begun to figure out some things, and when we opened up that new little Chevy we were amazed. Everything was absolutely junk! For example, the rocker arms were stamped out of thin, flimsy metal, and the moment we took one off and held it in our hand, it was suspect. We knew such a flimsy part would never hold up in a performance application. We saw all those little thin stamped timing covers, rocker arm covers, and other parts, and we immediately figured this little engine was hopeless.

We were used to working with big Cadillac, Buick, and Oldsmobile engines, and those things were very solid and very strong. Those components could survive pretty well, given the circumstances. But this new Chevy, the moment you put serious stress on the engine, it was probably going to scatter.

To be honest, when we looked at that little Chevy engine, we didn't see what it would become. Had no idea. We saw only the present, not the future. And the future was what this little engine was all about.

The world quickly began producing specialty parts that would replace all the flimsy factory stuff. Camshafts, rocker-arm assemblies, crankshafts, connecting rods, it became a massive industry, because Chevrolet ultimately sold a ton of those engines in classic cars such as the Tri-5 Chevy (1955-56-57), all the way through the next two or three decades.

Go karts became the latest rage around 1957, and I jumped on board to become a dealer. Boy, we were selling go karts like there was no tomorrow. I had the local market covered, as the authorized dealer of the official go kart brand as well as McCullough and Clinton engines.

The explosion of karting was way ahead of any kind of organized associations or structures. There were no regulations about where karts could be raced, and it was really just a bunch of local guys having fun.

Of course, every "car guy" wanted a go kart. Pretty soon I had one of my own, racing on deserted parking lots in the evenings against my friends and customers.

In late June of 1958 I was running a fast kart on a parking lot at 48th and O Street here in Lincoln. I had "tinkered" with this kart quite a bit, and that thing would really go. Somehow I managed to collide with a wall along the parking lot, and absolutely busted my ass.

My buddies piled me in the back of a pickup truck and drove me home. They carried me to the front door, and when Joyce answered the door she was greeted with the sight of all these guys carrying her husband, who looked like he had been ran over by a truck.

"Joyce, Bill had an accident on the go kart and hurt himself," they said. "What do you want us to do with him?"

Let's not go into details of what her reply was, because she had just come home from the hospital that week after delivering our third son, Clay. Now she had *me* to deal with, too. We both had a lot of pressure that night.

My fun night on the go kart had ended with a broken pelvis.

In addition to my speed shop, I was still very busy with buying and selling used cars. This was important, because it provided some margin and it also helped me stay on top of things mechanically.

If something was wrong with a car, by this time I had enough experience that I could fix it. Back then, one of the biggest problems was the transmission. For example, on a Ford automobile the transmission was the weakest link in the driveline. When somebody was hot rodding the car, the most likely thing to fail was the transmission. So I learned how to quickly drop the transmission and rebuilt it with about $15 worth of parts. There were no "rebuild kits," not yet. You figured out the individual parts you needed and that was that.

I viewed my speed shop and my car business in the same way; I figured Lincoln was a relatively small town, and word gets around quickly in a small town. If you cheat somebody with a car, or a part, pretty soon everybody in town knows that's how you operate. So I tried very hard not to play that game. Believe me, at this time the used car business had very little formal regulation. There were some crooks out there, with sawdust in the transmission and all that. Always.

If a guy felt like I had cheated him, he would never buy from me again. I couldn't afford that, because my market was already very small. Plus, it isn't right to do people that way. And, frankly,

I didn't like the idea of the guy coming back to my shop looking to knock my head off. That idea didn't appeal very much to me.

That kind of thing goes clear to the top, to the big boys. In the 1940s, Henry Ford sold big trucks with passenger car engines. These were 85 hp engines, pulling a 2.5-ton truck. You'd put a load of coal or crushed rock in one of those trucks, and that little engine could hardly move it. That's why the legendary Zora Arkus-Duntov was hired by Ford, and he developed the Ardun head that gave those little engines enough power to make the truck work. Previously, all those guys who bought those trucks wanted to slip that 2.5-ton vehicle into Henry's largest bodily opening. He wasn't getting favorable reviews, you might say.

There were always certain principles I believed in. If making a deal compromised one of those principles, it wasn't worth doing. I have always believed this: "A good deal has to be to the benefit of both parties, or it isn't a good deal." Both parties have to feel fairly satisfied. Sure, one is going to get the long end now and then, that's the way economics are. With that said, there has to be a good feeling.

The products I have sold through the years, all my life, none were life-giving or life-sustaining. They were somewhat frivolous in the big picture, items that simply made you feel good. So I've done a fairly good job of keeping people feeling good. I always figured I was something of a legalized drug dealer, so to speak: What I sold made people feel good, and they always wanted more.

One thing that is very obvious to me today is that regardless of somebody talking about "the good old days," there isn't a single car from the 1950s, '60s, or '70s that isn't dismally bad compared in any way to today's cars. They are so profoundly better today, it's amazing. The cars of that day had trouble with almost every component: brakes, suspension, engines, exhaust, starters, and so forth. Even the gasoline of that day wasn't very good. It's hard to describe to younger people just how fraught with trouble those older cars were.

10

Big Man, Big Character

By the mid-1950s I knew I was exactly where I was supposed to be. I loved the speed shop, because my business was almost like Christmas, every day. Everything you did was new, with very little repetition. You got a new product to sell, or met a new customer, or started building something new. Cars, cars, cars. Dragsters, circle track cars, hot rods, you name it. Constantly, one after another.

It was fun to take a challenge to build something that hadn't been built before. A Packard racing engine, for example, which a guy had me build for him.

One of my lifelong friends was right with me during this time, and he led me to some great adventures. I had known Marv Copple since junior high, and his dad was a banker here in town. Marv was a guy with a long list of amazing God-given talents. For example, I played in the high school band with Marv, and he was so talented on the trombone that, as a very young man, he was invited to sit in with Tommy Dorsey and his band when they came to Lincoln. Marv could have easily made music his career; he was good at everything he tried. But he loved cars and racing, just like I did.

Marv ultimately proved to be a very good race driver, but he didn't stay at it long enough to move up the line. In 1954 I built Marv a '55 Oldsmobile to race on the beach at Daytona, and he ultimately ran 14th. That's when they started nearly 50 cars, like a New York traffic jam.

Marv and I became as close as brothers, and I traveled with him to many stock car races at places like Toledo, Dayton, Des Moines, Milwaukee, Sedalia (Mo.), and North Platte (Neb.). Most events were unsanctioned, but a few were AAA races. Boy, those were fun adventures.

I was also running a jalopy here locally, a flathead Ford driven by Lloyd Beckman, and we raced two or three nights a week from the second week of May to early September. We were going pretty well, enough to subsidize my speed shop with our winnings. It wasn't just a figure of speech; we really were making money with our race car.

Bobby McKee was working for me in my shop, helping me build cars. Tiny Lund was living in Lincoln at the time, and the four of us — myself, Marv, Bobby, and Tiny — became very close friends.

Tiny was quite a character. He was a huge man, about 6-foot-7 and 280 pounds. He was fun-loving and gregarious, and a very loyal friend, but he could also get rough if he needed to. I never saw him hit a man with his fist — he would probably have killed somebody — but many times I saw him cuff a guy with the back of his hand. When he did that, it was like a grizzly bear swatted 'em; they'd reel backward six or eight feet.

I think I mentioned earlier I met Tiny back in 1948 at Hastings, Neb., when I drove a race car for the first time. From that point our paths would cross often at the race track, and we became great friends. When he moved to Lincoln, we were especially close.

Tiny was at the center of one of my embarrassing moments, something that could have become a domestic disaster.

We raced quite often at Playland Park in Council Bluffs, usually on Friday nights but sometimes on Saturday. The track was located right across the Missouri River from Omaha. Omaha is a huge town now, with something like 1.5 million people, and it was pretty big at the time, too. It's a river town, with stockyards, railroads, all the things that drove the economy in that era.

There were plenty of rough characters, too. Playland was an amusement park, literally right across the bridge from Omaha. From the bridge you could look down and see the races going on, within the amusement park.

Playland was the site of the first televised race in our part of the country, in 1951 or '52. I learned a lesson from that experience, something I would have sworn couldn't have been true. Before they began televising the races, they probably had 200, maybe 300 people in the stands on Friday night. I figured when they began televising the races people would say, "Well, I can stay home and drink my own beer, lay on the couch, and watch it for free!" But when they put 'er on TV, guess what happened? They tripled and quadrupled the attendance, because everybody wanted to see it live.

One night Joyce and I drove over to Playland to watch Tiny race. We were driving a brand new 1955 Chevrolet that I had just sold to my mother-in-law. This car was about as "plain Jane" as it gets; a pea-green 210-series sedan. She had paid me for the car but I hadn't yet delivered it.

During this period there was a traveling racing series that featured a bunch of car thieves from Chicago. I'm not kidding about this: These were rough, tough guys. They all had their deck lids and doors welded closed and they came ready to race or fight or both. Of course, they didn't mind too much if things got torn up, because they were racing their stolen cars. They'd just bring a different one out next week.

Tiny was driving a brand new Hudson Hornet for a dealer in his hometown of Harlan. The idea for Hudson, I think, was that racing could sell them a few cars. Hudsons were difficult cars to sell; they were expensive, and they looked a lot different than other cars. The perception for many people was that they were just too different, and perception is everything. The girls at the makeup counter deal in perception, every day. They're selling their products to boost the perception versus reality. So when the girl at the bar is all decked out in lipstick and rouge, it's about perception. Probably when you get home that night she'll be the worse you ever had, but the perception from looking at that makeup and lipstick, boy, you know it's going to be the *best* you ever had. Perception.

We got to the track that night, and I went to the pits while Joyce went up in the stands. Women weren't allowed in the pits in those days, which in my mind probably wouldn't be a bad idea yet today. But that's another story.

Tiny approached me, all excited.

"Billy," he said. "They're short of cars. I can get you $100 if you'll qualify your street car."

Now, at that time $100 seemed like a million dollars. I thought it over very carefully — for about two seconds — and said okay. I headed for the parking lot and drove the brand-new Chevy into the pits.

"Tiny, what am I gonna use for a helmet?" I asked. He gave me his.

"I need some kind of seat belt or something, to hold me in when I go through the corners. Got any ideas?"

He took the belt from his pants, and strung it around both me and the seat. So I was all set to qualify.

Up in the stands, Joyce was sitting with Marv Copple's wife Joan. She saw this distinctive pea-green '55 Chevy come out to qualify, and she turned to Joan and said, very cheerfully, "Oh, gee, that looks just like the car we sold my mom!"

Then she was quiet for a minute, and with her voice rising, she says, "Oh, God, that crazy bastard is racing my mother's new car!"

This is all pretty funny now but it didn't seem all that funny when we had the discussion after the race.

I qualified all right, and one of the guys running the circuit came over and said, "Are you gonna keep running that car?"

"No, I just qualified it."

"Well, if you run it, we've had trouble with those right front spindles breaking, tipping 'em over. You ought to put a heavier front hub on it."

"Well, I'm not gonna actually race it; I just wanted to get my qualifying money."

The guy looked at me kind of funny and walked away. Pretty soon Tiny came sauntering over.

"Hey, Bill, I forgot to tell you, but you've got to run your heat to get the $100."

"I can't do that! These guys will tear me to pieces!"

I finally talked them into letting me start last, so I wasn't in such danger of them knocking me into the next county. I drove a few laps and pulled in, and collected my $100.

The car survived without a scratch, and my mother-in-law never knew that the pea-green '55 Chevy she drove to prayer meetings was a grizzled veteran of the wild-and-wooly racing scene.

We stayed around to watch the feature that night, and I knew it was going to get rowdy. These guys were tough, and their cars were, too. One guy had a big Cadillac with an overhang out past the rear axle of maybe six feet. Huge. When he went down in the corner and pitched it on that fifth-mile track, it didn't leave much room for anybody else. It was just like Muhammad Ali hitting you upside the head; it would knock you clear through the outside wall.

The Hudson Hornet had more chrome strips than any other car on the market. It seemed like they had a chrome strip every couple of inches, someplace on the car. These guys got to roughing Tiny up — remember, with this circuit, these car thieves from Chicago were hard, professional racers — and when he was going down the straightaway his car got to looking like a ball of yarn, with so many strips of chrome hanging off it. It was bent, busted, and wrinkled, and it looked terrible.

They were really bouncing Tiny around. That usually didn't bother him much, because he was rough-and-tumble by nature. Rough *and* tumble. But they finally pissed him off, and when that happened, look out.

When the race was almost over, the leader was going down the backstretch while Tiny was on the front straightaway. Tiny suddenly turned left and drove 'er straight through the middle of the infield, and center-punched the guy leading the race. Now *that's* what the people came to see that night. It really was spectacular.

The two cars were all tangled up, parked on the track. The leader jumped out of his car, and he's looking to punch Tiny's lights out. The Hudson had kind of a chopped top, with narrow windows, and the man couldn't get the full appreciation of Tiny's profile until he got right there. He started to draw back, but as he looked into the car and saw nothing but this huge man filling that left seat, he had second thoughts. To him, I'll bet it looked like a gorilla. He just turned and walked back to his car. Good sense prevailed.

Those were good ol' boys and good ol' times.

Sometime in early 1956 Tiny decided he wanted to go South and race with NASCAR. He had driven Marv Copple's car on occasion in 1955, because Marv was too busy with his real estate and banking business to drive it himself. That was Marv's big challenge: He might have been a great race driver, but his business interests kept him from going out on the road. I built several cars for Marv to go out on the road and race, but he couldn't get away, and the car was ultimately sold to somebody else. For example, I built him a top-notch '56 Chrysler 300, but he never raced it.

Tiny had driven in a few NASCAR races, and the experience planted a seed in his mind, because from that point he was focused on trying to get something going that would allow him to race full-time with NASCAR.

NASCAR was nothing like it is today, but was a small, wandering series primarily focused in the Southeast. The emphasis was on "stock" cars, and very little modifications were allowed.

In fact, one of our cars—built by Speedway Motors—was once disqualified after winning a AAA race in Milwaukee simply because there was no oil in the air cleaner. The factory specs called for oil in the air cleaner, but our car didn't have any, so we were disqualified. End of discussion.

Tiny went to the bank and obtained a loan for a brand new '56 Pontiac. He immediately brought it to my shop, where I got busy building the engine, keeping in mind that few modifications were allowed. You could do a little work on the distributor, a little work on the carburetor, a little work on the right front hub, a little work on the shock absorbers on the right front, things like that. Overall, very few modifications were allowed. Some guys would get tricky by taking hydraulic lifters and making them solid, but it all depended on how much knowledge you had, and staying within the rules.

The Pontiac was a radio-delete car, stick shift, with no heater. Probably 90 percent of cars were built in that configuration in those days. The car had the total performance package, however, of two four-barrel carburetors. It was a "plain Jane" stripped-down two-door model. It was a Pontiac Chiefton, and looked very similar to a '56 Chevy.

Bobby McKee decided to go on the road as Tiny's mechanic. That was good, because Bobby was very sharp. Plus, I already knew Tiny was hard on equipment, so there would be some repair work needed on the car.

All of us worked hard to get the car ready and help Tiny and Bobby prepare to hit the road. It was like a brotherhood, we all did what we could to help make it happen. It wasn't as structured as it is in today's society. Everybody did everything; like you had a dozen brothers and everybody did whatever their talent would allow.

Finally, the car was ready and Tiny and Bobby were all packed up and ready to go. Just before they left, Joyce and I had them over for dinner. We were still living in the little upstairs apartment on the alley, so I can truthfully say our dinner was nothing fancy. In fact, Joyce was fixing peanut butter sandwiches.

Joyce went into the other room to look after baby Carson—I think we were expecting our second son Craig—and Tiny hid the peanut butter. He was such a practical joker, I watched him study Joyce as she came back into the kitchen while we sat at the table and talked. Joyce began looking all over for the peanut butter, talking to herself and wondering whatever could she have done with it.

Tiny was enjoying it immensely. Finally, very innocently, he said, "Joyce, what are you looking for?"

"I can't find the peanut butter!"

Of course he teased her about how could you lose something like a jar of peanut butter. She was just about frantic when he rose from his chair—he just about filled the kitchen with his imposing frame—and pulled the jar from the hiding place.

It really was great fun, and it's hard to describe today how good it felt. We had many great hardships; Tiny and Bobby were literally living in their tow car between races, Joyce and I living in that tiny apartment with two little children, and none of us having any money to speak of...yet, it was wonderful. It is so hard to explain yet so simple.

That was an interesting duo, Tiny and Bobby. Tiny was maybe the most charismatic man I ever met, completely outgoing. Bobby, on the other hand, was very quiet and soft-spoken.

I have known a great, great number of people who make their living in mechanical things. Car builders, designers, fabricators, gurus, engine builders, and so forth, but I have only known two men whom I consider to be a true mechanical genius. One was Howard Johansen, whom I'll talk about later; the other was Bobby McKee.

Bobby was originally from Palatine, Ill., and came to Lincoln when he was 18 to study engineering at the University of Nebraska. They had a very good engineering school, and in fact my son Carson later graduated from the engineering school there. Bobby started school in the early 1950s, but dropped out because it wasn't challenging enough. See, he is just so far ahead of what most others are thinking, it was difficult for him because he became bored. It simply wasn't challenging enough.

Eventually, Bobby went to work for me, and stayed with me for a little over a year. During that time we were doing engine conversions, and installing McCullough superchargers and building race cars. He helped build Tiny's Pontiac in my shop, then decided to go on the road.

In later years Bobby would build cars of his own design, and he created the McKee cars within sports car racing (never mind what I said earlier about sports car racers) that are still very well known. He went on to Le Mans, and was highly successful.

In recent years Bobby has become an expert in the field of electric cars, so he's done quite well to stay abreast of modern technology. He remains a dear friend, and a couple of times each year organizes a bus trip from the Chicago area to bring a bunch of guys to tour my museum.

Once Tiny and Bobby hit the road, we heard little from them. You had to pick up Chris Economaki's *National Speed Sport News* each week to see what was happening. Frankly, they often didn't run all that well, because Tiny was too tough on equipment. They tore up the car a lot. I looked back at the records some years later, and the most money they ever made was $365 for running fourth. Most of the time it was $100, sometimes as little as $25.

With that said, look at how much a NASCAR Sprint Cup (or Nextel Cup or Winston Cup, whatever) driver makes today. Just to qualify for a race makes almost $100,000. The difference between then and now is incredible.

One thing I remember was that Tiny's name was on the loan documents. Of course, if they had investigated his ability to repay the loan it probably would have never been approved. It would be like the people who sold houses and mortgages around the country this past couple of years. Not much of a trail on an ability to repay the loan.

In fact, I think they eventually wrote off the loan. I remember taking care of a couple of payments early on, but eventually Tiny just let it go and that was that. I doubt that's the first time that's happened in racing! In my mind, that doesn't reflect so badly on Tiny, because the fact is he truly didn't have the ability to pay. He was living hand-to-mouth, trying to survive.

Over time, they eventually tore up the Pontiac and brought it back to Lincoln, almost in pieces. Both Tiny and Bobby went back down South, because by that point the die was cast for their fortunes in stock-car racing.

Of course, that didn't end our friendship, as I stayed in touch with both men. In 1957 Bobby was hired by the Pontiac factory team, and they won the February race on the Daytona beach course. That was a wild-and-wooly event; a four-mile course, with two miles on paved Highway 1, and two miles back up the beach, with a couple of sandy corners to negotiate. Wow! If a car tipped over in the sand, they just left it there till the race was over. If the race lasted a little too long, the tide came in and approached the lane right where the cars were running. As the spectators drank beer, the good ol' Southern boys would get excited and run right out onto the track. "C'mon, Buick!" "C'mon, Pontiac!" "Go, Chevy!" "Go, Ford!"

Quite a spectacle, from a completely different time.

Each year I'd go to Daytona for the 500, and I'd team up with Tiny for a visit. He had it pretty tough in those early years, before he "made it" and earned enough to make a decent living.

I'm not exaggerating when I say he had it tough. I remember once meeting Tiny in Daytona when he was living in a $5 per week motel, and he had trench mouth so bad he could hardly talk. That was the result of eating in those horrible greasy spoon restaurants, because that's all he could afford.

In 1963 Tiny won the Daytona 500 in what was probably the greatest Cinderella story in the history of racing. He arrived in Daytona without a ride, and a week or so before the 500 as he was driving into the track he saw his friend Marvin Panch crash in a sports car, and the car burst into flames. Tiny, along with a few other men, ran directly into the flames to rescue Marvin and save his life. From his hospital bed, Marvin recommended to his car owners, the Wood Brothers, that they choose Tiny to replace him for the Daytona 500. Tiny then won the 500, launching him to stardom.

For many years Tiny was among the most popular drivers in NASCAR racing. He used his winnings to purchase a fishing camp in Cross, S.C., where he lived the rest of his life.

He remained very active in racing, and any time he came to Iowa—either to race, or visit his family—we always got together for a visit, either him coming to Lincoln or us going there. He was divorced from his first wife—they were married in front of the grandstands at Playland Park one night—and he later remarried and had a son. His second wife was considerably younger, I think. You've got to remember, these guys were all racers. To understand that, and what it means, you have to realize there were a lot of things going on that were outside the boundaries of routine people.

Tiny was a boy who never grew up. He was as hard on a race car as anyone I've ever known. Early on, he was fearless. And when you consider the kind of cars he drove in those early years—absolute deathtraps—it really meant something to be fearless.

One time I was with Tiny at Daytona and he was running a sportsman car. The race was 300 miles, and when the race began the crew had 35 tires mounted and ready. About halfway through the race, Tiny had used all those tires and had to retire. That isn't a cliché; he literally had to drop out of the race because they had no tires left. He drove Daytona like he did a county fair dirt track; run 'er down into the corner and give 'er a big slide. No man on the planet could ever have been more fearless than Tiny Lund.

That fearlessness stayed with him throughout his NASCAR career, and Tiny made the newspapers often. It usually wasn't for winning, but for being spectacular.

The bonds forged between Tiny and myself went all the way back to those early years when we both had almost nothing to our name. There were many times when neither of us had five cents between us, but we still had a good time. And there was something about Tiny that made people just naturally like him. He was like a big kid, always clowning around with practical jokes and having fun.

Even though he was a "Northerner" from Iowa, the Southern people embraced him. Believe me, that was no small feat in those days. There was a pronounced cultural bias that worked both ways. But Tiny overcame that, to the point of becoming one of the most popular drivers of his era.

All these years later, people who knew him still light up when they hear his name. When you can make people do that, you've really made an impact on them some way, somehow.

He was still racing in the 1970s, although not as frequently as before. We visited often, and I remember meeting his pet monkey. Long before the days when Tony Stewart had a pet monkey, Tiny had a pet monkey. He brought it over with him, and the damned thing just fell in love with me. It hung off my shoulder, picking the dandruff out of my hair, bothering me to no end. I'm not much of a guy with pets, and that monkey wore me out.

I talked to Tiny on the phone about a week before he was going to run the 1975 Talladega 500. It was the usual conversation, us giving each other a hard time, laughing. I hung up the phone that day with no idea that I'd spoken with my friend for the last time.

A week later, his race car got T-boned by another at Talladega and he was killed. Just like that, a great racer was dead.

I heard of his death over the radio. This was the days before cell phones and instant communication. I happened to turn on the radio and the guy was talking about Tiny getting killed, and there wasn't anything there to soften the blow.

What a sick feeling in my gut. To this day, I feel rotten when I think about it.

How would Tiny Lund fit into NASCAR, 2009? I'm not sure, really. I have long felt that if Tiny had been from this era, there would be nobody in the sport more charismatic. Almost from top to bottom, everybody loved him. From Bill France, Sr., to Bill France, Jr., to Cale Yarborough, to Tommy Pistone's dad who ran a restaurant in the infield at Daytona, they all admired and loved Tiny.

Tiny was a racer. When I call somebody a racer, it's not that they just drove the car. A racer is somebody who has been there, done that, and continues to do it all his life. Plays hard at the game. Damn the torpedoes, full speed ahead. That's a racer.

Tiny Lund was definitely a racer.

11

Brother Beckman

In the long, eventful period from 1948 to 1980, I hired a lot of race drivers. They ranged from tall to short, loud to quiet, polite to ornery. All were interesting and colorful human beings. I remained friends with nearly all of them, no matter how we parted: They quit, got fired, or we simply went our separate ways.

I have spent considerable time in later years trying to compile a complete list of these characters, but every time I think the list is complete I'm reminded of somebody else. Some lasted a long time, while others didn't even run the entire night for me.

I know of at least 87 drivers who have been in my race cars. As the years go along and I keep working the memory banks, I'll bet I think of a few more to add to the list.

I consider all of those guys — and one gal — my "step-children." Even when I bawled them out and fired them on the spot, I still cared about them, cared about their safety. They weren't really my kids, of course, but there was a fondness that goes beyond a routine friendship. At one time, we had a connection. It might have been for several years, or might have only been a matter of minutes. But we were connected, so I look at 'em like a "step-child."

With one exception: One driver and I became so close, so completely intertwined, that he was like my brother. Lloyd Beckman, the brother I never had.

When I hired Lloyd for the first time in 1953, I had my reservations. I was petrified of wild race drivers, because I didn't want anybody to tear up my car. Lloyd's reputation wasn't calm and easy; it was wild. So I wasn't sure if I was hiring the right guy.

However, once we got together we really clicked. We were completely different personalities, yet we had a bond, a closeness that was immediately obvious. He drove for me off and on, off and on again, spanning more than 30 years.

We fought, fussed and feuded, and loved each other just like brothers. He didn't like his God-given brother, or his God-given sister. In fact, Lloyd didn't like very many people at all. But he and I forged a friendship that endured.

It wasn't the kind of back-slapping, jovial friendship you often see. Lloyd was not that kind of person. He almost never showed his emotions, and you'd never get him to admit he liked something or somebody. That was just his way.

Yet, there was a bond, even though it was unspoken. I have a picture of me sitting in a wheelchair after a terrible accident that nearly killed me in 1968. I'm at the Nebraska State Fair, and Jerry Weld was driving my race car that day. But it was Lloyd who was pushing my wheelchair through the pits, looking out for me. He wasn't even driving my race car; Jerry Weld was driving my car. But Lloyd was there for me, like a brother.

Lloyd had a talent I never saw from anybody else in my life; he was quick as lighting. I always related him to Muhammad Ali, what'd he always say? "I float like a butterfly and sting like a bee." That describes Lloyd to a "T." He was quick, like a cat. Uncanny.

He was an alcoholic for much of his life, and later took the cure. He had been in the service, and went to the Veteran's Hospital for his treatment. He never relapsed, because once he quit drinking I never knew him to take another drink. He was clean and sober the rest of the way. When he decided he'd had enough, that was it.

Lloyd was a helluva race driver. The best "short-track" driver I ever knew. Period. Although he never fully understood how talented he was, he managed to have a tremendous career, one of the very best racers this country has ever produced.

But there was one thing Lloyd lacked: self-confidence. Had he been self-confident, he could have gone so much further as a race driver. That's a problem for many people in this world. I know this, because in my early days I didn't have self-confidence. I wasn't certain of what I could do in those days, and I didn't see any talents in myself. I have damn few, so it's pretty hard to see any when you have damn few.

Boy, did we fuss and fight. We'd get along for periods of time, then we'd have a big falling out and separate. We'd stay pissed at each other for something or other, but inevitably we'd get over it and he'd wind up back in my car. And that described our relationship, too. We'd be mad at each other, but we'd always wind up being friends again.

When Lloyd was driving for me he started making quite a bit of money. Naturally, Lloyd didn't think he needed to have a job, and he just hung around town all day. I figured he should be working, to keep himself occupied and out of trouble, so I insisted he come to work for me at Speedway Motors.

My idea was to have him sell parts in Omaha and the surrounding area. I bought him a fancy carrying case for all the catalogs, and really set him up in first-class style.

Lloyd a salesman? Judging from his rough, tough features and character, you might think he'd be better suited as a bill collector. But while Lloyd was tough — physically and mentally tough — he never started fights. He finished a few, but he didn't start 'em. So I figured he'd be all right to just talk to people about parts and do some selling.

That sure didn't last long. In no time at all Lloyd was back to just hanging out during the week, waiting on the next race.

My experience trying to turn Lloyd into a working man was short-lived. I was still learning, too, about human nature and the real world. My idea sounded good, but it wasn't a good idea at all. You can't make somebody be something they're not. Lloyd wasn't a 9-to-5 man. He was a free-spirit, impossible to tame, like a tiger or lion. You can spend all day thinking how that lion ought to act, and how he ought to be, and even try to train the lion to do what you think he should do. But in the end, the lion will do what he damned well pleases. That defines Lloyd exactly.

When I hired Lloyd the first time, he was making the transition from motorcycles to auto racing. Lloyd raced an Indian motorcycle, while I rode a BSA. We never actually raced against each other, because he was racing in Iowa and I was racing in southern Nebraska.

Lloyd was scheduled to make his debut in a roaring roadster at Belleville one Sunday, and for some reason he wasn't able to make the trip down. They put somebody else in the car, and the guy promptly got himself killed in the car Lloyd was supposed to be driving. Could have been Lloyd, but it wasn't. Thank goodness.

That was sure a different time. Back then, when you got killed in a race car, it hardly merited a mention in the newspaper. It was like, "Oh, by the way, George got killed at Belleville." As you look through many of my old clippings, you notice right away that racing was "hazardous to your health." Very, very dangerous, so much so that it's impossible for a young person today to grasp just how dangerous. People were getting whacked and maimed just about every other week. And I don't mean just a broken arm or something; I'm talking about catastrophic injuries that shaped the rest of their life. I know guys who are yet today in institutions from accidents in the '50s and '60s. Those were bad, bad times in that regard.

That's why so many guys—like my pal Woody Brinkman—raced under an assumed name. If your wife found out, she figured she was married to a dead man. If your employer found out, forget it, you were done. All done. You couldn't tell anybody what you were doing. It was as if you were robbing banks or something.

Lloyd had a demeanor that scared away 99 percent of the people he encountered. Even though my sons grew up around him, he scared them to death. He was stern, with a glare that could cut right through you. There was something menacing about him, and he had the gruffness to make it real.

Even with me, he was gruff. Not as much as he was with everybody else, but still gruff. However, it's worth noting that I never got hit by him. We would squabble and fuss, but he never reared back to take a swing at me. There was a lot of mutual respect, I think, and that's what kept us together, kept us close. I probably didn't recognize this early on because I was not yet wise enough to understand things.

Not long after I hired Lloyd we decided to go racing down at Playland Park. They were televising the races, drawing huge crowds. Bud Burdick and his pals were hard to beat at Playland, and we knew going in it would be a challenge.

The Burdicks were from south Omaha, and they were a tough bunch. That's a rough part of town, down around the stockyards. Bud had won the recent races at Playland, and had a big following.

During the race Lloyd tagged Bud and turned him over, and he rolled right up and into the television camera. Great footage!

After the race, all the fans and everybody else whose name was Burdick—Bobby Burdick was still just a kid, and a few years later he won a NASCAR race at Atlanta in his dad Roy's car—came calling on our pit area. They thought it would be a good idea to whip Lloyd and me, and anybody else standing around.

We just backed up to the fence, with our backs literally against the wall. We each picked up a jack handle, and said, "Step up, boys. Whatever needs to be, will be."

I'm a lover, not a fighter. That's been proven over and over again, because I always land on the floor, knocked out. It wasn't because I was running away, though. I was at least trying to challenge.

The Omaha boys were rugged, and they weren't just there to threaten. They were there to get some satisfaction. There were some fisticuffs, and then it kind of died down.

That's when I realized Lloyd was tough when it came to a scrap. Oh, man, was he tough. Years later I saw him fight a friend of his in the pits at Capitol Beach Speedway in Lincoln, because the guy accused Lloyd of doing his wife. Lloyd wasn't driving for me at the time, and during that period Lloyd would spend too much time before the races hanging around some bar in town. Both men had been drinking, and when they locked up in a fight it lasted for almost a full hour. I've never seen two men fight that long, not even in a 15-round prize fight in a boxing ring.

But that's just how Lloyd was. If you pushed him too far, he was ready to fight. And if you got him started, he wasn't going to lose. It's as simple as that.

Thinking about that mob in Omaha made me remember something: Many of the guys involved in racing during this era ran salvage yards. I guess it was a natural connection, because those guys had a steady supply of cars and parts.

Many times the whole family would show up with the guy from the salvage yard, and often the whole bunch was rough and tough.

For example, in Auburn, Neb., there was a family of red-haired people who were involved in local racing. This was a big family, easily more than 20 people, and they all had distinctive red hair. My good friend Gene Barnett was promoting races there and he invited me to "help him out" as a flagman. His regular flagman had been run over by a car the previous week.

I had raced at Auburn years earlier, but it wasn't a good situation. They kept picking on my car because they thought we were running a locked rear end, and finally one day after we won the race they decided to check us. The officials jacked up one rear wheel, and my driver was still sitting in the car. He put his foot on the brake, and the car rolled off the jack.

Immediately, all these red-haired people were raising hell, saying our rear end was locked. It wasn't locked, but they were sure quick to believe it was. That's another time when we had to fight our way out of the race track. You'd fight your way in, and fight your way out.

When Gene asked me to help him out with flagging, I had already gained a little experience. Some time earlier my friend Richard Lawrence and I drove my '32 Ford two-door down to Beatrice, where he would drive the car in the race and I would flag. These were full-fendered roadsters, with the glass still in place and everything. Truly "stock cars," right off the street. You weren't even allowed to roll the windows down, and I'm talking plate glass windows, long before the advent of safety glass. You'd cover the panes with masking tape, because, after all, you can easily cut your head off if you stuff it through those old plate glass panes. I made $20 for flagging the race, and he made $7.50 driving in the race. Then, after the race, we hopped in our "stock car" and drove it 50 miles back to Lincoln.

Incidentally, I got my opportunity to flag at Beatrice because that flagman — a man named Boggs — had been run over a week earlier at a roaring roadster race. Did I mention that this racing stuff can be hazardous to your health?

Gene and I flew down to Auburn in his small airplane, and it was a fun trip. The farmers were out in the fields, and Gene would buzz them from behind and they'd almost fall off their tractors.

They called a pit meeting to talk about the day's program, and during the meeting the leader of the red-haired clan says, "Barnett, we told you we were gonna run over your flagman last week, and even though you got a new flagman, we're gonna run over him, too."

Well, now. This was one minor detail Gene had neglected to mention! These guys were sore about something the flagman had done, and had sworn revenge. I guess that's why Gene hired me…better me than him. Right about then I'm wondering what I'd gotten myself into.

The method of flagging was simple: You'd stand at the inner edge of the track, wave the starting flag as they come out of the fourth turn, then run like hell into the infield to a two-story paddock building.

The first race, here comes all those redheads. I'm nervous as hell, holding the flag, preparing for the start. As they come off the fourth turn, I waved the green flag, and immediately realized they've got 'er turned left into the infield, coming right at me. I ran like a maniac for the paddock, barely making it as the cars roared past, and it seemed like they were right on my heels.

Survivor, I think the game is called.

Racing was in a period of transition in the 1950s, and I remember it well. The roadsters faded from prominence, and lots of guys moved away from jalopies. Stock car racing was taking off, going in a different direction. Some of us began stripping parts off the stock cars, and immediately those cars were known as a modified.

This was an early version of the cars that eventually evolved into sprint cars. The early cars were a full-bodied car with an overhead-valve engine, usually an Oldsmobile, Buick, or Cadillac.

This same scenario was playing out in pockets all around the country. Racing people didn't travel much in those days, and we were insulated from what was going on elsewhere. If your region had a strong, successful track, their rules usually set the tone for the entire area. Whatever form of cars that track promoted, that's what the racers built. Like a beehive, or an anthill. A racing community, informally bound together by common rules.

The roadsters fell out of fashion because they had to be hand-built, and were quite labor intensive. It took a fair investment of time, and certainly talent and money, to build one. Plus, they were dangerous; those cars killed an inordinate number of drivers. Remember, they had no roll cages, and no roof. All forms of racing were dangerous, but roadsters were particularly lethal.

In my mind, the modified was the most successful car in the history of auto racing. From the standpoint of good racing, affordability, and popular appeal, the modified was a big hit. They energized fans across the entire Great Plains, forever changing the course of auto racing.

The modified was the best-handling race car we ever ran. This isn't just Speedy Bill talking, this is from a lot of great drivers whose opinion I respect.

After we transitioned to the modified, one day in early 1960 I began to think about things. I had been racing for more than 10 years, and had begun to figure some things out. I knew some basic truths: lighter was better, and a short wheelbase was better. I also knew that if everybody is running the same widget, one little advantage can mean a lot.

I decided to build a new car, from a clean sheet of paper. I had some various ideas I wanted to try, so I got busy.

There were a number of rules governing modified racing at this time, and I had to figure out how to do what I wanted within the scope of the rules. Really, if you're creative you can often figure a way to build what you want and still not break the rules.

For example, the local rules stipulated that you couldn't move the engine back from the front cross-member more than a certain number of inches. So I left the cross-member in place, and moved the front axle forward. I was still within the rules, but I had the engine where I wanted it. This really helped the car's balance.

One thing everybody talks about in racing is balance. That's what I was looking for: balance. Well, this new car ultimately had it, believe me.

I placed the seat in the center of the car, instead of on the left side, because I wanted to use a center-steering setup. I then installed a 12:1 Ross steering gear that steered off the right front instead of the left front.

I used a buggy-spring front and rear suspension, and a hoop section for the belly pan that would stabilize the car, taking some of the twist out of the frame. I mounted a stainless steel WWII-surplus oxygen bottle over the left rear, and that was my fuel tank.

The rear suspension had a Model A cross member with adjusting bolts that allowed me to easily change the wedge in the car. Every time I ran the car, I took the front and rear springs off and polished them smoother. Then I'd cover them with Vaseline and wrap them with tape. The suspension was so soft and smooth, you could press down on the front with maybe 60 pounds of force, and it would gently bounce, almost like a baby buggy. The front had a pin that came out of the cross member, and the spring plate rode on that pin.

The entire package worked perfectly. I used magnesium hubs, and two-piece magnesium wheels. I also used oversized brakes, because Lloyd used a lot of brake. He'd lightly use the brakes to help work the car, so naturally that took a great amount of maintenance.

The car was light, maybe 1,900 pounds. Most everybody else weighed between 2,100 and 2,200. I had trimmed everything off the car I could, and sectioned the body to take about six inches from the profile. It was a clever car, it really was. During its lifetime no other modified ever came close to comparing in terms of innovation or success.

I installed a 350-ci Chevrolet engine, and fitted the car with a '32 Ford sedan body. It looked like a funeral hearse compared to the rest of the cars. It looked different and it damn sure ran differently. Of course it was painted purple like all my race cars.

"The Sedan" was born. Now we were ready to go racing.

We debuted the car at Capitol Beach Speedway on July 4, 1960. We won that first night, and I was elated. Then, one week later, we won again. The following week, we won again. With this great car, and Lloyd's great driving, it was now clear that everybody else was completely outclassed.

They always started us on the tail of the 24-car field as a handicap, but it didn't matter. Lloyd would just drive right to the front, like it was easy, without putting a mark on the car. We won every feature race at Capitol Beach for the rest of the year, and I was about to learn two very important lessons.

One, people love to cheer against a winner. Once we got on our win streak, the stands were packed each week. If you didn't get there by 2 p.m. (for an 8 p.m. race), you didn't get a seat. All those people crowded into those stands, sitting in the hot afternoon sun, just to cheer against Lloyd. They desperately wanted to see him get beat.

It wasn't that they didn't like Lloyd; they not only liked him, they respected him. But they didn't want the same driver to win all the time. The more we won, the louder — and more emphatic — the boos became.

The second lesson had to do with Speedway Motors. By this time I was selling a lot of stuff to my competitors; many kept their cars going with parts purchased from me. However, when we started really kicking ass, my business began to dry up. The perception among the racers was that we were cheating, or perhaps I was selling them inferior parts in order to beat them every week.

This was very hard on my business. Very hard.

Still, it was a dynamic time for our local racing scene. Our win streak generated great controversy, and created a real buzz. To this day, some 47 years later, I still have guys tell me about being a young kid and riding their bicycle six, eight miles out to the track at noon, climbing into the trees around the track because they didn't have money for a ticket. It takes a lot to inspire people to want to see a race that badly, and then remember it the rest of their lives.

It didn't hurt that Lloyd really egged it on. He was getting booed so badly, and him being the tenacious guy he was, on the cool-down lap after the feature he would stick his arm out the window and give the entire grandstand the No. 1 sign with his middle finger. And they would go crazy, booing him even louder.

We won the remainder of the races that season at Capitol Beach, making it 11 straight victories. We clinched the Nebraska Modified Racing Ass'n title as well.

That offseason was the weakest my business could have imagined. Plus, the fans were sure riled up. I couldn't go to the grocery without somebody raising hell about my "cheating" race car. Old friends were hardly speaking to me, angry that we were winning all the races.

We rolled into the Capitol Beach pits for the season opener in 1961, and I diplomatically suggested to Beckman that maybe he ought to take it easy. Well, that was like waving a red flag in front of a bull. It pissed him off to no end; now he didn't just want to win, he wanted to lap the entire field.

Victory number 12 came that night, and I realized I was really in trouble. I mean, what was I going to do? I certainly couldn't fire Beckman for winning too many races. But my business was slowly circling the drain, and Lloyd is out there trying to kick their ass.

I made an executive decision. I pulled the 350-ci Chevy, and replaced it with a tired old 302-inch Chevy instead. Boy, now Beckman was *really* pissed.

After winning our 16th straight feature, the following week the old 302 finally gave up. The crowd went berserk, cheering and roaring and dancing in the aisles.

It must have been the break I needed, because after that my business started getting back to normal. I replaced the engine, and Beckman and I went back to winning, but not 16 in a row.

Bill Smith the racer wanted to win all the races. However, Bill Smith of Speedway Motors realized too much winning isn't good for business. At all.

We began traveling a little more after our 1960 season, and late in the year went to Spencer, Iowa, for the big five-state championship event. Lloyd won it easily, and that's when I began to realize that we could compete with anybody in modified racing. We also won our second straight NMRA title.

The guys at Spencer were definitely not slugs. It was guys like Scratch (Jerry) and Itch (Don) Daniels, and Jerry Richert, who went on to win the Knoxville Nationals the following August. They were damned good, and I respected them as much as I did anybody. But Lloyd did a great job, the car performed well, and we won it.

It was during this stretch when I began to realize that we pretty much had it figured out. We got pretty good, at least I thought we were pretty good, and our results were there to support that. Maybe I thought we were better than we really were, I don't know. Racing is a humbling exercise for sure. You can be good today, and good tomorrow, but next week it might all turn completely flat. All life experiences are like that, I think.

In 1961 I began building "different" supermodifieds. This was another transition I was in the middle of, and just like before we didn't realize it was an evolution. Everybody followed along and before you know we were racing a new type of car.

The supermodifieds were very similar to modifieds, but were slimmed down with a different body configuration. You might see doodlebug bodies, or just a couple of narrow panels on the sides. The chassis had a roll cage, and was shortened and narrowed from the previous modified configuration.

At least that was the progression in our part of the country. People sometimes referred to these cars as "sprint cars," and they were similar. These cars raced at a number of area tracks, most notably Knoxville Raceway in Iowa.

True sprint cars, of course, were much more sophisticated, and only USAC (and AAA, prior to that) or IMCA raced those cars. They often had chrome, and fancy paint, and a car might be in competition for 10, 15 years. That was unheard of in our world. Our progression would never allow a car to stay competitive for such a length of time.

At some point — and nobody can pinpoint exactly when this happened — the sprint cars and supermodifieds merged. They became one, the same animal.

Nearly all of the USAC sprint cars in the late 1950s were still using the Offenhauser engine. However, the development of the Chevrolet small block engine forever displaced the Offy in sprint-car racing.

Hell, we were using overhead-valve V8 engines in our modifieds a good 10 years before anybody in sprint-car racing. And we were racing *a lot*; they were racing seldom. The overhead-valve V8 proved to be the hot ticket in sprint car racing, and we farm boys from the Plains were well ahead of the curve on that one.

This was one of the most exciting periods in my life, certainly in my racing career. Racing seemed to be going places, and I was right in the middle of things, glad to be along for the ride.

12

Hitting the Road

Something else was happening with me in the early 1960s, aside from the evolution to a different type of race car. I guess you might say I was getting restless, because more and more I wanted to take our car out on the road to see how we'd do against other competition.

Each week in *National Speed Sport News* I read about the bigger purses at events farther away from Lincoln. I raced for the money, and that was the bottom line. It was a business proposition. If my car could win more money, I could invest more back into Speedway Motors.

So I expanded my range, by a lot. Places such as Knoxville — along with Belleville and Topeka — became common destinations. Towing was still an adventure at that time, and although our equipment was primitive and we were soon turning 70,000 miles each year on the odometer, I never had any mishaps.

For many years we raced every Saturday night at Knoxville. That was a 500-mile round-trip tow from Lincoln, and Lloyd and I would leave around 10 a.m. on Saturday morning. We'd stop about halfway at a roadside picnic stand to eat a lunch Joyce had prepared for us.

This was before Interstate highways, of course. The state highways were narrow, two-lane roads with curbs on each side. Most racers were in half-ton pickup trucks towing a single-axle, open-wheel trailer.

Hwy. 92 was our main route across Iowa, and I'll bet I could drive that stretch in my sleep.

Knoxville was a place you didn't have to worry about arriving too early, because they didn't seem to care how late they raced. We would often race until one, two, three o'clock in the morning, and nobody seemed to mind. That made for some late drives home through the night, because we had to get back to Lincoln in order to race at Capitol Beach on Sunday night.

On those hot nights, we all drank our share of beer after the races. Why did we drink beer? To stay cool, among other things. It was hot, hot, hot in the summertime around these parts. You'd pull into Belleville, around 10 a.m. to get signed in, unload in your pit area, unhook and park your tow vehicle, and get ready to go. That meant you were standing in that extreme heat from 10 a.m. until late afternoon.

Belleville is typically 100 degrees, 105 degrees, 110 degrees. Hot, baby. Try that for an afternoon or two, and you'll know what hot is all about. When you literally could feel the sweat come off your gonads and roll past your knees, you knew you were sweating pretty good.

When you were all done racing you climbed into your tow car or truck and started down the road, looking at a 400- or 500-mile tow on a two-lane highway to the next race. To say you "turned on the air," meant that you opened the windows and turned the wing vents to point straight back at you.

If you stopped somewhere for the night, it was a $5-per-night motel in a little town somewhere like Winterset, Iowa. Your room had no fans, and no air conditioning. You were dead tired, and dirty as a pig from being in the dust all day, sweat pouring off you.

Even late at night, it might still be 85 degrees. The only way to get cool, and get some sleep, was to put a bed sheet in the bathtub and soak it with cold water, then roll up in the sheet and go to sleep. That's an old trick, and if you're thinking it doesn't sound comfortable, believe me, it isn't. This stuff is what you learn by doing, not by sitting at home reading comic books.

One thing I learned was that to run first, first you must finish. Preparing the car so it would last 10 laps, 20 laps, 50 laps, whatever, was the objective. That was a problem back then; places like Knoxville typically ran a 15-lap feature, because if they ran 20 or 25 all the cars would fall out.

That's because nearly everybody's car was home built. There were still only a limited number of "racing" parts I could sell these guys, because few companies had developed a line of racing products. You could buy rear ends, and steering gears, for example, but lots of other pieces still came from salvage yards.

That meant everybody's car looked different, which was neat. People called many of the Knoxville cars "hoodoo wagons," because they looked all cut-up and different, almost like a Chevy truck cab. When Pappy Weld brought his cars up from Kansas City, they looked still different. Pappy's cars were almost like a roaring roadster, built with square tubing and with no top on the body. Kind of funny looking. Actually, all the cars were funny looking. Everybody had their own interpretation of how the cars should look.

As we traveled around the country, each venue had an entirely different look. It was a very interesting time. They were running these hoodoo wagons down around Topeka, and for a long time Knoxville had very few local drivers because they attracted all these racers from outside the state.

Probably everyone in racing today knows of the Knoxville Nationals, but few realize that the very first nationals were held in Topeka. Through fate and the right people, the biggest event wound up at Knoxville.

The first time I raced at Knoxville — and I'm guessing it was 1961 — I used a Chevrolet engine with three carburetors. We were beaten that first weekend by Dean Sylvester's Ardun-equipped flathead Ford.

The next week we showed up with six carburetors, which ultimately led to some excitement on my part. Beckman was always afraid of the throttle sticking open, almost to the point of paranoia. He wasn't fond of big tracks like Knoxville to begin with, and the idea of a stuck throttle as he was going into the corner didn't seem very appealing to Lloyd.

He took one look at those six carburetors and was immediately skeptical. "You go out and hot lap the car," he said. "And you can qualify it, too."

So out I go to hot lap the car, and as I get to the backstretch I pushed the throttle pedal to the floor. Well, the linkage went over center, and the throttle stuck wide open. I knew I didn't have time to get to the kill switch, so I just focused on trying to make it through the corner. Luckily I made it, and I got it shut off on the front straight before I killed myself.

I immediately said to myself, "Hey, there is nothing to this, guys! I know you can drive through three and four wide open here, because I've done it!"

That moment of panic gave me lots of ammunition with many of my drivers down through the years.

In fact, that was an important moment in another respect. Lloyd wasn't a great qualifier, so I began qualifying the car every week. It got to the point that people got us mixed up. They'd see me in the pits and say, "Hi, Lloyd!" And they'd see Lloyd and say, "Hi, Bill!"

One thing I didn't tell anybody about was one of my supermodified creations: It was built with lightweight exhaust tubing throughout the frame.

This was a car like CAE had designed, which was a very popular car in those days. Basically it was a bunch of tubing with a couple of flat tin sides. However, Jim Culbert of CAE used very heavy tubing, and I elected to go with exhaust tubing because it is much thinner and therefore lighter. Remember, at that time we were doing a ton of exhaust work at Speedway Motors, and we were accustomed to working with that material.

Today, of course, we know that isn't safe. But in 1963, hell, things were wide open. I knew light was always faster than heavy, so why not? I not only used exhaust tubing, but lightened everything else on the car.

Which, aside from the use of exhaust tubing in the frame, we were ahead of the times with this car. The lightweight axle housing and tube, driveline, hubs, spindles, these were all speed secrets that later swept through every form of auto racing.

I don't think anybody realized how light we were. Today they even weigh the driver's wallet before he gets into the car, so the awareness of weight is very keen. That wasn't the case when I built this car.

The first time we raced the car was at the Iowa State Fair in Des Moines on a Saturday afternoon, and later that night took it to Knoxville. That same day Joyce and one of my mechanics, Marty Bassett, took my modified to race at David City, Neb., with Bobby Burdick behind the wheel. They had Lloyd's wife, Shirley, with them. They didn't win, and as the stories came out later it was evident a good time was had by the entire bunch.

(Bobby Burdick, by the way, was a very good race driver. He was a terror on the IMCA stock-car circuit when he was still a very young man, and nearly won the championship when he was just 20 years old. He was from Omaha, and was a championship motorcycle racer before he got involved in auto racing. His dad, Roy, was a great rival of ours, but later we became good friends with all the Burdicks. Bobby later raced with NASCAR and won the Southern 500 in 1961. We're proud to display the winning trophy from that race in our museum!)

Lloyd qualified for the trophy dash that night at Knoxville, while I was watching from the infield. Earl Wagner was driving a car with a big-block Lincoln engine, and he spun coming off turn four. Lloyd launched over Earl's front end and flipped 13 times in the air. It was spectacular and scary, all at the same time.

I'm there all by myself, with no help. When I saw my car flipping through the air, I immediately had dreadful thoughts. All of a sudden, the fact that I had built it out of exhaust tubing was very big in my mind. "This is the end of Lloyd," I remember thinking.

I was so shaken that I walked over to my tow truck and sat behind the wheel. A million things were going through my mind, and I was trying not to get emotional. So I thought about the practical elements of the situation.

"Now, when you take a dead guy from Knoxville to Lincoln, do you sit him up in the seat alongside you, or do you lay him in the back of the pickup bed?" Those kinds of practical thoughts.

All of a sudden here comes the 16-year-old ambulance driver, hurrying to our pit. He finds me and says, "Lloyd wants you to go to the hospital with him."

The first thing out of my mouth is, "He's *alive??!!*"

At the conclusion of World War II some years earlier Knoxville was somehow on the recipient list when the military got rid of a bunch of surplus vehicles, and the town ended up with a very nice '41 Packard ambulance, painted Air Force blue. In fact, I think the military signage was still on the side.

I climbed in the back of the ambulance, and discovered it had no medical supplies or equipment, just a flat floor to transport you to the local hospital. No gurney, nothing.

Lloyd was lying on his back, kind of in a daze. He looked up at me and said, "My feet are hot...take off my shoes."

He always wore boxing shoes, because they had a thin sole and he could better feel the throttle. This was an era long before my buddy Bill Simpson invented fireproof racing shoes. Lloyd's boxing shoes laced clear up to his knee, and I started unlacing the shoes while the kid behind the wheel of the ambulance raced to the hospital.

These were the days before storm sewers, when streets were built with a noticeable crown to allow them to drain properly. When you came across these intersections, the road was very uneven. With a long-wheelbase vehicle like this Packard, the front is a little bump but the back is a helluva ride through those uneven intersections.

Lloyd and I were rolling in the back like a pair of bowling balls, him moaning and groaning and me cussing like a sailor. The kid was oblivious, trying to see what this Packard would do.

As I mentioned earlier, racing was awfully dangerous in those days. And, of all race tracks, it seemed that Knoxville was particularly hazardous. At their local hospital, the doctors and nurses had figured out that on Saturday night there was a very real possibility of seeing a maimed racer come through the doors of the emergency room. Doctors are smart people, and soon they were taking Saturday nights off to avoid the carnage.

When we made our way into the emergency room, we discovered there was only one person working in the entire place, an elderly woman. I helped get Lloyd up on an examination table, and the lady took his vital signs and things like that. She looked at him for about 15, 20 minutes, and finally left us to sit quietly.

After about an hour she comes back in, looks at Lloyd and smiles, and says, "Well, sonny, looks like you're gonna be okay. You can go now." It was like, "Well, if you haven't died by now, you're probably not gonna."

The kid in the ambulance had long ago gone, so there we were with no transportation. Luckily one of my friends came by to check on Lloyd, and he gave us a ride back to the track. My buddies had loaded what was left of the car onto my trailer, and we sat Lloyd in the cab of the truck and started back toward Lincoln. By this time it's 2 a.m.

Lloyd was acting kind of goofy, and he told me he wanted a cigar. I hadn't known Lloyd to ever smoke a cigar, but I managed to get one from somebody and he stuck it in his mouth.

We're rolling through Council Bluffs, around 4:30, maybe 5 a.m., preparing to cross the Missouri River on the old South Omaha Bridge. Beckman is puffing the cigar, talking goofy, and I'm trying to stay awake.

As we're crossing the bridge he looks over at me.

"What time do you think we'll get there?"

"Get where?"

"Knoxville!"

"Lloyd, we've already been to Knoxville. You crashed, there ain't anything left of the car, and you got beat up pretty bad."

Finally we got back to Lincoln, and got Lloyd into his house. It was well into Sunday morning, and I was completely exhausted.

The following Tuesday Lloyd finally went to see a real doctor, who discovered that both arms were broken. Just a minor detail overlooked by the nice lady at the Knoxville hospital. So now my regular driver was parked for a few weeks.

I had several local drivers fill in the rest of August, but I needed a driver for the big modified race at Capitol Beach on Labor Day. I called Woody Brinkman and told him about the situation. The fair circuit was going on in our region, and a number of racers were in town for the IMCA sprint car races at the state fairgrounds that afternoon.

"Who can I get, Woody? Is there anybody at the fair who doesn't have a ride? I need somebody who won't tear up my car."

"Well," Woody began, thinking it over. "You can get a guy named Gordon Woolley, an IMCA champion from Texas. He's raced a lot of modifieds down in that area. Another choice is a young kid, also from Texas, named Johnny Rutherford."

"Which one doesn't tear cars up?" I asked.

"Well…Rutherford is pretty young," Woody explained.

"Get me Woolley," I said. Then I got busy getting my sedan— not the supermodified Lloyd had crashed, but my two-door modified—ready for that night's race.

That happened to be the end-of-season championship at the Beach. If I didn't show up, one of my best buddies would clinch the title by default. So I wasn't going to miss this race for anything.

I got everything set up with my new driver, who had to start last because he was new to the track and had no points. I wasn't sure how well he'd do, because even though Gordon was nice enough I didn't know whether he had any talent.

I was running two-piece magnesium wheels on my car, and as Gordon went up through the field it looked like the fourth of July, with those mag wheels grinding against everybody else's steel wheels. Gordon won the race, and immediately here comes all my best friends and customers, ready to kick the shit out of me for hiring a professional driver to spank the boys and run into them in the process. Luckily I talked them out of any physical violence, even though most weren't in a talkative mood.

Since we had beaten everybody so handily the year before at the big race at Spencer, Iowa, I had to hold up my image of the "tough guy on the block" at that event. You know, the "big dog pissin' contest" we all play. I had to get another driver and make another try. So I hired Woolley to run Spencer.

Their county fair, by the way, is billed as the largest county fair in the world. It really is quite the happening, and that's where they filmed the movie, "State Fair." The fair and the big race are held each year in October.

I took Gordon up to Spencer, along with a bunch of my buddies—a pretty wild bunch of cats—and for some reason I decided to take a spare engine. I rarely did this, because I didn't normally *have* a spare engine. In fact, it wasn't really a spare, it was the engine from my lightweight supermodified, the only thing I managed to salvage from the car after Lloyd's big crash at Knoxville.

The afternoon of the race my buddies went hunting, and afterward came by to take a look at our race car. I'm parked a couple of blocks from the track, busily trying to get the car ready. Nearby was Spencer's big water tower, and one of the guys had the bright idea that if you shot the tower with your 30-30 rifle, you'd see streams of water shooting out. The guys were fascinated with such a possibility. I tried to explain to them that this really wasn't a good idea at all; all the while, I'm hustling trying to work on my car. Luckily nobody took any target practice; but once again, the "leader of the band" wasn't having much fun at all.

We got into the pits and pretty soon it was time to warm up. We pushed Gordon off, but he chug-a-lugged the motor and spit a connecting rod right out of the side of the block. I saw it happen, because I was standing right next to the car. He came in and I leaned over the cockpit.

"How's it running, Gordon?"

"Great!"

"Well, that's funny…you kicked a rod out the side when you started it."

"Naw, I didn't."

"Get out and I'll show you!"

Which I did.

"Didn't anybody ever teach you how to start one of these cars?" I demanded. I was really not in a good mood by this time.

He had been driving sprint cars, and they were light enough that this wasn't an issue. But with these heavier sedans, you had to be more careful, holding the brake, bringing the fuel carefully to the fire, so they didn't kick back. In fairness to Gordon, he just didn't know.

So now we've got to change engines, and away we went, working as fast we could. Pretty quickly we had a bigger crowd in the pits watching us than in the grandstand. People had never before seen anybody try to change an engine at the race track, and it was certainly the first time we had done it. It took us about 45 minutes, and later when we were running sprint cars with the World of Outlaws, we could change an engine in 15 minutes. Today, they can probably do it in five.

End of story, we changed our engine and kicked their ass for the second straight year. I forgave Gordon, because he redeemed himself by winning the race. We had won the five-state championship for modifieds two years running, with two different drivers.

That's what I was there for. To win. That's what owners like to brag about!

Lloyd eventually healed up, and was none the worse for wear. In fact, that was probably one of the most serious injuries anybody ever had in my race car. Some years later Ray Lee Goodwin had some serious eye injuries in a bad spill in the Speedway Motors car at Knoxville. That accident ended Ray Lee's racing career, and it was a devastating time for all of us.

Bob Coulter migrated to the Indy area from California in the early 1960s, and in 1963 he won the Little 500 at Anderson, Ind. as a relief driver to Johnny White. Bob and family then moved to Lincoln, where he bounced around driving several local cars, including John Marsh's car. Bob joined the Speedway Motors team in 1965, and we raced with IMCA quite a bit. I had purchased and rebuilt a sprinter that had been A.J. Foyt's first racing ride (other than jalopies), and this was the car we ran with IMCA. They were racing at Topeka, and Bob was involved in a crash that left him with a broken back, which was the end of his racing career. He and his family moved back to Long Beach, Calif., and he was later a successful businessman and also campaigned sprint cars for many years. We still stay in touch.

(By the way, our crew chief for the IMCA sprint car was Bob Lawton. Yes, the same Bob Lawton who later owned IMCA for a time, "Promoter of the Year," and owner and promoter of the famous IMCA Speedway Motors Super Nationals at Boone, Iowa for the past 20 or so years. In those early days before his great promotional success, Lawtie was just an eager young guy who wanted to be around race cars.)

Still, I led a charmed life when it came to guys getting hurt in my car. Overall we were very, very fortunate.

I had some close calls, though. I had Sonny Helms, a driver from Des Moines, drive my car at Eagle one Saturday night, and the very next day he was killed at Bloomfield, Iowa, driving Bill Moyer's car. I'll never forget the date: July 12, 1964.

See, that was always very much on my mind. As much as I loved racing, I was petrified of anybody getting killed in my car. It weighed on my mind, every time we raced. I never talked about it or even admitted it publicly, but it was there. Every minute.

It was there for Lloyd, too. Even though he was a great race driver, and seemed to be fearless, the danger of what we were doing worked on his emotions and mind.

Some of that was Lloyd's personality. Many times after a race, particularly when it was hot, he would come in after the race so totally exhausted he could hardly move. A lot of this was because he was so uptight, literally, it fatigued his muscles. He couldn't control his adrenaline, his juices. Many times when he drove my supermodified or sprint car, he'd walk to the back of the car to throw up right before climbing in the cockpit. It was like someone with stage fright. It happens to race drivers, too.

It was just a very powerful nervous condition Lloyd suffered with. He got to where he detested running Knoxville or Belleville, because he was petrified at the big, high-speed tracks. Yet when he was on his game, he was as good as anyone has ever been at those tracks.

During the period when we raced together, we witnessed a lot of carnage. We never talked about it much, but he wasn't blind. He'd see other guys getting whacked and he knew he was at risk, too. Many times he would not talk to me at all during the drive to Knoxville on Saturday morning. That's four-and-a-half hours, and he wouldn't say one word. When it was like that, I almost felt like I was taking a guy to the gallows. He just clammed up and wanted to be in his own world. That was just Lloyd's way of dealing with it.

I've often thought that if Lloyd would have had a little different personality — and maybe that's not the right word to use — or maybe a different demeanor, maybe he could have taken his God-given talents and become the greatest racer there ever was.

Of course, at the time we didn't talk about such dreams. We just talked about the racing of the day, and how we could win. Or we'd be in the middle of a big spat, and not be on speaking terms for a few weeks at a time.

I should have known that's how things were going to be, because almost from the beginning Lloyd didn't hesitate to quit me if he thought he had a better deal someplace else. The first time it happened, I was still in my original Speedway Motors location on O Street, building flathead Ford motors to stay alive. One of my part-time employees, Don Lincoln, was a bread salesman during the day, and he'd come by to relieve me in the evening so I could work on my engines.

I stayed open until 9 p.m., thinking I might be able to catch one more customer. Don came in and worked the counter, allowing me to stay open yet get some engine work done.

Don decided he wanted to build a jalopy, and I ended up building him a motor. He talked Beckman into coming and driving for him. I hired somebody else, but through the course of that season I blew up several of my motors. In the meantime, Beckman and Don went all year long without one engine failure, and won a lot of races. I obviously gave 'em the wrong engine!

But over time, Lloyd and I were back together. It was always like that. Fight one day, make up the next.

One afternoon we were racing at Belleville at the North Central Kansas Free Fair, and we had 'em covered. It was very dusty, and Lloyd mistook the white flag for the yellow and slowed up. Grady Wade passed him to take the win, and I was furious. So furious, in fact, that I fired him on the spot. I loaded my car on the trailer and left him to find his own damned way home, some 120 miles away.

I don't know how Lloyd got home from Belleville. Hitched a ride, I guess. We were sore at each other for a while on that one. When you're brothers, that happens. I never had brothers, but I've seen my sons poke each other in the nose, yet they love each other the next day, and they get along well. That seems to be a normal thing for brothers; it was certainly the way it was for me and Lloyd.

I didn't have Lloyd to run the next day at our Nebraska State Fair, so I hired Don Brown. This was a very neat offset roadster I had built, and Don ran well but didn't win. He came in and said, "That's the best-handling race car I have ever driven on dirt." And he promptly set out building the three mechanical rabbits, but that's a story for another time.

One time, some years later, Lloyd quit me to drive a car for a guy who used to work for me. That pissed me off, of course. We were racing at Capitol Beach, and that night when I saw Lloyd come through the pit gate I could see that he had been drinking.

He went out for hot laps, so I jumped into my car for the hot lap session. I don't remember who was driving for me, but I was a pretty good hot-lapper.

The city of Lincoln is built where it is because during pre-historic times the basin was a great salt lake. All the creeks and water here, to this day, are salty. When the railroad began coming through in the 1850s, they needed salt to feed the animals and to preserve the meat. So this became a spot to stop and buy salt.

Capitol Beach was built on the west end of Lincoln, where an amusement park was located. Just outside of turn two was a salt lake, and to prevent cars from getting out of the track and into the lake they sank 10-by-10 timbers into the ground to form a wall. They had been hit more than a few times and by this time were pretty crooked.

I'm in my car that night, and I'm thinking, "You know, Beckman, I'm pissed at you. You haven't been treatin' me right, so I think I'll just park you out in that pond."

I drove up alongside him to make sure he could see it was me, and then I set about putting him in the lake. But guess who wound up in the pond that night? That's right, it was Speedy Bill.

The fact is, Beckman had more skill drunk than I had sober. You learn a lot from these little life experiences.

Lloyd and I continued to race together — off and on — throughout the 1970s, until I retired as a car owner in 1980. Right about the time I quit, Lloyd decided he'd retire from racing.

A year or so after I quit, my oldest son Carson — a licensed mechanical engineer — discovered an experimental sprinter I had built years earlier with the idea of Jan Opperman driving it at the IMCA afternoon sprint car races. I had never finished the car, and it was stored at my fiberglass plant. Carson got the bug to go racing, and he approached me and asked if I'd let him run the car here locally.

"Who you gonna get to drive it?" I asked.

He named some wild young kid, and I shook my head.

"No, that won't work," I explained. "He'll tear it up every week, and you'll spend all your time and money fixing the race car. And you'll sure get tired of that."

"Will you let me race it if I can find somebody else?" he asked.

"Yeah, if it's somebody who can get the job done."

"Who would you get?"

"Go talk to Lloyd and see if you can talk him out of retirement."

"Lloyd??!! Well...he's awful old." I could see that Carson was skeptical.

"That isn't going to make any difference," I assured him.

Carson worked up the nerve to call Lloyd — remember, my boys were scared to death of gruff, tough Lloyd Beckman — and asked if he'd consider driving the car. Lloyd said, "Well, let's have coffee and talk about it."

Lloyd and some of the local boys always had breakfast at a local truck stop, so Carson went out and they had a talk. Carson came back to me and said, "Lloyd said he'd drive the car if you'll come to the races and not do any of the work, just stand in the pits and watch."

What Lloyd wanted was for me to spot for him, tell him what the race track was doing, things like that. Just like I had done for years; it was a level of trust Lloyd and I had developed in each other. I agreed, and Lloyd and Carson were all set to go racing.

They won the opener at Midwest Speedway, a track here in Lincoln that had been built in the 1960s. Ironically enough, Lloyd and I won the very first race ever held at the track about 20 years earlier, and a couple of track championships there as well.

Carson and Lloyd kept winning, and by the middle of the season had already clinched the season championship. Even though it had been 29 years since I first hired Lloyd, he was obviously still able to get it done. I've always thought that was impressive as hell.

After several seasons Carson had the sprint-car bug out of his system and went on to all kinds of racing. Lloyd evidently still wanted to race, as he ran for car owner and mechanic Gary Swenson here in town, a man who has been racing for something like five decades and who worked with my team when we were having great success.

In the summer of 1995 Lloyd was in his home away from home, his Freightliner 18-wheeler, driving from Chicago to Los Angeles. He got a call from the father of Danny Young, a promising young racer from Des Moines. Danny was away running a World of Outlaws car, and his father needed a driver for the 360-inch sprint car races at Webster City, Iowa.

This was probably 10-plus years since Lloyd had "retired." But he drove to Webster City, 18-wheeler and all, and got in the 360 for the very first time and won. Race fans are still talking about that one!

Sadly, a few weeks later Danny Young was killed in a sprint car accident at Knoxville.

In the 1990s Lloyd ran the Masters Classic at Knoxville several times. This is a race for "over 50" drivers, using winged sprint cars. I thought that was interesting, because throughout his career Lloyd rarely raced with a wing, and of course he didn't like fast tracks like Knoxville. Yet, at the Masters Classic when he was well into his 60s, Lloyd was turning laps in the 17- and 18-second bracket. Hell, in all those prior years he never ran faster than the 20s! So here is this older guy, very late in his life, running faster than ever before.

In fact, in 1995 Lloyd set a new track record for the Masters Classic!

Lloyd was truly a special person in my mind, and always will be. He was well-respected by the fans, who enjoyed his talent. They used to say the only thing that attracted fans to the races was to see all the gore, to see the wrecks, to see somebody get killed. But a good race fan doesn't want to see any of that. They want to see the talent. It's like some of the stick-and-ball sports; fans have an appreciation for the talents of a Michael Jordan or a Peyton Manning, somebody who has the skill to excel at what they do.

After a while, race fans become like family with the racers. You watch a guy race all those years, and you get to know him. Often a racer gets to know the fans equally well, gets to know their kids and says hello when they greet them in the pits after the races. And here in Lincoln we always had very loyal fans. They understood the race cars, and racing, and they didn't need things explained to them. They were sharp.

They liked Lloyd, and respected him, even if they booed him. That was very obvious in later years because Lloyd had such a big following.

Yet, he never felt comfortable around people. For example, in the early years he often came by my shop and visited with me. As my business grew, however, he came by less frequently. It wasn't because we weren't friends; he just didn't like being around all the people hanging out at my shop. He wasn't a social person, and people were always asking him questions, picking at him. He didn't like any of that. He didn't even like people taking pictures of him, particularly before a race.

Once we were both completely and officially retired from racing, then it boiled down to just our friendship. We were no longer racing together, and no longer having any formal business relationship, but we remained friends. He began his job driving the 18-wheeler, going clear out west from Chicago each week. Every time he came through Lincoln, he would stop at the local truck stop just west of town, and he'd call me. Joyce and I would go out and meet him for coffee or lunch.

Toward the end of his life, Lloyd was living on cigarettes and coffee. He lived in the truck, and had very little interaction with people. It was sad, but that's what Lloyd wanted.

One day in January 2000, as he was parked at a Kansas truck stop, Lloyd died quietly. They found him there; the truck idled out of fuel, off the side of a busy highway. It was kind of an odd ending for a guy who had led such an eventful, rough-and-tumble life.

Not long ago, I sponsored a very nice memorial bench at Belleville in Lloyd's name. It really is a nice thing, and I'm proud to help people remember Lloyd Beckman.

He was, after all, my brother.

13

"Tinted windows? Cool, man!"

The mid-1960s were an amazing, eventful time, at least in my little corner of the world. I was as busy in racing as I would ever be, often building and maintaining several different types of race cars at a time, sending one out on the road and running one locally. I was also very busy at home, as Joyce and I were busy raising four young sons.

At the time, something was happening, something so subtle I'm not sure I caught on immediately. Our business, Speedway Motors, was quietly becoming a real company. A real business, and not just a mom-and-pop type of business. We had employees, a machine shop, a fiberglass plant, bookkeepers, shippers, and a growing customer base from our emerging catalog offerings. Prior to that, for our first 10 to 15 years, it was just me doing everything from cleaning the toilets to working with the customers.

Our business had changed, right along with the rest of the world. I was no longer just building flathead engines in the back of my shop; I had expanded to shipping products around the country, and carrying a growing number of performance items. And I was more than just a reseller; I focused a lot of energy on developing and manufacturing specialty parts myself.

Most of our growth came because I was still very careful with a dollar, and I continued to invest everything back into the company. Plus, my race team still did very well, and that was a revenue stream as well.

In 1962 or so we doubled the size of our shop on N Street. We acquired the property to the east, and that boosted us to a three-bay dual-exhaust muffler installation setup.

I had a hard time getting that property. The man living in the small house there was an old German, maybe 90 years old. He had come from the old country, and in his culture you never sold a piece of land. You kept it until you died. In fact, after he passed on his family held onto several parcels of land, which I think they still hold today. But when the elderly man died his son agreed to sell me the parcel next door, which I needed in order to expand.

Our store was starting to get busy, and I needed the shop space and the parking. Not only was my retail business growing, but I was manufacturing more parts, and was taking on more of a role as a wholesaler.

For example, one morning in the late 1950s I arrived at my shop to see a Chevrolet convertible parked outside. As I pulled up the car door slowly opened, and out stepped George Hurst. He had developed a new aftermarket shifter, and had driven to Lincoln to see me. He had arrived late the night before, but rather than pay for a motel room he slept in his car.

George offered me the rights to become the exclusive warehouse distributor of the Hurst shifter, from the Canadian border to the Gulf of Mexico, from the Mississippi River to the Rocky Mountains. All those boys in Minnesota, Dallas, Kansas City, they had to buy that product from me. I capitalized on that relationship for quite a while, until George eventually opened it up to allow every gas station in America to become a dealer.

The aftermarket shifter was one of the first performance products to really boom. Probably less than 10 percent of American cars had automatic transmissions, meaning there were a ton of manual transmissions out there. Pretty soon, it was considered much cooler to have the shifter on the floor instead of the steering column, and it was infinitely more efficient in terms of quick shifting. Plus, the advent of the 4-speed transmission meant floor shifting was definitely in style.

Next to the exhaust business, the shifter quickly became the second really big retail component of the speed-shop business. Plus, many people needed installation help; it wasn't easy to chop a hole in the floorboard, cut the mat, install and adjust the shifter and linkage, and get the boot around it properly. We did hundreds — maybe thousands — of shifter installations in the '60s and '70s.

One thing I continued to believe in was inventory. When a man wants a performance part, he wants it right now. It's kind of an impulse purchase, so you have to be ready to supply the customer what they need, right away. That's why it was so critical that I continue to invest in inventory.

A lot of factory reps can remember our shop during that period, crammed full with inventory. I mean, we packed every square foot with parts and materials. If somebody needed a set of headers, our guy had to literally swing through the rafters like a monkey to get the product, because we had stuff stacked clear to the ceiling.

In the beginning, Speedway Motors was simply a door and a parts counter, catering to local people. If you couldn't walk through my door in Lincoln, it was going to be difficult to land you as a customer.

I dabbled with the concept of a "catalog" as early as 1956, when a friend of mine put together a parts list for me and took it to Lincoln High School, where they had a mimeograph machine. This was about the most basic copying technology you'll ever see; it was a white sheet of paper with simple blue letters.

(Actually, the first time we printed one the guy somehow messed up with the ink exposure and the copies were printed in bright purple! I took one look at this and my eyes lit up like a kid at Christmas.)

But doing business with customers outside a close geographic circle was very difficult at that time. Long-distance calls were very expensive, and people weren't accustomed to purchasing something they couldn't first see and feel, something they couldn't hold in their hands. Plus, we didn't even have ZIP codes yet. The concept of an efficient way to communicate with people on a widespread basis just didn't exist. Not yet.

That began to change, little by little, beginning sometime in the early 1960s. Plus, I finally began to understand that if Speedway Motors was ever going to grow, I had to find a way to expand beyond Lincoln.

One day I came to the realization that if I left the front door of my shop open all night, allowing anybody to come in and steal anything they wanted, only a small percentage of the 75,000 people in Lincoln would think I had anything worth stealing. Even as a gift.

So that meant my entire customer base was maybe 1,000 to 1,500 people. My *entire* customer base. That's awfully small, and it became crystal clear to me that I had to find some way to reach outside that base into a much larger population.

See, that's the challenge in the performance business; you're always working with a small percentage of the American population. And I had the double-whammy: I was working on a small percentage of a small population base. Pretty tough to make that work. As I've said before, there were probably more cows and pigs in a 200-mile radius of Lincoln than there were people. You aren't going to sell exhaust systems and shifters to cows and pigs.

This realization kind of got me back to the drawing board. How was I going to sell more things? Am I going to have to expand my offerings, and reach outside the performance world? Or am I going to have to figure out how to broaden my customer base?

Today the performance industry has all kinds of statistics and marketing information to help you reach your customers. But in the early 1960s there was no such information available. How many customers out there are looking for a new gearshift knob? Or a hot camshaft? It was all a guess. An educated guess, maybe, but still a guess.

I was advertising in *Hot Rod Magazine*, trying to attract more customers. I looked into publishing a for-real catalog, but boy, that looked expensive. At that time all such catalogs were sold, maybe from $2 to $5 each. Nobody gave them away, because they were too expensive to produce and mail. The big question to anyone contemplating doing a catalog was this: Were you going to sell that customer one single item from the catalog, after going to all the trouble of producing and printing and distribution? Even today, that's a big challenge in my business. How do you get a return on your investment of printing and distributing the catalog?

But I finally bit the bullet and began printing a catalog, and through my ads in *Hot Rod* began to reach out across the country.

I guess it was just as hard then, maybe harder, than it is today. It was hard to find anybody with the need for what I was selling. You had to do something to capture their attention; either offer it at a competitive price, or offer added value of some sort, to make it worthwhile for them to order from you.

In the beginning, I never wanted to be called a "mail-order" company. At that time the mail-order industry was very much looked down upon, like a fly-by-night enterprise. Local merchant associations had all kinds of ads telling people not to buy from mail order. "They might cheat you, you might not get the product, it won't be exactly like you ordered, it might be of second quality, etc."

The Better Business Bureau preached it all that time. "Don't buy from mail order." Well, guess what? The BBB was serving the local merchants, and mail order wasn't in their best interests. I guess the BBB should have told consumers when Sam Walton came to town some years later, "Don't buy from Wal-Mart." Because in five or 10 years, there weren't any more local merchants left. This is a truism, and I don't think I'm telling stories out of school.

Something else that really helped build my catalog-related business was that I was racing much farther from home. I was really getting outside my circle, and that proved to be very helpful.

I'd go to Kansas, or Colorado, or Indiana, or Florida, and meet various people. They figured out I was in the performance business, and they'd say, "Are you carrying those new wheels?" "Do you carry points for a Vertex magneto? The guy who sold me the mag doesn't carry any points." "Have you got a header kit, with flanges and bolts?" "Where can I get some gaskets for these double-flanged headers?" "Do you have gears for my quick-change rear end? I busted my ring-and-pinion tonight, can you guys ship me a new set?"

I'd smile and tell 'em what they wanted to hear: "Sure, I can do that."

But that brought another challenge. I always believed in treating people like I wanted to be treated; I knew if somebody was looking for a particular part or piece, they probably needed it sooner rather than later. So I set about shipping their order as quickly as possible.

That proved to be one of the biggest challenges in the early years of Speedway Motors.

In the 1960s there was no UPS service in Lincoln. The federal government tightly controlled ICC permits, and they decreed that the region from Texas to the Canadian border would have no UPS service. Simple as that. It would be a number of years before UPS was in all of the lower 48, in fact.

That made it very difficult, because when somebody ordered a part from me, how was I going to get it to them? I tried Parcel Post from the U.S. Postal Service, but that proved to be not workable. They weren't very dependable at that time; it was maybe 50/50 whether the package would even arrive. Plus, there were other issues: You couldn't ship a box labeled "Iskendarian," for example, through Chicago because I guarantee it would be stolen. Guarantee, it will never show up.

So I had to figure another way. I began using Greyhound bus and Continental bus to ship a lot of orders. It wasn't convenient for me *or* the customer, but it was workable. Both bus companies gave us overnight service within a 500-mile radius. That gave us coverage east all the way to Chicago, west all the way to Denver, south all the way to Dallas, and north to Sioux Falls and Minneapolis.

The bus service at that time was incredible. They stopped at every small town in the country! We knew their schedules, and if we could get the order on the bus in the late afternoon, the customer would have it in the morning.

Every evening you'd see me driving to the bus station at 10th and P Street in my pickup truck, loaded with packages. There were two depots, located across the street from one another.

I had to do all the paperwork myself, because inevitably they had just hired a kid from college that morning to work the counter, and he didn't even know how to button up his pants yet.

The bus driver was usually so lazy he wouldn't get down to help me load the freight, which went in the baggage compartment in the lower section of the bus. After I loaded the freight, I'd hand the driver the paperwork.

One night I was down at the station with a '56 Pontiac engine I had sold to someone in Des Moines. I had the engine carefully packaged in a big crate, and that thing was heavy. I dragged it to the side of the bus, and the driver looked down at me.

"How you gonna get that in there?" he laughed.

It pissed me off, because not only would he not help me, but now the guy is laughing.

"Watch me," I said. I spent the next few minutes lifting and tugging and huffing and puffing, and figured out how to get the crate up into the baggage compartment. I walked onto the bus and handed the guy the paperwork.

"Now, smartass, how are you gonna get it down when you get to Des Moines?" I asked him. He didn't seem to think that was quite as humorous. As it turns out, the customer was waiting in Des Moines and he got it down himself.

Doing business by shipping to my customers expanded my business, but it was definitely a challenge, no doubt about it.

One idea that always intrigued me was creating a product that everyone in the world would want. I purchased a lot of products from various manufacturers, and I always struggled to get enough margins to survive. But if I created and manufactured the product myself, I would have a much greater margin. So I was always looking for ideas that might bring the world to Lincoln.

In the early 1960s I hit upon an idea that was like a dream come true.

For a while.

Drag racing cars were running Plexiglas side windows during this time, and a lot of them ran at night, particularly in California. You'd see cars like a '34 Ford coupe with a plastic windshield and side windows, heavily tinted. Orange, green, red, all kinds of colors. They would often light up the inside of the car, so you would see those colors very clearly when the car went down the strip.

Many performance and appearance products have roots in drag racing; if they saw it on the strip, they wanted it on their street car. It's all about ego, and being "cool." They wanted people to think their street car had been raced on the strip. Big tires on the back, small tires on the front. "Big and littles," they call that in the performance business.

It's the same reason Michael Jordan sold a lot of athletic shoes; if you saw Michael wearing them, you wanted to wear them, too. Emulation.

Everybody was buzzing about these drag racing cars with tinted windows, and how cool they looked. It got me to thinking: What if I came up with something that easily allowed people to tint the glass in their street car? Problem was, how do you tint glass? There were already people out there selling various tinting products, but they weren't very good.

I came up with the idea of putting a tinting agent in an aerosol can, so that almost anybody could apply it. I came up with all kinds of wild colors, with wild names to boot. Greens, blues, and reds.

Boy, I figured this product would really be something! Everybody would want it!

I came up with a catchy name: "Cool Man Glass Tint." Everybody wanted to be a cool man, right?

But now I had to figure out how to get it out there, and bring the product to market. I knew exactly the person I needed: Herb Goldstein.

Herbie's dad was an old-time auto parts and accessory salesman out of Chicago, and Herbie took up the business from his dad. He later became famous as "Mr. Phone," and he was a phenomenon that is hard to describe. Herbie could sell a monkey a new tail, and was just about as dynamic as anyone I've ever known.

I met Herbie through my relationship with Ray Bleiweis, who owned a bumper replating shop which began selling chrome wheels. This was very early in the chrome business, and these guys were taking wheels out of junkyards and chroming them without first taking the center out of the wheel. Anybody who knows the chrome process now knows that if you do this, it leaves all kinds of yellow hue around where the center meets the rim. But it was a function of price, and I could sell a chrome wheel in Lincoln for $14.95 each, and people stood in line to get them. Herbie was the salesman for Bleiweis, and that's how I got to know him.

I bought a lot of those chrome wheels from Herb, and now it was time to get him over on my side. He agreed, and came on to help me market Cool Man Glass Tint.

I found a company in Connecticut that manufactured aerosol products, and made a deal for them to make Cool Man Glass Tint. The product was actually pretty simple: clear lacquer with a tinting agent added. Our installation instructions were simple, too. Just like when you wash your driveway with a sweeping motion on the water hose; you apply the tint the same way. Keep the can moving, and the liquid flowing, to cover the glass from top to bottom.

Of course, some people were more talented in doing this than others. The end results were kind of mixed; some of it looked like a three-year-old kid had applied it, and some of it looked pretty good.

It was probably hell to get the stuff off your windows later on when you changed your mind, but nobody complained in those days. Today would be a completely different story, of course. Today it's all about complaining. People complain about things from the time they wake up until they go to bed at night.

Herbie got busy on the sales end, and next thing you know this thing really took off. Everybody wanted Cool Man Glass Tint! Nobody else had it, and they wanted it because it made their car — and them — look cool. They would put up with the difficulty of installing it properly, or the difficulty of removing it down the road, because they wanted to be cool today. It was something that changed their car to something that made people say, "Oh, gee, that is a 'Cool Man Tint' job!"

Pretty soon I was literally ordering it by the boxcar load. It was an amazing process. Herb would sell 50 cases to a guy in Chicago, and one week later would call me back saying, "Bill, send that guy another 50 cases!"

"He can't be selling it that fast, Herbie…he must be throwing it in the lake up there! You can't sell it to customers that fast!"

Herbie was a real go-getter. He would ship the guy another 50 cases whether he ordered them or not, and then talk him into keeping it. Whatever it took to make the deal, Herbie could make it happen. And believe it or not, I had no trouble getting paid.

I was paying Herbie a 15-percent commission on everything he sold. A typical factory rep at that time made anywhere from three to seven percent; that was the going rate. Exhaust systems, seat covers, whatever, as a factory rep that was the range of your percentage. Obviously I was paying Herbie quite a premium, but I always figured that if I'd pay the guy more, he'd perform better. That was my thinking, and it worked perfectly with Herbie.

We had success with Cool Man Glass Tint for a year, maybe 18 months, before the fad began to wane. It sold for $5.95 per can, and of course when it became wildly popular the competition began to appear. Pretty soon people were selling similar products for $3.95 per can. Soon enough, the demand faded and the product died away and became nothing but a memory.

But I made enough money from Cool Man Glass Tint that when I bought the race track here in Lincoln (as a sucker for a bargain) for $5,000 from my former partners, I used my Cool Man profits to make the purchase. Of course I eventually lost all my money in the track, so it's another of those "easy-come, easy-go" stories.

Soon enough I was back to my bread and butter, selling gear shift knobs and lug nuts. It was another one of those "up" periods, and through all the years the ups and downs have leveled out pretty well.

My experience with Cool Man Glass Tint was something I would see repeated many times in my business. Almost all products have a life cycle; some are very short, some are very long. Someone has a new idea, creates a product, has some success reaching the market, and here comes the competition. The price is driven down, the market become oversaturated, people lose interest, and that's the end. Next thing you know, people say, "That's old; I want something different."

It's been that way in the clothing business forever: high-button shoes, hats with wide brims, hats with small brims, no hats at all. It constantly evolves. Everything is faddish.

Cars, naturally, have experienced this. Wheels you can see, wheels you can't see, big wheels, small wheels, bright colors, subtle colors, boxy lines, sweeping lines.

Some product segments are so faddish, in fact, they're downright brutal in terms of trying to market within that segment. The aftermarket wheel business is like that today, and is probably the most treacherous of any segment in the automotive industry. Its way beyond other segments in terms of complexity, and the challenge of efficiently providing products in a rapidly changing market.

Sure, you'll sell four at a time to a customer, but it's terribly difficult to get the product in front of the guy who wants to buy it, and it's a high-priced item. Then you have the various manufacturers, styles, sizes, applications...just on and on. It's almost beyond anybody's capability of servicing a market like that. You see huge companies struggle in that arena, and you see lots of turnover among the competitors because the market and the market cycle are very tough.

One thing I realized was that the simpler the product installation, the larger the potential customer base becomes.

A product like Cool Man Glass Tint, for example, was not intimidating to install. Compared to changing intake manifolds, for example, it's downright simple. You've got to have some knowledge and tools to install a new intake; but anybody could use an aerosol can.

But it's still all about getting your product to market. It was challenging then, and even more challenging today. How can I get my product in front of somebody who really wants it? How do I find my buyers? What kind of pipeline? Do I sell it wholesale to dealers around the country, who do the same things I do? Or do I use jobbers, wholesalers, retailers, whatever? How do I get it out there?

I don't care how big you are, or how smart you think you are, it's still tough. When you see somebody like Sears Roebuck, once the largest retailer in the world, get knocked off the pedestal by somebody who goes to market in a different direction, using different methods, it tells you something. That sort of thing happens all the time; it's still all about getting products to market.

The Internet came along and changed the whole marketplace. Fast food came along and changed the entire restaurant industry. Markets change constantly, like clouds. You have to be aware of how the market moves, and how you're going to get your product there. It's not an easy task, believe me.

If I had a nickel for every person who came to me with an idea for a new product, I'd have a lot of nickels. "Say, I've got this great product I came up with, and if you put it in your catalog we'll both become rich and famous." But it's hard to spot winners, even though you're in the game every day and playing it as hard as anybody could ever play it. There are no guarantees.

I'm not ashamed to admit that sometimes I've been completely wrong about whether a product would work or not. For example, in the 1950s they came out with a product called "port-o-walls," which were inexpensive rubber strips that installed between your rim and tire and made it look like you had whitewall tires. I thought that was the dumbest thing anybody had ever come up with. They made them in colors like white, red, pink, yellow, green, and blue.

"Boy, that'll never sell!" I said. I ended up ordering them by the semi-truck load, because every used car dealer in town put a set of these on every car on his lot in order to jazz up his inventory. It made the buying public think each car had expensive tires, and it caught their eye. It was the sizzle on the steak.

I would have never guessed that. But it proves that no matter how much you think you know, and how sure you think you are, it's difficult to truly foresee what will work.

From the time I began my business in 1952, I always tried to learn from the success of others in the performance industry. Early on, a company I really admired was Cal Customs.

The Krause family owned the company, and by the early 1960s I had met several of the family members. In the beginning I bought products from their father's retail store in southern California, paying full retail. I could still make it work because the product was unique enough, and nobody knew where to get it directly. After I paid the postage on the item my margin was tiny, however.

Alex Krause actually offered me a job in the early 1960s, and I almost took him up on his offer. Boy, would life be different today if I had done this!

I met Alex at the big auto accessory show in Chicago, where they always had a big display. Cal Customs came out with a tubular grille for a '50 Ford, and Alex and I were talking. I told him about a similar grille I made, only I used plastic so it could be molded in various colors.

Alex's eyes kind of lit up, and he said, "You wouldn't want a job, would you?"

I thought about it, and talked it over with Joyce. It would sure be simpler than being the chief cook and bottle washer at my place, with all the worries and stress on my shoulders.

After talking about it for a little while we decided that moving to southern California wasn't really what we wanted, so we stayed put. We had four small boys, and such a move would have been far beyond anything we could have handled at the time.

In the 1950s and '60s life was almost scripted for people, much more than today. You did things based on what people *thought* you were supposed to do. When you graduated from college you were supposed to do two things: get a job and get married. If you didn't do that, people actually kind of looked at you funny, like you weren't "normal."

It was like the rules of life were written in stone, and that's the way you were supposed to live it. From your parents and your friends, from everybody around you, that's just what they thought.

I followed many of those ideas, but not all. I got married, and kept the same gal around for more than 50 years. Went to church, stayed out of jail, paid my bills, did the things you're "supposed" to do.

But in my own way, I followed my own path. My mom always got after me, saying, "When are you gonna forget those cars and get a real job?" But I did the two things I loved: racing, and owning a speed shop. I know that made me awfully "different" to a lot of people, but that's who I was. No doubt about it, and as the years pass I'm more sure than ever I followed the right path.

Alex's job offer was interesting, though. Of course it inflates your ego, to hear a job offer. I've always had the "I'm from Nebraska" syndrome, which is kind of an inferiority complex. That was a detriment then, and it still is today. It hangs something around your neck that says you must not be very smart if you're from Nebraska and you're still there. And this goes back to everything you do.

You could be the wizard of all time, but you wouldn't be recognized because of where you are. "If he was any good at all, he wouldn't still be there." That's the conventional wisdom, and for many people it's very real. I've always known that, and felt that, and that's one of the reasons it was always so sweet to stand on the winner's podium in racing and have someone say, "Where you guys from?" "Lincoln, Nebraska."

They couldn't have come within five states of putting their finger on the map to find Nebraska. That's just the way things are. I guess some things never change. For example, when Harry

Truman became president, he was considered by many to be a country bumpkin because he was from Missouri. Perception is everything.

But by the late 1960s, I was proud I was doing okay in my own right. My business was slowly but steadily expanding, and even doing more business outside Nebraska through my growing catalog operation.

In a way, I was a lot like a race driver. I knew lots of bad things could happen, but never figured they would happen to me. I was happily married, had four great kids, my business was pretty solid, and my race cars were kicking ass.

I was working hard, yes, but I was happy. I figured life was going along just fine, and I couldn't imagine any kind of serious interruption.

Then came a flash of movement, a massive impact, and the realization that life is fleeting. It can end awfully quickly, before you even have a chance to think about it.

Eagle Raceway, 1968. Hard and painful memories, those.

14

Code Blue

Rocks and pebbles pressed against my back, and everything was a blur. There was still a dull roar in the air, and dust swirled around me. I could hear shouting, and in a moment people were standing over me, looking down at me with a mixture of amazement and concern.

Something was under my head, making my neck crane at a painful angle. As I gathered my senses I realized it was my right foot. Immediately, I knew something was seriously wrong, because I'm not nearly that limber. I knew my foot couldn't go there.

It was Eagle Raceway in Nebraska, July 22, 1968. It was a very rare race on a Monday night, a benefit race for Mark Crear, a local driver who had been killed a week or so earlier in a motorcycle accident.

It took a few moments to fully grasp what had happened, but I was in serious trouble. A wheel and suspension had come off one of the race cars and sailed into the pit area, hitting me. It nearly tore my right leg off, and knocked me a good 25 feet from the spot where I had been standing.

This was a very real brush with death. It was one of those moments where you look back and easily surmise that if things had been just slightly different, you're dead.

It was chaos for a few minutes, until somebody thought to get me into an ancient ambulance and take me to the hospital. I never lost consciousness; I wish I would have, because the pain was nearly unbearable. One of the guys on the scene tried to put a splint on my leg, but he actually put it in the wrong place. My femur—the large bone running from the hip to the knee—was shattered, but he thought my leg was broken below the knee.

Never mind, just get me the hell out of here! They tossed me in the old ambulance, wheeled by a young kid. He took off for

Methodist Hospital in Lincoln, and every time he'd turn a corner it felt like the ambulance was going so fast it might turn over. I was yelling to the kid, "I ain't dead yet, but if you keep it up we're both gonna be! Slow down!"

I had been kneeling just outside a wire mesh fence separating the pit area from the race track. That's where all of us in the pits watched the race; we squatted or knelt behind the fence, hooking our fingers through the fence to balance ourselves. We were shoulder to shoulder, all along the fence, maybe half-a-block long.

I was watching Keith Hightshoe in my race car, and he had just gone through the corner, running second in the feature race. Just behind him, the front axle of the third-place car broke as the car was coming through the corner. The hub, wheel, and tire sailed through the air, probably going a hundred miles an hour.

Out of the corner of my eye I saw it coming. In a split-second I instinctively took my fingers from the fence, which was a good thing because it would have taken my fingers right off. I'm left-handed, and as I started to turn to my left the wheel hit my right side, just below the hip. If it would have hit anywhere else — my chest or head — there is no doubt it would have killed me instantly.

The guy on my right was hit in the face by the fence, and was knocked cold. The guy on my left was also hit by the fence, but it didn't knock him out.

Joyce wasn't at the race that night, because she stayed home to type out the statements for our Cool Man Glass Tint accounts all over the country. However, Lloyd Beckman and his wife, Shirley, were at the track; Shirley called Joyce immediately and said I was in trouble, and Joyce rushed to the hospital. When she arrived they had put me into this steel cage contraption, trying to put traction on my leg to straighten it out.

I was bare naked, because they had cut all my clothes off. My leg had already swollen so badly it almost made Joyce sick, literally. She kept telling me, "Bill, please, pass out! If you don't, I'm going to!"

They weren't able to operate for 24 hours, so the first day was pretty tough. Finally they got me into surgery, and cut a hole in my butt cheek where they inserted a long steel rod down the length of the femur. The bone had just exploded from the impact, and to this day I have a big knot at the location of the break from all the tiny fragments that all healed together.

One of the residual problems from all this was that my right leg was now two-and-a-half inches shorter than the left, and for many years I had to wear an elevated shoe on my right foot.

Years later I had a double hip replacement, and they got things back in the proper alignment.

Two weeks after the accident, I was still hospitalized but doing better. Around 9 a.m. my doctor came by to see me, and he saved my life.

Normally I'd see my doctor, along with other specialists, between 6:30 and 7 a.m. These guys were all familiar with the various medical issues I had dealt with all my life, and they were like my dad. They liked me better than they liked anybody, it seemed. They took an interest in me and were very good to me.

But for some reason my doctor didn't show up until much later that day, which was a godsend because that's when I needed him. I was already down in therapy, and one of my fraternity brothers whom I hadn't seen for 20 years was the therapist. He and I were talking, catching up on old times. He was going to teach me how to use crutches.

I was sitting in a chair, talking with him, feeling fine, when all of a sudden the ceiling went one full revolution and I passed out cold.

A piece of bone, or tissue of some kind, had passed through my bloodstream and stuck in my heart, and it immediately stopped beating.

The therapist had the foresight to wrap a sheet tightly around me and turn me upside down, getting the blood to flow to my head. They called "Code Blue," alerting everyone that I was in dire straits.

At that very moment my doctor walked through the door for my regular visit. So he was right there, at the right time. It was meant to be.

They got me upstairs and starting putting blood thinner in me, and they got it so thin it was running out of my nose, ears, anyplace that had a thin membrane. For several days I couldn't brush my teeth because of the bleeding.

I had to lie perfectly still because they couldn't find the aneurism. X-rays didn't show anything, and after a while they figured it must have dissolved.

There was a weird side-effect, too. I suddenly had a terrible pain in my left foot, much worse than the pain from my fracture. I could feel the pain moving slowly all the way up my body, from my left foot. This was over a period of about three days. It moved all the way into my right shoulder, down my arm, into my right hand, and to this day two of my fingers are completely numb. Very strange.

After five weeks in the hospital I was able to return home, and get back to business, back to racing. Even before my accident it had been something of a difficult year in racing, by my standards.

I started the year with big ideas, big plans. Chevrolet had developed a 427-inch big-block V8, and it was being used in a few racing applications at that time. The original configuration was developed for use in heavy trucks, but GM quickly figured out that the engine had great potential in the performance world.

I had the idea that I wanted to put one in a sprint car. One of the challenges, however, was that it was too large to fit in a traditional sprint car frame. A year earlier I began to use a car built by Don Edmunds, who had a shop in California.

A lot of my time was spent thinking about this new car, and I was confident. I couldn't imagine it wouldn't be an absolute killer. There is no substitute for cubic inches, I knew that for sure. So this big-block car should be one that makes the other guys not even think about coming to race.

Somehow, through hook and crook, I managed to secure an aluminum 427 engine block, which were being used in Trans Am racing at the time. This was a very rare and hard-to-get piece.

I called Edmunds and told him what I wanted. One of the problems with his cars was that from the firewall forward they were too floppy. The softer cars seemed to work better out West, but on our tracks we needed something more rigid. When you're out here in the Plains racing on tracks full of ruts and holes five feet deep, you have to have a car that doesn't flex so much.

Most sprint cars still used the old spring-front suspension, but Edmunds was using an early four-bar torsion bar design.

I explained to Edmunds what I wanted, describing to him how the chassis needed a couple of particular bars added to stiffen it up. He agreed, and said he'd get busy right away on my new car.

We got the engine built, and I was excited. As time passed, however, Edmunds still hadn't finished my car. When I'd call, it was, "Yeah, we're just finishing it, we'll have it on the truck by Friday." For a month and a half, it was always "next Friday."

Marty Bassett, my welder and a trusted friend who helped with my race cars, was planning a vacation trip to California with his wife Janice. I asked Marty to stop by Edmunds' shop and see what the hell was going on with my new car. A couple of days later Marty called.

"They haven't started on it," he said. "They've just got two frame rails laying on the floor."

So Marty finished welding it up, and we air-freighted it to Kansas City for our season opener. One thing that really pissed me off was that somebody in the shop out there had written "Race Truck" on the dash of the car, making fun because the 427 was originally a truck engine.

We thrashed to get the engine installed and the rest of the car finished. The car had real promise, but we had some teething issues, and issues with the fit. The engine installed on the motor plate at the same height as a small block Chevy, but the oil pan on the big block is about six inches deeper. We immediately had trouble because the pan would actually drag the ground in the corners, and almost stop the car.

But, man, was that 427 loud! I ran a megaphone exhaust on it, and when we went to St. Louis the people in the grandstand complained because this thing deafened 'em. Lots of compression, big pipes, it was worse than the Novi at the Speedway.

Beckman and I had split up during this period, and I had Grady Wade in my car. Grady was a very good driver from Wichita, Kan. In no time at all this new car was a real issue for Grady, because he felt like my experiment wasn't working. Finally one day he climbed from the car and said, "Bill, I'm gonna quit if you don't take that motor out." Plus, all my help was disgusted, threatening to quit as well.

So, under duress, I took out the big block and put a traditional small block back in. All my thinking, all my engineering, it was all for naught.

What a frustration! I had gone from what I thought would be a killer car, back to square one.

After we got the small block back in, we took the car to Midwest Speedway one Saturday afternoon to shake it down. I got into the car to take a couple of laps, and I guess my anger got the best of me. I didn't have a helmet on, and didn't even have safety belts on. What was supposed to be a few laps at idle turned into me just ripping around the race track, wide open, flailing that damned car for all it was worth. What a sight that must have been; me without a helmet, banging around that track in full anger. All of the frustration of my aborted big-block adventure, I was venting it all on the race car.

The following night Grady came up to run at Midwest. He got into the car for hot laps, and ran it hard down into the first corner.

The way you adjust a Hilborn fuel injection setup is to loosen the throttle blades, set the barrel valve, lock the screws all down, then lock the barrel valve down. One of the screws apparently fell out, and when Grady opened 'er up that first time the throttle blade rolled over the screw and locked the throttle wide open.

Grady hit the wall in turn three so hard that it ricocheted the car clear into the infield, some 35 feet. It knocked him cold, and bent the entire car into a pretzel.

I've often thought about something: What if that throttle had stuck when I was taking my hot laps the day before, without a helmet or belts? I'd probably still be flipping to California, but without my head. That was one of those close calls.

Don Brown, "The Prince of Darkness," said, "Hey, Bill, we can fix that car! You get Pete Leikam to let us use his frame machine at the body shop, and we'll straighten 'er right out!"

Pete and his crew did a lot of repair work, particularly with heavy trucks, and had just bought a very advanced frame machine. But our car was made out of 4130 chrome moly steel, and that stuff is hard to bend.

We put our car on the frame machine, and for two weeks we were still working on it. Brown had every hook and chain from Pete's shop hanging on that car. You couldn't even see the frame from all the hooks and chains.

Brown and I argued about whether or not to use heat on the frame. He didn't want to, but eventually I prevailed and got out the torch. We did get the car straight, but it was just another chapter in a frustrating period.

Amid all the heartache and disappointment of 1968, it's easy to spot the highlight of the entire year. That was the moment when I first heard the name Jan Opperman.

When I was still hospitalized with my shattered leg, I got a surprising phone call. Yogi was on the phone. He says, "I've found the damnedest race driver you have ever seen, Bill. We're going to come back and run the fair."

Yogi was my long-lost employee, Jerry Jansen, calling from Hayward, Calif. He had worked for me for quite some time, but some weeks earlier had flat disappeared, without a trace. Even his wife didn't know where he was. Yogi was quite the free spirit, and he ended up in California, hanging out with the hippies.

This was actually a problem for me, because at that moment — amid a difficult racing season and damn near getting killed — I was going through a withholding tax audit with the state. They insisted that the guys who helped on my race car were to be paid overtime, and my assertion was that they were just friends of mine, helping me go racing, and not acting in the same capacity as an employee. All of my guys gladly signed off on that scenario, except I couldn't find Yogi to get him to sign the form.

See, I told you it was a frustrating period!

I'm lying there in the hospital bed, listening to Yogi raving on the phone about this driver, Jan Opperman, and how good he was going to do in my car at the Nebraska State Fair.

"Bill, this guy Opperman, he's a great competitor," he said. "He's been in the rodeo business, raced motorcycles, and now he's a sprint car driver. Just wait till you see him!"

"Yogi, I'm just trying to stay alive," I tried to tell him. "I got hit, almost got my leg torn off, had a blood clot or something that stopped my heart...I'm in a helluva shape."

"Yeah, but Bill, we're coming back anyways. We want to run the fair."

"Don't come back, I've quit racing," I told Yogi.

Sure enough, Yogi and Opperman showed up at the fair, where I was slowly making my way around in a wheelchair. My race car was there, and Jerry "Butch" Weld was driving. We didn't do well that day, but at least I didn't get ran over or anything.

Incidentally, that's the event where Beckman pushed me around all afternoon in my wheelchair. Good ol' Lloyd...even though we were split up, he was still my buddy.

I've always been fascinated with the concept of a four-wheel drive sprint car, because I figured that would be the ultimate. Butch's dad, Pappy (Taylor) Weld, was interested in four-wheel drive, too. When we were finished that day he said, "Let me take your car back to Kansas City, and over the winter I'll make it four-wheel drive."

"That's a good idea, Pappy," I said. "Because I've got a lot of healing up to do this winter."

Unbeknownst to me, a few weeks later Butch (who was Pappy's oldest son) got the bright idea to take my car to Phoenix, for the very first Western World Championship. He put my car on one of their ratty old trailers and a young kid named Freddy Vance would drive the tow rig from Kansas City to Phoenix.

As Freddy was driving through the mountains, the trailer came loose and went over the side. It plunged over a 1,000-foot cliff, but by pure luck snagged on a little tree and was saved. They managed to drag it back onto the roadway, hook it back up, and continue on to Phoenix, where they didn't do much in the race.

Like I said, I didn't hear about any of this until long after the fact. Just another episode where racing people tend to play just a little bit out of bounds.

Incidentally, Freddy Vance is still in Kansas City, building parts for me. He uses a cheap band saw from Sears and lovingly refers to it as his CNC machine. Recently Freddy delivered some parts and stopped by my office and with a little encouragement from Joyce, Freddy retold the Kansas City-to-Phoenix story from 1968. The story gets better with each telling, and we laughed just as hard as we always have.

However, I am glad I didn't know anything about it at the time.

That first Western World, by the way, was won by Bob Cleberg. Cleberg is a memorable character; actually, his wife, Teo, was a memorable character, too. She always helped him with the race car, just like a mechanic. Often they had to park outside the pit area because women weren't allowed in the pits. When Bob raced she would run around like she was absolutely insane with fear that he was going to get killed in the race car. Insane! Boy, she was wacky as a pet coon.

It was that 1968 Labor Day race at the Nebraska State Fair— while I was rolling around in my wheelchair—when Opperman and Yogi hooked up with my great rival Bob Trostle and Jan drove his car. Jan raced for Trostle a few more times that season, and showed us that he had some ability.

Trostle and I were rivals for many years. Always, really. There were lots of other car owners, but for some reason Bob and I were particularly keen on beating each other.

Bob began building race cars, and I built a lot of fiberglass panels for sprint cars in my shop. Therefore, I knew the exact measurements of all the various chassis—Edmunds, Trostle, CAE, etc.—and I knew who was copying from whom.

Bob and I had done some business, and had gotten crossways on some things, so there were some tensions there. So there he is, out there racing in the same territory as me, and naturally I took particular pride in beating my rival. And, when he beat me, I took particular misery in that.

I could see Opperman's talent, and I wanted to see if we could work together. We put a deal together for 1969, and he talked Big Bill Chadborne and John Levernz into something of a partnership for the first couple of months of the season, because I didn't yet have the car I wanted. Big Bill and John were good race car mechanics who had come from northern California with Opperman. They had a very old sprint car; in fact, it was the car in which Bob Slater was killed at Des Moines in 1956. But the car was still solid, and they updated it enough to be competitive.

We ran it as car No. 4x while we waited on a new car from Roger Beck. Roger was a great California craftsman who built top-quality race cars. This was just before Roger moved to Indianapolis to work for George Bignotti. Roger's stuff was top-notch, and he was the perfect solution after I had decided to go in another direction after my frustration with Edmunds a year earlier.

The car I ordered from Roger was a spring-front car, with a cross-torsion rear. Roger got the car to us just after Memorial Day, when we won a big race at Des Moines called the Hawkeye Futurity.

Along with having Opperman in my car, I also hired Yogi back at Speedway Motors. I guess I'm forgiving, if nothing else.

Yogi was an interesting guy, definitely a guy who marched to his own beat. He had come to me several years earlier when he was operating heavy machinery. We call those guys, "Cat skinners." Yogi came from Tulsa, a tough town if there ever was one. He was making good money operating machinery, but when he got laid off that winter he needed to find employment right away. He came to see me about a job installing mufflers.

"Do you know how to weld?" I asked.

"A little bit," he said.

"What were you making when they laid you off?"

He told me, and I shook my head.

"Well, I don't even pay half that."

"Yeah, but I want a job this winter."

I shook my head again.

"No, because I'll teach you the trade, and when spring comes you'll take your old job back and be gone."

"No," he insisted. "If you'll hire me, I'll stick. I won't leave."

I took Yogi's word and hired him. He kept his promise; he didn't leave in the spring. He got involved with our race car, and also became a damned good muffler man. He could put a muffler on faster than anybody I've ever seen. We would time the guys, and Yogi was by far the fastest. Put the car on the rack, run it up, cut the old muffler off, put the new muffler on, and have it on the ground in just a couple of minutes. Of course, that was only on "time trials," because we didn't work on any customer's car like that.

Jan Opperman was a very special race driver. Did I see that right away? Well, sort of. He was still pretty young, and he wasn't a particularly good driver in the beginning. He was rough on equipment, and rough on the other racers.

In fact, we quickly realized the need for much heavier nerf bars—the bars on the side of the car that keep you from getting tangled up with the other guy's wheels—for Opperman, because he'd tear the standard bars off in just one race. We called the heavier bars, "Opperman bars." Most guys didn't often bend those bars—also known as "kick-off" bars—because they didn't like getting that close to the other cars. Hell, Jan would rub against the other cars, constantly. He defied all common sense in that regard.

We began making Opperman bars out of 1.75-inch .095-wall chrome moly, and we'd make six at a time because he went through 'em so quickly.

Opperman used his competitors to slingshot off them. If you had the standard set of bars, they'd just wad up and stick into the tires, tear up the steering gear, stuff like that.

Were guys sore at him for racing that way? Absolutely.

Here's a story from when we ran the mile track at Sedalia, Mo. Jan ran into Jay Woodside and knocked him clear off the track and into the parking lot. Now, Jay was a Native American, and was a very big guy. He had been hurt terribly at Topeka, and had recovered to race again after something like a year in the hospital. So this was one tough puppy, and he carried a limp from that wreck.

After the incident at Sedalia I saw Woodside coming back over the fence, barging into the infield. "Oh, man, this is gonna be something!" I thought. "Shit, he's gonna tear Opperman's head off!" I was so certain it was going to be a disaster, I actually took off the other way, and I'm not even the guy who knocked him off the track. But I figured Jay might see me first and take it out on me.

But ten minutes later, Jay and Jan were walking around arm-in-arm, the best of friends. That's because Opperman was charismatic like nobody I had ever met before. Right at that moment, watching him easily diffuse the situation with a very angry racer and immediately turn the guy into his friend, that made a big impression on me. I mean, Woodside had fire coming out of his ears when he came storming into our pit. But Jan was so charismatic, he completely calmed Jay and convinced him that everything was wonderful.

Around women, Jan was especially charismatic. Women had no chance around Jan. Zero. None. Jan could talk a woman out of her pants quicker than any man I've ever known.

And that, right there, was one of the constant contradictions to Jan Opperman. He was an outspoken advocate of the Christian faith, so much so that he led lots of people to Christianity. Yet, just when you assumed he was sweet and innocent, you'd see him sneaking off with a new woman, or going into a back room to smoke dope with his friends.

Not everybody was enamored with Jan. To be honest, I didn't enjoy racing with Jan at our local track, Midwest Speedway, because he would knock some of my longtime friends clear off the track. It wasn't good for my local business, that's for sure. Many people — particularly Lloyd Beckman — had no respect for Jan. In Lloyd's case it was because Jan was so rough on the track. Beckman was the complete opposite: smooth and steady.

There were other things, too. Jan grew his hair long and wore Indian moccasins and leather clothes with beads, like a hippie. There were always rumors about Jan smoking pot, and of course it was true. That sort of thing was very controversial in 1969, and it turned many people off. However, people who met Jan personally always seemed to like him. He had an ability to make almost anybody like him.

We began winning frequently that summer, and in August I figured we could finally win an event that had eluded me for quite some time: the Knoxville Nationals. Opperman was leading when Kenny Gritz passed him with just three laps left, and we finished second. That was a bitter pill to swallow.

Sprint-car racing was in the midst of a great debate at this point, centered on whether roll cages should become mandatory. Some places allowed them, while others did not. Knoxville, for example, allowed cages, and many guys ran 'em. However, IMCA, the prominent sprint-car group in the Plains, did not allow them.

Two weeks after the Nationals, I was standing in the infield here in Lincoln at the State Fair, watching the races. This was an IMCA race, and the boys had all taken their cages off. I was standing about 20 yards from the track when Gritz crashed, right in front of me. Somehow it hit a guardrail while upside down in mid-air, and Kenny was nearly decapitated. The car continued flipping in the air, and the scene suddenly turned a peculiar pinkish tint for a second or two. It wasn't for a moment before I realized it was blood.

It was a very shocking moment, one these old eyes could have done without.

That pretty much ended the debate about roll cages. From that point forward, sprint cars in our area used cages. Period.

Opperman was a con artist, super-deluxe. He could almost talk you out of anything you had. In fact, he was going to lead some of the folks here in town to a settlement out in the mountains of Montana, where they were going to live in a cult. One of my best friends was almost ready to go with him. Jan had that magnetic power about him that was amazing.

However, I've always believed that a good con artist is easy to con by a better con artist.

We had a really good season in 1969 with Jan. We won the Big Car Racing Ass'n (BCRA) title (both driver and car owner), and a bunch of races. We finished second at the Knoxville Nationals and finished seventh in IMCA points, even though we didn't run all the races.

That's why I was very surprised when Opperman told me that winter he was leaving to go to Pennsylvania to race. A promoter out there, Jack Gunn, had recognized the appeal of promoting such an off-beat character, and offered Jan a deal that would require him to move to Pennsylvania.

Personally, I thought it was just a promoter conning Jan. They turned him into a freak show, in my opinion. Who had seen a guy like that, a hard-core, dope-smoking hippie in a sprint car? Long hair, wearing moccasins, talking about Jesus, he was unlike anybody else, and that's what Gunn was counting on.

Although I was disappointed, Jan and I still had a good relationship. In fact, he continued to drive my car when his schedule allowed. That arrangement lasted for several years, and we continued to win quite a few races together.

One of my real objections, and I voiced this very clearly to Jan, was that he was getting into cars that were nowhere near the quality of my car. I've always prided myself on building a good race car, and performance wasn't my only criteria. Workmanship, appearance, safety, I wouldn't compromise in any of those areas.

But the cars Jan drove back East were so horrible, I wouldn't put my worst enemy in them. Absolutely horrible! In fact, when he won the Western World in one of those cars in 1971 or '72, he stopped by to visit us on his way back from Phoenix. He parked his tow rig and trailer three blocks from our shop, hidden, so we wouldn't go look at the race car. He was embarrassed for us to know he would even drive such a piece of shit.

I never stopped liking Jan, even when he quit racing for me full-time. From 1969 until 1976 we still raced quite a few races together, and we remained close friends. Oh, we'd have a spat now and then, but it was usually nothing and we'd be over it in a couple of hours. Besides, you couldn't stay mad at Jan, because he'd turn on the charm and you'd forget why you were even upset.

Except that time at Phoenix...oh, yeah, Phoenix. *That* one pissed me off, for sure, enough that I was hopping mad. All these years later, it still aggravates me just to think about it...

15

Adventures With Opperman

I'm a competitive guy, and when I set my mind to winning something I usually don't rest until I've done it. Good or bad, that's how I'm wired.

From the first event in 1968, the Western World Championship at Manzanita Speedway in Phoenix was one of the big events in sprint car racing. At the time it was a groundbreaking event; it was one of the first events outside the Knoxville Nationals to attract sprint car guys from all over the country. It wasn't a USAC event, and in my opinion the Western World helped prove that a traveling "outlaw" sprint car series might be viable.

I really wanted to win the Western. Phoenix is a long way from Lincoln, but I wasn't shy about hauling my car out there. Besides, by this time my car was traveling much farther away, from Florida to Washington state. We were playing with some damn tough competitors, and it was hard to win those big races like the Western or the Knoxville Nationals.

In 1969 we had as good a shot as I ever had at the Western. Jan Opperman and Yogi took my car out to Phoenix, and qualified real well. They had sewn up a good starting spot, and I was excited because I knew we could win it.

I was too busy with my business to travel all the time with the car, so the plan was I would fly to Phoenix the morning of the race. I was excited and nervous on the flight, because I was all fired up about winning the Western. I just *knew* we were gonna win it, because we were having a good year and I was confident.

Jan had arranged to get a free motel room at the Kontiki Motel, which these days is in a very tough section of Phoenix. Jan was to have somebody pick me up at the airport, and I was surprised to find nobody waiting for me when my plane landed.

I waited around a little while, growing more irritated with each passing minute. Where the hell were those guys? Finally I got a cab and rode over to the Kontiki.

As we turned the corner into the motel, I saw my car parked way out back, in a field that wasn't even part of the parking lot. It looked like it hadn't been washed in a month, which rankled the hell out of me. I'm a stickler on keeping the car sharp and clean, because I think it's a psychological advantage when your competitor believes he's racing against a top-notch, well-maintained machine. Plus, I want the car to look nice for the fans.

After paying the cab fare, I walked over to the car. I was shocked to see they had completely changed the fuel injection system. The whole thing looked like a mess, and by now I was not in a good mood.

I stormed over to the motel and found the front desk, and got the room number for Jan and Yogi. It was on the second floor, and I found the room and used my key, barging right in.

The room was filled with about 10 people, and marijuana smoke was so thick you could hardly make anything out, like a dense fog. A woman who hung out with the racers—I guess you'd call her a groupie—was bumping some guy on one of the beds. Everybody else was sitting around, in a complete daze, oblivious that I had even walked into the room.

I was livid, just madder than hell. We were supposed to race tonight! I yelled for everybody to get the hell out of the room, and pretty soon had the place cleared out. Opperman just gave me that innocent smile.

"Hey, Bill," he says. "Good to see you."

I didn't want to hear it.

"What the hell is with the injectors? Why did you change the injectors?"

He starts telling me about his buddy from the Bay Area of California who says he is an expert on injectors, and he told Jan he could really make the car go. I just threw my hands up in disgust and stomped out of the room.

I was so pissed I refused to ride with Jan and Yogi to the race track. A buddy of mine was also staying at the motel, and he offered me a ride. He says, "Gee, you guys ought to do good tonight, with a starting spot on the front row!"

"Aw, that son-of-a-bitch probably won't even start."

"What are you talkin' about? You qualified real well!"

"It won't even start. Just watch."

The Western World always drew a big field of cars, so they weren't able to hot lap everybody at the same time. They hot lapped in stages, and the feature starters would typically hot lap before the C-main ran.

Opperman got in the car, and we rolled him out to the starting lane. A push truck shoved him onto the track, and stayed behind him for two full laps, trying to get the car to fire. It burped and coughed, with fire running out of the injector stacks, and the engine got hotter than hell.

Finally, when the car couldn't get underway on its own power, the push truck brought it back to our pit. Man, I was livid!

I pulled the hood off and used a screwdriver to remove the upper radiator hose, pointing the flood of steaming water in the general vicinity of Yogi and Jan's buddy, the "expert."

I definitely got their attention. Their eyes widened and I screamed, "Get the hell outta here!"

That probably wasn't the brightest idea, because now I didn't have any help. Roger Beck, a first-class mechanical guy who was a friend of mine, was sitting a little ways off on a lawn chair, watching the races with his wife. He came over to see if he could help, and the two of us pulled the new injector off and replaced it with the unit we normally run.

We finally got the car running, and Jan eventually finished 25th.

I was so frustrated I didn't talk to anybody after the race. I just went back to the motel and hit the sack, so upset I couldn't see straight.

The next morning I found Opperman and Yogi, and I didn't mince any words.

"You two guys are obviously not capable of running this race car by yourselves," I said. "Get this car back to Lincoln right away, and then you're both fired. I'm through with the both of you."

I flew back to Lincoln, and went back to work. I figured they'd get back with the car around Tuesday, maybe Wednesday or

Thursday if they were really poking along. However, by Friday there was still no sign of 'em.

There were no cell phones to call, no e-mails to send. They were out there somewhere, with my race car, and I had no idea where.

Was I mad? Hell yes I was mad! Mad enough that I called the highway patrol, and reported the whole setup — the tow rig, the trailer, the race car — as stolen. They issued an all-points bulletin and told me they'd call me when they'd located the culprits.

What I didn't know was this: Right after our heart-to-heart talk in Phoenix, Jan and Yogi decided I didn't really mean it. I was just upset in the moment, they figured, and I'd change my mind when I cooled off. In fact, they were sure I wouldn't mind if they went ahead and drove my tow rig and race car to California, where Jan would drive somebody else's car at a big race in Sacramento that following weekend.

Of course, they didn't bother to call and fill me on these minor details. I'm pacing the floor back home, wondering what the hell has become of my race team.

It was about a week later when they finally straggled back home. How they got by without the cops picking them up, I'll never know. Good thing they did, too; if the cops would have arrested them, I was just about mad enough to let 'em both sit in jail for a while.

I sat them both down and they told me about their adventure. I gave them an ass chewing that would just about take the paint off the walls, but of course it had no effect on those two impossible guys. Yogi and Opperman were two of a kind, dancing to their own drummer. My ass chewings were like air drifting past, and they were completely oblivious.

They just gave me that blank stare, smiled, and said something like, "Okay, Bill!"

And of course they talked me into not firing them, and things were fine again. God, they were frustrating. I laugh now as I think about this, but I wasn't laughing at the time. Those two guys were the ultimate in high maintenance.

How was it I had surrounded myself with such personalities? Yogi, Opperman, Don Brown, Don Maxwell...they took years off my life with the worries they inspired.

Unfortunately, Yogi's life came to a sad and premature ending a few years later. He continued to work for me in the shop, and one very hot day in Lincoln we were getting ready to break for lunch.

Yogi never wore a belt, and his pants hung so low on his hips you could always see the crack of his ass. He walked over and showed me this mole on his belly, which was all red and swollen. His pants had been rubbing against the mole, and it had really irritated the skin.

"This thing hurts," he said. He walked over to the workbench and grabbed a pair of side-cutters, and snipped the mole right off. "There…no more mole."

A year later he was dead, a victim of cancer.

It was a very sad ending, and he's buried out near Beaver Crossing in an unmarked grave, next to Jan's brother, Jay, who was killed in a racing accident in Knoxville.

When Jan later left me to go race in Pennsylvania at the end of the 1969 season, I began doing some USAC Champ Dirt racing. I bought a Ronnie Ward-built chassis from California. Ron was Indy 500 winner Rodger Ward's brother. I hired Don Nordhorn, a driver from southern Indiana who ran a body shop, and we ran a few races together. Don was one of the few drivers I had who actually had a real job in addition to driving a race car. Don was a very good driver, with a nice following of fans from the Indiana area. We ran a few of the USAC races, although USAC had an extremely limited schedule at that time, something like four or five races a year.

In 1974 I built an all-new Champ Dirt car. This was a turbocharged Offy, a specially built chassis, designed by myself, Warren "Jelly" Wilhelm of Wichita, Carl Cindric, and Don Brown. We ran the USAC Hoosier Hundred with Larry Dickson driving. This was our only outing in the turbo-charged car. My good friend, Jackie "Lucky" Howerton of Indianapolis, actually won the race in the only other turbo-powered Offy, built by George Bignotti.

This was the first year anybody had tried the turbo-Offy in the Champ Dirt division. They held so much promise; by July 4 of that season USAC had already outlawed them in the future, but allowed them to be used for the balance of that season.

I was interested in racing more with USAC, even though they frustrated the hell out of me. There was an attitude within the organization that's hard to explain, sort of an arrogance yet incompetence at the same time. They clearly distrusted outsiders, and as I mentioned earlier they made sure — again, this is the world according to Bill — to protect their regulars.

Yet I saw great potential with USAC. So much so that, against my better judgment, I campaigned for a position on the car-owner board of advisors. I felt like I had something to offer, because of my background. I had driven, built race cars, promoted events, promoted tracks, and ran a successful business. I didn't really have time to get involved in a lot of meetings and committees, but I believed that with the right advice and direction, USAC could become much bigger than it was at the time.

However, the owners felt differently, and they elected Boston Louis Seymour to the position. After that, I didn't pursue the idea any further.

But I do credit USAC with one very important thing: my trademark hat.

When I decided to campaign for the position on the advisory board, I figured one challenge was that most of my fellow car owners didn't know who I was. How could I get them to notice me, and remember me when it came time to vote?

I decided I needed something to help me stand out. So I began wearing a black hat.

Even though it didn't help me win the election, it quickly caught on. More and more people were mentioning the hat, and it was obvious the people I encountered across the country at racing and hot rod events were noticing it.

I'm always looking for a way to build visibility for Speedway Motors, so I figured the hat might help me do that. Sure enough, 30-some years later, the hat has become a fixture, both on my head and within some of our Speedway Motors logos.

During the time when I had the USAC cars, we still raced locally with a different race car. In 1970 I had several guys in the car...Ron Perkins, Roy Bryant, Tom Corbin, Jay East, and Opperman ran for me a few times as well.

In 1971 I built a new sprint car, and teamed up once again with Lloyd Beckman. We raced with NMRA and BCRA, and won a few races and the NMRA season title. The following year Lloyd set a record by winning four-straight features at Eagle, and in '73 I had Eddie Leavitt in my car.

The "local" car also raced at many of the weekly shows in our area. In fact, we won a championship at one of the local tracks one year and they awarded both Lloyd and me a new passenger car. I think Lloyd got a Mercury Cougar, which was neat.

Down through all of my sprint car years, I raced quite often with IMCA. The IMCA sprint cars were a very strong series through the 1940s to the early 1980s or so, and they were a mainstay in our area. Their travel schedule was quite extensive, long before the World of Outlaws came along. My car visited a lot of faraway tracks on the IMCA schedule.

When you traveled with IMCA, you traveled what was called the "fair circuit." Minnesota, North Dakota, South Dakota, Kansas, Nebraska, Iowa, Missouri, Oklahoma, and more. The auto races were run during the State Fair, and the fair circuit would go non-stop for two months. You can't have all the fairs at the same time, because there aren't that many carnival companies to service them.

You also ran "special events," such as the Florida State Fair, Des Moines, and Spencer.

Typically the state fairgrounds had a half-mile or bigger dirt oval, and that's where you'd run the races. The Nebraska State Fair track is a five-eighths-mile, and like most of these ovals was built for horse racing. The surface is a mixture of clay and sand, although the original surface was a yellow clay. The horse people insisted they mix sand with the clay so it wouldn't stick to the horse's hooves. If the horse is stamping around and it's damp and his hoof gets as big as a football, he doesn't run very well. So here comes the sand. This was common at the fair tracks.

When our cars raced on those surfaces, it was horrible in terms of traction. Absolutely horrible, particularly on a 115-degree afternoon race. Even by Labor Day it's still damned hot in Nebraska.

When the fairs came around, many of the traveling racers found their way to my speed shop. They might pick up a few parts, or use my shop facility to repair their car. I'll bet we had more racers passing through Lincoln than anyplace else in the country. The combination of the fair circuit and the great Midwest racing around Lincoln, Knoxville, Topeka and Belleville made us an ideal stopping point.

By the time the fair circuit came to our town on Labor Day, lots of the racers needed help. They had been going up and down the road beating the hell out of their equipment, and things were just about worn out.

That's how I met Rollie Beale, for example. These were the days before Rollie became a great USAC champion, and he was following the IMCA circuit. Despite what many people might think, IMCA paid pretty good purses, and guys always followed the money. Rollie's car broke down, and they used my shop to get going again.

I met all kinds of guys like that. The California guys, they came back to the Midwest because the races paid well. They could take a few weeks off of their job, like a vacation, and come here and race almost non-stop for several weeks straight.

There was a distinct advantage to having all these racers come by my shop. Of course, some of it was that I enjoyed making friends with many different people who shared my passion, make no mistake about it. However, I also took the opportunity to study what they were doing, and learn.

I can't invent the wheel, but I can sure try to re-invent the wheel. When they had the oil pan and heads off their Traco-built engine, I could look in and see what Mr. Traco was doing. Then when I had to run against all the Traco engines in the 1970s, I knew what I was up against.

That was a big transition for me, when I began racing some USAC races. The rules were very different back then, and USAC allowed only 302-inch V8s, much smaller than our engines out here. I had been running a 4-by-4 400-inch Chevy for more than 10 years at that point, and I had to figure out how to build a competitive 302-inch engine to compete with the Traco.

My 4-by-4 engine was something of a "speed secret." A 4-by-4 is an engine with a four-inch bore and a four-inch stroke, which is a good-sized small block. I had a guy named Gilliam in Detroit who was forging crankshafts for Chevrolet engines who made me a crankshaft that had a four-inch stroke. You put one of these into a four-inch bore 327 block, and you've got a 4-by-4.

Such a block had never seen such a crankshaft. That's because there are big issues with clearance, and I had to make my own connecting rods to make it work. I took rods from a Buick V8, then cut the rod and plated it on both sides to make it stronger. Then I had to make special rod bolts to hold the caps in place yet clear the camshaft. The trick was to run a very small-diameter camshaft with a small-diameter roller, which I got my friends at Iskendarian to make. Isky's rollers were the only ones I found that could live if you moved the roller that far in the boss of the block. All the rest I tried would turn sideways, and a roller doesn't roll if it's turned sideways. Not very well, anyways.

This was all a trial-and-error process that went through the early 1960s. Gilliam made me some custom crankshafts, and every now and then he'd call me on the phone.

"Bill, I've got a guy who wants to buy one of those crankshafts I made for you...tell me again how you did that so I can make another."

Well, I wasn't interested in telling anybody how we were doing this. I'd just laugh and say, "I told you once how I did it, and I'm not telling you any more!"

Why would you tell anybody?

The nice thing about the 400-inch small block is that there is no substitute for cubic inches. You can be racing on a hot afternoon, and pick the gear 50 points wrong, but that horsepower makes up the difference. It can make you look good even if you're bad. And it will cover a lot of mistakes. A spark plug wire falls off and we're running on seven cylinders, but we're just as good as the guy running eight. Cubic inches can make up for a lot of sins.

Plus, I found that it made the car a lot more drivable. The racing we did was not stab-and-steer like much of the racing on dirt today. Traction was very different then, and it was more complicated to figure out how to get fast.

Even though I tried to have the absolute best car I could, I still had to have a great driver. The quotient of the driver meant more in my day of racing than it does today, I think. Certainly these guys today are the finest in the world, but the quotient of the driver and his ability to adapt was even more critical back in my day.

I've always said that Steve Kinser's best quality is his ability to pick his race track more quickly than anybody else in all situations. Whether it's winged, non-winged, whatever. You don't win 12 Knoxville Nationals without a keen ability to pick that race track.

A dirt track can change every 30 feet, although that's less true today. With every passing minute it changes more. If you don't have the ability to study the track and pick your launching pad, you're not going to win. Not now, and definitely not back in the day.

It was fun traveling the IMCA circuit during those years, because their schedule was full of interesting tracks and their pit area was filled with interesting people. There were two promoters you dealt with on the IMCA tour, and they were very different from each other. Al Sweeney was a pleasant guy, while Frank Winkley was much more of a hard-nosed guy. If you sneezed at the pit meeting, he'd threaten to throw you out. He'd lock the pit gate very early, and if a driver got there late he wouldn't let him in. He was a hard-nosed, tough dude.

One of the tracks we visited was at St. Paul, Minn. That's where I once again damn near got myself killed, and aside from my serious accident at Eagle, St. Paul was probably the closest I came to "lights out."

They had just paved the St. Paul track, and we were there as part of a combination show with stock cars. They placed barriers along the pit lane to keep cars out of the pit area, great big cast concrete barriers that it would take a big truck to move.

A Mopar got upside down coming off turn four in the stock car race, and came sliding toward the pit area on its roof. It seemed like it picked up speed as it was sliding along, and was still going very fast. It hit that cement barrier and just blew apart, launching over the barrier and coming straight into the pits.

I was standing with a bunch of people along the infield stage, watching the race. We looked up and here comes that Mopar, and of course in an instant there was chaos with people scrambling to get out of the way. I reached up to grab something to pull myself up onto the stage, when somebody literally stood on my shoulders, using me for the ladder. Drove me right down into the ground!

The car came flying straight at me, and literally stopped less than five feet away. I came within a few feet of getting completely smashed between the car and the stage. Luckily everybody was okay, but it sure got my adrenaline going.

Another interesting stop on the IMCA tour in the 1960s was the Little 500 in Anderson, Ind. This race intrigued the hell out of me, and no matter how hard I tried I wasn't able to win it. It's a 500-lap race on a quarter-mile high-banked asphalt track, starting 33 sprint cars in 11 rows of three. Quite the spectacle.

In 1965 the Little 500 was the first race Bob Coulter drove for me. Coulter was something of an unknown in IMCA, because he was from California. He had won the Little 500 as a relief driver with Johnny White in 1963, and in 1965 he got $200 in show-up money to come run the race again. So he and I went to Anderson for the race. Boy, what an adventure.

They had kind of a screwy set-up, because you went out there to qualify two weeks before the race. That was a long way just to qualify! But that was the setup, so off we went to Anderson.

I bought a brand new M&H tire to qualify on, even though I hate buying tires. It's hard to make any money with the race car when you're spending it all on tires. We drove through the night to Anderson and then went to sleep there in the parking lot, waiting on the track to open for qualifying.

Early in the morning a kid tapped on our window and says, "Are you guys gonna run that tire on your car, the one on the right side?"

"Yeah...what's wrong?"

"Well, the trailer rubbed a hole through the sidewall!"

So I was in a great mood, right off. That was an expensive tire! We took it off and tried to find some way to at least use it in qualifying. I'm not sure what we did, but I'm sure it was something that you shouldn't be doing. All the tires already had tubes, because there wasn't a steel wheel made back then that would hold a tubeless tire. Especially a Halibrand wheel; they wouldn't hold air, period.

(Ted Halibrand called me one day when he was making wheels for Carroll Shelby, and said, "Speedy, I can't get these things to seal. What should I do?" I thought for a minute and suggested, "Why don't you try painting them?" He painted them green, if you can imagine that. My fault for suggesting he paint 'em.)

We managed to get the car qualified, and then drove all the way back to Lincoln. Two weeks later we came back for the race, and I had some engine trouble.

Greg Weld was running for the USAC sprint car championship (he ultimately finished second to Johnny Rutherford) that season, so he spent a lot of time in the Indiana area. He came to watch the Little 500, driving a brand new Chevrolet pickup truck.

I needed a new set of rocker arms and push rods, and in my great wisdom I realized that parts on Greg's new tow truck would fit perfectly! Luckily he agreed, and I literally took the parts from his truck and ran them in the Little 500. The downside was after the race when I had to work in that dark parking lot to reassemble his tow truck so he could go on to Winchester. Ugh! You don't do things like that today.

Coulter had lined up Hal Minyard as a backup driver, a really neat guy from California. These were the days before power steering, and this race was one tough chore for a driver. The plan was to let Hal relieve Bob if we had a red flag, but it turned out there were no red flags and Bob went the distance.

Part of the reason for no red flags was that this race was absolutely impossible to score. If you threw the red, you had to come up with a detailed restart order, which was impossible. You could have 100 difference scorers doing the race, and they would come up with 100 different scenarios. So unless the entire track was blocked, they kept driving around under caution if there was an accident.

Coulter wound up getting collected in a pile-up that involved eight or 10 cars, and he was parked up in the corner, backward on the track. The car wasn't hurt, he just needed to be restarted. Meanwhile the field kept idling around the track, putting us more laps down.

My friend Keith Barker and I scrambled up the high bank to try and get him restarted, all the while with cars whizzing past. Keith has a wooden leg, and my hip joints have always been marginal, and there we were trying to walk up those steep banks.

Coulter is yelling at us, "Get me turned around and get me started!" It was really a pretty funny scene. Now, not then. We ended up finishing 16th, which wasn't funny then or now.

I took Ron Perkins to the Little 500 in 1970, and while we didn't do very well we did make Dick Wallen's "Sprint Car Spectacular" film. Since it was crash footage, I would have preferred we not be in the film.

I preached and preached to Perkins, "Don't race anybody until after 400 laps. Just maintain a good pace, and race the last 100 laps. No matter what."

They had just repaved the track, and during the race the oil came up from the surface and the track began to come apart. The rocks and gravel from the asphalt were really a problem, and the surface was treacherous.

Halfway through the race Perkins got to racing with somebody, and the track was just miserable. He spun in turn four, near the track entrance, and hit the opening a ton. It pushed the right front wheel all the way back to the cockpit. Perkins was knocked out, and his foot pressed down on the throttle. The car bounced off the wall and headed for the infield pit area on three wheels, with people scattering in all directions. Boy, I thought it was going to be a holocaust, but luckily the car finally stopped without hitting anyone.

Needless to say our Little 500 adventure wasn't good that year, either.

I had another brilliant idea at the Little 500 one year, and it's only a matter of luck that it didn't end in dire circumstances.

One element of the race that's different than all other sprint car races is that you have to fuel your car during the race. I decided, in all my wisdom, that we needed to have a really quick fuel stop. I put a 55-gallon barrel on a stand I had made, maybe 10, 12 feet in the air. It had a big hose with a mechanism like you'd see at a gas station, which I figured would be a great improvement. Pouring fuel in by the can was not only slower, but also messy and dangerous because the crew would often spill some on the car, on themselves, and so forth.

So I came up with the idea of the gravity-feed fueling barrel. Oh, did I mention the fact that when we got it set up in Anderson we couldn't get the tank to vent properly? The only way we found to vent it was to take the top end off the barrel.

Which means you've got 55 gallons of methanol in what is essentially an open bucket, 10 feet off the ground, sitting there in the infield. Are you getting nervous yet? I am, just telling the story.

We got the first pit stall located right past the start-finish line, toward turn one. We're not far from the track itself, maybe 15, 20 yards. By the way, it used to be hazardous to your health to hang out at places like that.

The start of the Little 500 is rather, uh, busy, what with 33 sprint cars three-abreast on that quarter-mile track. Busy, and unpredictable. On the first lap a guy in the second or third row spins, and guess where he comes? Backwards, going as fast as he was forward, toward our pit. Oh, shit!

Even though it was only a few seconds for all of this to take place, my mind was already thinking about that 55 gallons of methanol getting dumped all over the area, and the fact that Speedy Bill was probably going to be in big trouble.

Here he comes, and he hits the corner of my fueling rig. He hit it pretty hard, and it bent the leg about a foot, but it didn't knock it over. I couldn't believe our good luck. If that had knocked the barrel over, boy, they'd still be trying to put out the fire. Whew!

One of the great annual adventures during my racing years was going to Florida each February for the annual "big dog pissin' contest." That's where we all showed up in Tampa to try and out-run, out-brag, and out-last all the other big dogs.

The roots of this event go way, way back to the early years of IMCA. I began going sometime in the 1960s, and on my first trip I had Harold Leep of Wichita, as my driver.

I wanted somebody who wouldn't tear up my car, because that's a long way to go just to crash. My buddy Warren "Jelly" Wilhelm had been running Harold in his supermod in their area with great success. They spanked all the boys, using an early small block Chevy. Jelly assured me Harold wouldn't tear up my car, so we put a deal together to go to Tampa.

Jelly rode down with me, and Harold met us there. It was sure a long ride from Lincoln to Tampa, particularly on those old pre-Interstate two-lane highways.

Harold didn't have a good qualifying lap that first day. We drew a late number, went out late, all the things that won't get you to the front in an afternoon race. So we're in the donkey race, the hooligan, with all the slugs, starting about 20th.

It was dusty and slick, and I was standing at the edge of the track along the front straightaway. It was so slick Harold went past me going about 35 mph, so slow I actually waved at him and he waved back.

The cars disappeared into a cloud of dust in turn one, and I couldn't see a thing. All of a sudden the announcer on the loudspeaker yells, "Big wreck in turn one...Harold Leep is involved!"

I'm thinking, "How could he be involved, he's running 20th going 35 mph?!"

The guy leading the race had spun, and was driving backward through the field and hit Harold head-on. Great luck, eh?

So now I'm standing in the middle of Florida wondering what to do with a badly wrecked race car. We didn't have a semi-trailer full of spares, by the way, such as axles and engines and spindles and the like. You're there with your two-axle trailer and pickup truck.

What could I do? I had no tools, no welder, nothing.

Suddenly I remembered that my old buddy Buzz Barton lived in Tampa. I could fix my car at his place!

We loaded everything back on my trailer and headed for Buzz's place. I have to tell this story, even though it's terribly off-color, because it's a perfect Buzz Barton story. We pulled into the driveway, and I walked up to the shop door. The lights were on and the door was unlocked, so I went on in.

Buzz was sitting there at his desk, with a young woman giving him, uh, service while he's sitting in the chair. I'm absolutely dumfounded with surprise and shock, and Buzz looks up at me and waves.

"Hi, Bill! Come on in!"

"Uh...well, Buzz, maybe I should come back later..."

"Naw, she's all finished. Say, honey, you've got to go now, okay? Well, come on in, Bill!"

He just acted like it was nothing out of the ordinary. That was Buzz. I'll admit I was embarrassed as hell, but it sure didn't bother him. Oh, the colorful characters of our sport!

The good news was we got our car fixed in his shop, and Harold ran the rest of the races that week without any more crashes. Although we didn't have much success together, Harold continued to drive for me off and on throughout the rest of that season.

Harold was a good race driver. He was great to work with, and I'll never forget this: You could ask him, "Well, what do we need to change, Harold?" I was looking to make the car better for him...do we need more gear, more caster, do we need a ribbed tire on the left front, change the brakes...what do we need?

He'd always say, "Oh, I think it will be all right. I'll just adapt."

Now, not too many drivers—even in my era—could do that. That was impressive. When we first raced together and he said that, I instantly respected his ability to adjust. I was not at all skeptical because I thought he could do it, and I was confident in his ability.

Really, I respected the ability of nearly all of my 87-some drivers down through the years. If I didn't think they could get the job done, I wouldn't have put them in my race car.

I looked at racing differently than many people, I think. For a lot of people, they looked at racing like they were going fishing. "Oh, we're going fishing this afternoon, and we'll sit at the lake with our friends and if I catch one or not, who cares? We'll have fun."

My attitude was different. I looked at it and said, "I've spent all this time and effort, and my kids are home and my speed shop needs a shot of monetary adrenaline, and I'm gonna try and win this race!"

When I got to winning a lot of them I got a little cocky. I'd look around as I came through the gate and said to myself, "I wonder why the rest of these guys even come...I'm here."

16

Accidental Auction

In the late 1960s, I added a new dimension to my business interests, and it was completely by accident.

Not long after I got ran over at Eagle Raceway and nearly killed, the track closed (it had nothing to do with my accident). The track was located on leased land, and they decided to have an auction to find somebody who wanted to buy the track and have a go at it.

The auction was on a Saturday morning, and I told Joyce I'd go see how it went. She had been around me long enough to know that, well, this might be a problem! I was constantly going to an auction and buying a car, buying a bunch of junk, whatever. I couldn't pass up a good deal, you know.

As I went out the door that morning, Joyce called out, "If you buy that race track, don't even bother coming home!"

I think she meant it.

It had only been a couple of years that we had gotten over our experience of being an owner of Raceway Park, located on 14th Street in Lincoln. This was located just north of the state fairgrounds, on state fair property. I leased the land, and owned the improvements.

I held this lease until I sold the grandstands to a guy who moved them to Whitehead Speedway, just across the Missouri River from Nebraska City. I had painted the grandstand orange, and was planning it to be the finest track in the world. Well, it didn't work out that way. That venture went broke, so my experience wasn't good.

A funny story about that orange paint: The grandstands were located at Raceway Park, and we painted everything nice and fresh for our grand opening. However, the humidity was very high, and the paint was a lot slower drying than I counted on.

All the people came in for our first race, and when it was over everybody got up to leave. I was pretty surprised to see people walking out with orange paint all over their ass!

Next day angry people were showing up at Speedway Motors with their clothes, dotted with orange paint. Joyce handled the situation real well, and just told people to get them cleaned and send us the bill. What else could we do?

However, once it dried that orange paint was awfully durable. For years and years afterward, we would see that orange paint off in the distance as we drove past, long after Whitehead Speedway had closed. That's probably the most durable paint I've ever seen!

Actually, I would have probably went completely broke from all those race track adventures of that era, except for the timing of my very successful Cool Man Glass Tint product, which saved my ass. Lucky timing.

I was also involved in the ownership of the Capitol Beach track, with three partners: Bob Lundberg, Art Stuber, and Paul Saenz. We bought the track from Jake Singer and his buddies. Lundberg and I got out first, leaving the two others to continue on their own. They eventually closed and moved the grandstands to Raceway Park. So that grandstand had three homes: Capitol Beach, Raceway Park, and across from Nebraska City.

Then, like today, race track owners didn't have a good history. When it's all said and done, only a few succeed. Bruton Smith and the France family have obviously been exceptions to that rule, of course. Ontario Speedway in California went broke something like nine times before it finally closed for good. Texas World Speedway closed, and many other big tracks have failed a time or two. I know, because I've lost money in a half-dozen of those damned things.

So Joyce didn't have anything to worry about that morning. I didn't want to get back into a race track experience, in any way. By then I knew I wasn't very good at that, and it always cost me a pile of money.

I was merely a spectator that morning at Eagle, watching the track go under the gavel for something like $25,000.

As I was driving home I saw a bunch of people gathered in the parking lot of an old building at 33rd and O Street. There had been a bread company called Smith Baking Company (no relation) there when I was a kid, but that business had been gone for many years and the building was sitting empty. As I cruised past I spotted a friend of mine who is an auctioneer.

"Gee, they must be having an auction," I said, turning my car around. "I think I'll stop and have a look."

A real estate auction is typically very different than those of machinery and other products. In a real estate auction they'll call out that they have a bid in X amount, and they'll go silent and talk to two or three guys who might have an interest in bidding. It's not biff-bam-boom.

My friend asked me if I'd ever been in the building. I said yes, I used to come in and buy donuts through the front door, but I'd never been in the back part of the building. So I walked inside and looked it over. It was an old building, quite a nice size, big enough that they had parked their delivery trucks inside. There was also plenty of parking outside.

"What's the bid on this place?" I asked.

"$90,000."

I walked around and looked it over some more. I thought it was a good buy at $90,000.

"Who is bidding on it?" I asked.

They told me it was Mr. Mahoney, who had been a partner of my good friend Roger Anderson's father in a building downtown. Mahoney was in the construction business, and up by Omaha there is a state park that bears his name. So this fellow was a big player in our area.

Mahoney was kind of rough and tumble. He was sitting in his Cadillac, parked in front of the building, with a roll of barbed wire on the back seat. His car door was open, and he was waiting on the auction to end.

"I'll bid $95,000," I said.

Mahoney came right back with a bid of $100,000. A few minutes passed.

We had been the only two bidders, and the auctioneer was getting ready to close it down. A kid from Kansas City was there, the recipient of the auction. The building had been willed to him, and all he was wanting was to cash Grandpa's building out and get on the road in his Corvette. He was champing at the bit.

"$105,000," I said.

The auctioneer called out the bid, and Mahoney immediately slammed the door of his Cadillac, started it up, and headed down the street.

The auctioneer kind of looked around, and said, "Well, I guess the auction's over. You bought it."

I was happy, naturally, because I had won the race. Competitive, remember?

I was very excited, and I called Joyce from a pay phone. I had completely forgotten about the auction at Eagle. I was laughing and feeling good about my purchase.

Joyce answered the phone, and I said, "Guess what? I bought something!"

"You didn't buy that race track," she said, crestfallen. "Don't you come home if you did."

"Oh, no," I insisted. "I bought something else."

Now, I don't know if she had *all* my clothes packed and sitting at the front door by the time I got home, but it was almost to that point. I kept trying to reassure her that I didn't buy the track, and offered to drive her over to show what I had really bought. Finally she relented, and we took a ride over to our new building.

That was our very first venture in the commercial real estate market. Today, we have invested in about 300 properties in Lincoln. It's been a good way for us to diversify, and it helps us continue to be a part of the community. It's worked out very well, all because I happened to stop at an auction.

I do know one thing: I'm glad I didn't buy that race track. So is Joyce.

Within a day or two of my property purchase, I began to realize something: Once you purchase a commercial property, you have to figure out what to do with it.

One of the ideas rolling around in my head was the idea of becoming a dealer for new cars. This was very different than the used car business; it's a little more prestigious, a little higher-profile. And of course I was confident I was up to the task.

But you can't just wave a magic wand and be in the new car business. You have to make a deal with a manufacturer to carry their line, and by this time most of the established brands had a big dealer network. I couldn't just become a Chevrolet dealer, for example, because Chevy had already established local dealerships.

The Misle family was prominent in Lincoln, and they had owned many of the major automobile dealerships in town. Chevrolet, GMC, Cadillac, Pontiac, they had several brands, and over time expanded to included Mazda, Jaguar, Rolls Royce, and several more. They apparently wanted to own 'em all.

Not long after I bought the building, I heard that the Misle people had flown to France to talk with Renault about establishing that line in Lincoln. Renault was making some noise about selling cars in the USA, and had recently introduced the

Renault R5. They apparently wanted to build a dealer network similar to the American manufacturers.

But Renault didn't want their dealers carrying other lines at the same location, because they felt that confused the buyer. When I heard this, I figured I would apply. After all, I didn't have any other lines. There would be no confusion.

I guess I was a little surprised when Renault took me up on my offer. Soon enough I started remodeling the old building and got ready to receive my first shipment of brand new cars.

I was going to become a Renault dealer! I'm going to become legitimate! Rather than simply being a used car bum, I'm going to be a respectable new-car dealer.

I was genuinely excited about this. I was getting in on the ground floor of Renault's launch in the USA, and who knows? Maybe this was going to be the next big thing.

I knew I couldn't run Speedway Motors and also run a new car dealership, so I hired a couple of guys to run the dealership. These guys were hustlers, and in that business you've got to be a hustler. Pretty soon, we were fifth in the nation in Renault sales.

However, it was very hard to make money in that business. My cost for these little Renault's was around $3,150 each and we sold them for $3,299. Larger cars typically have a much bigger margin, but with a value-priced small car it was awfully tight. Still, we sold a bunch of 'em.

By this time it was the early 1970s, and conversion vans became the rage. I added a line of conversion vans to the car agency, and we were doing okay with that, too.

Really, if you'd taken my business temperature in late 1972, you'd find me with cheery cheeks and a big smile on my face. My business interests were growing nicely, and with the advent of muscle cars ruling the streets, Speedway Motors was selling more and more performance equipment.

The performance industry was really picking up steam. My race cars were running well, with success almost everywhere we went.

I had no idea that the most catastrophic period the industry had ever experienced was right around the corner.

Did I see it coming? No way. Was I ready for it? Maybe, but only because I was lucky. Ready or not, here comes the crunch of 1973. Survival of the fittest was about to begin.

17

Surviving the Crunch

It was Anaheim, Calif., on a sunny late-autumn afternoon. My mood was bleak that November day in 1973, because the world seemed to be going to hell in a hand basket.

The stock market had dropped a bunch throughout 1973, and the U.S. was in the midst of a serious recession. Inflation was on the rise, and if all this wasn't enough, the Arabs decided they wouldn't sell us any more oil.

Anybody who was an adult in late 1973 has never forgotten that period. Sure, we've been through recessions and wars and natural disasters, but for the first time in about 30 years, it looked like we were going to run short on gasoline.

Gasoline, if you haven't figured out by now, fueled every element of my life. My hobbies, my passions, my business. Like all car guys, the very thought of being cut off from gasoline left me cold.

That's why the newspaper reports of the day shook me to the bottom of my shoes. The report was that the government was looking at rationing, allowing each family something like three gallons per week until we could figure out what was going to happen with our oil supply.

I lived through rationing once, as a kid growing up in Lincoln during World War II. I knew what rationing meant: black markets, and a lifestyle where most people simply stayed home.

I was in Anaheim for the SEMA show, a national trade group focused on the automotive performance industry. Everybody at the show was in a complete funk, with the combination of the difficult economic situation and the possibility of gas rationing.

The Anaheim Holiday Inn was just a short hop from the show, and I vividly remember going back to my room that afternoon. I had seen with my own eyes vivid proof that dramatic things were happening; long lines stretched around the block at many California gas stations, something we hadn't yet experienced in Lincoln.

I walked into my room, and stepped into the bathroom without turning on the light. In the dim afternoon light I leaned over the sink and stared at myself in the mirror. The room was quiet, and there was nothing but me staring into that mirror, wondering if my world was falling apart.

"This is the end of the world," I said out loud. "I've been in business for 20 years, and now I'm going to be broke because nobody is going to buy anything."

I stood there and stared into my own eyes. Then I began to think: I'm a racer myself, with a couple of very active race cars and ambitious plans for 1974. Was I ready to quit racing, just because of the way things were?

No, I won't quit. I'll save my three gallons of gasoline each week, and I'll walk to work so I can save my gasoline allocation to go racing that weekend. Or do hot rod stuff. I'm gonna race, I'm gonna continue to build parts for my car, and I'm gonna continue to mess with hot rods. This is my hobby, my passion, my life; nothing is going to stop me from fulfilling my passion.

That's human nature; our hobby and our passions are what really intrigue us, and give us a zest to keep living. Whether it's hunting, fishing, racing, basketball, hot rods, whatever, our passions are the only thing we can truly feel are ours alone. We can share it with others, but it's *our* thing. We'll stick by our hobbies and passions almost to eternity.

As I stood there, I began to feel better. Sure, things were tough. But in my heart I knew our country could get through it, Speedway Motors could get through it, and I could get through it.

The next couple of years weren't easy, not for me nor anybody else. But you know what? Not only did we get through it, but I discovered there is truth to that old adage about "opportunity in the midst of difficulty," or however it goes. Even though our economy was struggling, that didn't mean there weren't opportunities in business.

Did I see the crunch of 1973 coming? No. The '60s were great years, with lots of things going on and lots of growth, not only in our business but throughout the racing and performance industries.

But the industry was not "big" in the 1960s, not yet. Not when compared to today. And, frankly, it wasn't big when compared to other industries. I was always amazed, for example, by the people I got to know who were in the motorcycle industry, and how much larger they were than anybody in the hot rod or race car industry during that time. What they were able to spend on fluff, and show vehicles, was way more than we did in automotive performance. And the shows themselves; the motorcycle show in Indianapolis, for example, used to blow away any show I had ever seen, even the SEMA show.

Our industry began to really grow, it seems, when we began to see more automotive-related things on television. As auto racing began to be seen on weekend afternoons in the 1960s, it seemed to inspire more people to care about cars. Plus, we began to see far more magazines related to cars and hot rods, and racing. The media was beginning to expose everybody to what was going on in our world.

As that happened, what was an isolated pocket began to expand. A young man would read about custom cars, or whatever, and might be drawn to find out more. He might hook up with somebody locally who was into hot rods, and that was enough to get him involved in building a car of his own.

As the racing and hot rod industries slowly began to grow, I realized that it was very important to know my customer. Not just individually, but collectively. I had to understand him, and know how he thinks. Because pleasing that customer was the reason for the existence of my business...I had to devote myself to figuring out how to make the customer happy and give him what he wants, even when he isn't sure himself what he wants.

One way to do this was simply getting to know more people, and listening to them. In the speed shop business, that's pretty easy to do. A good businessman doesn't stand aloof from his customers, but rather gets to know them, and participates in the arena where they're playing.

I've always prided myself that I know my customer, sometimes better than he knows himself. In both arenas: race cars and hot rods. The reason I know them, of course, is simple: I can relate, because that's me. I've been there myself.

I know what it feels like to build and race a successful race car. I know what it's like to pour my heart and soul into making a street car everything it can be, with my own loving hands. I've busted my knuckles, scalded myself, cut myself, smashed my fingers, cussed, and struggled just like every racer or hot rodder in the world.

When my customer uses something he bought from me for his race car or hot rod and it makes him faster or better or nicer or whatever, I know exactly how he feels. Been there, done that, as they say.

The crunch of '73-'74 was real, but it took some time to really understand what was happening. Nobody really knew what was around the corner, and everybody scrambled to figure out how to proceed.

I actually put an ad in the Lincoln newspaper that if rationing came, I would buy gas stamps. I looked back at my experience working for Blackie at his gas station during WWII, so I had some idea about how the game was going to be played. Luckily rationing never came, so at least we didn't have that draconian issue to deal with.

But the crunch slowed down the business community, a lot. Particularly with large items, such as automobiles. The car manufacturers had a tough time during this period.

This had big implications for my Renault dealership at 33rd and O Street. We were among the fortunate dealers who actually had a viable offering during the fuel crisis; those little Renaults got pretty good gas mileage, compared to most of the cars on the market.

But I could see the handwriting on the wall, as far as the automotive business. I was already on the fence on whether it would be a viable business, when a couple of developments kind of made up my mind for me.

First, I had a chance to sell the building at 33rd and O. I wasn't thinking of selling, but it was one of those situations where somebody came out of nowhere with an offer, and they clearly wanted it more than I did. I sold it and purchased a building right across the street, and moved the Renault agency over there.

However, Renault was talking about merging with AMC, and since there was already a big AMC dealer in Lincoln, I knew my days were numbered. I had an opportunity to sell the Renault agency to the AMC dealer, and that was that. I was officially out of the new car business.

The conversion van business was much more difficult. Boy, did it get hammered by the gas crisis! Those vans were going great guns before the oil embargo, but with the jump in gasoline prices the market evaporated overnight.

The manufacturing process for those vans was simple; you buy very basic panel vans (known as the "tin can" in that business), then you install all the accessories and interior. I had just finished a batch of these vans when the fuel crisis hit, and they sat on my lot for quite some time.

It's amazing how quickly the market for something can go away. Everybody in the van business was caught in a tough spot, and they hurried to unload their inventory.

I took all my vans to the auction to get rid of them. I had about $10,000 in each vehicle, and I was just looking to break even. But they wouldn't bring even half what I had in them, because the market was just dead for these things. So I withdrew them from the auction and brought 'em home. I had some storage space at Speedway Motors, so I parked 'em nose-to-tail inside a big building, and let them sit. About a year later, the van market suddenly came back, and I just washed 'em off, rolled 'em outside, and sold them at a profit.

It was very fortunate I didn't owe money on those vans. If I had, I would have been forced to sell them for half what they were worth, just to pay off the note. I would have taken a terrible bath. But because I had no debt, I could hunker down and didn't get hurt at all.

That's a great illustration on why debt is so hazardous to your financial health. A perfect formula for going broke is when debt forces you to make terrible business decisions. Debt might not let you wait for a more favorable market, forcing you to make a disastrous move too early.

As the crunch wore on into 1974, the racing season got underway. Everybody was holding their breath, wondering if the sport would survive this economic downturn.

But guess what? Just like I figured, racers still wanted to race. Some cut their travel, some held off buying new stuff, but they still raced.

Where I saw the biggest change was with my suppliers. Because of all the uncertainty, a lot of people ran scared.

With our product line of hard-core racing parts, you're talking about many items that only a very narrow niche is looking for. Rear ends, ring-and-pinion gears, steering gears, etc., these are parts only sold through probably 12 to 15 warehouses across the entire country.

Many of the manufacturers of these parts were not really into mass production, because the quantity they produced was relatively small. Many hadn't invested in newer technology, and still used antiquated lathes and drill presses, punch presses, etc.

They typically invested money in the late summer in raw materials, and spent the fall and winter building up their inventory for the late-winter and spring rush. In the fall you basically do no business, because all the racers typically wait until winter to build a new car or update their existing stuff.

So if you're a manufacturer—or retailer, for that matter— operating on a shoestring, trying to feed your family, it's pretty tough to come up with the money to spend on raw materials or products. Even in a strong economy, cash flow in this business is very difficult. *Very* difficult.

You can't just press a button in February and suddenly have 50 rear axles on your receiving dock. You would call the supplier and order 50 axles, and then he'd go out and get the raw materials, build the product, and then ship it to you. It took time—sometimes quite a while—to build 50 rear axles.

I had long ago figured out that in order to prepare for the spring rush, I had to stockpile the stuff from September to March. I couldn't just pick up the phone and order the parts and get them the next week.

(By the way, it's still like that today with most of our products. You operate on a very close margin, and there isn't much room for mistakes. You can't be wrong on your production run very often, or you'll go broke. You can't produce a thousand pieces and only sell a hundred. Almost every other business operates on a stronger margin, but in our world it's much more challenging.)

But as we entered the winter of 1973-74, I continued buying product just like I always had. Although there was very much a question about what the future held, my instincts told me that in the spring people were still going to be racing, still going to be building hot rods. So I went about building my pool of inventory just as I always had.

Then a funny thing happened: When springtime came, our sales volume doubled. *Doubled!* That old adage is true, "You can't do business out of an empty wagon." I was one of the few companies selling hardcore parts that had inventory, because so many suppliers, wholesalers, and retailers had cut back that winter.

Guys called me from New York with a tough, gruff voice (you have to be tough to even *exist* in New York), "Well, they told me you're the only guy that's got the ring-and-pinion set I need...I called 20 places, and somebody says you're the only guy. How much are they?"

I gave 'em my price — and I didn't raise any of my prices, because I wouldn't have liked that if I'd been sitting on the other side of the table — and the guy said, "Where you at?"

Of course, if you live east of the Mississippi and west of the Rocky Mountains, you're not going to know where Lincoln is. I'll guarantee 90 percent of my new customers couldn't put their finger on the state unless it's got the name on it. And the guy said, "Go ahead and ship it."

As it turns out, it was a crucial period for Speedway Motors. I had inventory, and I increased my business. Simple as that. It was the first really big burst of growth my company experienced, and it proves once again that even in adversity, there is opportunity.

In the end, I was right: My customers didn't stop racing. They didn't stop building and running hot rods. Even though times were tough, they didn't abandon their passion.

And, I might add, I don't think they ever will.

18

Free Spirits

If you were to look around the racing pit area during the "economic crunch" years of 1974 and '75, it would have been difficult to spot much difference from the previous few years.

In fact, the economic downturn didn't seem to make a dent in our travel schedules. Maybe early in the 1974 season people were hesitant to travel quite as far, but as fears of gas rationing eased and the gasoline supply became a little more certain, racers were back at it, as hard as ever.

By this time our travel range in sprint car racing had expanded by a bunch. The game was changing, and it was laying the groundwork for what would eventually become the World of Outlaws. Our roster of tracks was now scattered all across the country: Skagit, Wash.; Sacramento; West Memphis, Ark.; Williams Grove, Pa. It was the traveling freak show, I guess.

We got to where my driver, Jan Opperman, was getting show-up money, along with a few other notable racers like Rick Ferkel. This was sometimes in the range of $1,000, maybe $2,000. Not insignificant money.

We had a great run in Florida in February to start the 1974 season. Remember what I called the wintertime Florida races? The "big dog pissin' contest." By this time you'd see the *really* big dogs from all over the country make their way to Florida. Dick Tobias and the boys from Pennsylvania; three-time USAC sprint car champion Pancho Carter and the rest of the top USAC guys; the tough guys from our area of the Midwest. It wasn't unusual to have over 100 cars in the pits.

Bob Weikert from Pennsylvania would have his cannons loaded with Kenny Weld, as well as the coal-miner car owner, Al Hamilton. Al hated to get beat by me, and I once built him a car he tried to use to beat me. I think that guy would have spent a million dollars to beat us, but he never got it done, at least not that year. We won all but one of the races.

Boy, that fired me up, beating all those big dogs. I remember walking across the infield as we arrived at the track the first night, and seeing Duke Cook standing there looking at me. Duke is a loud, blustery guy, and he's always needling somebody. He had it in his mind that the USAC guys were superior to God, and he always let you know it.

"Hey, Speedy," he yelled, getting everybody's attention. "You're gonna get your ass kicked today! Pancho is here!"

I was actually embarrassed, because he was so loud, causing everybody to stare.

"Duke, just wait till the race is over," I said, real quiet, "and we'll see who gets their ass kicked."

Luckily, Jan did a great job for us and we kicked their ass that week. Just another little point of pride for the car owner, quieting down those who don't think you can get it done.

By this time in the early 1970s the cars had completely transitioned to sprint cars. For several years we raced a combination of sprint cars and supermodifieds; many of us often raced the same car for both styles of competition although it was a lot of work and wasn't particularly effective.

I had different body combinations I used, and different roll cage combinations. This was possible because roll cages were still a bolt-on accessory. Of course the respective sanctioning bodies wanted you to use their "style" exclusively; supermodified series didn't want any sprint cars, and sprint car associations didn't want any supermodifieds. Still, many of us cheated the system somewhat and changed our cars around as needed.

In fact, sometimes people tried to invent ways to disqualify you. For example, my friends and customers at Eagle Raceway did that to me for a period of time. We got to winning a good percentage of the afternoon races at Belleville, and by the time you finished up, kissed the trophy girl, and got your money, it was 5 or 6 o'clock. You've got to really hustle to get to Eagle in time to race, and with the three-hour drive we were cutting it close on many nights.

Pretty soon my "friends" at Eagle made a rule that if you weren't at the track gate by 7:30 p.m., you weren't allowed to race. Of course the track—and the competitors—would just as soon we miss the race, because they had a very hard time beating us. I spent a lot of anxious hours on the highway from Belleville to Eagle, leaned over the steering wheel of my truck, putting the hammer down to make it in time.

When they throw a rule like that at me, that does nothing but motivate my ass. I like to win, and the more they try to prevent me from winning, the more I want it. I don't ever let up, you know? Even in my business negotiations, I go about that the same way. I'm fair, and I'll play by the rules, but I'll also work as hard as I can to be successful. I don't win 'em all, but I want 'em to know I was there.

From 1974 to '76 Opperman ran a lot of races for us, but he wasn't full-time. He raced some with USAC in other cars, and he ran some championship races. Still, we raced often enough with IMCA that we finished second in the 1975 standings.

We came up with a master plan that year, because winning the IMCA crown required extensive travel. I distinctly remember the Des Moines race being very close to the one in Topeka, and the Sedalia, race was very close to the one in St. Paul, and South Dakota was very close to the one in Lincoln. These were all state fair races, and to get the car from point A to B to C to D was very difficult.

We figured out we'd need two cars, one stationed here and one stationed there. We raced in Des Moines, then jumped in my buddy's private plane to fly to Topeka, and so forth. That's the only way we could figure out how to avoid missing any of the races, and therefore miss out on the IMCA points.

It's always been tough to get much publicity from our local newspaper — this is probably not unlike your local paper — because Lincoln is a college football town. I think I could win the Indy 500 with an all-Lincoln team, and call our sports desk and say, "I just won the Indy 500!" The girl on the desk would probably say, "We don't put horse racing results in the paper."

Believe it or not, this conversation actually happened! When I've called with results from big sprint car races we've won, that's what they told me.

But the *Omaha World Herald* picked up on the story of Opperman and me flying from race to race, and ran a big feature story in the Sunday paper with a human-interest angle. It was refreshing to actually see a newspaper give short-track racing some respect.

When Opperman couldn't run the car, we had several other good drivers in the seat. Ray Lee Goodwin, for example, raced quite often with us during this period, and did a good job.

One of the growing challenges in racing at this time was rising costs. I had been building and racing cars for 25 years at this point, and I felt like I was as good at it as anybody. However, it was becoming harder and harder to make money, because there was a mindset creeping into the sport that you threw money at everything in order to get faster.

Listen, this was a serious issue for me. I had always counted on my race cars for a revenue stream; those things made money, and without my race car Speedway Motors could never have survived. I began to see something I didn't like: If race cars were becoming a break-even proposition, or even a money loser, how could I justify that? It affected my four rug rats and my business, and that's why I always worked so hard to win races.

It actually began to affect how drivers looked at me, and my cars. Drivers sometimes got mad because I wouldn't buy 'em all the new tires in the world, or the fanciest motors, whatever.

When Jan and I won the '76 Tony Hulman Classic — the race that truly changed all of sprint car racing — we were running a $375 out-of-pocket engine. If I had tried to hire any other USAC driver that day to drive my car, they would have asked, "Where did you get the engine in your car?"

"I built it myself."

"See you later, alligator."

That was the mindset of the time. Unless you had the $5,500 California 302-inch engine built by Traco, you could not win. That was the mindset. You couldn't hire a driver, period, if you didn't have the Traco, because in his mind how could you win? But Opperman didn't know the difference, and he won races anyway.

One of the greatest rivalries in the history of racing was between Opperman and Kenny Weld, of the famed racing family of that name in Kansas City. It began when Opperman went to Pennsylvania in 1970, where he raced against Kenny every week. Their rivalry literally lasted until the end of their careers.

They were complete opposites; Jan was the long-haired free-spirit, while Kenny was the button-down, no-nonsense type. They were both great racers, however, and when you have two big fish swimming in the same pond, there are bound to be problems.

I was right in the middle of some of that, because through the early 1970s Jan raced often in my car. Plus, I had known Kenny's dad, Pappy Weld, and many other family members for years. Our paths crossed constantly.

I can remember one incident very well. Jan and I had been racing somewhere in Ohio or Indiana on a Saturday night, and drove through the night headed for Topeka. Early that next morning we were driving through St. Louis, and we stopped at a Holiday Inn restaurant for breakfast. We were tired and worn out, eager for a break.

It just so happened that Kenny and three of his crew members had stopped at the same restaurant. Just as we walked in, our eyes met and Kenny saw Jan walking in with me. I could see that the waitress had just brought their food.

Kenny immediately stood up, said something to his guys, and left. He was so intense in his dislike for Jan, he wouldn't even be in the same restaurant with us!

They walked past us without saying a word. As they went through the door Jan and I kind of looked at each other and arched our eyebrows in amazement.

Jan kind of chuckled.

"You know, Bill, we're going to have to spend a little more time on our focus of beating those guys!"

But that's just the way Kenny was. He woke up in the morning and from that moment until the time he went to sleep that night, he was totally focused on beating Jan Opperman. Every time we ran against him, that was his call to duty. Kenny was probably as fierce a competitor as I've ever known in all these years.

I knew Pappy well, and I knew Kenny's oldest brother Jerry (they called him Butch). I also became very close with younger brother Greg Weld, but I didn't really get to know Kenny until long after his rivalry with Jan had faded.

The three Weld brothers were great racers, but very different personalities. *Very* different.

All were intense, but Greg learned to channel that intensity better than the other two. Butch, for example, was about as rough-and-tumble as they come, and was absolutely fearless. In fact, Butch met an early end when he was chasing a guy from a tavern with a pool cue, and they ran out into the street and Butch was struck and killed by a car.

In the late 1970s Kenny's driving career began to wane, and he was kind of lost. He began to transition to building cars, and his creative genius really showed. He and Don Brown developed a modified that absolutely destroyed the competition at Syracuse in 1980, a car known as the "Lincoln Continental." This car was so far ahead of everybody else it was amazing.

That's about the time I got to know Kenny a little better. By then Jan wasn't racing for me any longer, so I guess Kenny figured it was okay to talk to me again!

Kenny took a couple of wrong turns and was eventually arrested for dealing narcotics in the early 1980s, and went to Federal prison. When he was released a few years later he started a company that did CNC machining of cylinder heads, and did very well. Unfortunately he was diagnosed with non-Hodgkin's lymphoma and died in 1997.

A lot of people have asked me over the years if Kenny's stint in prison changed him as a person. I suppose in many ways it did change him, but it didn't change who he was. He was still very competitive, and he just put his focus in a different direction.

I see that a lot. It's just like the monkey they tried to raise as a human; he's not a human, he's a monkey. So he still acts like a monkey. You can put him in confinement, you can spank him, you can do whatever you want to do, but you never really change him. Those traits, those gifts, everything that makes you what you are, they're still there and they don't go away.

When Kenny changed his focus to his new idea of using a computerized CNC machine, he was as creative as anybody who had come down the pike. And as bulldog-tough as ever. The idea of using a computer to port cylinder heads, however, wasn't Kenny's original idea. I had some good customers in Germany two or three years prior who ran the Porsche racing team, and I supplied them with spring raters and other tools not available from anybody else. I had quite a few interesting conversations with those guys, and they told me about CNC porting their heads quite some time before Kenny started his business.

And I say this not to take away from Kenny's accomplishment, in any way. Who cares if it was his original idea or not? He still managed to successfully get the concept into business practice, which is damned difficult. Ideas are easy. Making them work commercially is the challenge. And you have to give Kenny complete credit for creating the business, and making it so successful. Plus, you have to give his wife and daughter credit as well, because after Kenny's passing they kept the business viable and it's still going to this day.

September 11, 1976. I know that date by heart, and I still get a cold chill and an empty feeling in my gut when I think about it.

I'm not a Bible thumper, but I do go to church. I graduated from a Methodist college, and I was exposed all my life to church thinking and ideas, but I've always thought you have to make out of life what you can, and not just wait on some other force to make it for you.

However, I do believe there is something that puts you where you are supposed to be at a certain time, with no explanation. That's what I'll always believe when it comes to thinking about Jan Opperman, and the day the magic was all taken away.

After Jan and I won the big sprint car race at Terre Haute in May 1976, he went on later that month to drive in the Indianapolis 500. After that he bummed around Indy for a while, ran my sprint car a couple of times, and was also racing for Bobby Hillin.

Hillin had a USAC Champ Dirt car with a new engine built by Donnie Ray Everett. The car itself was an antique, probably as antique as any car on the race track at that time, a spring-front Champ Dirt car. But the engine was very strong; they were using slide-port injectors, which had previously been used on the big V8 engines in Formula 5000 racing. It was a neat piece that used roller bearings, and was really slick. Boy, did those injectors wake up that little 302-inch small block Chevy engine!

I was working back here in Lincoln, running my business and racing my car locally with Lloyd Beckman. Jan and I stayed in touch, but we were both kind of doing our own thing. September rolled around, and our racing season began to taper off. On the Thursday before the Hoosier Hundred at Indy, Jan called me.

"Why don't you come back and watch me run the Hoosier Hundred?" he said. All of a sudden that sounded like a great idea; my friend Roger Beck had built a new Champ Dirt car for Bubby Jones to drive at the Hoosier Hundred, and in addition to visiting with Jan I could see how Roger and Bubby did with their new car, too.

These were the days when you could lay your money down and buy an airline ticket just like a bus ticket, without all the massive charges and fees. So I drove to the airport, bought a ticket and headed for Indianapolis.

Bubby and I were staying at the same hotel, the Holiday Inn near the airport. On race day I made my way to the Indiana State Fairgrounds, where they would race the Hoosier Hundred on the mile oval.

I was there as a spectator, more to watch Bubby run Roger's car than anything. Roger and I were great friends, going back to when he built a car for Jan to run when I first hired him in 1969.

I had raced at the Hoosier Hundred in the past with Larry Dickson and Don Nordhorn, so I knew it was a great event, and I liked the way Tony Hulman took care of the politicians. Many high-ranking statesmen were on hand at this race. Plus all the big racing studs of the day were there: A.J. Foyt, Jim Hurtubise, Little Joe Saldana, Jim McElreath; it was a stout field.

In a way, I was out of my element that day. I had no race car to take care of, so it was a leisurely time. When I raced I never wandered around much, or went very far from my pit area. But with no car to take care of, I kind of puttered around, talked with people and watched the racing.

The cars pitted just inside the front straightaway, and when they rolled out for the feature race I decided to walk down into turn three to watch. I just picked a spot and stood by myself.

Johnny Parsons was in the lead from the start, and pretty soon Jan was right on his back bumper, with Bubby close behind. They ran like that for a while, but around lap 50 Parsons got over the cushion and bobbled, in full view of where I was standing.

Jan was close enough behind that he couldn't avoid him, and he ran over Parson's left front wheel and flipped, out of my sight. The car lay on its side, with Jan's roll cage pointed toward the fence. Bubby slid into Parsons, flattening his headers and knocking the front end out of Bubby's car.

Jan was starting to unhook his belts. Bubby yelled to him, "Are you okay?"

Jan answered, "Yes!"

A bunch of cars behind them all managed to miss them under the yellow, but one car was on the outside and he hit Jan dead square. Apparently Jan's head was struck by the left-front wheel.

I hurried over, and they took Jan out of his car. I climbed into the ambulance with him, and we rushed to Methodist Hospital. On the way, the medical attendant pronounced Jan dead.

But once we got there, they detected a pulse and whisked Jan away. Bubby was all torn up emotionally, and he changed his clothes and came to the hospital right away. We found Jan in a room with his uniform cut off, lying on a gurney, and he looked like a dead man. But the doctors told us, "No, he's not dead." But he was sure solid quiet.

We stayed at the hospital through the night, Bubby and I, and around midnight we went down to the chapel to say a little prayer for Jan.

Eventually, he survived.

But I'll always be amazed at how ironic it was that I would be there when all that happened, with no real *reason* to be there. Just fate, I guess, or whatever else you want to call it.

Even today, I get chills when I think about that day. Everything was so unusual, and out of character, it just makes me wonder why I was there.

Jan spent much of the next year trying to recover from the crash. He had suffered a very serious blow to the head, and the injury was extensive.

His mother and dad, Mops and Griz, were living in Jan's home in Beaver Crossing, Neb., just 40 miles from my office. The entire family often lived together, kind of like hill people. With a lot of love and attention from his parents and many friends, Jan was beginning to get better.

Mops came by my office to talk to me, asking me how he could possibly make a living going forward.

"What should Jan do?" she asked. Keep in mind, this was a man who had never filed income taxes, never paid Social Security, never had any kind of skill or trade other than driving a race car.

"Well, he could sell a monkey a new tail, so he could easily become a salesman," I told her. And he could've: I could envision him selling something in the racing industry, because with his charisma and all the people who knew him, I believed he could be very successful.

But that wouldn't have been the revenue stream like racing had been. So, as he got better, they decided Jan could go back to racing.

The only problem was, the crash had taken the God-given talent from Jan. No doubt about it.

Think about this: For eight years I knew that guy as well as if he were my brother, traveling and racing together and becoming very close. Yet, after the accident he didn't know my name. We had traveled 50,000 miles a year together, yet he couldn't remember me. And it wasn't just me; he couldn't remember lots of names and faces. He covered it up very well, and called me "pal" or "buddy," but not Bill.

He had been a phenomenon far beyond just being a great racing driver, but so much of it had been taken away with that blow to the head.

The following year I had taken my turbo-Offy out of my Champ car, replacing it with a Chevy engine. I hadn't raced it much that year, and late in the fall Jan called me on the phone.

"I've got a deal with Goodyear where they'll buy my tires," he said, all excited. "Would you bring your car to Syracuse and let me run it?"

"You bet I will," I said.

Syracuse, N.Y., is about a two-and-a-half day tow from Lincoln, and away we went. We got the car to the track on race day, and pretty soon Jan arrived as well. They were ready to begin the program, and Jan got his suit on and prepared for hot laps. Then he inexplicably walked to the wrong car and climbed in.

He laughed it off, saying he was playing a joke on us. So I got him in my car, and was leaning in the cockpit to help him adjust the belts and get comfortable. As I'm leaning in close I looked into his eyes, and it was as if I had looked into a long black tunnel. There was nobody home.

A cold shiver went down my back, and I instantly thought, "If I let this guy drive my car, he'll get killed, and guess who will be the bad guy?"

I didn't care what anybody else thought; but I sure knew how I would feel about it. I couldn't lay my head down on the pillow if that happened, not ever again. How would you live with yourself?

And, as fate or whatever would have it, we suddenly got a rainstorm and they called the race. Thank God!

I loaded the car, and began the long drive back to Lincoln. We were planning on running the sprint car at the Western World Championship in Phoenix that following weekend with Shane Carson, and I told Jan I didn't think they'd reschedule Syracuse, so he never did drive for me again.

Jan put a deal together with some doctor in Florida to buy my Champ Dirt car, and Jan came to Lincoln and picked it up that next spring. He arrived on a Thursday afternoon, and they took it and ran Springfield, Ill., a couple of days later. That car was about as ready to race as my passenger car; absolutely no preparation.

I didn't have much interaction with Jan after that; he wandered back to Pennsylvania and began racing sprint cars again, but not with any real success.

In June 1981 I got a call from Don Maxwell with some very bad news. Jan had been in a bad accident at a URC race in Jennerstown, Pa., and suffered another serious head injury.

When I heard this, I knew Jan's situation was very bad. There is something about the brain that makes a second injury particularly damaging. Only a brain specialist could explain this properly, but it's like your brain says after the first incident, "That was kind of mean, so don't do it again." They don't want to be hurt twice. If you do, it's often really bad.

The second time for Jan was the end. He was a complete vegetable, requiring around-the-clock care.

Even when Jan was at the peak of his winning power, he and his family never had any money to speak of. So with Jan's earning power now completely gone, they were in a world of financial hurt. The racing community rallied to try and help them, and it did make a difference in Jan's living conditions.

Dick Berggren helped raise money through *Open Wheel Magazine* to allow the Opperman family to move to Florida, where Jan could swim in a pool for physical therapy. Don Maxwell and I put together a van with a wheelchair lift and gave it to the family.

Before they relocated, Mops had him in California for a while, and on one of my trips out there I called to see if I could visit. I was only about a hundred miles from where they were living, and I really wanted to see Jan.

"Don't come over," Mops urged me. "He doesn't know me, and he won't know you. When he sees somebody new it gets him over-stimulated, like a cornered animal." She explained that after a visit he would get mean and angry, because he couldn't figure out what was going on. It was very frustrating to him, and tough for his family because it often took an entire day to get him settled back down.

"If you come over," she explained, "tomorrow he'll say, 'Bill was here!' And he'll remember for a little while tomorrow, and that's it."

So I stayed away. I didn't want to make more hardship for Mops and Griz, just to satisfy my desire of visiting with Jan.

Jan never really improved, and his loyal parents stuck with him and tried to make his life as good as they could, all the way to the end. In 1997 Jan died quietly at his home in Florida, his parents by his side.

I was in Boone, Iowa, at the time for the IMCA Super Nationals when I got the news. Even though his passing was a blessing, I couldn't help but feel a great sadness at the loss of a special friend.

There was nobody quite like Jan Opperman. Nobody.

19

High-Maintenance Friends

At the time of Jan Opperman's devastating crash in 1976, I was heavily involved with Don Maxwell, building sprint cars out of my Lincoln shop. Don was a brilliant fabricator, and would ultimately become a lifelong friend, but boy, was he high maintenance!

Don was from Albuquerque, where he spent some time working for Al Unser. Don was originally a race driver, and like so many drivers seeking to expand their careers, pulled up stakes and relocated to the Midwest. He and his wife Sandy drove up to Lincoln, because by the 1960s and '70s this area was hot with racing. We ran three, four, five nights a week, at places like Lincoln, Knoxville, Topeka, and a number of other great tracks in this area. If you wanted to improve, you came where the racing was.

Don's real skill was not in driving, but in creating things with his hands. He truly had a gift in that regard. He went to work for LaVern Nance for a short while in Wichita, and crossed paths with my friend Jelly (Warren Wilhelm). Jelly built my USAC Champ Dirt car with a turbocharged Offy built by Carl Cindric.

Jelly told Don he ought to come to Lincoln to see if he could get a job with me, and the next thing you know I hired Maxwell and we had big plans of building race cars together.

I've brought many talented people to Lincoln in the course of my life, and many have fit in very nicely. Randy Hunt, for example, is a very creative guy who came here from the California Bay area with Jan Opperman, and today he builds many of our racing seats at Speedway Motors. Randy still has that artistic, creative edge, and sometimes you have to remember that people who are creative aren't like the rest of the world. They have special talents, and special needs. As a manager you have to recognize that. They never reform; till the day they die, they are what they are. So forget trying to change them.

That said, I can honestly say this: Don Maxwell was unmanageable. From the very start, it was a problem. I explained to him that we come to work at 9 a.m. and we go home at 6 p.m.; he'd show up at 11 a.m. and work until midnight. Our staff would see Don shuffling in at 11 a.m. and they'd raise hell. If he gets to come in at 11 a.m., why can't they?

It was kind of like teaching school; if you have a class of 20 kids, and you let one get by with everything, guess what? They all want to get by with it, too. I put up with Maxwell's schedule for quite a while, and talked to him many times about the issue. He'd listen, and nod his head and agree to work on his punctuality, and then show up the next day at 11 a.m. sharp.

When Maxwell and I got started, there weren't many players out there building sprint cars, certainly nothing like today. There was Don Edmunds and CAE, building cars on the West Coast, and I had bought and sold cars from both. I was nearly always competing on the race track against the cars I sold.

Finally I decided to build my own cars, and that's where Don Maxwell came in. We had purchased a car from Roger Beck when Opperman and I got together in 1969, because that's the car Jan wanted. Roger built a great car; a spring-front cross-torsion rear, and his work was top-notch. He made his own halves of the fuel tank, and there were damned few fabricators at that time with the ability to do aluminum noses and cowlings as nicely as Roger. Later on we duplicated many of his ideas in fiberglass. Eventually we built another car similar to Roger's, incorporating some changes we wanted.

When Maxwell came along we cleared out some space behind our fiberglass shop and set him up to build cars. We weren't looking to "mass produce" cars in the pure sense of the word, but we did want to build a certain quantity.

Don loved tools, and we were all the time going to auction sales to buy mills and drill presses and everything you needed to build race cars. I didn't mind, because I like tools, too.

Don was a really smart guy. His mother was a schoolteacher, so I think he was exposed to lots of good things as a kid, and he was blessed with a brilliant mind. As a fabricator and a designer, he was spectacular. He would often get off on some crazy zigzag project, because he was artistic. Artistic people, the Don Maxwell characters of the world, have a very high IQ and a rare creative talent, and they're typically horribly hard to manage. And horribly hard to fit into any kind of an organized network or structured system that works.

That said, I recognized his talent. Don Maxwell was obviously a talented man, and talent is hard to find.

However, the most significant issue with Don is that he took a *long* time to build a race car. The design and workmanship of the product was excellent, almost to the point of perfection.

But in business you have to live with the realities of the marketplace. When somebody ordered a new car, they typically needed it right away. But Don might take two months to get it built, and that was a best-case scenario.

Somewhere along the mid to late 1970s, Gary Stanton got into the chassis business, and he did very, very well. In fact, in many ways Gary changed the complexion of the world of sprint car construction, because he developed a way to quickly build cars and pieces, providing customers with quick turnaround and a quality product.

Some years later Gary told me, "You know why I got into the chassis business? Because the cars you guys were building were perfect, but it took too long to get them."

Don approached each car as a work of art, and not as a commercial product. It had to be perfect. Perfect is good in art, but in business you have to work on a reasonable timeframe in response to your customer's needs. And we weren't fulfilling the customer's needs in that regard. We were creating works of art, and the customer didn't want art. They wanted a solid race car that worked nicely on the track, and they wanted it delivered within a reasonable timeframe.

Stanton saw this and addressed it accordingly, and I give him all the credit in the world.

This sort of thing was ultimately a challenge for Don. He later moved into several different business ventures, but none were really successful. For all his brilliance in terms of design and fabrication, he struggled with business issues. He held a bunch of patents—more than anyone I've ever known—but he didn't score commercially on any of them.

In the workplace at Speedway Motors, Don's free-spirit schedule got to be too much of a problem. My guys in the fiberglass plant were constantly on my ass that it wasn't fair that they had to come to work at 9 a.m., and Maxwell didn't.

Eventually, after lots and lots of conversations about his work schedule, Don made a suggestion. I had purchased the building across the street from our fiberglass plant, and there was some space available in the front half of the building. Don suggested I rent him that space, and he would go into business for himself and would build me what I needed.

"Okay, we'll do it that way," I said. By then I realized I couldn't control him and his work habits. Although we redefined our business relationship, Don and I never did "part ways." We stayed connected in many capacities for the rest of his life.

For the next 25 years there probably wasn't a two- or three-week stretch where my phone didn't ring at two or three in the morning, and Don wanted to talk about something for a couple of hours.

Did I mind him calling me in the middle of the night? It didn't matter, not when you're friends with a free spirited genius. He was like so many people who have come through my doors down through the years. They don't fit the mold like average people. They don't dance to the same drummer. They don't conform, they won't fall into line. They are truly different.

Through the years Don approached me with this idea, that idea, on his new business venture. Even though I knew it was unlikely I'd ever see the money again, I'd usually ante up and help him get going. Why? Because I cared a lot for Don, and I wanted to help him.

Sometimes people look at gifted people with respect, but other times it's more like jealousy. I don't think Don was recognized properly for his amazing ability to build and create. It's like seeing somebody do something so easily; you sometimes take it for granted that it isn't all that difficult. Kind of like Tiger Woods, making a million dollars on a nice Sunday afternoon. We've all tried to swing the golf club that same way, but somehow it doesn't work like that for us. It isn't as easy as it looks.

In his later years, Don designed and built portable stages and sets for country stars in Nashville. These sets were amazing, and could be quickly assembled and disassembled for these acts when they traveled on the road. One night he called and asked us to come see a "masterpiece" before it was shipped out. It was a work of a genius, I'm not kidding.

One of the challenges for people like Don is that they make things look easy. He was so brilliant, and so creative, people took him for granted. They didn't see the dedication, the effort, the incredible number of hours spent at his trade.

When Don died of cancer on July 8, 2006, he was still my friend. All the way to the end. He was a guy who lived life on his terms, and I sure admire that.

You know, as I'm sitting here thinking about Don Maxwell, I couldn't help but think about another brilliant free spirit whose friendship I enjoyed, Don Brown. Another great friend who was high maintenance!

Brown was originally from the West Coast, and he was also a driver who had some ambitions to get to the top of the ladder. He had a shop in California, and was a key player in the development of a power steering unit for race cars. Somebody had hired Brown to drive a Championship car, which had an experimental power steering unit manufactured by Saginaw. The car owner was from back East, and he sent Brown and the car out on the road. They ran Phoenix, Sacramento, places like that.

Don took the car back to his shop in California, and he and a fellow named Tommy Lee were intrigued by that power steering unit. They took it apart and started looking it over, and discovered that it was actually very straightforward, and used basic Saginaw parts. From that point Tommy began building power steering pumps for racing, and the advent of power steering extended the career for an untold number of race drivers.

Brown was eventually drawn to Lincoln by the racing action here, and he started hanging around Joe Saldana's place. Joe, like all great racers, was very hospitable. He'd welcome people, offer to help them, take them pheasant hunting. Joe took Brown under his wing, and Don ended up sticking around.

Pretty soon Brown built the dumbest-looking supermodified I had ever seen. It had a door in which you'd get in and out of! The car didn't work worth a damn, by the way.

Then came the day in 1967 when I fired Lloyd Beckman at Belleville for mistaking the white flag for the yellow and slowing down, costing us the race. I needed a driver the next day to run the state fair race here in Lincoln, and I put Brown in my offset roadster, a square-tube car I had built.

Brown ran real well, and although he didn't win, he climbed from that car with the biggest grin you could imagine, proclaiming, "That's the best-handling race car I've ever driven on dirt!"

Don went to work building an offset roadster for himself, and ultimately built three. They had great success, with drivers such as Greg Weld and Joe Saldana winning many races over the next couple of years. These cars were known as the "mechanical rabbits" and were arguably the most innovative sprint cars during that period.

Incidentally, at that time we were falsifying the roadster as a sprint car, even though it was technically not a sprint car. Remember what I said earlier about all these associations that tried to keep sprint cars and supermodifieds from mixing? IMCA and BCRA, and many others, had very strict rules about that sort of thing.

It was all about trying to hold their core groups in place. If somebody came in from outside and won the money, it was bad for their business. So they dreamed up all these bullshit rules such as requiring outsiders to provide Magnaflux papers for the entire front end: spindles, axles, steering gear, all those things.

Which was impossible! There were only two Magnaflux stations in the entire country; one was in Indy, and the other was in Kansas City at Greg Weld's shop. So I just had Greg falsify the papers for me.

Simple enough; throw your bullshit rules at me, and I'll jump through the hoops. No problem.

The secret to those roadsters, I think, was the fact that they drove off the left rear much more than most sprint cars did at that time. It had a narrow rear end, and the driver sat to the left. The weight bias was very favorable, and the whole package was a hit.

Brown put Chevrolet spindles on the car, which was very unique at that time, because almost everybody was using the heavier International spindles. In those days if you lost a spindle you usually lost the car *and* the driver, but Don figured out how to make the Chevrolet spindles work and changed the way we looked at things.

Brown was a fabulous fabricator and craftsman, particularly when it came to building bodies and other sheet metal components.

(Incidentally, when Don came to Lincoln he brought Carl Cindric with him, and Carl married a local girl, Janice, and settled here. Sometime later, championship mechanic Judd Phillips hired Carl, and Carl and family moved to Indianapolis. Carl was then instrumental in developing the Cosworth Indy engine. He later went on to develop the Judd Indy engine. Always an engine man, Carl is known and respected to this day.

Today his son Tim is the heir apparent at Penske Racing. In fact, Tim's mother Janice still lives here in Lincoln.)

Brown eventually moved to Indianapolis and curtailed his driving to focus on his mechanical work. He ultimately gained quite a reputation as a guy who could not only fabricate, but his repair work was amazing.

He had the most God-awful work hours you'd ever see. Brown would literally work through the night, going to bed at daylight. After a few hours sleep he'd be back at it in the afternoon, working until the following morning. The ultimate night owl.

Pretty soon he was known as the "Prince of Darkness." What a perfect nickname! You'd drop off a wrecked race car in the evening, and by morning it would be repaired. It was as though he couldn't venture out into the light; like some kind of Dracula or something. But boy, did he do great work.

He did a lot of work for me when he was in Lincoln, and I hated to see him move to Indianapolis. It was one of the reasons I kind of resented the Indianapolis Motor Speedway. I can't begin to count the skilled guys who would leave to go to Indianapolis, because the money was good there.

While I'm on the topic of some of the interesting characters that enhanced my life, I'd be remiss if I didn't tell some tales on Pete Leikam. Pete came into my life in the late '40s when I was looking for a local body shop to paint my jalopy. Naturally, economics figured into things; I needed the lowest price and Pete came through.

"Pete's Body Shop" became a key part of my education of the ways of the world, even before Speedway Motors had been thought of. Pete helped me paint cars for some 30 years, maybe more. Race car parts, hot rods, race cars, or used cars…whatever the topic, we became very close friends.

Pete was about 15 years older than I was, so I looked up to him. He was a tough, tough guy and he knew the body shop business. His wife Leona worked with him through all of his endeavors…body shop, promoting Midwest Speedway, and all of his later ventures. She was a real task master and stood by him in many difficult situations.

During my serious health problems in the 1950s, I needed a unit of blood each week. There was no blood bank at the time, so we had to pay for every unit. Pete got all the boys from his body shop to donate blood, which was a wonderful gesture and a financial godsend for Joyce and I.

Those body shop guys were a rough and tumble, hard-drinking bunch, and they really came through for me. I often wondered, though…does all the alcohol in a guy's bloodstream transfer with the blood he donates?

By the late '50s, Pete decided he wanted to get his pilot's license. He bought a "Stinson Station Wagon," which was a high-wing, fabric-covered airplane with a top speed of 75 to 80 mph. That wasn't fast enough for Pete, so he soon traded up for a Cessna 182, which would cruise at 130 mph.

Pete and I spent hundreds of hours together in that airplane. We flew all over the country…through northern snow storms all the way south to Daytona. In 1959 Joyce and I joined Pete and Leona as we flew to Daytona for the grand opening of the Daytona Intl. Speedway.

Boy, the adventures we had in that plane.

Pete and I flew to I-70 Speedway, just east of Kansas City, Mo., and landed on a grass airstrip at dusk just in time to watch the races. Things finished up around midnight, so Pete and I took off in complete darkness. I was tired, sitting in the co-pilot seat, and I quickly dozed off. A few minutes later Pete woke me up and pointed toward some lights on the ground.

"Is that St. Joe, or Springfield? I think we got off the runway in the wrong direction."

I hadn't been asleep very long, but I sure as hell had no idea where we were. Which wasn't a problem, except that neither did Pete.

Some time later we spotted an airfield and headed down. We made a nice landing and taxied toward the hangars, when all of a sudden a bunch of floodlights came on, with alarms going off.

A big loudspeaker started blaring, "What in the hell are you doing here? This is the U.S. Air Force base in Topeka, Kansas! Get out of here immediately!"

Which wasn't all bad, because now we knew exactly where we were. Pete quickly turned around and we took off, now going in the right direction toward Lincoln.

On another occasion Pete and I, along with Lloyd Beckman and my dad, flew to Des Moines for the Iowa State Fair races. After the races had finished we piled back into the plane, but as we took off I saw something fall off. We figured we had lost a wheel on our landing gear, so Pete got on the radio to tell the Lincoln airport that we'd be one-wheel on our landing. When we arrived at the airport the rescue squad was in place—complete with fire trucks and emergency vehicles—prepared for a crash landing. As it turns out it was only the hub cab that I saw fall off, not the wheel itself.

Our best flying adventure came in the mid-1960s.

The famous Buzz Gregory—who would later win the Little 500—came from California to Lincoln and ended up working at Speedway Motors. Buzz spent the winter living with us in Lincoln, and in the spring it was decided that Buzz should return to California because his hope of driving the Speedway Motors race car probably wasn't going to work out.

Pete and I decided to fly to Phoenix to watch the USAC championship cars race. A friend and former driver of mine, Dick Bloom, decided to tag along. We figured we'd take Buzz with us, getting him going toward California.

Pete had his pilot's license, but no instrument rating. His small plane required refueling quite often, and many times we had "experiences" because Pete had trouble reading the fuel gauge.

We were well on our way to Phoenix, flying over Lake Powell, which is located along the Arizona-Utah border. Suddenly the engine went "Sput!" Pete quietly looked at us and said, "We're almost out of gas." Down we go to find a place to land, and quickly. We spotted a sand beach, and as luck would have it the Army had been using the area for training maneuvers with amphibious "ducks" and had put down mesh webbing on the beach.

Many fishermen and their families were on the beach, and as we came down they thought we were buzzing them, so they just waved. But we were out of gas! Pete got us down okay, and we determined that the nearest gas station was 15 miles down the road. One of the fishermen offered to drive to the gas station and bring back some fuel.

After we had refueled, we were ready to take off. However, with four people in the plane and a good bit of fuel on, the beach runway was too short. We pushed the plane to the very end of the beach, and Pete opened the throttle as we all held on to the elevator, letting the engine build plenty of power. He went roaring off, barely clearing the treetops at the other end.

The fisherman quickly followed him by visual reckoning, with all of us hanging on for dear life in the bed of his truck. Pete flew about 15 miles to a straight paved highway, and sat the plane down there. We climbed back aboard, and went on to Phoenix. I've often wondered what that fisherman told his grandchildren!

We watched A.J. Foyt win at Phoenix, then turned Buzz over to A.J.'s wife and after a couple of days of racing it was time to head home. Except that Dick Bloom had had so much fun on the way down, he decided to fly commercial back to Lincoln. On the way home we encountered a big snowstorm, and had to do some tricky "flying around."

Dick and I relive that trip each winter when we see each other at the Chili Bowl in Tulsa. I think we're both happy to still be around to tell the tale!

I mentioned earlier how racing was changing in the 1970s, and one element that was different was the introduction of corporate sponsorship in short-track racing. When that happened, it ultimately changed the entire game.

Auto racing had always had the element of sponsorship, of course, but things changed dramatically in 1971 when Winston signed on as the sponsor of the NASCAR Grand National series, and it became Winston Cup.

Winston spent a lot of money on the sport, and it filtered down to grass roots racing as well. NASCAR got involved at I-70 Speedway, and Winston put up a big billboard on the freeway and so forth.

That's when I met Jim Hunter, who today remains as a very influential guy at NASCAR. Jim is a really smart guy, and knows a great deal about racing. I used to go down to Florida a day or two before the trade show and the Daytona 500, and Jim would invite me to the NASCAR corporate offices at the Daytona Intl. Speedway.

Jim was heavily involved in grass roots racing for NASCAR, and he was responsible for their involvement in our region. Those guys would pick my brain for a couple of days on what was happening in the Heartland. They were looking for my perspective because I was selling a lot of racing parts in my region, probably the majority of the parts sold in this part of the country. Plus I was very active in racing, campaigning a car locally and one on the road.

With Opperman's big crash in late '76, I was back to looking for another driver. I spent 1977 with a variety of guys in the seat, and still did okay. However, I was on the brink of hiring another truly great racer, a guy who would ultimately land in the Hall of Fame.

His name was Doug Wolfgang, and if you'd have seen him in the beginning you'd have never dreamed this guy would go on to become one of the greatest sprint car drivers of all time.

But history was on his side: My racing life was still full-bore, right in the midst of great change in the sport.

Was it fun? Boy, it was stressful, and it was a lot of work. But we won a lot, and I guess that made it fun. 1978 was going to be a raucous, rock-and-roll year for sprint car racing, and we were right at the forefront. Just like driving a race car: Get in, shut up, and hold 'er wide open.

20

Wolfgang and Knoxville

One of the great racing events that eluded me for many years was the Knoxville Nationals. That's the Indy 500 for sprint car racing, and for nearly 20 years I took my best stuff there, hired the best driver, and still didn't win. I could almost write a book from all the "shoulda-woulda-coulda" stories from the Nationals.

In the 1960s I went there with Lloyd Beckman several times, and had some good finishes. But we didn't win.

In 1969 Jan Opperman and I were having a great year, and when we went to Knoxville in August I felt like we had everybody covered. And we did, too, until luck intervened. Luck, as in *bad* luck. Opperman had been sleeping outside on the ground that weekend in his hippie style, and on race day woke up with a stuffy nose. That night during the race his congestion caused snot to get all over his goggles, and he had to slow down while leading because he couldn't see. With just three laps to go Kenny Gritz got by us, and we finished second. We should have won the race easily.

In 1974 Opperman led 29 laps of the 30-lap race, and I was standing in the infield, watching him all the way. In the very last corner Dick Gaines got past, but Opperman was still ahead by a nose at the flag stand, and I thought we won it. But they quickly informed me that the actual finish line wasn't the flag stand, but was well down the track past the flag stand. If I close my eyes I can still see Gaines pull alongside in the final corner of the race. Nobody knew the actual location of the finish line; they said I was beaten by six inches, the width of our front tire. Boy, that was devastating!

But the Nationals couldn't deny me forever. I would finally win it in 1978, when I teamed up with a quiet, talented driver from South Dakota named Doug Wolfgang. Of all my 87 or so drivers, I had a warm and close relationship with Doug, a relationship that continues to this day. Not just because we won a lot or races together, either. It was because we clicked. We both greatly respected each other's talent. In fact, I refer to Doug as my "fifth son."

It wasn't something immediate, however. Because when I first met Doug, I still had Opperman in my car, and we were one badass team, the best in the country. Not bragging; just stating the facts of life according to Speedy Bill.

When Don Maxwell was building cars in my building at 1719 N Street in Lincoln, Doug was a struggling racer trying desperately to break into the sport. He had won a lot of modified races in South Dakota, and his ambition led him to hire on with Don as a very talented welder.

There were many out-of-state racers hanging around Lincoln during that period. We had a lot of racing around here, so it made sense for Doug and his wife Geri to put down temporary roots here in town, at least during the racing season.

You generally didn't notice somebody unless he was good. In Doug's case, in his early days he was not particularly good. And he will be the first to admit that: I'm not telling stories out of school. But through tenacity and sheer desire, and putting 150-percent effort toward everything he did, he got to the top. That's what you have to do, in my experience, to truly excel. God-given talent will only get you so far, and what do you do if you don't have God-given talent? You have to work for it.

When Doug worked for Maxwell, sometimes around noon he'd come from the chassis shop to my office to visit. We hardly knew each other, and Doug is actually kind of a shy guy, but he worked through his shyness because he really wanted to drive my race car.

Doug would come into my office, and give me that grin of his, and say something like, "You ought to hire me to run your car!"

Now, think about it: At the time I had Jan Opperman, the best sprint car driver in the nation. No, the best in the *world*. And I'm gonna fire Jan to put an unknown kid from South Dakota in my car?

But you had to love Doug's tenacity. I'd just smile at him and say, "Maybe you ought to get a little experience first." I had watched Doug race a couple of times, and he was basically not what I thought a race driver was.

Then again, I've told a lot of drivers this, that they weren't exactly what I perceived a good race driver should be. One was Eddie Leavitt; he ran good for me one night at Knoxville, and thought sure he'd get to drive my car the next night at Lincoln.

"Well, maybe someday when you get better than you are now," I told him. Boy, that lit a fire in Eddie's ass. He used that against me every time he won at Knoxville or Manzanita or any of the big tracks. Any time he won, the first guy he looked up was me.

"Do you think I'm good enough now, Speedy?"

He did indeed drive for me many times later on. But he never forgot what I told him that night, and I know for a fact that it motivated him.

But that's all right. When somebody doesn't give you the respect you feel you deserve, it's perfectly all right to get fired up about it, and I'm not just talking race drivers. I don't care what kind of work you do; it's all right to let adversity motivate you, and drive you to work harder and never give up. Eddie had something to prove, and it probably made him a better race driver.

Early in 1976 Doug got a call from Bob Trostle, who wanted to hire him both as a welder in his shop in Des Moines, but also to drive his race car. So Doug and Geri and their two young girls left Lincoln and moved to Des Moines, and pretty soon he and Trostle were winning races.

They had a good season in 1976, and were even better the following year when they won a bunch of races. However, the way I perceive it was they cherry-picked their races, and went where there wasn't a lot of competition. And Doug tore up a lot of stuff that year. If he would have been driving for me at that point, he would have been out of the car. But he learned a lot of things while driving for Bob.

I watched Doug run Knoxville, and he scared me to death. And he wasn't even in my car! He got to the point where he could run a car with a torsion bar that was slightly smaller than almost anybody, because it allowed him to feel the traction his car was gaining, feel it in the seat of his pants and in his foot. Knoxville is typically a heavy track, and when he'd come off the corner, the car would take a set and he'd guide it with his foot, driving the car off the right rear. When he'd decelerate for the next corner, it would take a big turn to the left, and then go to the right. That scared me to death. He'd come off the corner all hooked up, then let up and veer toward the infield, wide open.

Well, sure, he and Bob cherry-picked some of those wins. And sure, Doug tore up a lot of cars. And sure, at times he scared me. But I was intrigued; there was something about him that really got me going, and I worked hard to put a deal together to hire him for 1978.

And I don't just mean hire him to drive my sprint car. It was much more than that; I wanted to help him get to the Indianapolis 500, which was his life ambition. I also wanted to help him get established in the sport, and build something solid for himself and Geri and their family.

I had gone through a number of drivers in 1977, and I wasn't satisfied with anybody in particular. In fairness to them, it's awfully hard to replace Jan Opperman. So it was a changing time for my race team, and I was eager to get back on track with a driver I could groom and develop to create something lasting.

I talked earlier about how sponsorship was changing NASCAR and Indy-car racing. However, it hadn't yet arrived in sprint car racing. But in early 1978 I was about to change that.

The Peterson family owned the Vise-Grip company, located in Dewitt, Neb. It was a very successful old-line manufacturing company, marketing a line of tools all over the world. I approached them with the idea of putting their name on my race car, and they were receptive.

I asked for $25,000 for the year, and told them I'd win the Knoxville Nationals and the World of Outlaws championship, and would generate as much publicity for them as possible. At the time they were purchasing advertising on the Johnny Carson television show, costing them something like $20,000 per night. I promised I'd get them as much publicity as their deal with Johnny Carson.

Now that's a tall order! However, in due course we did that, and I was very proud of that fact. Bragging about something is one thing; actually *doing* it is usually a whole other thing. In this case we actually did it.

I also did something very different with Doug, something very few people knew about. It was something I had never thought about with any other driver.

Ever since Jan's devastating crash in late '76, I had been more concerned than ever with the fear of somebody getting hurt in my car. I wanted to structure something that would help take care of Doug in case he got hurt and couldn't drive again.

Doug was an excellent craftsman in his own right, and he could build a very nice race car. By this time Don Maxwell was doing many other things, and he wasn't really building cars for me any longer. So Wolfgang and I put our heads together and hatched a plan to have Doug build our cars, and we created a company called Winners, Inc. as a "brand" on the car.

We planned on building a few cars, but mainly just for ourselves. However, if something happened and Doug couldn't race, he could take this chassis business and pursue it full-time, giving him some kind of a survival plan. It was something he could pursue the rest of his life if he wanted, but at least we'd have a plan.

Hey, sprint car racing was still plenty violent; it wasn't a sissy sport. We lost two guys in one accident at Knoxville in 1979, in fact. There were no wings on the cars most of the time, and these things were hazardous to your health, big time.

When I hired Doug, he wanted to be more involved in the construction of the cars and the running of the team. He had worked directly for Maxwell a couple of years earlier, but he felt there were some things he wanted to do differently.

1978 marked the very first season for the World of Outlaws. Boy, talk about a challenging schedule! We were traveling some really long distances, and there were times when we ran 40 races in 50-some days. It was an intense, frantic schedule.

The extended travel was a new experience for most teams. Even though my teams had followed IMCA and had logged a ton of road miles over the past 25-plus years, it was a little different for us, too. In the past you might be gone for several days at a time; now, people could be gone several weeks or even *months* at a time.

Naturally, that kind of travel was out of the question for me personally. Speedway Motors was in the midst of a major expansion during this period, and the demands on my time were great. But I still wanted to stay involved, and not just be a long-distance owner. I still wanted to be hands-on. Not only because I enjoyed it, but because I wanted to better control our destiny. I didn't want the team to get out of control.

228 / FAST COMPANY

We had Tommy Sanders as our traveling mechanic for a while, and later John Singer.

The road, boy, that was tough on relationships. On one occasion Doug and Tommy and their wives climbed into the truck here in Lincoln for an extended racing tour, and they were all happy-happy as they drove away, the best of friends. By the time they got back to Lincoln a month or two later, they were all so mad at each other that when they got out of the truck Doug and Tommy were actually in a fight.

I remember it vividly. It was a Saturday morning, and they pulled into the alley behind my fiberglass plant, where the racing shop was located. When they got out of the truck they were actually whaling on each other. Just too much togetherness.

That's what the road does to you, particularly when you add in the normal stress of racing. They got to the point where when they stopped at a restaurant, they would all sit in separate booths, trying to get some space. The guys usually had their wives with them, so you had four separate personalities in the mix.

Doug was always very dedicated to his craft, very dedicated to keeping himself in shape to be a racer. I never saw that kind of determination in anyone else.

He let nothing stand in his way when it came to his fitness regimen. I remember one terrible winter day in Lincoln when the whole town was snowed in, and none of my help made it to work because of the weather. I was sitting in the store by myself, and I looked up to see Doug running down the street in a path a truck had made. Extremely dedicated.

This was before anybody talked about fitness. Most racers were smokers and drinkers, there was no such thing as a physically fit race driver. That was an anomaly. Overweight, bad eating habits, smokers, just a mess. But not Doug. In the early days there was always this debate on whether a race driver was an athlete; well, let me tell you, Doug Wolfgang was an athlete.

I guess that's one of the things that made him so different. Racers were a free-spirited bunch, and you never knew what to expect. Many were so consumed with themselves, they weren't very trustworthy. Chasing women, partying, whatever, you really didn't know what to expect from racers.

With Doug, you didn't have to worry about any of that. He didn't run around with other women, and he and Geri were very close. He didn't party or drink, and he was impeccably honest with money.

And his work ethic was very strong. *Very* strong! He would do whatever it took to prepare the car, prepare the team, and prepare himself to win.

So when you send a guy like that out on the road with your race team, it's kind of a nice luxury that you don't have to worry about things being done properly.

In August of 1978 we had our first opportunity to deliver on our promise to the Vise-Grip people. The Knoxville Nationals were up, and I was on pins and needles once again, hoping like hell this was going to be the year we finally won it.

Wolfgang came into the event as the defending champion, because he had won it one year previous with Trostle, while my car finished third behind Doug and Lealand McSpadden. Bubby Jones was my driver that night in '77, and it was the only time Bubby had driven for me. My car lost a cylinder during the race, and we finished the race running on seven.   After the race, Bubby apologized for running third. I said, "Hell, it wasn't your fault, pal, it was mine…I didn't have the car hitting on all eight."

With such a big event, it's always a sick feeling when you fall short because it's another year before you get another chance.

Going into the '78 Nationals I felt like we had them covered. But then again, there had been plenty of times at Knoxville where I figured we had them covered, and we didn't win.

There is a picture of me before the race, leaning over the hood of my car with my hand on my chin. When I look at that picture, my confidence at that moment was visible.

I took my usual spot in the infield, watching as the race got started. As I look back now, it was almost anti-climactic, because we led every lap and won.

There was no lightning bolt of excitement that swept through me. We had led all the way, we were never threatened, or affected by the yellow or red flags that can throw you a curve. It was just one of those times when I figured we had it won almost from when we started. I was very confident.

We celebrated until three or four in the morning, of course. I had some of my pals in town, including Dick Martin from Portland, Ore. We celebrated and enjoyed the victory, but I don't remember the celebration being overly spectacular. Like I said, the whole thing seemed anti-climactic.

I didn't sit around and savor it for long, because Monday morning I was back at work. And the race team was back on the road, thinking about the next race. There wasn't much time for the celebration to linger.

It felt great to win it, yes; but at the same time, you don't really allow the highs to affect you, just like you don't let the lows get you down. When you're playing the game as hard as we were playing it, you don't really have those highs and lows, not like others might have. Ask Karl Kinser about dealing with the ups and downs; they don't mean a thing, it's almost just another day in the office.

And it wasn't like winning the Nationals brought a big windfall of money. When we won the race that year, we made $5,000. (Today the winner of the Nationals gets $150,000, by the way.) It was almost just another race in terms of money, but certainly not in prestige. No matter what it paid, it was still the one event everybody wanted to win.

Someone might suppose that because Doug won the Knoxville Nationals for me, that's why he and I had such a close friendship. The fact is, our friendship would have been the same whether he won Knoxville or not. Our friendship was based on lots of reasons, and not just winning a sprint car race.

For one thing, Doug is about the same age as my sons. I met him when he was a young man, and I've been associated with him through many different chapters and phases of his life and his career.

His success came fairly quickly, starting with Trostle, and he had a lot of things to keep in perspective. What's that old saying about nothing tests a man's mettle like success? Well, he had a lot of success to deal with, and a lot of adversity, and he never let it change who he was or what he was about.

It wasn't an easy road for Doug and his family. The man's dedication was amazing, both physically and mentally.

From the moment I hired him, we forged a relationship that was very personal. We'd have Doug and his family over to our house, and when he drove my car he and Geri moved to Lincoln. We became very close.

I took Doug to the SEMA show in Las Vegas to try and raise his visibility, try to help him get to Indianapolis. That never happened, but he had a great career anyway.

I really enjoyed his talent, especially during that 1978 season. We could go almost anywhere and have a good showing. I didn't worry about him cheating me on the gasoline for the tow rig, or in any other area. He was impeccably honest. I was, as a car owner, getting what I paid for: 100 percent effort, and 100 percent honesty. When you get what you pay for, you don't second-guess anything. You're happy.

He was much younger than me, and had grown up at a different time, but we got along nicely. When he'd win a big race, I was the first guy he'd call on the phone, even later when he wasn't driving my car. I'd ask him why he didn't call his dad.

"He wouldn't understand like you do," he told me. We shared a passion, and he was right, I *did* understand.

Maybe that's why Doug and I clicked so well. We were like-minded when it came to being competitive, and wanting so desperately to win.

I wish I could describe that feeling to you, but I can't. When you really, really want to win a race, and you fall short, it's a disappointment so intense you can't describe it. Sometimes you're so emotionally crushed you literally feel physical pain and sickness. You want to cry, you want to get angry and lash out, you want to go hide because you feel so disheartened.

I've seen Doug finish second in a big race, after a tremendous drive from the back of the field. It was sensational, truly above and beyond. By rights, a man should be proud of such a great showing. After the race, when Doug took off his helmet, people hurried over to shake his hand and congratulate him, heaping words of praise on him and his ability.

He was gracious and kind to them, but if you looked closely you could see a teardrop running down his cheek for an instant before he could brush it away. The man was so utterly disappointed that he didn't win, he was literally fighting back tears. A tough, grown man, reduced to tears over not winning a race.

If you've been there, you know.

He hated running second almost worse than death!

And that, friends, is how I always felt. When I drove race cars, when I owned race cars, in business, in anything I've ever done, I'm probably as competitive as anybody I've ever known. There is something about losing that affects me, just like it affected Doug.

Everything I ever did, from shooting marbles in the schoolyard to whatever, I wanted to win. I used to play a lot of poker and shoot a lot of craps, and one time I lost pretty big, almost lost a piece of property I'd put up for collateral in a high-stakes poker game. I ultimately didn't lose the property, but I lost enough that it hurt. Not just hurt my wallet, but hurt me personally, so I quit.

To me, to lose a contest is to lose face. To lose at anything is disastrous.

So much of this goes back to my childhood. When I went through my health ordeals and challenges, I wasn't able to participate in any kind of athletics. So I channeled my competitiveness to other things.

Winning on the race track, or winning in business, was a way for me to rise above the health difficulties of my life, and prove I could compete. For any competitive person, that's extremely important, to at least compete.

That's why I understood Doug perfectly when he nearly cried after finishing second. So many times in those situations, I wanted to cry, too.

Throughout 1978 Doug went up and down the highway with my race car, and it was a challenge. John Singer was traveling with him as a mechanic, and those two were constantly in the middle of a spat.

Doug would fire Singer, and Singer would fire Doug. They were bickering all the time. Singer built a nice new car, and Doug tipped it over at Kansas City and bent the cage maybe a quarter of an inch. Singer was livid, because he was such a perfectionist. He couldn't stand to see a driver bend his stuff, he was even more fierce about it than I was.

Part of the problem was too much togetherness, and not enough personal space as they traveled and worked together. But another issue was that Doug had decided he didn't like Singer. Frankly, along about that time I don't think Doug liked anyone. And again, I'm not telling tales out of school; Doug will admit that he was so intensely focused on winning races that he often overlooked his relationships with the people around him.

I remember traveling to Phoenix late in the season, and Doug picked me up at the airport.

"John got the car ready and I fired him yesterday," Doug told me. So I spent the next few hours smoothing things over, trying to keep these guys together to finish out the season. Once again, the leader of the band wasn't having much fun.

We were all pretty much worn out on each other by the end of the '78 season, so we decided to split up. No hard feelings;

fact is, Doug and I never had hard feelings for each other. We just all agreed to call it quits for a while.

We fell short on winning the World of Outlaws title, but by then I realized I didn't really want to pursue that much travel anyway.

For the '79 season Doug went back to Trostle, and I hired Shane Carson, who had driven for my rival Trostle the year before. It led to a funny season in which Trostle and I unofficially traded drivers several times. My stuff would get torn up and we'd park for a while, then regroup with Doug back in the car. Same with Shane and Trostle.

Eventually Doug moved on, and in 1980 I decided it was time to park the race cars and focus on Speedway Motors. But Doug and I stayed in close contact, and we maintain a great friendship even to this day.

In the mid-1980s Doug drove for Bob Weikert in Pennsylvania, and they had great success together. I remember them winning the Knoxville Nationals, and I happened to be standing next to John Singer as Doug and his crew were celebrating in victory lane.

John looked at me and smiled.

"We made a good race driver out of him, didn't we?" he said. We were both proud of Doug, and proud that we played a role in helping develop his career.

Boy, did Doug struggle to fit in with the fans in Pennsylvania! People today can't understand how hard he had to work to make all of that a success. He was living in a little farmhouse out there for a while, and I visited him. He and Geri and their two daughters (they later had two more children) had hardly a stick of furniture in the house, living like paupers. They weren't poor, of course, because they were winning a lot of races. But they sure didn't live luxuriously.

For some reason the fans there were tough on Wolfgang. His phone would ring late at night, and some "fan" would make death threats on Doug. I guess they felt he was an outsider, coming in and winning all the races. I know this was very hard on Doug emotionally, and he struggled to fit in there.

The dedication Doug put into his career...there are damned few people in this world willing to work that hard. It's amazing how hard he had to work, and it's hard to understand it if you haven't been there.

234 / FAST COMPANY

In 1992 Doug was involved in a terrible fire at Lakeside, Kan., and suffered catastrophic injuries. He ultimately sued the track and the World of Outlaws for inadequate safety precautions, and he won. His lawsuit brought a tremendous amount of resentment from some people in the sport, and some were good friends of mine.

It was a difficult situation. I didn't like arguing with my friends, but no way was I going to condemn Doug. Until you've walked in his shoes — and in this case, just about had your legs burned off — you don't know what you would do. You can *say* what you'd do, but you don't know. Until it's your skin they're peeling off in big strips while you lay there in agony, you don't know. You just don't.

I stood behind Doug all the way, and I still do. He's my friend. Period.

Geri was very supportive, and not just through the recovery from the fire. She was there from the very beginning, even though at the moment of the crash she was almost eight months pregnant. To her credit, she held everything together and later delivered their fourth child on the day Doug woke up from his coma. You can't overstate what a difficult time that must have been for the entire family, particularly Geri.

Doug wasn't a guy who would chase women or run around, but the whole thing of being a race driver's wife is very difficult. All those miles, watching your husband get beat up in the car now and then, it wasn't easy.

Geri kind of got to where she didn't like it, and I don't blame her. She'd come to an event and not even get out of the motor home to watch the race, because it was too hard to watch, too scary, too…just too much. Togetherness is great, but too much is too much.

When I got the call that day in 1992 telling me of Doug's accident, it was a sick feeling. That was the one thing I had always feared, through all my years as a car owner. I feared somebody getting killed or maimed in my car. By 1992, of course, I had long ago stopped racing, but that sick feeling was the same.

You get to know these guys almost as well as your wife, and better than your kids. When you're bouncing around and traveling with them, going up and down the road, you develop an attachment and of course you don't want to see them get hurt.

I talked earlier about building that early-60s car out of exhaust tubing, the one in which Lloyd Beckman broke his arms at

Knoxville. I learned from that car, and I can honestly say I never once sacrificed weight or quality in any component of my car if it meant compromising on safety.

Part of that was my fear of somebody getting killed in my car, or in one of the cars I had built. If I cheated on weight, or quality, and it cost somebody his life, I would have a hard time sleeping. I've spent over a year of my life doing sheet time, so I understand what it does to your demeanor, your self-esteem, all those things. I didn't want to impose that on someone just because they had a desire to race.

In the late 1970s weight became a big topic in sprint car racing, and everybody was building cars and components with that in mind. It wasn't long before people were building frames and roll cage out of thinner tubing in order to save weight. That's asking for it.

In 1979 there was a terrible accident at Knoxville that killed Daryl Dawley and Roger Larson. It was a particularly violent crash, and the damage to the cars was massive. Doug was an eyewitness to the crash, and was actually on the track racing someone else's car.

He and I had just decided to go racing together again. Doug was going to be driving my car, and it was a car he had not personally built. That night, after the crash, he approached me.

"Hey, Speedy," he said, "what size tubing do you make your roll cages out of?"

I didn't hesitate.

"One-twenty, pal," I insisted. We used .120 tubing, instead of the .065 tubing some guys were experimenting with at the time.

I would not sacrifice safety just because a driver thought the car might be too heavy. Listen, you can go take a crap and you'll make about as much difference as using .065 tubing instead of .120. There is no way such a small gain in performance is worth such a terrible sacrifice in terms of safety. No way!

If somebody got killed because I used tubing that was too thin, what am I going to think about every time I look at myself in the mirror?

Wolfgang's extremely good physical conditioning was the key to his survival from those terrible injuries in 1992. No doubt in my mind about that. I had seen him use his conditioning to win races during the last five laps of a 40-lap feature, when the other drivers were falling out of the seat.

Doug never completely recovered from the fire in Kansas City. Oh, he raced again, but that old magic was gone after 1992. He raced locally for a while, then had a neck injury in 1997 that led him to quit racing.

These days he's building sprint cars in South Dakota, raising his kids and grandkids. He has a great family, and Joyce and I enjoy seeing them all now and again.

There probably isn't a month that goes by I don't call Doug, or he calls me. As soon as I hear his voice, it's like it's 1978 all over again; I feel like we're just as close as ever.

Racers are a complicated bunch, that's for sure. I've seen more than my share down through the years. It's funny, some of the guys who had great success on the race track never had any success anywhere else. They had a hard time adjusting to life outside racing. Jobs, family, social circumstances, they struggled in those surroundings.

Doug was always different in that regard. Yeah, he was one of the greatest racers of all time, but away from the track he was a good man. He had a solid work ethic, he got along nicely with people, and he was a great family man. A *great* family man. He was dedicated to his wife and kids, and that's why their family is today so close and strong.

He got beat up pretty badly, too, and he still has plenty of scars to prove it.

Doug worked his ass off to get where he is in life. Above all else, I probably respect hard work as much as I do anything.

But Doug was one of the lucky ones. Even though he was badly nicked up, he's got a good life these days.

He'll always be one of my special friends. More than anything else, I understand him. And he understands me. And that ain't easy.

21

Renewed Focus

As 1980 dawned, we were all set for another great racing season. In fact, I was fired up because I had an exciting new "Master Plan."

Racing was suddenly all about sponsorship. If you could attract the top sponsors, and therefore have a bigger budget, you could win more races. That's the way I saw it, anyway. But how do you attract sponsors? You offer them guaranteed exposure for their products.

In 1979 I began hearing about Cheryl Glass, a young black woman who was racing sprint cars out in the Northwest, near Seattle. She won a local championship, and this impressed me because I knew the competition up there was good.

They had two or three car builders in the region, speed shops and the like, and I had several customers there. It was a nice pocket of sprint car racing, even though it was a long way from Lincoln.

Suddenly I had an intriguing idea: If I could hire a black female racer and make her a winner in national competition, that would be a dynamite package. Nobody had ever heard or seen anything like this! It would move sprint car racing closer to the mainstream, and maybe even build a whole new audience.

I could also secure sponsorship from people who traditionally had never been approached before, such as *Ebony* magazine, with products marketed to the black community. What a win-win situation!

I decided to give it a try. We would form a two-car team, and this was long before the days of Richard Childress or Rick Hendrick, I assure you. A two-car sprint car team was unheard of in 1980.

Our other driver would be Ron Shuman, a very talented driver from Arizona. I figured it would be good to team Cheryl, who had relatively little experience, with a seasoned veteran.

I made the deal to hire them both for the 1980 season, then got busy putting everything together. I hired Ty Berger to do our publicity, and Lee Kunzman to manage the team. I still had to make a living running Speedway Motors, and knew I wouldn't have time to give the new team the oversight it needed.

We had Cheryl come to Lincoln for a couple of weeks in January while we prepared the cars, then we were off to Florida for the Winternationals in Tampa.

At first, everybody in racing figured I had lost my mind. Yes, my idea was a little far-fetched, but then again, not really. Cheryl clearly had some experience, so why not hire her? Jan Opperman had very little experience when I hired him, so why was it such a stretch to think Cheryl might be able to do this?

Most of my friends kidded me throughout that winter, and I think many people believed this was some kind of novelty. I assure you it wasn't. If I didn't think she could at least be competitive, I wouldn't have done it.

I ultimately lost some friendships over this project. When we got to Florida, Cheryl spun in hot laps, and Lee Osborne went over her front end and flipped clear out of the place. Of course, everything my driver ever did on the track, everybody said it was *my* fault. Hey, I wasn't driving the car; but the heat comes with the territory.

It was probably a couple of years later before Osborne would speak to me again. And we had been good friends, traveling together in 1978 when Doug Wolfgang ran my car with the World of Outlaws. Lee was a good guy and I hated that he was mad at me.

Just as quickly as everything had come together, it started to come apart. Cheryl was not improving like she should, and almost immediately there was friction.

Part of the reason she didn't succeed — this is the world according to Bill — was that she brought her father along. Her parents were highly educated, and Cheryl was also well-educated and intelligent. She succeeded in many arenas as a young girl, dancing and so forth. She also won a huge number of quarter-midget races, so she was an accomplished racer at a young age.

But as we went along her dad kept insisting we were somehow giving Cheryl inferior equipment, something less than we were giving Shuman. This was absurd; I had so much invested in making this work, why would I not give Cheryl every possible tool to succeed?

It galled her dad to watch Shuman run well while Cheryl struggled. Naturally, it *had* to be the equipment, right? Never mind that Shuman was an excellent, experienced racer, the Knoxville Nationals winner in 1979.

There was absolutely no difference in the two cars. The same chassis, the same equipment, period. They were exactly equal. Still, her dad complained.

That works on a racer's head. When your dad is telling you something, you listen. Even if he's wrong, you listen. Pretty soon Cheryl was complaining, too, saying she wasn't getting a fair shake.

Her dad had a big chip on his shoulder. I hadn't been exposed to any of that attitude, to be honest. I came from a totally white world, and seeing someone with a chip on their shoulder because of race, well, I didn't know how to deal with that.

We soldiered on for a little while, until it became obvious this wasn't going to work. Like those 80-some drivers before her, Cheryl went her way, and I went mine. We continued on with Shuman.

One day not long after, I got a call from my friend from Indiana, Charlie Patterson.

"I hear you had Cheryl Glass drive for you," he said.

"Yes, I did."

"Tell me about her."

"Well, Charlie, she has a lot of talent."

And she *did* have a lot of talent. If these two eyes—which have seen about as much racing as any other human in history—can do anything at all, they can spot talent.

But I cautioned Charlie; there would be trouble if she brought her dad along with her.

Charlie hired her anyway, and they went racing. I suspect he had the same grandiose ideas I did, and he saw the obvious marketing potential. But guess what? Some things never change. They didn't have much success on the track, and eventually parted ways.

Not long after Cheryl and I split, I made the most difficult decision I've ever made in my business life: I decided to quit racing altogether.

It wasn't simply because of my experience with Cheryl. Honestly, that had nothing to do with my decision.

My reasoning was based on a simple but painful realization: I had lost the ability to properly manage and control a race team. I was personally spread too thin, and couldn't manage things like a good team owner should. So we continued to run Ron in our car until June or so, and then I folded it up.

You have to remember one other thing: From the time I made $22 at my first race at Hastings, Neb., in 1948, I had made money with my race cars. It was a revenue stream, not a revenue drain.

But now things had changed. The costs were soaring in sprint car racing, and it was hopeless to turn a profit. Corporate sponsorship had nowhere near caught up with the rising costs. You didn't have to be a genius to see it happening.

My race cars had advertised Speedway Motors, but the return from the advertising wouldn't have paid any of the bills. I needed the purse money to make it. And when we reached the point where the purse money wouldn't cover our costs — even if we won — it made no sense to keep doing it.

Why not just scale back, instead of quitting altogether? Because I had to be hands-on. It was an all-or-nothing proposition. Either run the team with my oversight, or turn it over completely to someone else to manage, which I could not do. It would have made me just like all the car owners out there today: Throw the billfold on the table and let the boys sort through it.

That held no appeal to me. Racing was supposed to be fun, and fun meant trying to figure out how to beat my competitor, and win. Suddenly it was all about who had the biggest billfold.

So I quit. Cold turkey.

Boy, it was tough. For a while I hated to go to a race, because my stomach would still grind. I'd sit in the grandstand — where I'd never sat before — and watch other people race, and it was not fun. You'd see people doing things you figured were dumb, and naturally you're saying, "They should have done this, they should have done that…"

I did discover this truth: It looks a lot easier from the grandstand seats.

Over time, I began to "heal up" from my racing addiction. I was still very much into the sport, but I learned to enjoy it in a different way, in a different role.

I never stopped loving racing; to this day, I have an almost endless passion for racing of all kinds. But the stars aligned that summer of 1980 where everything told me it was time for a change.

My business was in the midst of an important growth period, and in my heart I knew I needed to give Speedway Motors my undivided attention. It's simple, really; why would you devote yourself to something you didn't even enjoy all that much anymore, when you know you're needed elsewhere?

In racing, nothing is forever. Nothing, and nobody. I was no different. My time had come, and I walked away from being a hands-on car owner. Simple as that.

Looking back, I'm more convinced than ever I made the right decision at the right time. All the factors were in place, and the timing was right. The sport had changed, and I wouldn't have been happy with racing in that manner. Too much money, too little control, and very little fun.

My whole life had been consumed by racing, and at times my business was almost secondary in terms of time and energy. Now, things were changing. I had more ambitions for my business, and I wanted to grow it, too. I realized I couldn't do both. There just wasn't enough time. Or at least I'm not smart enough to figure out how to make more than 24 hours in a day.

I raced from the 1940s through the early 1980s; my footsteps spanned five different decades. There were too many highs to mention; and as far as the lows, well, no need to dwell on those.

We won a bunch of races, and had some awfully good times. I wouldn't change one day of any of it, even if I could.

22

A New Era For Speedway Motors

A round 1980, Speedway Motors really began to take off as a company. Was that related to my decision to quit racing, or was it a coincidence? I'll never know, but it's like anything else: To make something successful, whether you're growing flowers or raising kids, you have to focus. Spend some time and attention and focus on that objective.

I had focused on racing very intensely for many years, and ran my business at the same time. But as the business began to grow more quickly — remember, I doubled the size of my business in the first year of the economic crunch in 1973 and '74 — I knew I had better pay more attention to business.

There are many different aspects to any business, but managing growth is one of the most important. You can either let outside forces control your growth, or you can choose to take specific steps to control the pace of your growth from within your company.

Growing at the proper pace is actually much harder than simply gaining market share. If you can control your growth, and still keep up with the market, that's the ideal situation. But it's very difficult to do. If there is somebody who knows exactly how to do this, I'd love to listen to them tell me how, because it's a very tough thing to do.

Naturally, you fight your competitors for market share, and as the markets grow you naturally get more competition. Whether everybody can survive or not, who knows. But you have to keep things in balance in terms of growth, because not every day is going to be sunshine. You're going to have bad weather in business, just as you do in life. If you have a solid foundation, and control growth properly, you can usually outlast the inevitable perils that come along.

Our growth from the mid-1970s—aside from the big gain in 1974—had been about 10 to 20 percent each year, which is manageable. Of course, as you go along the overall number gets bigger, and harder. But manageable. I still manage that rate of growth; only today it's a much bigger number. These days it takes four sons and my wife and 300 good people to make it happen.

My oldest son Carson was the first son to "return to the nest" at Speedway Motors. He brought with him a vast knowledge of both big business and computerization. Carson, a professional mechanical engineer, had been with Caterpillar and later with Charmin Paper Company, in Green Bay, Wis., when he returned to Lincoln. His qualifications and experience were just what we needed to grow our business. Plus, he was family.

A little later my second son, Craig, came out of the Univ. of Nebraska, specializing in architecture, advertising, and design. He came on board and took over our fledgling advertising department. He has great artistic talent, and was just what the company needed at that point.

(Today, the equipment in this area is amazing. Computers can render things I can hardly visualize. They use PhotoShop, a program that can do almost anything. We have several people these days using cad-cam technology to draw products, as well as our Internet work. In fact, one has a doctorate. So it's come a long way from those old paste-up catalogs!)

The use of computers in business was becoming critical by the early 1980s. It was obvious the computer would allow you to gain so much—efficiency, management information, creative processes, and so much more—that you could no longer deny that computers were here to stay.

But they were terribly expensive, both for the equipment and the programs you needed. When we began to figure out how to enter the computer age—and our sons were critical in this process—I quickly realized that this was going to be a very expensive proposition, a big investment for our company.

That's one of the key challenges in a company; you have to fund the tools needed to grow. The economics of business today are such that by the time you pay taxes and people, do all the things you need to deliver the product to the customer, there aren't many dollars left on the bottom line, and not a lot of dollars

244 / FAST COMPANY

to invest in growth. So you have to manage that part of business very carefully.

If you expand too quickly, your debt load will likely bury you. Especially if you have a hiccup in the economy, because you lose a lot of sales and growth.

It's like a giant ball you're trying to balance on the end of a stick; it's difficult, but after a while you begin to figure out the techniques and it gets slightly easier.

So my challenge in the early 1980s was this: I knew we needed to invest in a major computer system, but how should I go about paying for it?

All through my life, I was completely averse to borrowing money. Period, end of story! Banks were a place you *deposited* money, not borrowed money. In my mind, borrowing money was a sign of failure, and that was very troubling to me.

But it quickly became obvious it would be wise to use a business loan to invest in our new computer system. Again, try to think smart: If you use all your capital to invest in one segment of your business, you're very vulnerable to having cash flow issues. Cash flow issues kill more businesses than any other factor, hands down. So I knew — reluctantly — that it made sense to use a business loan for this key step for our company.

I guess one thing that had softened me up a little was the fact that, in a sense, I had borrowed money in a different way down through the years. Each time we bought a commercial property, for example, the transaction typically involved a contract with the existing owner. There was no financial institution involved; the transaction was between buyer and seller, and the seller made the interest.

Early on I recognized this as the reality of commercial real estate, so I reconciled it in my mind. However, when I bought a piece of property, I never really looked at it as a large debt. I saw the payment amount, I saw the possible rental income, and knew that at some point five to 10 years down the line, I would have the property paid off.

That's a completely different proposition — in my mind anyway — than walking into a bank and signing a loan document for a large amount. The concept of owing money to a bank frightened me to death.

I didn't want to owe money to anybody! For example, many people in our business use "dating" for buying inventory, but I never did. Dating is where you buy inventory on credit, hoping you'll have the product sold before the payment is due. It's a balancing act, and it's very easy to get trapped if the product doesn't sell. Everybody's situation is different, of course, and there is no road map that works for everybody.

When we finally made the decision to finance our big computer project through a business loan, I accepted the reality. Still, I was so upset with the idea that I couldn't bring myself to actually go to the bank. Joyce had to go in alone, because I just couldn't. I couldn't get over the powerful sense of failure I had that we were borrowing money.

One of the elements I've always been keen on is understanding my customer, and understanding my market. Long before computers, I always tried to study what was happening in our business and throughout the industry, and figure out how to get more business.

Kind of like being a racer; you're always looking at the race car, thinking of tweaks and changes that will make you faster. Winning the race has many different forms, you know.

With my tough geographic location, I always had to fight for market share. If you draw a circle that's 1,000 miles across with Lincoln in the center, you'll get to the outskirts of Chicago, the outskirts of Dallas, the outskirts of Denver, and going north you'll get to Canada, with very little in between. That circle will encompass only 15 percent of the U.S. population.

If you take that same 1,000-mile circle anywhere else in the East, whether it's Cleveland, Detroit, Chattanooga, Columbus, or wherever, you'll get 75 percent of the U.S. population. The difference between 15 percent and 75 percent is a big, big number.

I've never been able to sell a race car wheel to a pig or a cow. I can't sell a chrome hood scoop or gearshift knob to a pig or a cow. I have to sell to human beings who have an interest in my products.

I've never sold anything to anybody that extended their life, or did anything other than make them feel good when they bought it and used it. But if you're an outsider looking in, you might think, 'Gee, this looks like an easy business!" Evidently it does look easy, because today I have more competitors than 10 years ago. I thought the competition was so fierce 10 years ago that it couldn't get any tougher. But it has.

When I closely analyzed my business in the early 1980s, I saw I was primarily selling to the racer. I already knew that; but it's good to analyze things every so often just to be sure.

The good news was that racing was experiencing healthy growth, so my market was expanding. One of the big reasons for the growth of racing, in my opinion, was because it was being exposed more and more on television. In the mid-1970s you could only watch two races in full length on television: one was the Indianapolis 500, and the other was the big race I won in 1976, the Tony Hulman Classic. Other races were shown in parts and pieces, even the Daytona 500.

By the 1980s the cable channels had greatly expanded racing's presence on television. The rest of the world was suddenly exposed to what guys like me had been doing for the past 30 years. People could see races from the comfort of their living room, races I had been chasing all my life. So racing was growing, and that helped my business. More interest always brings more competitors to the sport.

At the same time, the hot rod industry was growing, too. Hot rodding is a hobbyist sport, just like racing. People love their hobbies, whether it's a double-barrel shotgun to go hunting with, a fishing rod to go fishing with, whether it's a blond at the bar, people love their hobbies.

We're all human beings, alike in many ways, with wives, kids, girl friends — all the things that continue to make humanity work — but the one thing that makes us feel unique is our hobbies. Not everybody can go hunting, fishing, whatever. And one thing that's truly interesting to me is the great number of people who migrated from racing to the hot rod-street rod industry.

If you're involved in racing in some capacity, age will typically limit your hands-on involvement. For example, you typically aren't still driving a sprint car at age 60. With that in mind, I've seen dozens of my friends who once made their livelihood in racing, and as they matured they eventually moved into building street rods and hot rods. This continues to happen, every day.

I call it the "world of wheels" syndrome. They have wheels in their brain as a small kid, and get into racing, and continue right on through and into street rods. Many of them are good craftsmen, and as they learned about racing they became good welders, metal smiths, engine builders, and so on. When they stopped racing, they couldn't just give up on those talents, so they changed direction and applied themselves on something different, such as a street rod or hot rod. They merely redirected their interests.

And that sums up exactly how these two markets — racing and hot rods — fit my glove perfectly. I address all those things! I've built hot rods, I've built race cars, and I love both. Plus, there is a technical tie-in too; a tie-rod end for a Saturday-night racer is pretty much the same tie-rod end for a street rod.

I suppose I'm getting ahead of myself with all this talk of growth in the early 1980s. In retrospect the biggest step in my early years, I think, was when I made the decision to get into the fiberglass business in the 1950s.

My buddy, Leroy Snyder, built a fiberglass boat in his dad's barn five miles north of Lincoln. The concept of making and using fiberglass — tiny fibers of glass matted and glued together by various resins — was in its infancy; it was quite a novelty and I was fascinated with Leroy's new boat.

Immediately I pictured building a fiberglass Model T body. Think of the possibilities! Lighter than steel, no rust to deal with, it's a brand new piece, make as many as you need, on and on.

I was intrigued by the business potential. And, as a "gearhead," I was fascinated with the manufacturing process involved, even though working with fiberglass is a dirty, rotten, stinking business. It's nasty stuff; you get little slivers in your body if you work around it, and it's not much fun. However, the things you produce are definitely fun!

I told Leroy about my idea, and he built me a few Model T bodies then went away to college. That's part of why I found Leroy to be so impressive; when he figured out the fiberglass process he was still in school, a typical young man wondering what to do with his life.

Within a couple of years he had received his master's degree at a business college in Phoenix, and he called me on the phone.

"I'm not coming back to Lincoln," he explained. "I'm going to get a job out here in Phoenix. So I won't be able to make any more bodies for you."

"I think that's a mistake, Leroy," I told him. "You've got a tiger by the tail with your fiberglass business. I think that industry is going to be very good."

"You really think so?"

"I sure do."

We talked a little more, and I finally convinced him to return to Lincoln and expand his fiberglass business. His little enterprise eventually became Snyder Industries, and Leroy became the largest in the world in centrifugal molding, building tanks to hold water and feed for farm use. He also made fuel tanks for military vehicles, and many other government applications. He built a huge company!

Leroy and I made a deal where I invested in some tooling, and he would then build bodies and things for me. However, during the startup period he had a terrible fire, and I lost all my tooling.

Leroy's plant burned to the ground in 45 minutes, and afterward there wasn't anything standing higher than your knees. Static electricity came up one of the spray guns and sparked a fire, and the operator instantly dropped the gun and ran for the door. In the two or three seconds it took to get there, the fire was already so intense that the door handle was almost too hot to handle, and he barely escaped. Luckily nobody was hurt, but the building and all contents were destroyed.

Now, fiberglass is only as good as your tooling. It's like making Jell-O; unless you put it in a nice mold, it just looks like a bunch of crumbled-up cubes. If I were serious about the potential of those fiberglass bodies, I had no choice but to invest in new tooling. It was the only way to continue in that business.

I had already learned a lot about building a product to a price. Long before Sam Walton came along, I had learned that "price sells," and you also have to have the item in stock. Since I was in a tough geographic location, and didn't have a million people walking past looking to buy something, I had to make sure my products were priced competitively.

My T-bucket bodies were priced at $59 back then, and I still sell them for under $500. Very competitive.

However, even at a lower price I didn't want to compromise quality. Leroy was moving into manufacturing shower stalls, pig feeders, and other such products that didn't require nearly the same level of quality as an automobile body. I was still insisting on both price and quality, and finally by the early 1960s Leroy said he couldn't give me both.

That forced my hand, and I had no choice but to create my own fiberglass manufacturing facility. I began looking around for buildings, and of course the property had to be cheap in order to make the business viable. This wasn't a retail outlet, so location didn't much matter. I finally found an older building in the Haymarket area of Lincoln that had been used as a millwright business, and the tenants had moved out looking for newer facilities.

On a cold winter day with snow up to the door handle, I bought the building at 610 L Street. I bought it on contract, which, as I mentioned earlier, I viewed as very different from a loan. It was a very simple transaction, almost to the point of being a handshake deal.

We got busy preparing the location, and buying the tools needed. I still had my tooling, which was a big head start, but now I needed chopper guns, fans, and a fair number of other things required to make fiberglass.

Like all new businesses, hiring talent is always tough. Fortunately, a young man, Ivan Anderson, was attending the University of Nebraska at this time working on his degree in accounting. He needed a part-time job, and he came on board, graduated from the university, and that solved my challenge of finding good people for the right job. After all these years, Ivan and his wife Sandy are still managing that division!

Once we got going, the bulk of our production was bodies. I built the first fiberglass '32 Ford roadster body, and the first '34 Ford roadster body, which I'm very proud of. I also began manufacturing hood scoops, supermodified bodies, noses, hoods, and many other smaller items. I didn't subcontract work for others, and everything I produced was to sell directly to my customers.

Opening the fiberglass shop was probably the first real step in the growth of Speedway Motors. I moved the company into something more than simply being a retailer; we were a legitimate manufacturer. Not only were my margins better on the things I manufactured, but I could also carefully control the quality and make sure it was up to my customer's standards.

It's hard to describe the enormous impact fiberglass had within the performance hobby. The '27 Model T body I built was particularly important, because the guy who bought it — the very first T body produced in fiberglass — became a world champion drag racer that very next year. I still have his letter around here somewhere, thanking me for building the body and telling me what a difference it made on his race car.

At that time — and this is difficult for younger guys to imagine — you could buy steel Model T bodies all day long for peanuts. They were plentiful, literally laying around in ditches and alleys. So my idea of a fiberglass body had nothing to do with filling a supply issue; it was all about *weight*.

Drag racing cars were still primitive at that time, and most cars were built on a standard automotive chassis with a 120-inch wheelbase. This was before Don Garlits stretched the wheelbase and created the first "rail" dragster, of course. You'd run the biggest engine you could get — typically a big Oldsmobile or Cadillac, or maybe a flathead Ford — and you moved your seat over the rear axle. You'd drape some kind of body around you, usually a Model T or Austin or Anglia, and away you went down the quarter-mile.

If you replaced that 450-pound steel Model T body with my 50-pound fiberglass body, you could be a *champion*. I can say that with conviction, because that's exactly what happened with my very first customer.

This guy purchased the body through a speed shop around Detroit somewhere, and of course everybody saw what was happening and they wanted one, too. The next year I sold a body to a guy in Tennessee, who became the champion that season.

Later I built a '31 Austin roadster body, which was even smaller than the '27 T. That Austin body design is still used to this day in the Altered classes of drag racing.

It felt good that our fiberglass products were really taking off. However, the downside to such success is that it immediately attracted copycats. And fiberglass, in particular, is fairly easy to dub. The startup companies came out of the woodwork! It isn't all that difficult to start a fiberglass operation; all you needed was a garage, some glass mat, and some resin, and you could produce a product. Of course, the quality of this stuff was all over the map, but that's a different discussion.

I've probably been more copied than almost anybody on the planet when it comes to speed equipment. But I always took pride in being the originator. In fact, for years and years my catalogs proclaimed, "The originator, not the imitator."

Now that I'm thinking about the fiberglass shop I remember a great story about buying another fiberglass operation. This was long after I had started my own facility, and by then I figured I knew a little bit about the business.

I'm a sucker for a bargain. That's a fact. I've always got my antennae up for a deal I can get on the cheap that has a nice upside, even if there is significant risk. I've been blessed with pretty good instincts on such things, and with just a couple of exceptions I was able to take a troubled entity and make it part of the Speedway Motors family, and turn things around.

(The exception—and it's still a pain in my side to admit this— was the race track business. Everything worked except that. Damn it anyways.)

I heard that a fiberglass company, Kellison Fiberglass in Lincoln, Calif., was for sale. I was excited, because I figured this was the kind of deal "tailor-made" for Speedy Bill! I was familiar with some of the company's products, and they had been turning out some nice pieces.

This transaction was another learning experience. I bought the entire operation — inventory, tooling, molds, everything — sight unseen, lock, stock and barrel, and sent Lloyd Beckman (my race car driver!) to California to pick it up. They loaded everything into a railway freight car, and rolled 'er into Fremont, Neb., onto a siding with the Union Pacific Railroad.

I drove up to look it over, quite proud of the great bargain I had scored. However — and remember that old rule I talked about learning as a young boy? Know the rules before you play the game? — unbeknownst to me somebody had slid all the good stuff out before I bought it. I started looking at all this tooling, and nearly all of it was junk.

The quality of the product coming from that tooling would have been awful, and I didn't want the rest of the world to get hold of it and turn out bad pieces. If you've ever assembled a car with fiberglass pieces, you understand how frustrating it is to deal with an inferior product with terrible fit.

I kept just a few small pieces that were okay, and moved all the rest out alongside the siding on the ground. Then I paid a guy in a tractor to drive over and crush the entire lot. That was Speedy Bill's public service of the day, I guess. Sure was an expensive public service!

On another occasion I bought out a guy in Kansas, and he had tooling that stretched out almost a quarter of a city block. This was a bankruptcy auction, and I bought the lot. The price was cheap, and I knew going in it was nearly all junk. However, if this bad tooling had fallen into the wrong hands, some poor guy would be trying to put a fender on his '40 Ford that would no more fit than fly.

It was actually kind of fun, destroying all that tooling; it was probably more fun than losing the same amount at the crap tables in Las Vegas.

Yes, I love a bargain, and yes, I like to make money. But this was a matter of principle: Any self-respecting car guy has a moral responsibility to help keep junk out of the marketplace. I'm a car guy, above anything else; this was just a car guy doing his public duty.

23

"Hey Speedy! I just got your catalog!"

If I were writing the corporate history of Speedway Motors—and I'll bet corporate histories would be pretty dry compared to the "people" history—I would probably pinpoint the development of a product catalog as a key turning point in our business.

I can't point to one historic day when we suddenly decided to create a "catalog" and fulfill orders from all over the world. It was more of a learning process over many, many years where we gradually realized the potential of something and then focused more and more energy toward it.

As I've said before, Speedway Motors started out in a very small building at 2232 O Street in Lincoln with a small parts counter and a place out back to install parts. In the beginning, every transaction was on a face-to-face basis.

Today, our business is like a giant hub, far beyond anything I could have imagined in 1952. The Speedway Motors facility is 750,000 square feet, on a 65-acre campus near downtown Lincoln. The main building is filled with a vast inventory to service customer's immediate needs. A sophisticated fulfillment system (surpassing any in the industry) is in place, and orders come in from a variety of technologies. We quickly process the order, and immediately ship products to the customer.

Obviously, it's been a complete transformation from our 1952 debut on O Street. This transformation took place not overnight, but over the past 57-plus years. And this is not unique to Speedway Motors; there isn't a segment in American business—really, worldwide business—that operates today like it did in 1952. Customer habits change and businesses have to change with them.

I mentioned earlier our first experiment with a "catalog," the mimeographed sheet of paper with the accidental purple ink. From that first attempt, we always had at least some form of printed document to promote sales.

Even as far back as 1955 I can see references to our "catalog" in my ads at trade shows. But this was still a tiny percentage; customers who walked through our front door still represented the bulk of our business.

By the late 1950s and early '60s, I realized I was selling a lot of parts at the race track each weekend. A guy would see me in Iowa on Saturday night and say, "Hey, Bill, when you get back to Lincoln, could you ship me a new set of No. 6 quick-change gears?" Or a new master cylinder. Or a new 31-inch axle.

I quickly realized I was doing more than just selling parts. I was providing a service to that man, making his hobby — racing — a little bit easier and more enjoyable. Plus, by doing business on a face-to-face basis, I became the face of Speedway Motors. The guy wasn't buying something from "a company," he was buying it from his friend. And, on the flip side, I didn't just have "a customer." Likewise, I viewed that man as a friend.

And another thing: I was as hands-on as anybody in those days, so I understood perfectly what some of these tasks were all about. When somebody asked about a ring-and-pinion gear, I knew he would also need lots of other pieces to complete the puzzle. Bearings, seals, gaskets, bolts and so forth. I'd put together all the items he needed and sold everything in package form. So the fellow was happy to have all the pieces in the puzzle right there, ready to assemble. It's all about service.

As you go down this road in business, your reputation precedes you. No matter how good you are, no matter what other factors are involved, that reputation is what *you* have created. I lived and died on my reputation back then, just as I do today.

Our catalog efforts gradually began to get a little bigger, a little better, and a little more polished. But let me tell you, they were still a far cry from our catalog today. That was true of everybody in every form of business: Communications with your customers are so advanced today it makes our old days look primitive.

But in the beginning, there was another very challenging element to the catalog portion of our business. Even if somebody from far away wanted to buy something from me, there wasn't an easy way to ship it.

I talked earlier about using the bus lines to ship products, and while that was somewhat workable it had its own challenges. The fact is, for many years there simply was not a viable way to ship product on a large scale. I know this because I tried just about everything.

This is impossible — and I do mean impossible — for younger people to understand, but in the late 1960s there was no UPS service of any kind here in the Midwest. Fed-Ex? The company hadn't even been founded yet.

I don't know exactly how all this was set about, but during the 1960s Lady Bird Johnson — wife of president Lyndon Johnson — was involved in some Federal bureaucracy that decreed there would be no Interstate Commerce Commission permits issued for UPS to operate in the Plains states.

It was some silly federal mandate and that was that. In fact — and this is still an amazing thing to ponder — it wasn't until 1975 that *any* private shipping company had the authority to deliver packages in all the lower 48 states. UPS was the first, and today there is plenty of competition in the shipping industry. Today we take shipping for granted, but believe me, it's a relatively new phenomenon in business.

This is what I meant when I said this whole issue of our catalog was a long process. It wouldn't have done any good to have a huge, national catalog in 1965, for example, because we couldn't have effectively delivered the product to the customer anyway.

Plus, in those days there was a negative connotation to being in the "mail order" business. The perception of "mail order" typically involved somebody reading about some seedy product in the back of a magazine, and sending a check to a blind P.O. Box to get something in a plain brown wrapper.

Obviously, that's not what Speedway Motors was about. We worked hard to build a good reputation and good products, so I sure as hell didn't want to be painted with a bad label.

Plus, the public's attitude changed down through the years. While people once insisted on holding something in their hands before they bought it, today most of us have very little reluctance to order a product from the catalog of a reputable company. That's because we know the company and we've had good experiences with them. Now my customers are comfortable ordering a $50,000 item without touch and feel. So when you have customers like that, you've earned their trust.

Even in our early efforts, we worked to create a nice-looking catalog to let the customer know our history, and that we were serious about customer service. Whether it was me selling a ring-and-pinion set at the race track, or a guy from Alaska ordering a part today, the principle is the same: I do business the right way, and I'll take care of my customers.

The truth is, we receive only a tiny percentage of our orders via "mail order." From the beginning we developed a relationship with our far-away customers on the telephone, and today we've expanded that to e-mail and the Internet. To this day, only a very tiny percentage of our orders arrive here at Speedway through the mail.

Business is complicated, and timing is really important. I guess that's why I've always enjoyed business, because it's never a black-and-white, cut-and-dried formula. It's a complex series of decisions based on a rapidly changing environment, and no matter how smart you are you never get it just right.

If we had introduced a big, husky catalog in the 1950s, we would have gone broke from the printing and distribution costs. The timing wouldn't have been right.

Likewise, if I had ignored the concept of catalog sales when the world began to change, and focused on running our business only through a front door and a parts counter, Speedway Motors would still be a very small enterprise.

That's the challenge for any business: Studying the environment around you, the market, the products, the customer, and looking into the future to see what's coming and where you should be in order to take advantage of it. You can't *wait* for it to change, and then react to it; by then it's too late.

The racer has a mindset like that, and there isn't any doubt in my mind that such a mindset helped me in business. From my first race car, I realized I had to think ahead, and not wait to see what everybody else was doing. Be proactive, not reactive. Racing or business, it's the same principle.

The Speedway Motors catalog eventually became a bigger and bigger part of our business. As the catalog went, so did the business. And as we became more sophisticated with our catalog design, my son Craig's artistic talent really made a difference.

Next thing you know, we had customers all over the world. The catalog did something I could never have done personally: It developed a link between me and the people far outside my geographic circle.

It was a very neat feeling when I would run into my friends at the race track or at the hot rod show or wherever, and they'd smile and wave.

"Hey Speedy!" they'd call out. "I just got your new catalog!"

The real key to the growth of Speedway Motors was the great people who came on board in those early years, many of whom spent their entire career at Speedway.

Jim Gessford was a roaring roadster builder, driver and engine machine specialist.

Marty Bassett was our welder and fabricator — the best welder in Lincoln — as well as being an engine specialist and top-notch tuner. Marty went racing with us all over the Midwest, and was a big part of our racing success. Marty recently retired from Speedway after 40-plus years.

John Larson was a dragster driver, engine specialist, and top tuner. He built a large number of engines for Speedway customers.

John Marsh was our engine balancer specialist, as well as a great injector and supercharger specialist. He came on board in 1961, and in 1970 John returned to college and earned his engineering/education degree at Univ. of Nebraska-Lincoln. He joined the staff at Milford Trade School, an outstanding automotive school here in Nebraska, and eventually John became Dean of the college. A great accomplishment for my good friend!

Jerry "Yogi" Jansen was our welder, exhaust specialist, and race car pit strategist. He was a great free spirit and a big part of our racing program.

Ron Scheinost was an exhaust specialist and eager student of the high-performance trade. Ron came from a small town, and after high school moved to Lincoln to become part of the Speedway family. He worked on our race cars and traveled with our crew all over the Midwest. At Ron's 60th birthday party this past summer, he told me that working at Speedway was the most fun he had ever experienced in his life. Boy, what a wonderful compliment that was!

There are so many more, I can't possibly name them all. But from those early years, I think so fondly of Bob Anderson, Dick Wells, Larry Kruse, Bill Franklin, Les Bock…gee, so many great people were a part of Speedway Motors down through the years.

In the 1960s I took another step that laid the groundwork for Speedway Motors expansion for years to come when I purchased the Getz Gear Company, which was the first company to create and market performance ring-and-pinion gear sets.

A.J. Getz, the founder, was an interesting man. He retired from Perfection Gear in Chicago, which was building ring-and-pinion gear sets for the Ford Motor Company. Building ring-and-pinion gears is a difficult process, because you must forge them, grind them, heat-treat them. It's a complex and detailed scenario. An old German, by the way, owned Perfection; it seems that many of the technologies we still use today are rooted in the old countries of Europe.

When A.J. retired, he took all the company's obsolete, special-run gears they no longer were interested in and cataloged them. It was an interesting assortment; gears for Oldsmobile and Packard, all kinds of stuff. Pretty soon A.J. recognized the business opportunity, and he began making ring-and-pinion sets for jalopy racing, which primarily used '35 to '48 Ford rear ends.

These were very high-ratio gears. For example, when I owned jalopies we used 6:17 and 6:66 gears. These ratios were never available from Ford, of course, because the application was just too far-fetched for passenger cars. The highest they carried were usually 4:88 or maybe even 4:11, and that didn't work for us.

Pretty soon A.J. had a nice inventory, and he invested in the forging dies to make other gear sets. Eventually he retired again or whatever, and the company ended up back in the hands of Perfection's owner, who decided it was too much of a niche and wanted to sell it off.

It was a perfect addition to Speedway Motors. Again, it was all about building the company and controlling our own destiny to a certain extent; now I knew I had an adequate supply of high-quality ring-and-pinion sets, which is a key component in both racing and automotive performance. This was an important item in my catalog.

Even though I now owned the product line, I kept the Getz name. I never give up a name; some companies simply fold the old brand name into their brand, but I don't do that. I feel like when your company acquires a brand, it makes sense to enjoy the reputation and recognition of that brand.

I still have Getz gear, and still use the brand name associated with their products. I never give up, I'm like a junkyard dog. Clench down and don't let up!

Boy, the memories. As I thought of Getz Gear a moment ago I instantly thought about Pee Wee Erlbacher, one of the most interesting characters I've had the pleasure of calling my friend. Pee Wee liked me so much, I actually thought he was trying to kill me one afternoon at DuQuoin, Ill.

After I purchased Getz Gear and began building ring and pinion gear sets, I discovered a need for change gears that could be used in racing applications. Racers need a quick-change rear end, and they need a wide array of gears for various track configurations.

As I said earlier, gear manufacturing is tricky business because of the special tools and skill set required. As I scouted around for someone with the expertise in this area, I quickly realized that few people understood the process.

Somehow I crossed paths with Pee Wee, who operated Erlbacher Machine in Cape Girardeau, Mo. Pee Wee had the knowledge and the tooling to produce just what we needed, and we were soon doing business together.

In addition to the business side, we became good friends. Pee Wee is a lot of fun to be around, a gearhead and a hardcore lover of cars and racing just like me. He also had an airplane, which would come in handy.

In the early 1970s I was scheduled to race my USAC Champ Dirt car on the one-mile oval at the DuQuoin State Fair in Illinois. Pee Wee and I decided that I would catch a commercial flight to St. Louis, where he would pick me up and fly us to DuQuoin.

Everything was going along without a hitch, and we were quickly flying along, happily chatting away. I could see the track in the distance, and I spoke up.

"Say, Pee Wee, there's the track…where's the nearest landing strip?"

"Oh, it's about 20 miles away, but I'm not going to mess with that. I'm going to land on the backstretch of the race track."

My eyes widened a bit, but I figured he knew what he was doing. We came in for a nice, easy approach, and you'd have thought we were coming in from outer space. Suddenly everybody was running out onto the track, waving their arms, trying to wave us off.

Pee Wee looked over at me and said, "I guess they don't want us to land here. That's all right, Speedy. We'll just land over here on the parking lot."

We circled around, and I saw the parking lot. Now, I'm no pilot; but there was no damn way we could land in an area that small. Now my eyes were *really* wide!

If you've ever been in a small plane, you'll know there is something called a "stall alarm." This handy little device tells you that you're just about to drop right out of the sky because you're going too slow to generate enough lift to keep you airborne. Pee Wee had our air speed way, way down, trying to get in on this tiny parking lot. The stall alarm was screaming, and I realized we were flying at a level *under* the nearby light wires.

He flopped it onto the parking lot, and we somehow didn't hit anything or anybody. Boy, was it a thrill! Thrills like that, however, I'd prefer to only experience one time.

We ran the race, and didn't win. Pee Wee and I walked out to the plane, and I began to realize something: How was Pee Wee going to generate enough speed to take off from that tiny parking lot?

"Speedy, you'll have to catch a ride to the airstrip, and I'll pick you up there," he said casually. "Too much weight for such a short takeoff."

Pretty soon a crowd had gathered, wondering how this guy was going to get his airplane out of the parking lot. A bunch of us held the elevator of the plane while Pee Wee firewalled the throttle, building up power. We let go and off he went, racing along the parking lot, the nose of the plane suddenly jumping in the air.

He probably didn't clear the light wires by more than a couple of feet. It was nerve-wracking, and at that moment I would have probably been willing to *walk* back to Lincoln.

I caught a ride to the airstrip, where Pee Wee was waiting, like nothing had happened.

With friends like these, nobody needs an enemy! Pee Wee and I still laugh about that story, and we still do lots of business with Erlbacher Machine.

In the years since that very first "brand" acquisition, I've bought lots of various companies and product lines. I acquired Safety Racing, which was a wheel and rear-end manufacturer in Michigan. I bought the Deco Company from Dick Etchison in Anderson, Ind.

I also bought Pro Racer's Supply, but that one didn't work out like I planned. I had always sold lots of racing helmets, and was often the second- or third-leading outlet of helmets in the entire country. Bell Helmets was owned by Roy Richter — they later sold out to Wynn's Friction Proofing — and pretty soon they got into the manufacturing of motorcycle helmets, which outsell racing helmets by something like 100-to-1.

I was hoping to become a master distributor for Bell, because I could see the potential of selling these helmets. However, they awarded the distributorship to Bill Tempero, an Indy 500 driver from Colorado, who created Pro Racer's Supply as a new business entity. I later made a deal with Bill to purchase the company, and I was all set to become a major outlet for Bell Helmets.

However, right after the purchase, Bell decided to completely change its distribution. Instead of selling through master distributors, Bell opened it to up allow every gas station in the U.S. to sell their helmets. You could get the dealership privileges for nothing.

So ultimately my purchase of Pro Racer Supply didn't gain me what I had hoped. Sometimes you win and sometimes you lose; I lost that one.

Mr. Roadster was a well-known manufacturer of street rod parts, and when the opportunity came along to acquire the company I jumped at the chance. They had a lot of neat products and a great reputation, and they were a great addition to the Speedway Motors family.

I still use their name, too, along with Pro Racer Supply. Pro Racer Supply is now a wholesale entity, and Mr. Roadster is a wholesale entity for street rod parts.

Here's a story I like to tell: Mr. Roadster had long made vintage windshield frames for 1909 to 1936 Fords. They had special tubing dies, which cost about $20,000 each to create, and then the frames must be formed and welded and polished.

When Ford had its 100th anniversary celebration a few years ago, they recreated seven 1914 Fords to the tune of $1 million — *each!* They recreated the tooling for the engines and the bodies themselves, but all of the windshield frames came from Speedway Motors.

So even the Ford Motor Company buys parts from Speedy Bill! I loved it!

If you're in business there are many ways of "keeping score" on how you're doing within your industry. Obviously, sales and revenue are probably the two key numbers that "rank" you.

I've talked elsewhere here about the "Nebraska syndrome," and how I always felt a little bit "smaller" than the big operators in California or on the East Coast. Even though that element was always present, particularly in our early years, I made it a point to stay involved in the "big picture" of the industry as much as possible.

I'm proud I was involved in a couple of very important organizations that — to this day — serve an important role in the world of automotive performance. I could have been timid and sat on the sidelines, but I didn't do that. I rolled up my sleeves with several other key people and got involved, and I'm glad I did. It opened my eyes a great deal to industry issues, and it also provided friendships that have lasted many decades.

In the early 1960s a group of California guys involved in manufacturing performance parts started sharing information about who didn't pay their bills. The government takes a dim view of such activity, of course, but human nature tends to take a natural course sometimes. These guys were trying to survive with the deck sometimes stacked against them, trying to identify a few unsavory retailers who intentionally stiffed vendors after they had shipped the product.

From that nucleus of manufacturers it became obvious there was a need for an industry organization, to help the industry with all sorts of issues. They quietly dropped the idea of sharing information you're not supposed to, and began to focus on how to build a legitimate industry organization to serve all parties. They began to invite people from other segments of the industry, such as warehousers and jobbers, to their meetings, and the organization began to get some traction.

That's when I began attending the meetings, and it was my first real experience on a national level in our industry. The early meetings were heavily stacked with drag racing people, because that's what was primarily happening in California. But as time passed the mix began to include people from all walks of the performance industry.

This organization eventually became SEMA. The original name was Speed Equipment Manufacturers Ass'n but it was later changed to Specialty Equipment Market Ass'n.

SEMA eventually began offering a trade show — this was probably later in the '60s — but it was tiny compared to the SEMA show of today. In fact, everything about SEMA is vastly larger today than it was in the beginning. Business members number more than 7,000 companies, and the trade show is one of the largest in the world. The early shows were in Anaheim, but later moved to the current home at the Las Vegas Convention Center, the only facility in the world large enough to host the show. Huge!

I'll admit that I'm probably like everybody else from those formative years when I say that the show is way beyond anything I could have imagined, both in size and scope. Last year, for example, more than 150 different manufacturers of wheels and tires had exhibits at the show. Plus, the show now encompasses far more elements than just the speed business, because there are electronics, stereos and music, everything.

In recent years we've seen a new movement involving "tuner" cars, all under the same SEMA umbrella. It's been a complete evolution from the days of it simply being focused on hard-core performance parts.

But the impact of SEMA goes way beyond how the show has grown. The organization has been an important voice for all of us who love cars, because it's helped us navigate the difficult road involving politics.

For example, if a politician introduces a bill that has the potential of hurting our hobby, it's important that there be a voice to help that politician see the implications of his bill. Without an organized response, that bill might become law without anyone even knowing about it.

I'm proud I was involved at an early stage, and I'm especially proud to have been elected to the SEMA Board of Directors, and later was honored with an induction into its Hall of Fame in 1984.

No matter what industry you're in, it's a good thing to get involved in things that help the overall picture. My involvement was very rewarding, and was way beyond simple dollars and cents. It was all about giving back to the industry, and creating a strong enough industry that my sons — and everybody in future generations — can enjoy it for many years to come.

Another key moment for me was the foundation of the Performance Warehouse Ass'n in 1971. The PWA is still going strong today, and it all came out of a couple of us having a conversation that we ought to organize a little bit and figure out a smart way to do business with each other.

PWA is actually the result of a second attempt at such an organization. In the '60s I was vice-president of a similar group, but it lasted only a couple of meetings and quietly disbanded due to lack of momentum. Listen, trying to get people together from all over the country, and organize something nobody had done before, is plenty tough.

But by 1971 the time was right to try again. Myself, Angelo Giampetroni, Jack Harris of Midwest Auto Supply (Cleveland, Ohio), and two or three others got together and this time the idea stuck.

PWA really helped in the development of our industry. In the very early days there were manufacturers and retailers, and that was it. But as our industry evolved another couple of segments developed, the warehouse/distributor and the dealer/ jobber. It became much more complicated than a two-step distribution system.

For anyone doing business with a lot of different partners, life became complicated because everybody had their own way of doing things. Forms, processes, everybody was all over the place. PWA came along and helped standardize the distribution process, smoothing things such as orders, returns, invoicing, and so forth.

It's paid great dividends to all of us, because it made us so much more professional and efficient, and I'm proud to say I was there from the "get-go."

Even though we were starting to grow by the 1960s, Speedway Motors was still relatively small when compared to companies such as Warshawski's and Honest Charlie's. I had only a fraction of the buying power of those much larger companies.

I came up with the idea of a buying group, and enlisted the help of my friends Angelo Giampetroni and Don Hampton. Angelo operated Gratiot Auto Supply, a chain of eight stores selling accessories and speed equipment, while Don had five or six similar stores around Oklahoma City.

The three of us created Pro Stock Buying Group. At first we were simply trying to get more margin in order to survive, but we discovered many other benefits to combined purchasing. Collectively, we were now big enough to order private label products, which we marketed under the Pro Stock brand. Headers, tires, wheels, all kinds of products.

Unfortunately, Angelo was in a big expansion mode just as the economic crunch of '73 and '74 came along, and his bank went bust and took him down. At the time he was the largest such chain in the U.S.; no small player by any means.

We continued the buying group with 12 to 14 warehouse members until the early 1980s, when it quietly went away. The big issue was finding someone to run the organization. If you don't have the right person up there waving the baton, the musicians won't play properly.

None of the early days of these organizations—SEMA, PWA, Pro Stock Buying Group—were easy. There was lots of in fighting and arguing and yelling, because you're talking about a lot of strong-minded entrepreneurs and their firm ideas on how to do things. We'd fight and grouse at each other, but in the end, things got done. Good things, positive things, things that pay dividends today for people who weren't even born when those early scuffles and arguments took place.

Yet, when it was all said and done those guys I'd fuss and argue with turned out to be my best friends. For example, I still see Angelo at various industry functions, and I count him among my closest friends. I guess a friendship that's been forged on mutual experiences is the strongest kind, and that's sure been the case with Angelo and me. Really, with all my friends. We've gone shoulder to shoulder through a lot of years and a lot of tough situations!

When this group of entrepreneurs started the evolution in the performance industry, they were truly a fascinating cast of characters. To name a few: Joe Hrudka of Mr. Gasket; Els Lohn of Eelco; Louis Senter of Ansen; Robert E. Petersen of Petersen Publishing (*Hot Rod Magazine*); Dean Moon; Mickey Thompson; Ed Iskendarian; Vic Edelbrock; George Hurst; Aaron Fenton; Phil Weiand; Bruce Crower; Ted Halibrand; Bill Simpson; Ed Cholokian; and Joe Mondelo. These pioneers of our industry will never be duplicated; they threw the molds away on the whole bunch!

24

Opportunities Seized, Opportunities Missed

Since the very beginning, one of the constants for Speedway Motors has been the mix between our racing business and our hot rod business. I've always considered myself fortunate in that the two industries — separate, yet similar — allowed some diversity in our operations.

Through much of the early years, racing represented 75 percent of our business, and hot rods were 25 percent. One reason why, I suspect, is that I was very active in racing through those early years. *Very* active. Nearly every weekend would find me in the pit area somewhere with my race car, and naturally that influenced the direction of our efforts.

Plus, the hot rod industry was a little slower to come around, to build and mature. We've seen lots of peaks and valleys, booms and busts over the past 60 years.

In the very beginning, you could almost say the performance industry was the "Ford" industry. When I became immersed in the world of automobiles in the 1940s, Ford was the overwhelming choice for car guys. There were lots more of them around, with a small but growing number of aftermarket performance parts available.

When you walk through my museum you realize that the performance industry actually dates back to the turn of the last century. When cars began to be mass-produced, a few pioneers immediately began building parts to improve them.

One of the groundbreaking cars in our history was the 1940 Ford, particularly the coupe. That was a nice car. The later cars of the '40s were heavier, bigger, and didn't handle and ride nearly as well. The '40 Ford was an enduring design that remains popular to this day.

With the advent of the 1955 Chevy — and the Chevrolet small block V8 engine — it inspired a lot of people to get excited about cars again. That led to the era of the Detroit muscle car, which fueled great interest in performance automotive issues and inspired another generation of "car guys."

The horsepower race among Ford, GM, and Chrysler during this era was really something. Each was introducing new models and new engines every 90 days; not once a year, but every 90 days. Other companies trying to keep up were literally overwhelmed. Studebaker, Packard, Nash, Rambler, and a few others were buried by the Big Three. Put 'em clear out of business.

But in the early 1970s the government threw a wet blanket over the whole thing. Emission regulations were the start, and insurance companies finished it off with much tighter rules related to performance cars. Then came the recession and fuel crisis of '73-'74, and it took a while for the industry to find its way through the mess.

Somewhere along that time the name "hot rod" sort of evolved into "street rod." "Hot rod" was only visible on my friend Pete Petersen's magazine of that name. There was a negative connotation to that name, kind of like the word "biker." There's a big difference between a guy who rides a Harley and a biker. Perception is a big deal, and nobody likes the perception of "biker."

The street rod name seemed more acceptable, and it caught on. In fact, in the early years Petersen almost changed the title of his magazine because of the negative connotation. I doubt it would have been "street rod" because that name wasn't yet in our vocabulary.

Dick Wells, who worked for me, and whom Petersen later hired to run *Hot Rod Magazine* and *Motor Trend* and the like, started the National Street Rod Ass'n in the '70s. He lined up some investors and got the thing going, and that was a key moment for our industry.

Today, our business mix at Speedway Motors is about 50/50 between racing and street rods. The street rod market has come full circle, and has grown into a very significant industry.

I want to give a shout out to Dick Wells, because he's made a huge contribution to our industry for many years. When I hired him as a counter man in the 1950s, he was a young, excited "car guy," and he ultimately made the performance industry his life.

When I first met Dick he worked for Hank's Auto Store here in Lincoln, and Hank had his guys wear white pants and a white jacket, just like the guy behind the soda fountain at the drug store. Dick walked into my shop one day to pick up some parts for Hank's, and I said, "Hey, kid, what drug store are you from?" I didn't pick up any points that day.

Later on I hired him, and while he was with me he was heavily involved with local car clubs, drag racing, and writing articles for various publications. In 1960 Dick got a call from Wally Parks to come to California and start Wally's new publication, *National Dragster*.

Dick has been living in California ever since, and you'd be hard-pressed to find anyone more dedicated to our industry over the past few decades. He's served on numerous boards, ran Pro-Stock, ran PWA, and was instrumental in the growth of SEMA. He's worn almost *all* the important hats, and worn them well.

We've stayed the best of friends all these years, and I'm proud I helped Dick get started. It's guys like him who have not only made our industry strong, but a pleasure to be a part of.

It's been fun to live through all the ups and downs in our industry, and see it with my own eyes and be totally involved. Whether times were good or bad, I kind of stuck to certain principles, and that's probably been the key to my survival. Many of my friends and rivals fell by the wayside down through the years, because that old path is treacherous.

It's good to stick to your principles, especially things like honesty, hard work, and treating others with respect. However, there were also times when my principles prevented me from taking advantage of lucrative opportunities that were presented.

For example, as I said earlier, I never believed in debt. *Never.* If I didn't have the money on hand to buy something, I didn't buy it. Period. The idea of going into debt frightened me so badly, I would have no part of it.

That required me to grow Speedway Motors very slowly, very steadily, in a controlled fashion. Today, I understand that controlled growth is far and away the safest and most desirable way to grow. However, I had no choice but to grow slowly, because I wouldn't borrow money, and without a loan I didn't have the capital lying around to finance rapid expansion and growth.

In hindsight, however, there were times I should have borrowed money in order to take advantage of an opportunity. For example, in 1970 my very good friend, Charlie Card, approached me with a very generous offer. Charlie owned Honest Charlie's in Chattanooga, Tenn., one of the largest performance mail-order companies in the U.S.

I met Charlie through industry meetings and the like, and we hit it off nicely. One day he decided to move away from the mail-order segment of his business in order to focus on developing retail stores. The cost of printing and mailing catalogs was soaring, as well as increases in prices from our suppliers. These were seemingly insignificant increases — probably two to five percent — but he was playing so close on his margins that such an increase made the difference between winning and losing, between a black number and a red number.

Charlie and his family hoped to become an entity similar to Western Auto or Super Shops, selling performance parts through retail locations. They began turning their focus in that direction.

Charlie was a very good friend, and he was kind to me. He offered to give me his mailing list of 75,000 customers. Not sell; *give*.

The mailing list is the most important asset for every mail-order business. Today, I have mine insured for $3 million in case somebody accidentally purged it. So this was a very generous thing for Charlie to offer.

The idea was I would mail each of his customers a postcard offering them our catalog for $3, and hopefully some would begin buying from me. I quickly did the math in my head: Postage for a postcard was 10 cents, and at 75,000 names we're talking $7,500 in postage alone, plus the cost of printing the postcard.

At that moment I didn't have $7,500. So I had to decline Charlie's offer, because I couldn't pull it off. Simple scenario. That's the way it was.

Our business would have been much better if I would have just borrowed the $7,500 and did the mailing, and gained more market share. We had nice growth in later years, but it would've come much faster, I think, had I been able to capitalize on Charlie's offer.

Another missed opportunity came in the late '50s or early '60s by way of Ed Almquist of New Jersey. Ed probably did as good a job as anybody in the business with his catalog operation, which carried the Almquist name. Ed also created and owned the Sparkomatic line of products, which was a big success.

Ed was obsessed with spark plugs with multiple electrodes, gadgets to improve gas mileage, this that or the other. I think he had a little "carney" in him. He was a very smart guy, with a lot of experience. He had been a pilot during World War II, and was one of those guys who was good at everything he tried.

When George Hurst introduced his floor shifter, it was by far the top item in terms of volume in any speed shop. Not long after, Ed developed a low-cost shifter to compete with the Hurst.

I began offering the Sparkomatic shifter, and it really took off. In the meantime Ed began developing many other performance parts, and pretty soon his business was booming.

We did something a little different with the shifter, and it worked out very nicely. Most shifters were sold only in a package: shifter, stick, knob, boot and plate, and so forth. We broke the Sparkomatic package apart and sold the parts separately, which almost nobody else would do. This really helped the guy who didn't need the whole package, but maybe just needed the boot because his was torn. I advertised in *Hot Rod Magazine*, and we did a big volume.

One day — and again, I think this was the 1970s — Ed Almquist sold the shifter division of his company to a couple of guys from New York. He came to me and offered me the rest of his product line for $75,000. It was a great opportunity, but once again I didn't have $75,000. More importantly, I didn't have the guts to try and borrow the money or raise it through investors.

As I look back, those are probably the two biggest missed opportunities I ever had. I wasn't able to seize them, and I missed out. I can see now that acting on those two opportunities would have moved Speedway Motors much more quickly into a growth pattern. But shame on me.

Opportunities *seized*, and opportunities *missed*. That's what it's all about.

There were a couple of times I was pretty sure my business was going to explode with growth, just take off beyond anything I could have imagined. It never worked out like that, of course.

Before SEMA was created, there were a few auto accessory shows in places like Chicago and Los Angeles. Noel Carpenter had an early version of such a show in Anaheim, the predecessor of the SEMA show. My buddy Joe Hrudka was just getting started with his Mr. Gasket Co., and Joe called and said he wanted to get a booth at Noel's show, but they wanted $300 for the booth space. Would I be interested in splitting the booth rental with Joe?

I said I'd be glad to do this, so Joe and I worked the show, just the two of us. I showed up with a fiberglass T-bucket body, and my Cool Man Glass Tint, and maybe another goofy thing or two. Joe had his gaskets and a few other products.

Believe it or not, neither of us had one single buyer that weekend. Not one. I almost had to give my T-bucket body to a friend of mine from Texas, because I didn't want to pay the expense of shipping it home.

But the show was not a bust. It was all about making contacts, building relationships, raising visibility. It might not be immediately evident, but many times things are happening as a result of the contacts you made at those early shows. As I look back I can see it was these kinds of shows that created relationships I continue to enjoy today. I was laying the groundwork that still exists to this day, and it was a critical part of our business.

The people in our business in those earlier years, I think, were driven more by the automotive passion than the idea of making a lot of money. That's why I became such good friends with so many of those early pioneers—we shared a genuine passion for cars, and the industry. If you happened to hit it big and get rich, that's fine, but even if you didn't, you enjoyed what you were doing.

Somehow, and maybe it was a show like Noel's in Anaheim, I got hooked up with Roy Warshawski from Chicago, the granddaddy of all automotive catalog businesses.

For many years I received monthly letters from Warshawski, looking for new items to add to the catalog. Their catalog was larger—by a multiplier of 20—than any in the business. Honest Charlie, Ed Almquist in the East, the California guys—Neuhouse, Moon, Bell, and others—nobody had an offering the size of Warshawski. Warshawski was larger by a bunch, and his penetration was strong. If you signed up for their catalog you got it until you died, and they might have even forwarded it to the hereafter. And they published constantly, putting out a catalog every 30 days, it seemed. Every time you turned around another catalog appeared in your mailbox.

The Warshawski catalog, along with their sister company J.C. Whitney, sold every conceivable type of automotive item. Replacement parts, custom parts, used parts, everything. Roy's dad was in the salvage business in the very early days, and I can remember ordering a used engine and transmission out of the Warshawski catalog in 1952.

And their catalogs were amazingly detailed: If they took on a line of Holley carburetors, for example, the catalog would list every line item. The catalog was illustrated with line drawings, and no photographs. That's how you went to market in those days: nothing fancy.

Because they did such a huge volume, Warshawski could undersell everybody by almost half. Roy had a lot of buying power, and therefore he got margins. If you got your item listed in their catalog, they immediately became your biggest customer because of their amazing reach and volume. He was like Sears in the early days, or maybe like Wal-Mart today. They controlled their vendors, and almost told them what they were going to pay for their product.

At one of the shows Roy told me he printed his catalog by the boxcar load, and I remember thinking, "Boy, if I could just get enough money to buy the *paper* for a boxcar load of catalogs…" It was beyond anything I could imagine.

One day I had a conversation with Roy about adding my fiberglass T-bucket roadster bodies to their catalog. This product was a genuine breakthrough in our industry, and I was proud of those bodies. They were well made, and quite beautiful in deep metal flake colors.

When Roy agreed to carry the bodies in his catalog, I truly thought I had *arrived*. I was suddenly going to become a fantastic success with these bodies, and maybe my business would double in size…maybe triple! I kind of wondered how I was going to spend all that money.

I was about to learn a big, big lesson: Maybe being the biggest wasn't the best thing for ol' Speedy Bill.

From the start, things were difficult. Warshawski would receive and process the orders, and I would drop-ship the product to the customer. It had to go via truck because of the size, and they'd usually run a forklift through the side of the body or something, and I had to deal with all that. If the guy needed to return it, it came directly back to me.

But the biggest issue was financial. Warshawski was very slow in paying me, and this was a time in my business when I needed to get paid *yesterday* because my cash flow was so tight. *Very* tight. I had no cash flow, period. Cash was something that must have been stopped at the border, because it was sure scarce around my place.

Luckily, I recognized what was happening: This deal with Warshawski was about to do me in. I could see right away how a guy could go broke: Invest in materials and labor, build the product, get it shipped, deal with customer service, all that, and in the meantime no payments for months.

Unless you've got lots of cash, volume doesn't help you in that scenario. In fact, volume just kills you more quickly.

I quietly ended my deal with Warshawski, and my bodies were no longer in their catalog.

Those grandiose ideas of spectacular success are the stuff dreams are made of, especially among young and inexperienced people like I was at the time. I had very little knowledge of how the real world operates.

Today I know that business isn't a fairy tale, and if the Fairy Godmother comes along you'd better be careful because she might send you up the river without a paddle.

For example, let's say Wal-Mart called and wanted to carry a few of our parts in every one of its stores. Some years ago I'd be in euphoria at such a conversation, thinking I had it made. Today, however, I'm much more cautious and realistic, because I know there is a dark lining in every silver cloud. Hate to be pessimistic, but that's reality. Deals are never without challenges, and some challenges are so big they'll eat you alive.

Remember this: It's never, ever as easy as it looks.

Just to say, "Here, we're gonna do it..." without keeping your eye on the ball, boy, that's dangerous. That lesson my dad taught me as a small boy — "Keep your eye on the ball" — still holds true today. Stay focused, and keep things in perspective.

I mentioned Joe Hrudka a moment ago, and he was one of the most interesting players to come along in the performance business. Joe and I had a good friendship, and a lot of mutual respect. We spent quite a lot of time talking and traveling together in those early years. Joe came out of a rough, tough neighborhood in Cleveland; Cleveland is a tough town, baby, just about as tough as New York or Chicago.

I was Joe's first customer of his Mr. Gasket product line, his first and only product line at the time. It was an intake manifold gasket made of a special material that was not available in the automotive industry. Joe was a drag racing builder/driver who saw the need, created the product, and started his business in his home garage. His mother was his first employee, so to say he had humble beginnings is a fact.

In the late '60s Joe had an idea he could grow his company, Mr. Gasket, by greatly expanding his product line. He and I had long conversations about which products he should develop, how to go about it, and so forth.

In fact, when I damn near got killed at Eagle Raceway in 1968, Joe called me every night in the hospital to talk business. He had a buddy who worked at the phone company, and after midnight Joe had the guy patch his call — without long-distance charges, of course — into my hospital room. We'd talk for two or three hours about his product line, and this went on for several weeks until my doctors found out. They said it was impairing my recovery, and they made the nurses unhook my phone.

The first 165 items Joe developed came from those conversations. What parts were needed, the product specs, where to have them manufactured, how to price them; we spent hours talking it all over.

For example, when you banged a Hurst 4-speed shifter from second to third gear while powershifting, you'd blow out the little nylon bushing on the shifter rod. The clip would pop off, the rod would fall out of the shifter ear, and you're dead in the water. I'd say, "You know, Joe, it would be great if somebody would manufacturer a graphite bushing for the Hurst shifter, and make the clip out of spring steel instead of mild steel…"

And off Joe would go, making it happen. Next thing you know he had an upgrade package for the Hurst shifter. Plus, he developed his own Mr. Gasket shifter, too.

Another of Joe's early products was a locking lug nut to prevent somebody from stealing your mag wheels. I went with him to Chicago to purchase the little company manufacturing the part; Joe was doing the buying, I was there for moral support. Joe was smart, and aggressive, but he wasn't really good at talking to people at that early stage.

I hooked Joe up with Herb Goldstein, who had successfully sold my Cool Man Glass Tint. Herbie was a good fit for Joe, and they were together for many years. It was funny, they would fight like cats, and Joe was forever threatening to fire Herbie. And Herbie *was* a loose cannon, one of those guys who was difficult to manage. But they were good for each other, and I was constantly intervening to keep them together. This combo was clearly the recipe for success.

I've been in that situation a lot. People ask my help or advice, and I'll give them the best I've got. Not because it makes me money, but because it's the right thing to do. I want people to be helpful to me, so I want to treat them the same way. That's the way I think.

Eventually Joe sold his company, and made a bunch of money. But a few years later, when the company was struggling, he bought it back for pennies on the dollar. It was recently sold again, and they took the company from public status to private. At one time Joe's stock was worth $50 million, when $50 million was a lot of money.

As Joe went up the line, he kicked a lot of rungs out of the ladder. We hardly have any conversations these days, because he's moved on to purchase a chain of restaurants and our lives have gone in different directions. But Joe was definitely a major player in our industry, and he did all right for a blue-collar guy who was working as a bartender in the beginning. He had a lot of smart people around him, and a lot of desire.

I've met a lot of guys who were really smart, or really good at what they do. But few have been what I call a true mechanical genius, like Howard Johansen.

I first met Howard over the telephone in the early 1950s. I was doing a lot of engine work at the time, experimentation and learning at the same time. It was very helpful when somebody with knowledge could share time with me, and Howard was a pioneering force in camshaft design.

His California company, Howards Cams, was well known at that period, at least among gearheads like me. He was a huge presence in drag racing, but his knowledge was much more broad.

Most camshaft specialists focused on drag racing, which is all about acceleration over a specific distance. But we soon discovered that various engine applications require a completely different camshaft design. In oval racing, for example, you have to keep the engine together more than 10 or 15 seconds, and the power band is completely different. Howard recognized the differences in these various applications long before most other cam specialists.

Howard was a great mentor to me, and he shortened my learning curve by a lot with my race cars. Compression ratios, camshaft lift and duration, all those things. Later I learned that Howard was originally from David City, Neb., and had gone west to California in 1941 to look for work in the defense plants. He landed as a welder in a California shipyard, and put down roots.

I quickly began using Howard's cams in my race cars, and recommended them to my customers. They weren't as well advertised as some of his competitors, but his products were as good or better.

Howard was a racer, and the typical problem for a racer is that when he produces his own products, his own racing often gets in the way and usually his business suffers. The passion for most racers is in development and competition, not business administration and marketing and advertising. Howard was a little like that, and so was I. In fact, many of us racers had that problem. We're off racing somewhere, usually not spending the attention we should on our business.

There were other people doing innovative work in camshafts during the 1950s. Crower, Iskendarian, Giovanni, there were probably a dozen manufacturers. In California you could buy a cam grinder—which looks like a big lathe—very easily, and make your own product. You could turn out a camshaft in 45 minutes, and get $20 to $30 for it, which was a day's wage at that time. Tools like this were readily available in southern California in the late 1940s and early '50s because many were war surplus.

The defense industry was a huge influence in the hot rod explosion just after the war. All that knowledge from the defense plants, all the new materials that had been developed, all that surplus machinery, it all combined to allow a bunch of various manufacturers to make their mark, and create an industry.

Pretty soon little support industries were cropping up, supplying tools and raw materials and other stuff, and that began the essential support system to those fledgling performance manufacturers.

One of the prominent names that also came from that early period was Ed Iskendarian. He came from an Armenian family, and was knowledgeable in technical workings of engines. He learned how to sell merchandise, how to advertise, and he stayed out in front of the customer. He created the perception that his stuff was the leading edge of technology, and created a lot of catchy logos and so forth.

In addition to his passion for performance, Ed had a passion for collecting tools. He bought lots of used mills and lathes, things like that, at auction sales. Pretty soon he filled his entire shop with the stuff.

I realized early on that certain guys in the business of camshaft design were much more advanced than others in their field. It wasn't just about advertising and logos; it was about product, and performance. Howard Johansen was very strong in that area; Bruce Crower was another wizard.

Many times the people who started the business—the guy who was the heart-and-soul of the place—didn't stay hands-on long enough. They became an absentee owner, and that is very hard to make work. The hands-on part is what keeps you humble and barefoot.

In those early days, the shops turning out all these performance products were tiny operations. Even names that are big today — Edelbrock, Iskendarian, and others — started out with two guys in a small shop, turning out parts as fast as they could. There were no CNC milling machines, no computers, very few tools, and efficiency was nothing like it is today. It took a long time to make things because you did everything by hand.

In the early years I took a trip to California, and saw many of these shops firsthand. Boy, was I shocked; I had envisioned California as some sort of paradise, and these shops as something like the Taj Mahal. But they were just little shops, a lot like my operation back in Nebraska.

I remember my eyes really being opened on that trip. I was thinking, "Gee, I'm doing all right after all!"

I mentioned the Edelbrock name a moment ago, and it reminded me of the first time I met Vic Edelbrock, Sr. He was still in a humble situation at that time, and his company was still just a small southern California concern.

Vic made quite a name for himself in 1937 by building parts for the Ford V8-60 engine. Just prior to WWII, Ford introduced a 60-hp V8 that was designed to use less gasoline than the standard 85-hp Ford V8. It was built from 1937 to '40, and it quickly became a favorite among home-built midget racers.

If your grandma left you the farm, you had the money to get a shiny Offy engine, all aluminum, which would outrun 99 percent of the home-built midgets. But for everybody else, they had to look for something less expensive. That's where the Ford V8-60 came in.

Just before the war, and in the half-dozen years after, midget racing thrived in pockets throughout the country. One of those pockets was southern California, with their big population base and nice weather that allowed a very long racing season. Plus, there was plenty of industry in the region.

Vic began building manifolds and cylinder heads for these V8-60s, and was quite successful. He was also one of the first to experiment with nitromethane, and found that a 20 percent mixture in the fuel made 30 to 40 percent more horsepower.

Several V8-60 cars in Vic's back yard were successful against the Offy-powered cars, and pretty soon the little Fords began appearing at midget races throughout the country. Racing has always been monkey-see, monkey-do, so when people saw Vic's parts on those V8-60s, it created an immediate demand for his stuff.

That was the genesis for Edelbrock, which today is a major player in the performance industry.

I was thinking about what I said a moment ago about talking with Howard Johansen on the phone, and him taking the time to answer my questions.

The help he gave me...all I can hope is that history has repeated itself through the years, and in turn I have helped others with their questions about our hobby. Whenever I got such questions, I've always been completely honest with my answers. I like to lay my head down at night and not have any remorse or guilt for saying something that wasn't true.

I think there are probably a large number of customers and enthusiasts who have learned something from what I learned, and shared with them. I still travel to a lot of industry events — both racing and street rodding — each year, and I'm deluged with questions on flathead Fords and the like.

I do my best to answer them, and steer people in the right direction. That's what Howard did for me, and I want to keep the chain going, to the next generation.

25

An Expanding Circle

In 1986 I was invited to join several Ford Motor Co. executives on a trip to Taiwan. This was during a period when many U.S. companies began expanding their business relationship with worldwide companies, particularly those in the Far East.

This was by far the longest trip I had ever taken. I struggled with jet lag, and for an entire week I hardly slept a wink at night because my body clock was so out of whack. I never did get adjusted to the time difference.

Everything I saw from the time we landed is stuck in my mind. When I walked off the plane into a huge airport at Taipai, it was full of people but was eerily quiet. The people went about their business in a very orderly fashion, with a constant state of calmness.

The people were slender and fit, and nobody was obese. No big guts or fat asses; they looked like we ought to look. They were a petite, small people.

They smoked a lot, though; that's the first thing I noticed that was different.

We were accompanied at all times by a translator, which made things much easier. We were met at the airport by the owner of a company in Tainan City, located at the far southern end of the island of Taiwan. This was probably a 150-mile drive, maybe as far as 200 miles. We were riding in a big Mercedes, rolling down the highway at a hundred miles an hour.

When we arrived we had a small breakfast. I immediately noticed that the portions were tiny compared to what I was used to. I guess that explained the petite build of the Taiwanese.

After breakfast we went to visit their manufacturing plant. As we approached the main gate, I realized it was closed. We're running along about 75 mph, and that gate was coming up pretty damned fast. I thought, "Boy, that gate isn't going to open in time!"

The driver never lifted, and the gate swung open in the nick of time. It kind of illustrated everything I saw in Taiwan: There was a quiet precision and order to things.

I noticed throughout our trip that all of the big manufacturing facilities were fenced and gated. Most of the workers at such places lived on-site, in dormitories.

Our first visit was to the largest gasket manufacturing facility in the world, at least at that time. Three brothers were the principals of the company, which had been in business about 20 years.

In Taiwan nearly everybody, rich and poor, does a stint in the military as a young adult. These three brothers had done their term, and when their service ended returned to their father's rice farm, located about a block from the factory entrance. In fact, I saw the father's farm during our tour of the area.

These three brothers decided they didn't want to be rice farmers, so they looked around in search of a product they could manufacture. There must be 10 million motor scooters at every intersection in Taiwan, and the brothers decided they would make gaskets for motor scooters. For the oil pan, the head, and all that.

In a very short time they became the largest manufacturer of gaskets in the world. The *world*! Eventually they were supplying all the OEM gaskets to Japanese car manufacturers.

These three men were great guys, and very smart. Like most Taiwanese businesspeople, they watch you very closely during conversation, trying to figure out if you know anything. They are very suspect of sales agents. They give you lots of subtle tests while you're there, studying you very carefully.

While you're at lunch, for example, you might be casually visiting and enjoying the situation; while you're relaxing they're constantly studying and testing you.

One of the interesting things I noticed was that most big companies in Taiwan are actively involved with smaller companies, helping them gain more business and financing them.

For example, we visited a half-dozen smaller manufacturing firms, all connected to the large gasket manufacturer.

After the third or fourth day there, our hosts began calling me, "Uncle Bill."

"What's this all about?" I asked.

"You've been accepted into the family," one of their aides assured me. I had earned their trust, and they felt I was worth talking to. They still, to this day, call me "Uncle Bill."

From that moment on, everything changed 180 degrees. Our conversations were much more in-depth and revealing. I guess you'd say we started to get down to the nitty-gritty of things.

I'll never forget one "sleepless night." I was still trying to get adjusted to the time lag, and would leave the TV on all night. Even in Taiwan, they were televising America's great space liftoff with the schoolteacher, the *Challenger* space shuttle. There I was, a million miles from home and witnessed this great tragedy. Although I was so far away, it still broke my heart as an American.

Aside from that "downer," the entire trip was a great experience in many ways.

One way was that I actually invented a product while I was over there, a product of which I still sell 10,000 units each year. I saw the capabilities of their equipment, and one morning I asked them, "Could you make me a gasket that goes between the air cleaner and a four-barrel carburetor that would have the proper durometer rubber, with a steel liner inside?"

This had been a nagging problem in our business for years and years. This particular gasket had traditionally been made of paper, and once fuel sloshed all over the gasket, they became brittle. The first time you tightened the air cleaner too much, they broke.

When your car visited the shop, the mechanic threw the gasket away and put the air cleaner back on the carburetor without a gasket. That allowed air to bypass the air cleaner, filling your carburetor with dirt and junk. If you're running a race car, particularly on dirt, it's essential that you keep dirt out of the carburetor.

I presented my idea for this new gasket one afternoon, and the next morning when we visited the plant here they came with a sample…the gasket was perfectly designed! The following day they had the packaging done, and it too was perfect!

To this day, I am amazed at how they attack business when presented with such an idea. It wasn't, "Let's wait until tomorrow, and then maybe six months down the road we'll have it done if we aren't too busy going to the bar or watching a football game."

It was their devotion to detail that really impressed me, their attention to making money and being successful. I had never seen such focus in my life.

For example, when I began purchasing from them, their product might arrive in a wooden crate. If you looked at the wood closely, it was recycled, not fresh-cut. Which worked perfectly for the application.

If you examined the steel banding around the crate, you noticed a nice gold hue, and discovered it was made out of recycled tin cans.

They didn't miss a trick, and concentrated on the very basic things. It was amazing attention to detail.

When you opened the crate you found the products packaged in plastic that was very easy to see through, unlike the opaque material we often use here. Anybody with a degree of intelligence could look inside that package and see it was the right product. They didn't have to look at it twice, or think twice about it. Very quick and efficient.

Instead of packing things in quantities of 12 or 15, everything was done in multiples of 10. So even the simplest clerk who could count with their fingers could gather 10, 20, 30, 40, 50, very quickly. If the product is in lots of 12, and you need 50, now how am I going to figure that out? Even a young kid can figure out multiples of 10. That's why their system was so efficient.

I called all my employees together and showed them these things. I said, "You know, these guys could win the war of economics because they're thinking. They're doing things that we don't think need to be done."

That's the way I viewed it, in the world according to Bill.

There is one other key thing to talk about. In all my dealings with people in the Orient, they have proven themselves to be very honorable. If you have a problem, they don't say, "Well, we'll take care of it next year." Or, "It was your fault," or whatever. They step right up and say, "I will make it right."

Replace it, re-machine it, re-plate it, whatever it takes. They are extremely honorable people, at least in my view. And I've dealt with them a great deal.

The world has changed countless times since that trip almost 24 years ago. However, the people of Taiwan—as well as many other Asian countries—continue to prove themselves formidable businesspeople.

At Speedway Motors our business has grown to the point that we're doing business with people throughout the U.S. and Canada, and also Taiwan, China, India, and South Africa. It really is a global market, even for a little guy from Nebraska.

I used to do more business in India than I do today. I was heavily involved in India for about 20 years, but there were some quality issues there, even though they speak the King's English. They have problems with materials, and consistency.

The Japanese have always held a lot of influence over trade issues in India, mainly because of the control of so many key natural resources.

When you study the history of the world, you discover than the countries of the Far East were trading extensively among themselves while we were still rowing a boat. They were trading commodities such as leathers, silk, bamboo, salt, sugar, all those things. They are traders by nature, while we're more inclined to focus on our world, and trade within ourselves.

Read the history books: Throughout our history, the West never traded very well with the Orient because they always got the best of us. This goes back not just 100 years or 200 years, but maybe 2,000 years.

In the many years since that first trip, I still do a lot of business with the large gasket manufacturer. We've become very good friends, and I can honestly say — like nearly all of my dealings with the Asian people — they've been a pleasure to work with.

It's grown beyond simply being a business transaction. They have become friends with me, and my family. They have come to Lincoln to visit us, and played golf with my sons. One of the sons was the golf champion of Taiwan some 20 years ago.

There is so much we can learn from their culture, and the way they approach business. But instead of learning from others, too often we become defensive, and stubborn, and insist that we're the world leader in everything.

Well, as much as I hate to say it, in some things we're far from the world leader. Education, for example. Other cultures insist their kids pay attention in school and demand they earn a good education, while we often spoil our kids and "soften the blow" by relaxing our education standards. In many urban American cities, the schools are a complete disaster, with not even half the kids graduating high school.

Yet, we puff our chests out and say, "We're the greatest!" Even if we're not. Hey, just look at where the U.S. stands in the world rankings of education, and get back with me.

That kind of denial, I fear, is going to get us into big trouble down the road.

Another big difference is the context in which business is operated. In Asia, companies do things not just for the next year, or the next five years, but with an eye on the next *hundred* years.

Here in America you can't get executives to think beyond the current quarter, because every public company is under such intense pressure to build the stock price *now*. We've created a situation where American business — and our government — has sacrificed the long term in order to satisfy the short term.

You don't have to be an expert economist to see the folly in that.

Certainly I'm not bad-mouthing the United States; I'm an American, and I love my country. But it's troubling to see us slip into lazy and inefficient ways, because the day is coming — mark my words — when such attitudes will create a very difficult situation for our country.

I hope I'm wrong; I really do. But I wish everybody could visit a place like Taiwan and see what I saw. It was an eye-opening experience 26 years ago, I assure you.

26

Labor of Love

In March of 2009 I was honored to accept the Robert E. Petersen Lifetime Achievement Award in Indianapolis at the 11th Annual Hotrod & Restoration Trade Show. It was a very nice affair, and naturally it meant a lot to me because Pete Petersen was a good friend.

This ceremony was held at the Indianapolis Convention Center, and Joyce and my four sons accompanied me to the breakfast presentation where we were joined by nearly 1,000 trade show attendees.

Several of my old buddies joined me on stage at the presentation for an informal chat — I thought it might be a roast at first, but it was all in great fun — including Posie (Dutch Fenical), Angelo Giampetroni, Dick Messer of the Petersen museum, and the TV star and emcee Barry Meguiar.

It was a very proud moment, obviously, because it always feels good to be recognized. One thing I couldn't help but notice, however, is how my friends arched their eyebrows and widened their eyes when Messer told the audience about the Smith Collection Museum of American Speed back in Lincoln.

It seems that I've created something special!

Actually, that makes me even more proud. The collection and museum will out-live me, and that's a wonderful thing. I mean, how many of us have the satisfaction of knowing that we've created something for future generations to enjoy? Kind of like that old adage about planting a tree you'll never sit under. It's a very good feeling.

I have to confess something: The origin of the collection and museum is something of a great, wonderful accident. That sounds funny, but it's true.

When I started collecting all that stuff—I'm talking about the 1940s here—I never thought about the concept of a museum. How could I? I mean, how could a 15-year-old kid who simply hung on to things he liked ever envision people wanting to look at that piece some 60 years later?

Frankly, some 30 years ago I began to realize that the museum and collection was a significant amount of work and expense. Most people don't work toward creating something that's a lot of work and expense at the end of the trail. It's usually just the opposite!

However, I wanted the collection to be shared and shown properly, admired and enjoyed by people who have the same passion I do. Because this is a hardcore collection of performance memorabilia, for sure.

As a private collection, mine began as basically just piles of stuff. When I'd have my buddies in town and they wanted to see some of the pieces I had been describing, it came down to a couple of guys looking at just another pile of junk, stored in dirty boxes on the top shelf.

Some years ago I soon realized that if I were going to do the right thing with all this stuff, I needed to put it in some kind of presentable shape, something manageable, and make it something we can all be proud of.

Today, the Smith Collection Museum of American Speed covers 135,000 square feet in a three-story building adjacent to Speedway Motors. We have people coming through the museum every day, and it has become quite a center of activity.

I often hear a couple of familiar questions from people coming through the museum.

One question is: "How much is all this stuff worth?" I don't exactly know the answer, and it doesn't matter. Assembling the collection was never about money, or winning the "big-dog pissin' contest." It's always been about doing the right thing, and giving back to the world. That's far more important than money.

Here is the other question: "Why did you collect all this stuff, and why did you go to all this effort to showcase it so nicely?" That answer is complicated, because I know exactly why, but I can't explain it very well.

To begin with, it goes back to me falling in love with automobiles in the early 1940s. I was barely a teenager; when something hooks and inspires you at that age, it's usually a powerful experience.

That's how it was with me; I was so enthusiastic, so fascinated, so consumed...cars and racing were all I could think about.

Sound familiar?

From the first car I purchased — that Model T pickup when I was 14 — I found everything associated with repairing or improving the car to be a big effort. Grinding the valves, putting in new piston rings, getting something welded or fabricated, it was a challenge because nobody — or certainly very few people — knew how to do those things.

Then I might run across an old cylinder head from an old Model T that dated back some 30 years, with an overhead valve conversion or something unusual. Say, that was unique, and exciting!

I distinctly remember looking at such a piece and thinking, "How on earth did that guy get that done?" He didn't come from another planet, he didn't have some kind of superhuman powers or equipment, and yet he created something above and beyond anything I had ever seen.

That's the moment, I think, that instilled in me a powerful admiration and appreciation for that type of thinking. Different, and unusual. Creative.

My emotion took on a tangible form when I would try to acquire the unusual part, even if I knew I couldn't possibly use it on my car. I guess I had such a respect for the piece, and what it represented, that I wanted to own it.

Collecting is like looking at a book: You look at the cover, and the title, and it might intrigue you enough that you open the cover. If you start to read the text, does it have enough interesting things to hold you? If not, you'll probably close the book and find other things that interest you.

That's how it was with me, anyway. Once I managed to hold onto those first few unusual pieces, it honed my interest and gave me an appetite to become more and more interested and knowledgeable in automotive technology and history.

I suppose 99 percent of the world would have looked at that cylinder head and thought, "What's that piece of junk?" And maybe it is junk; the eye of the beholder and all that stuff.

Remember, my daddy didn't give me a big check just to wake up each morning. My grandmother didn't leave me a big farm. I was a guy of very modest means. Since I didn't have what they call "resources," I had to watch my pennies and choose carefully how I spent them.

That meant I might have to work another half-day in order to own that unusual piece, but that was all right. It didn't represent much money, but it did keep me working pretty hard to support what was soon a habit.

Some guys have a drug habit, or a gambling habit, or a drinking habit, or a "women" habit; my habit was acquiring unique and unusual pieces of automotive technology.

Along the way, one piece at a time, a couple things happened. One, I had a pretty good-sized pile of stuff. Two, by studying all of this, I acquired a good knowledge of the history of automotive technology, particularly related to the Ford Model T.

It was like a big puzzle; I knew of the pieces I had, and I knew of other things I'd seen and read about, and I had a desire to fill in my collection of stuff with the missing pieces.

There was a tremendous variety of parts out there. Some pieces came from Ford, some pieces from other entities, with many variations on the same theme. And again, it was all about my admiration for the people who came up with those variations. This piece was manufactured in Buffalo, N.Y., for example, while this other piece came from Anderson, Ind.

Today, I have the largest collection of Model T accessories in the world. By far and away. And my collection of performance and antique engines is the largest in the world. Sometime later I also grew interested in pedal cars, and toy race cars, because they were a natural extension of my interests. So I assembled quite a collection of those items as well.

Joyce and I never took vacations, sitting in the sand or playing golf, going fishing, whatever. Instead, we used almost every available "off" minute to continue our mission of collecting important and desirable pieces of automotive history. Swap meets, auctions, estate sales, or simply chasing a "hot tip" on an item, we were constantly on the hunt.

This took us literally all over the country, catching last-minute flights east, west, or anywhere in between. We would typically leave on Friday evening and get home late Sunday night in order to be back at work on Monday morning. This was when flying was easy; you walked up to the counter and bought a ticket, instead of making reservations months ahead.

Boy, the hours we spent in a rental car, half lost, trying to locate a race car, engine, sign, you name it. Then we'd have to figure out how to get it back to Lincoln. The shipping issue alone was good for quite a few adventures!

Pretty soon the word was out that Speedy Bill was looking to buy or trade for neat "old stuff." Today, not a day goes by without a phone call from somebody who wants to talk the talk and make a deal. You'd be amazed at what has come my way from those phone calls.

After sixty-plus years of such deals, one day I realized that I actually know more people all around the globe than I do in our own hometown!

One thing that amazes even me is the logistics it took to make this happen. For example, in the beginning I certainly didn't have a three-story building and a staff of people to help with my collection.

Early on I kept things in the garage at my folk's house, or in their basement. Later on, as I got involved in commercial property, I acquired some buildings where things could be stored.

I noticed that it wasn't fun to show my things to people, because everything was in piles. It looked like a junkyard, even to me. I've always been a proud person, and I like my things to look good. I'm proud of what I've got, whether it's a little or a lot. I don't want to apologize for it.

There was a constant nagging feeling, "Gee whiz, I wish I could show all this to people." And show it in a way that reflected the fact that I was very proud to have owned and preserved this collection.

All of those feelings became a reality in the late 1980s when we began to seriously plan for a way to house and display the material. Remember, everything was scattered in various nooks and crannies, and it was a big challenge to bring it all together in one location.

If I had known what a huge chore it would be, I probably would have crawled into a hole and pulled the lid over me! But we took it one bite at a time, and over several years got the building up and things assembled. Even the most wonderful, delicious steak can't be eaten in one bite. You have to take it one bite at a time, and that's what we did.

Some years ago I had the opportunity to meet Bill Harrah, owner of a magnificent and famous collection of vintage automobiles. Harrah had all the means in the world to build his collection, because he owned a casino in Reno, Nev.

By the late 1970s he had amassed by far the largest collection of vintage cars on the planet. Everybody had heard of him, and his collection. However, when Bill died in 1978 there had apparently been no arrangements made to keep the collection intact.

After his death Holiday Inn purchased Bill's hotel and casino, and the car collection came with the deal. What did Holiday Inn want with a collection of cars, anyway? So the entire collection was disbursed; some were donated to a smaller museum that is still active in Reno, but the bulk went out the door at several high-profile auctions.

What a travesty! To put the collection together as he did, with the means required to do so, and the desire and effort he expended over a long period of time...then to have it all scattered to the winds, under the auctioneer's gavel. A travesty!

As a kid going to Sunday school, there were many Christian ideas instilled in me. One was the principle that you're to leave this planet better than when you arrived. Later, as a student at Nebraska Wesleyan University, this idea was further reinforced.

I believe the collection I've been able to assemble and present will leave a good legacy for the rest of my family's life. Even past my sons, perhaps even past my grandchildren.

I truly hope the collection will live into eternity, long past anyone remembering a guy named Bill Smith. That sounds a little corny, but that's how I feel. I still believe in the idea of leaving things better than when I arrived, and I hope the museum will do that.

That's why we took specific steps to insure that the operation of the museum is secure well into the future. We formed a separate 501(c)3 foundation to oversee the collection and museum, and made endowments that will allow it to continue long after we're gone.

That's why, when people talk about "Bill's collection" I squirm just a little bit. Oh, I'm proud of the collection, and certainly I puff out my chest feathers when people are saying nice things about it. But this thing moved beyond just being "Bill's collection" several years ago.

This collection—and I mean this from my heart—belongs to anybody who loves cars, loves racing, loves history, loves the work of people who are gifted artistically and mechanically. It even belongs to people of coming generations, who haven't yet arrived.

Through the years, I have had fantastic and irreplaceable help from hundreds of friends, neighbors, competitors, employees and acquaintances from all over the world. This was especially

290 / FAST COMPANY

true when it came to getting items back to Lincoln. Countless times people would go above and beyond, offering to haul stuff halfway across the country to "help the cause."

There are too many individuals to name, but you know who you are. I'm sure you all have stories of your own to tell! I thank you with all my heart, because without everyone's help the museum could never have been possible.

However, I would be remiss if I didn't talk about Jim Schuman for a moment. In terms of the Smith Collection, Jim is one of our greatest assets. Jim is an old racing friend, customer, and employee.

His artistic talents were simply amazing. From researching engines, restoring parts and pieces, creating displays, he was wonderful. His real talent was this: he could envision what something could look like and make it reality. Sometimes I would describe my idea for a display in general, sketchy terms. Jim would listen, and come back a couple of days later with the most fantastic display, far beyond anything I could have imagined.

Jim worked very hard at making the museum a reality, until health problems required that he step away. If his health allowed, I know he'd be right there with us every day, inspiring us with his creative ideas.

Thanks, Jimmy.

My college degree was to be a schoolteacher, so inside me there is still this burning desire to impart knowledge onto others. I used to joke that if you didn't know anything about a subject, you wrote about it or taught it. But what I have found with physical examples — which describes everything in our museum — is that it's not about what somebody has said or heard, but is literally real.

A physical example doesn't embellish, lie, or stretch the truth. It doesn't revise history; it IS history. What you see is what you get.

That's why I think this collection will have such relevance to future generations. The history of automobile technology is right here, not to be embellished or diminished. It is presented exactly as it was created, 20 or 40 or 80 or 100 years ago. You can see it, touch it, feel it.

It is thousands and thousands of mechanical items that were created from the turn of the 20th century on, over a span of a hundred years. There were an awful lot of things that were discovered or designed during that period of time.

I've said this to my sons many times: You could not, in today's society, assemble such a collection again. So many of these items are one-offs, where the designer worked on one project for 10, 15, 20 years of his life. His tenacity, his desire, you can't replicate that. So what you see in our museum is truly irreplaceable.

Today the collecting hobby has been reshaped with the advent of things like the Internet, particularly eBay. I didn't have the luxury of any of those things, because 99 percent of my collection was acquired before the Internet became popular.

I have probably walked through the museum a thousand times, usually leading an entourage of visitors. But no matter how many times I walk through, I enjoy it.

Sometimes I walk through all alone, and I pause to carefully look over a particular exhibit.

I still stand in awe of someone's craftsmanship. I mean, all you've got to do is look at that particular piece and marvel. It's like a painting; you're an artist looking at someone else's work. You've painted, too, so you know what it's about, and that's why you admire their work so much. You know what kind of sweat and genius produced the end product.

I can feel it in my body, in a shiver that goes down my back, and I feel good in my tummy because somebody made this and it's a great creation.

I can walk through the museum and still get excited about Robert Roof's cylinder head I acquired when I was 15. Somebody made that piece in 1916 — that's 93 years ago — and it's still impressive. A marvelous piece of engineering.

Compared to today, of course, it is primitive. But it's still a marvelous piece for its time.

Today, almost everything we do — other than computerization — is reverse engineering. You see something that was made before — yesterday, a year ago, 10 years ago — and you improve on it. But when you look at those early guys who spent decades building and creating *new* things, you realize they didn't have any previous examples to work from.

It wasn't reverse engineering. It was creating something new, something never tried before. Those are the things that still intrigue me, and a physical example helps stimulate passion even among those who aren't quite as hardcore as I am.

There were no CNC machines, no CAD-CAM, no computers. Before World War II, we were about fifth or sixth in the world for creating and manufacturing. We couldn't weld, we couldn't cast, we couldn't do many of the basic things.

The war came along, and while it was devastating in terms of cost—both in economics and human suffering—the silver lining was that it moved America toward putting our heads together and making things happen. Nothing else could have united us like the war.

That's the story I see when I walk through the museum. It is the transformation of an entire nation, and how they pursued their passion for mechanical excellence.

That's the "world according to Bill," anyway.

Down through the years, I suppose there have been moments when I wondered why I went to so much trouble to assemble and display all the things in my collection. Frankly, it probably would have been easier to skip the whole process and put all that effort toward other things.

But if I ever had such thoughts, they were all completely erased one quiet Sunday afternoon when I was able to give a brief glimmer of pleasure to my dear, dying friend.

Howard Johansen and I had been good friends since the mid-1950s, and I counted him among my most cherished acquaintances. I admired his knowledge and experience, and I never forgot how he patiently spent time with me on the telephone in those early years, teaching me the dynamics of camshafts and other elements of horsepower.

Along the way we built a friendship based on mutual passion for the automobile. It's easy to share time with someone like-minded, and we spent many hours talking about cars, both past and present.

Sometime around 1988 Howard was diagnosed with throat cancer. I've lost plenty of friends down through the years, and I can tell you I was crushed when Howard told me of his ailment.

You can have too much money, you can have too much stuff, you can have too much ego, you can have too much of almost anything. But you can't have too many friends. Especially friends like Howard.

Howard and I talked a few times while he was fighting his illness, and I knew he wasn't doing very well. I saw him at Bonneville in August, and he said, "I'd sure like to come by your museum and see you, Bill." He was in obvious pain, and the look on his face was almost like a guy who had put his hand on a hot stove. It was very distressing for me to see my friend in that condition. The pain was so intense it had changed his look, his demeanor.

A few weeks later he was on his way to visit his family in David City, Neb., en route to attending the U.S. Nationals drag races in Indianapolis. He called me at my office on Saturday afternoon and asked if it would be possible to come by the following day, even though we're normally closed on Sunday.

"You got it, pal," I said.

He explained that he was in such pain he could probably only stay a half-hour, maybe 45 minutes. We made plans to meet that following morning.

I was excited about showing Howard the museum. I have paid tribute to several people — Howard, Harry Miller, Robert Roof — with special exhibits, and I hoped this would help Howard understand just how much I respected him and his work.

What an innovator Howard was...a mechanical genius, an inventor. I'm not sure I can come up with the right words to cover all he did. If you get into California and talk with old-timers in the performance world, there are more Howard Johansen stories than anybody around. He was a do-er, and he didn't just work on one project...he was involved in many different things. From boats to Bonneville to drag racing to circle track, and he was highly successful in all of them.

He is generally credited as the first man to create an aluminum connecting rod. Think about that for a minute: Something that is widespread in every form of automotive and marine performance today, yet he was the first. The innovator.

Howard ran Bonneville with two belly-tanks, side by side. The motor in one and him in the other. He ran a Cadillac overhead-valve engine in a roaring roadster. He ran hemi DeSoto engines in boats and Bonneville cars, while everybody else ran a hemi Chrysler.

Howard had that special mix of curiosity and brilliance; he would look at something and wonder how he could make it better, and then had the intelligence to actually do it.

So, yeah...I wanted to show him around my museum.

I met him at 10 the next morning at the front door, and my heart sank when I saw the pain on his face. We made our way up the front steps, and through the front entrance.

I have said this many times since then: If I never, ever get another accolade for the museum, it was all worth it by seeing the look on Howard's face when we walked inside the museum that morning. Despite the obvious pain, he stayed until 4 p.m., and he had a smile on his face the entire time.

During those six hours, it was all about two car guys sharing a deep, powerful passion for cars and mechanical things. Howard was proud of the display that honored him, yes, but you could see that he had just as much pride and joy in what *others* had done.

I'll never forget that day. We said goodbye that afternoon, and somehow I knew when I shook his hand that it really was goodbye.

Howard died a short time later.

Money? People talk about it a lot, but in some ways it's meaningless. Instead, I got the greatest reward a human being can ever receive: I put a smile on a friend's face, at a time in his life when he really needed it.

I hope I have told the story properly of my museum, and how much it means to me.

Sure, I like to brag about things I've done, and that's natural for anybody who has raced and been competitive. But when it comes to the museum, I take the idea of sharing my passion very seriously, and I learned a long time ago that it's way beyond just one guy. This is something for *all* of us.

If you're holding this book in your hands, you probably at least have a tiny bit of passion for cars, racing, hot rodding, performance, whatever. If you're ever in Lincoln, I hope you'll take the time to visit our museum, and I hope you get just as excited as I do every time I walk through. Remember, I built the museum for YOU!

27

The She Was a He and I've Got the Car

I will confess to a certain amount of lust when it comes to the cars I've added to our collection through the years. Often I'll see or read about a certain vehicle, and my immediate reaction is something along the lines of, "Oooohhh! I'd like to have that car!"

Cars are almost like ladies: They have a lot of curves and lines and personality. There's a lot of sizzle in the steak, so to speak.

Sometimes I'm fascinated by the history of a car; that can be as important as historical significance or artistic beauty. Each car in the museum has a story, of course, but some stories are downright amazing to the point of the bizarre.

In terms of colorful history, there is a small three-wheeled car parked in my museum that just might offer the most interesting story of all.

To tell this story properly, you have to put yourself back in time to the autumn of 1974, in the midst of the Arab oil embargo. Believe me, fear was running rampant here in America, because the idea of gasoline rationing was very much alive.

Out of the woodwork and into the national media came a 6-foot-1, 175-pound woman named Elizabeth Carmichael. Elizabeth said she was an engineer, and she was going to design and market a revolutionary three-wheeled automobile. Her car was going to get 70 miles per gallon, be capable of running 85 mph, and sell brand new for $1,995.

Now, anybody with a basic understanding of automotive engineering would say in 1974 that this was impossible. Was I skeptical? To the point of laughter. However, the media—and a

shocking number of people who ought to have known better —
lapped it up like a kitten at a bowl of milk.

Elizabeth hired a guy named Dale Clift to build a prototype,
and then Elizabeth went on the PR offensive. A Chicago
newspaper ran an extensive story about the car, and suddenly
Elizabeth was on national television, including a stint on the
Johnny Carson show where she reportedly had him reaching
for his checkbook to invest in her company.

"I have millions of dollars from investors," she claimed, and
she set up luxurious sales offices in a downtown bank building
in Los Angeles. Her company was called Twentieth Century
Motor Car Corp., and their new automobile would be called the
Dale. They would begin taking deposits *immediately* for this
exciting new car, which would be delivered, well...soon.

Let me tell you, it had been a loooonng time since anybody
had attempted to launch a new automobile brand independent
of the "Big Three" manufacturers. Not since Preston Tucker had
anyone come along to claim they were going to build a new
type of automobile.

I think that's what made all this work. The launch of the
Tucker automobile had been a spectacular failure in the late
1940s (I have a Tucker in my museum), and enough time had
passed that most people had forgotten how investors and
customers lost their shirts in that deal. What's that old adage:
"Those who are ignorant of history are doomed to repeat it," or
something like that. So, with little knowledge and good old
reckless enthusiasm, the American press — and a great deal of
the American public — fell for this story hook, line and sinker.

Elizabeth told everybody what they wanted to hear: $1,995, and
70 mpg. People were like sheep, flocking to the slaughterhouse.
She announced that 85,000 cars would be built the first year, and
possibly 250,000 the following year. All of this even though we
were in the midst of a serious economic downturn at the time.

By the way: If you were willing to put down more money in
advance of your order, you would move up in the queue. That
ratcheted up the excitement, and the flow of cash. Elizabeth soon
had the prototype proudly on display at their sales offices. One
of the big morning game shows had the car as a potential prize
for the winning contestant, and it seemed you couldn't pick up
the newspaper or turn on the TV without hearing about the Dale.

In due course long and lanky Elizabeth had several million
dollars in deposits.

Elizabeth explained that the cars were being assembled in a 150,000-sf factory in Burbank, where hundreds of people were employed. However, that's where the wheels began to come off, so to speak. One of the California television stations had a "Scoop Jackson" type reporter who started sniffing around, and he discovered that the only things inside the locked doors of the "factory" were a desk and a chair.

Pretty soon the scam was fully realized. But there's more: Elizabeth Carmichael, it turned out, was actually a man with the last name of Michael (get it? "Car" and "Michael?")

The jig was up, and there was scandal. The IRS got involved fairly quickly and seized several assets, including the Dale prototype. A guy from Watts bought the car at auction, hauled it back to his radiator shop, and hoisted it to the top of the rotating sign out front.

Elizabeth — Mr. Michael, I mean — became even more mysterious by disappearing somewhere along the way, and some years later was featured on the TV program, "Unsolved Mysteries."

Now do you know why I looked at that prototype and just *knew* I had to have it in our museum? I tracked down the guy with the radiator shop, and made a deal. I flew to California and arranged to have it literally taken down from the top of the sign and get it ready for transport back to Lincoln.

This was another time when I had to call on my friends and buddies for help. This time, it was the famous Dean Moon. His story on dismounting the car from the sign and getting it back to the Moon shop was one in a million.

As a car it wasn't much, even for a prototype: It was mostly made of foam, with the wheels bolted to a frame made of 2x4 wood.

Even after I got the car back to Lincoln, automotive writers still loved to write about it. I believe this car received more worldwide attention than the Tucker automobile. I was on radio shows all over the country, and people would call in and say, "If you're still going to produce that car, I still want one. I paid $2,000 down but I'll pay another $2,000 to get one."

It's hard to explain how people's minds work, isn't it?

I don't know what ever happened to Elizabeth/Michael. But I do know one thing: There was only one Dale built, and I've got it.

True story.

Over the years I've had some great adventures pursuing some of the vehicles in the collection.

298 / FAST COMPANY

Many years ago I read of the spectacular Bucciali, a French automobile whose design won the Paris auto show in 1932. The Paris show was once the premier auto show in the world, far above any show including New York or Detroit. However, although everyone raved about the design, the car never moved into full production. The concept car displayed at Paris was unfortunately destroyed during World War II.

In the late 1970s a fellow from California saw a photograph of the Bucciali and got the bug to recreate the car. This man had serious money in real estate, and was involved in premier properties in Los Angeles, New York, and Detroit. He was mesmerized by the fantastic lines of the car — I sympathize with such infatuation — and he absolutely had to have such a car.

He wasn't a car guy, so he had to find car guys to create his dream machine. Ultimately, he hooked up with some people with knowledge and ability and they got started.

I can tell you from experience, to create a new car from scratch is a monumental undertaking. Let me say it again: Monumental.

California Metal Shaping built the tooling, and when the car was completed in 1985 the price tag was $3 million-plus.

Special wheels had to be constructed to support the four-wheel-drive design. It had your everyday luxury upholstery made of ostrich, which probably cost a half-million dollars alone.

The car was actually quite a piece of engineering. I later talked to the electrical engineer who designed and constructed all the wiring, and he explained that it took him a full year. I don't know the pay scale for a California electrical engineer, but I'll bet over the course of that year it ran to several hundred thousand dollars if it was a penny.

It took eight years and more than 200 craftsmen to create the Bucciali, but finally the car was complete. The gentleman from California was elated; it's easy to see why, because the car was truly a work of art. It got quite a bit of press, and he decided to drive it across the country. Later he took it to Pebble Beach and the great concours celebration of automobiles.

He apparently arrived at Pebble Beach with his chest puffed out, which is understandable. You know, the "Look at me!" attitude to which I am well-accustomed. The rooster syndrome.

But the Pebble Beach crowd wasn't impressed, and they apparently turned a cold shoulder. The car wasn't "real," and therefore they weren't interested.

As you might guess, the gentleman was severely angry and disappointed. Maybe that's what led him to sell the car, and somewhere along the line the car ended up with a bank, and was sold to a man from Houston named Jerry J. Moore.

I had seen the Bucciali, and had a growing affection for it. So one day I called Jerry J. Moore, although I didn't know him from a pile of coal. I had asked around about him, and discovered that he was quite well-known in the commercial real estate world. He lived in Houston, just down the street from one Anthony Joseph Foyt.

Apparently Moore owned more real estate in Houston than the Phillips 66 oil company, and that company is fairly well-to-do. At that time Moore owned 76 shopping centers. He owned a little ol' tool company named Black & Decker. He kept two Boeing 747s at the Houston airport at his disposal. J.J. dabbled in many things, such as a Rolls Royce dealership, a Bentley dealership, and had just purchased the Sterling Automobile Manufacturing company from the British.

And, I discovered, he owned something like 800 classic cars.

Jerry J. Moore was a player, to say the least. But when I called him he was very nice on the telephone, and told me to come down and look the car over and maybe we could make a deal.

Joyce and I flew to Houston on a Saturday morning, and Jerry said he'd pick us up at the airport. I told him I'd be wearing a black hat, and you couldn't miss me. We deplaned and here comes a guy who looked like he should be pushing a grocery cart and picking up cans along the highway. He was a very small guy, wearing very plain everyday clothing: shorts, an old t-shirt, and tennis shoes.

We shook hands, and he said, "My car is at the front door." We walked outside and there was a Rolls Royce limousine that once belonged to the Queen of England, driven by Jerry's chauffeur.

After a short ride we arrived at Jerry's house, which was, in a word, spectacular. It was created from a castle in France, and Jerry said it was flown over here piece-by-piece and reassembled on his lot. It featured a full-size Olympic swimming pool, and a full-sized roller skating rink. The home was decorated with a stunning array of Louis XV art — harps, pianos, golden maidens, etc. It really was a memorable place.

Jerry introduced us to Mrs. Jones, and we sat down at their kitchen table to talk. He began telling me his story, and I found he was quite a fascinating character. And I really like fascinating characters.

Jerry explained he was a Russian Jew, and grew up from the cracks of the cement of Houston. He never graduated from high school, and it was apparent that he enjoyed telling you of his success, and telling you how he slicked somebody. He had just recently acquired a golf course south of Houston on the gulf, one of the finest in the world, and he was very excited about that.

He explained that during the crunch of the mid-1970s the banks were going to call his loans, which would have put him out of the real estate development business. He flew to New York for a meeting on the top floor of the World Bank. To prove how stupid bankers can be, he played a trick on 'em. They asked him how he got there, and he said, "I rode my horse in...I'm from Texas, and I ride a horse."

"No, you didn't," they scoffed.

"Yes I did, go look out the window," he insisted.

Well, they went to the window, and of course there was no horse tied to a hitching post in the front of the World Bank. But within the first minute of the meeting he had proven they were gullible enough to go for the trick. In a sense, he set the tone by proving he was smarter than they were.

That was probably how Jerry talked them out of pulling the sheet over him, and he survived with his loans intact. And we're probably talking billions, not millions.

He explained to Joyce and me that he recently got his high school diploma.

"Oh, did you go back and finish?" I asked.

"Oh, no, here's what happened," he grinned. "It was easy...they needed all new chairs and furniture at the local high school, so I bought all that and they gave me a diploma!"

I don't know if that's true or not, but he took great delight in telling the story.

So J.J. and Joyce and I sat at the kitchen table for four hours and negotiated, and I ended up trading him nine of my cars and a big box of money for the Bucciali. He later sent a hauler up to pick up my cars, and dropped off my new purchase.

Soon it came time to go to the airport, and Jerry decided to drive us himself. I noticed that when we went to lunch his wife insisted on driving separately — which I thought was odd — but once we got on the highway I completely understood. When Jerry got behind the wheel he became an absolute maniac!

I was riding in the death seat and Joyce was sitting in the back, and we're going down the highway at 100 mph. He's not even on the damned road; he was in the breakdown lane because traffic was heavy. He's craning his neck to talk to Joyce in the back seat.

"Jerry, you're going to kill us all," I yelled. "Get back on the goddam road!"

That next year they inducted Jerry into the Classic Car Hall of Fame in Auburn, Ind. They had inducted me a couple of years earlier; I almost called Jerry to point out that I got in ahead of him. You see, one-upsmanship still applies with Speedy Bill.

You've got to have a little fun in life, don't you?

28

My Four Sons

From the time our four boys were old enough to do anything, they worked at Speedway Motors in some capacity. I have a strong belief that anything you get, you should earn.

Remember that old saying of mine: "A dollar earned means more than a dollar given."

I didn't dole money out freely with my kids. However, I provided an opportunity; if they wanted money, all they had to do was work. They'd come down to Speedway Motors in the evening, or on weekends, and stuff envelopes, sweep the floors, put away the mufflers, and lots of other menial jobs. They washed cars, dusted parts, and cleaned the shelves in the showroom.

Today, they'd probably charge Joyce and me with some kind of abuse because we made our kids work. However, I would point out that the end result says something; all four are fine men, and good human beings.

I even had them work the counter sometimes, just for fun. Craig is probably the most "people" person of all the boys, and when he was eight or nine years old he was helping me on the counter one Saturday morning.

Kidding around, I asked him if he wanted to smoke a cigar while he was working the counter.

"Sure," he said. My grandfather had done that to me when I was a kid, stuck a cigar in my mouth and lit it. Of course I got sicker than a dog and fell on the ground.

I stuck that cigar in Craig's mouth and gave it a light. However, it didn't make him sick. In fact, it didn't do anything! He sat there calmly puffing away, smoking the cigar. It was kind of bizarre, and it was still one of the most amazing things I've ever seen.

Here's this kid, sitting on a high stool by the cash register, puffing on a cigar. When a customer came in, Craig said, "Hi, buddy, can I help you?" You talk about people doing a double-take! It was great.

When it comes to parenting, some things work and some things don't.

I've got to be completely up-front and give all the credit in the world to Joyce for how our sons turned out. I know lots of guys joke about this with their family, but in my case it's true.

All those nights and weekends I was off trying to make some money with that damned race car, Joyce was holding down our household and raising our sons. She had to do an awful lot on her own, and I can honestly look back and say she got nearly all of it right.

The fact that I'm a "car guy" was passed on to each of my boys. When they turned 16, of course they had to have a car. However, I insisted they earn the money to buy it. I also had right of first refusal, because I understand what it is to have teenaged car hormones in your brain. I put the kibosh on Corvettes and the like, even if they had enough money to buy one.

They still got some pretty nice iron, though. Carson bought a '68 Chevelle with a big-block engine and a rock-crusher 4-speed, and I think he put a clutch in that thing every four days or so. He was an absolute killer on those clutches.

I didn't require the boys work back in the shop, or learn to weld, because they were still too young. There was plenty of time for that later. And at times I realized that very basic things I took for granted are still a challenge for someone new to cars. For example, Clay's first car was a '68 Z/28 Camaro—he still has the car—and one day he called and said he had a flat and was having trouble getting the wheel off the car.

Clay is a very bright guy, and later he earned an engineering degree from Stanford, so he obviously has some mechanical smarts. I asked him where he was, and he explained he was about 40 blocks from our home. I drove over to help him, and discovered he was turning the lug wrench the wrong way.

I can tell a lot of stories on the boys, probably just like you could about any young man who is learning his way in the world.

I'll tell you a little bit about each of my boys. I'm proud of all of them, and there is no "ranking" from this dad. I love them all equally, and I've been equally mad at each of them at one time or another. Then again, it's probably mutual.

Carson is the oldest, and a very bright guy. He's very focused on what he does, and he's got an ideal engineering mind. Very analytical, very focused. If he's working on a project in the room, and the rest of the building fell down, he probably wouldn't notice because he's so focused.

He's done some magnificent things in racing. He built a car that broke the track record at Pikes Peak by such a large margin they thought the clocks had malfunctioned. He won the American Indy Car championship with Robby Unser driving his car. Chevrolet asked him to build a special truck for Pikes Peak, and he won the event again with that vehicle.

This isn't a case where dad did the science fair project for the kid; Carson did these things on his own. He's probably the best suspension guy — particularly independent suspension — I've ever known, and I've known a few. That's a combination of his education in mechanical engineering and his hands-on racing experience, and his high IQ. He's very good with chassis setup.

When he got the racing bug out of his system about 10 years ago, he walked away from the sport and doesn't have a need to be involved any more.

When Carson was still at the University of Nebraska, he worked as an intern for the Caterpillar company. Upon graduation he went to work for the Charmin paper company in Green Bay, Wis., running a million-dollar paper machine.

Carson was the first of my sons I recruited to come home and join me at Speedway. Our business was growing at a rapid rate, and I needed help. I was not computer literate, and I always believed that if I couldn't run the business from my head, I can't run it at all. I had always kept everything in my head; prices, inventory, everything, up until the late 1970s.

I finally realized the business had grown beyond that, and I needed help. But I didn't know how to go about it. I was about as computer illiterate as is possible.

But Carson was a key part of us moving into the computer age. Our first computer cost $85,000, and I had never bought a piece of mechanical equipment for anything like that kind of money. I was shocked at how much they cost!

Even the nice CNC machines with which we built products didn't cost that much. Balancing equipment, mills, lathes, nothing even came close to the computer in terms of cost. Plus, mechanical tools will actually appreciate as time goes on if you take good care of them, because you can use them so long.

But that first computer was an education for this businessman. I entered a realm where the machine immediately depreciated drastically over a very short time — and we're talking months — and it was quickly obsolete. What happens when it becomes obsolete? You'd better get ready to write another check.

It really was a struggle with that first computer. Ultimately we only got our mailing list on it, although that was quite a big breakthrough. Carson did all of the programming, and it was incredibly time consuming.

As far as I was concerned, they were just a pain in the ass. The computers, I mean. Not the sons.

The next son to come along was Craig. From the beginning, Craig showed a completely different set of skills. He's artistic, and loves to do architectural things. Designing buildings, designing rooms, that's the sort of thing that motivates and gets Craig very excited.

Like Carson, I eventually recruited Craig to join me at Speedway Motors. I figured he would fit perfectly in our advertising department, designing our catalog and doing things that are graphically driven. However, that didn't work. It was too boring, too monotonous, too mundane for Craig. He can sit down for five minutes, but not 50 minutes. He can't focus that long, that artistic mind of his is always racing along much faster than the world around him. He's got to be on the go, all the time.

Craig is very much a "people person." His friends mean more to him than anything, next to his family. Some of my buddies nicknamed him "J.R." because they said he was just like his dad. To this day, some of my old-time buddies still call him that.

Craig left the company for a while, and set out to make a million bucks before he was 30. He lived in Pakistan, which I'm sure was a fascinating experience. In fact, living overseas is probably something all of us should experience, because Craig discovered that the system in Pakistan was not like the system in the good old U.S.A. Over there, unless you were born with a certain name, that of a well-known family, you were probably going to be just another rug rat. Plus, there is so much more dealing under the table in those environments.

When Craig returned, we got him back to Speedway Motors and he got involved in the expansion of the real-estate portion of our business. Boy, he's been a big help in that area, because he's gifted when it comes to designing buildings and things. He's taken some old, run-down historic properties and created beautiful and lasting things.

Next was Clay, who is named after the great mechanical genius Clay Smith of California. Clay earned a degree in economics and a masters degree in industrial engineering, both at Stanford. He then went to work at Boos Allen, one of the largest consulting companies in the world. While at Boos he was involved in a project at Sprint when they were firing their CEO every two weeks and Clay wound up basically running the company.

Later he started his own investment company with three partners, and had the top floor of the Embarcadero building in downtown San Francisco. The first deal they did was one of the biggest such deals in history when they took Levi Straus from a publicly held company back to privately held.

He later left the company and bought Bojangles, the second-largest chain of chicken restaurants in the U.S. He sold that property, and was mulling over what he wanted to do next. He had several offers, including one from Warren Buffett and another from Dole (the pineapple people). He also had a job offer from Speedy Bill, and when it was all said and done he decided to come home to Lincoln and to Speedway Motors.

It was a good move on many counts, including the fact that he met his wife here. Beth, a Lincoln native, had worked as an assistant to President George H.W. Bush, and was sitting next to him during the trip to Japan when he got sick in the lap of the Japanese prime minister. She was one of the only women in the U.S. to lead a state Republican Party, which she did here in Nebraska.

Clay works with me in managing Speedway Motors, and our real estate concerns.

Jason is our youngest, and he is the only one of our sons to come to work for us right out of college. He had several offers, and nearly took a job with Maytag, and I was pleased when he decided to go with us instead.

Almost from the beginning, Jason has been like my left hand. He has a keen ability to read situations, and he and I think alike. When our company moved to a new facility — and I can't think of any greater challenge for a business — Jason was highly involved in everything about our logistics.

He's still very much involved in that area today. The way all of our logistical systems work, the way our warehouse works, he's very tuned in on that process. Today, our operation is probably one of the most advanced in the world in terms of computerization, automation, and efficiency. We're able to do jobs with one or two people that usually takes 10 people manually. Jason takes it personally that we have to try and be smarter every day.

Naturally, I can't sit in on those conversations when they're working on systems like our carousel picking systems and things like that. It's like listening to a foreign language, and I don't quite understand what they're talking about.

I love my boys, and I'm proud of all of them. I suppose I'm the proud papa who thinks his kids have special talents and are well above average in every category. But they *do* have some talent, and that's an honest, objective opinion.

In their early youth, the four of them were typical boys. But as they grew and matured with many different interests and talents, they became friends. This was the "key" to working together.

However, integrating all four into Speedway Motors was by far the most challenging thing I've ever done. It wasn't just an easy walk in the park, by any means. All of us are somewhat strong-willed and opinionated. Plus, the generation gap is hard to manage; experience versus youth and technical knowledge.

I've got to give a lot of credit to our sons, because they've certainly worked hard to make it all work.

We've tried to learn from the experience of others, but we were setting the precedent a little bit. For example, my sons saw many of their friends in similar situations, going to work in their family business. However, this didn't approach the magnitude of what we were trying to do; four is greater than three or two or one.

That's why what we were trying to do was so difficult, and why there is such a sense of satisfaction that we managed to pull it off. All four siblings are on board, and their spouses and children have bought into the idea as well. All of these diverse personalities, and this diverse set of skills, have managed to mesh and become one strong team.

My sons are all pretty vocal, and it's been hairy sometimes. Like I said earlier, I've seen my sons—at a much younger age, of course—poke each other in the nose and still love each other the next day. But among all these personalities you have to be strong to survive.

Our board meetings consist of six people: Joyce and me, and our sons. There are some intense discussions at those meetings on occasion, to be sure. We have an agreement that if the issue is of major importance, we won't proceed unless we get 100-percent approval from the entire board. Because if you don't have all the 20-mule-team pulling together, it's too difficult.

All deals in life have an upside, and a downside. Simple. If the upside far outweighs the downside, it's probably what you would call a good deal. If it is balanced, it's going to be a flip of the coin. If the downside is greater, it doesn't take a rocket scientist to figure that one out.

Sometimes one of us will put their feet on the ground with firm convictions on why we shouldn't do something. We'll reason it out from there, and if there is a reason to challenge his position, we'll talk that over. If he's right, we won't move forward. And I can name lots of projects and ideas where we decided not to move forward.

Along the way, guess who had to learn how to adjust? Bill had to adjust, a lot. In running a kingdom, the king rules. When you run a kingdom with your spouse, that's one thing. But trying to be the king with four sons and a spouse, that's a lot more challenging.

Again, I have to give lots of credit to Joyce, for lots of reasons. From a business perspective, she has been right there alongside me for 57 years. She doesn't needle me that I never did pay back that $300 I borrowed from her to start the business!

Even though she was a great mom, and did all the things a mom needs to do to raise children, she still found time to help me in the business. Believe me, I don't mean spending a few hours a week. She spent hours and hours and hours working with me.

There probably isn't any family, no matter how close, that can go on a camping trip or fishing trip or cruise or whatever and not come home and say, "God, I'm glad that's over...I need some space."

We've all heard that expression many times, and that's a normal feeling. But for our family, we don't have much "space." For us it's 24/7, almost all the time.

But we've adapted, and learned to get along, because that's the only way it works.

Just like those early days, I'm here to *win* the game, not just be a player. To win, I have to adapt. A lot. It's just like racing; you learn more in the hobby of racing on how to conduct your life and your business than you do in any other hobby, I think. You learn to quickly adapt and address rapidly changing situations; life is a lot like that, isn't it? If you don't adapt, you won't be around long. If you think you're so good you don't need to constantly improve your game, well, pretty soon they're going to spank your butt. That's just how it works. Again, I can't change the rules, but I can try and figure out how to play.

Our family situation at work has required an awful lot of give-and-take. I've probably had to compromise more than anyone, because I went from a situation where I had all the control to a situation where I had to give up some of that control in order to utilize the skills of my four sons. I've had to go with the flow: have control, lose control, gain control, and so on, buying into situations I would never dream of as a one-man band.

But it's been worth it, in spades. When I look around at what Speedway Motors has become, it would be silly to think I could have done all that on my own. It's taken everything I could do, everything Joyce could do, all of our employees and suppliers and vendors and other partners, to get it done.

So I give a tip of the hat to my sons and their partners: Carson and Jane, with Bill, Bob, Betsy and Ben; Craig and Cathy, with Lauren; Clay and Beth, with Sarah, Emily and Katherine; and Jason and Lisa, with Avery and Tucker.

My four sons, they're more than just my partners. They're, well, they're my sons. And I couldn't be prouder of them, individually and collectively. That's a father's right, you know!

29

A $300 Racing Engine? You're Kidding, Right?

Sometime in the late 1970s I heard about a new type of race car that had been developed in Iowa. The idea came from Keith Knaack, owner of IMCA. By this time IMCA had changed a great deal, moving from the days of a traveling "state fair" sprint car and stock car series to sanctioning weekly races throughout the Plains.

Keith's new car was a radical step, and as we look back, an important point in the history of auto racing in America.

The new car was based on the concept of creating a tight set of rules that allowed the average blue-collar guy to go racing, and *keep* racing. In the late 1970s we saw an amazing rise in the cost of racing in almost every division, and this was soon reflected in dwindling car counts, particularly among high-end weekly "late model" cars.

One of the key elements of a race car is the engine. The more you spend, the more horsepower you make; the limit usually isn't how much power, it's how much money. Naturally, that's where a lot of racers were spending the bulk of their budget.

Keith's proposal was this: you can spend whatever you want on your engine, but if you win the race you must be willing to sell it to another competitor for $300. The car would look a little bit different than any other cars out there, and from the beginning was known as an IMCA modified.

When I heard about the idea, I laughed. A $300 racing engine? For a minute I thought the story was a joke, I really did. I thought the whole concept was preposterous.

Luckily, I was wrong. I say luckily on two counts: One, the IMCA modified has been a tremendous boost to short-track racing in America, by any measure. Second, as the IMCA modified exploded in growth over the past 30 years, Speedway Motors has grown right along with it, selling parts and supplies to thousands of eager racers.

The cars have changed a lot since that first season of competition in the 1970s. The other day some IMCA racers stopped by our place with a couple of very early examples, and the cars had AMC engines with a ton of displacement.

I immediately thought, "You know, if I were building a car with a low-budget formula, that's how I would have done it." You can't beat displacement in making horsepower, and horsepower is a beautiful thing.

The cars have steadily evolved, and today's cars look very professional compared to the earlier versions. However, even as the car evolved IMCA has done a good job of keeping the costs under control.

Lord knows there probably hasn't been anybody on the planet who's sold more racing parts than I have, and I've seen racers try to buy wins and spend themselves into the poorhouse. But Keith and the IMCA created a series that works, and helps protect the racers from themselves.

From the very beginning, Speedway Motors was right in the thick of the growth of the IMCA modified. Yes, I was pretty skeptical early on, but I quickly began to see the potential of this thing. When you consider the dozens of smaller race tracks in middle America, this package was exactly the right formula.

By the early 1980s there were a ton of guys putting these cars together in their garages and shops. It was a mix — guys who had raced other types of cars, and guys completely new to the sport.

This was very important. A generation earlier, almost every man had some involvement under the hood of his daily driver. That mechanical experience was very important, because it helped interest young men in race cars. However, over the past 25 years automotive technology has progressed to the point where it's pretty tough for the average guy to work on his street car. As fewer young American men were interested in working on cars, there was a big worry about where the next generation of racers and mechanics would come from.

That's been a very encouraging element of the IMCA modified. Oh, I don't mean to imply that's the only entry-level division in racing; there are many types of cars across the country. But for a large group of today's racers, their first involvement was with an IMCA mod.

I've always prided myself on knowing my customer, and understanding how to help him. I put a lot of effort into building our inventory of parts and pieces for the IMCA car, making it easier to go racing, yet affordable enough that guys could stay with it.

We began building a wide range of parts and pieces, everything from an individual component to a car that was almost turnkey. Today almost every piece on the IMCA car — except the tires — can be found in the Speedway Motors catalog. A-frames, spindles, radiators, suspension pieces, steering parts, seats...I'm not kidding, almost every piece on the car.

In fact, we did a good enough job that in recent years IMCA has mandated that certain pieces come from Speedway Motors. Most of this is related to availability and quality, and we have committed to holding up our end of the agreement and hold down the cost. This is particularly important with some suspension and steering pieces, because they must be built to a very high standard of performance and safety.

Today you'll find all sorts of engines in IMCA racing. Early on we developed a successful Ford engine; I guess deep down inside I've always been something of a Ford guy, which probably stems from my early love for the Model T.

It isn't easy to be a Ford guy, at least not from the standpoint of volume. Since the advent of the small block Chevrolet engine in 1955, the numbers greatly favor the Chevy.

If you develop an aftermarket engine piece, you'll sell 10 Chevy pieces for every Ford or Dodge piece. Fact of life. However, I like seeing various makes of engines on the race track, so I believed it was important to at least help Ford have a presence in short-track racing.

I went to the various manufacturers — including Ford — and convinced them that if they'd reduce their prices to compete with the Chevy, there was a market there. Performance parts are like anything else; something selling in high volume is generally going to be less expensive to produce.

I believed — and I was right — that if the Ford could be competitively priced with the Chevy, there would be more competition on the track between brands.

If I couldn't find a supplier to agree to make the part at a lesser cost, I'd build it myself. And I did, many times. We got to where you could run a Ford engine for very close to the same cost as a Chevy. I believe that helped the series, because people like the Ford vs. Chevy vs. Dodge competition.

The original concept of the $300 "claimer" engine has evolved since the 1970s, just like everything else. The IMCA officials — and the racers themselves — have learned what works and what doesn't, and they've done a good job adjusting the rules to continue to be workable.

I'm proud that today Speedway Motors is more involved with these cars than ever. A few years ago we signed on as title sponsor at one of the biggest events, the IMCA Speedway Motors Super Nationals in Boone, Iowa. My longtime friend Bob Lawton is the promoter, and Bob and his crew do a great job at this event, which is truly a sight to behold. Hundreds and hundreds of race cars, roaring around the track every night for nearly a week. The competition is intense, and the atmosphere is exciting.

The series is as competitive as ever. This past year at Boone we saw a fantastic race, and I was standing in the infield watching, trying to figure out who was going to win this thing! Boy, it was great, because the action on the track was frantic. These old eyes have seen about as many races as anybody, and I know good racing when I see it.

There are many very talented guys racing IMCA modifieds, but no superstars. That's good, at least in the "world according to Bill." It's still a blue-collar sport, true to our roots. IMCA has figured out that it's best to keep these cars on the smaller tracks, and that's where the action is.

If I were going to build a race track today (don't worry, Joyce, I'm just saying *if*), it would be a high-banked third-mile oval like Eagle Raceway here in Nebraska. That track puts on a great show, for a variety of race cars. You can see a pretty damned entertaining race on a track like that.

You know what's funny? Today, at 80 years old, I can still strongly relate to that young kid working away on his race car, trying his best to get it ready for the next event.

In many ways the world is completely different than when I was that young boy. However, in many ways it's the same.

Even though I was only earning 25 cents an hour at the gas station back then, it didn't cost much to race. My stuff was cobbled together from junkyard parts, and I probably didn't have more than $100 in my race car. At $100, it took about 10 weeks of work to "buy" my race car.

An ordinary salary today is maybe $75 or $100 per day, and at that salary you'd have a hard time buying your helmet and driving suit and getting a race car to the track in that same time period.

I was thinking about all that a few years ago when I was invited to be the Grand Marshal down at Fayetteville, Ark., for an event called the "Hillbilly Nationals."

Now, any event with that name sounds like a lot of fun!

Joyce and I made the trip south to Fayetteville, and we couldn't have had more fun at the circus. They were going to have me lead the races in a pace car, waving to the crowd. They got a convertible from one of their sponsors, an old Pontiac that still had the price on the windshield in big neon letters. This car looked kind of suspect, and I wasn't looking forward to driving it around the track. Luckily it rained, and I was off the hook that first day.

The next day they arranged to have an older Corvette as our pace car. I was supposed to do one parade lap and then pull off, but the racers started the race before I could get off the track. Just as I'm flying toward the infield to get the hell out of the way of the race cars, I remembered the guy telling me, "The brakes are a little weak."

"A little weak?" They weren't there at all! I managed to get into the infield without killing myself or anybody else, so all was well. It was a thrill, though.

During the two days I was there, I walked through the pits and talked with many grass roots racing people. I noticed a kid parked in the pit area, working all alone on his race car, and I walked over to talk with him.

He explained he brought the car all by himself to the race track, and he was the driver, mechanic, crew chief, tow-truck driver…he did it all. I was intrigued because he sounded like a guy I knew from Lincoln, Neb., all those years ago. Me.

The boy explained that he ran here the previous year, and finished fifth or sixth in points. He was really proud of that. He told me about having engine trouble last year, but this year he wasn't gonna have that problem because he got another engine from a guy who had ran pretty well.

I asked him who helped him with all this work, because I know from experience that it's more than a one-man job. He said he used to have some buddies come along to the races, but they got married and got tired or whatever, and dropped out. As he's telling me this I remembered how I had worn out all *my* friends back in the old days.

His buddy had a salvage yard, and the boy kept his race car there. Each night when he got off work from his job as a delivery truck driver, he'd go over to the salvage yard to work on his car. This worked out pretty well because his buddy would help him on things that needed four hands rather than two.

I thought to myself, "Here is a guy who is doing a job that isn't really all that much fun. It's too much work to be fun."

What I saw in that kid was a lot of desire. He was making it happen on guts and sheer determination. I don't think there were any "gimme's" in his situation.

I still feel a kinship with a kid like that. Crawling around on the ground, working on the car, sweating, spending your last $100, with very little financial gain on the horizon. The wonderful emotions of doing well and winning, and the crushing disappointments when you fall short. A lot has changed over the past 60 years in the world of racing, but not the powerful emotions that are part of being a racer.

I never stopped being that kid. I understand his passions, and his feelings for the race car. *His* race car. I can look in the mirror, and instead of seeing me, I see that kid.

A few months ago at the Boone Super Nationals — oops, the IMCA *Speedway Motors* Super Nationals — a young guy introduced himself while I was sitting at the motel having breakfast. He saw my hat, and overheard a conversation I was having with a friend.

The boy said he found our conversation interesting. He was there for the races, traveling in from Ohio. He wondered if I ever raced my sprint car at New Bremen or Eldora, and I laughed and said, "Oh, yes, many times, especially Eldora."

He explained that he got into racing four years ago when his neighbor got a race car, and he went along to help out. Sounds familiar, doesn't it? That describes an awful lot of people in racing today; we kind of wander into the sport by accident and the next thing we know, we're addicted.

We had a nice conversation, and the boy mentioned our company, Speedway Motors. Joyce chimed in, "Let us send you a catalog!"

The boy said, "Oh, I've already got your catalog. I put brakes on my '57 Chevy, and I got 'em from you."

Instantly our bonds were even tighter. We shared an interest in not just racing, but also automotive things, and with that we somehow felt a greater respect and admiration for one another. That, my friends, is what life is all about. Having a great passion for something—in my case racing and rods and all things performance—and meeting other people who have that same passion.

Meeting folks like this young man is something that happens nearly every weekend for me, and that goes back almost 60 years. Boy, do I love that part of my job! I've always made the statement, "I've never met a racer or rodder I didn't like." That's essential, because you should like your customers. That's when you feel his happiness, his pain, his needs, and you understand how incredibly good it feels when he wins.

Been there, done that. That feeling of shared experience is much different than just viewing racing from a distance. You don't know that feeling unless you've lived it.

It's easy to take things for granted, and assume everything just happens by itself. Well, things don't just happen by themselves; the big resurgence in grass roots racing over the past 30 years wouldn't have happened without Keith Knaack's vision. Not just the idea and concept of an affordable race car, but putting the idea into action.

Keith was an interesting guy. He was a racer from way back, one of those passionate guys who never quite had the level of equipment to get to the top. I remember him racing a supermodified at Knoxville, against staunch competition.

I can't say enough about how outlandish his concept of a $300 engine was at the time. I mean, $300? Listen, if you go down to the junkyard and buy any old small block Chevy lying outside, you've got some work to do before it's ready to go around in circles. Hell, the oil pan and pump you need—and I'm talking about simply building an engine that will oil itself on an oval track—will set you back close to $300.

His thinking is obvious now: If a guy knows he has a chance of "losing" his engine for $300 at the end of the night, that will prevent him from bringing a high-dollar engine to the race track.

The concept of a claimer looked dumb to me. And, to be fair, it was a concept that had a lot of kinks to be worked out. At first guys used giant V8 engines, looking for cheap horsepower. The engines evolved to be more "cookie cutter," and that's when racers started claiming each other's engines. That nearly put everybody out of business, it was so widespread. Guys were getting claimed a dozen times in a season, and you couldn't find enough money to replace your engines that often.

IMCA continued to tweak the rule, and time has proven that Keith's concept was sound. Look at the Super Nationals: 300-plus IMCA modifieds on hand. It's a major, major event by any measure, and yet it represents only a small percentage of modified racing on the national scene. There are hundreds and hundreds of those cars across the nation.

It's been a tremendous boost to the sport, because it brings people to the entry level. You can still experiment and see if you like it, without investing your life savings.

The beauty is, these aren't cookie-cutter cars. They aren't identical, not by a long shot. They are widely adjustable, and one top guy can't just jump into another guy's car and go fast. You have a lot of work to do to fine-tune the car to your liking. You're on a smaller tire, and traction is difficult. You have to move the weight of the car around, and the throttle steers the car more than the steering wheel.

It's impressive to watch these guys get a handle on it, because the cars are wicked to drive. Actually, let me say it like this: They're wicked to drive *well*. If you're going to win, you've got to drive it very, very hard, and that takes talent.

Sometimes I hear people in the stands laugh about the cars at this level, calling them junk or jalopies. That upsets me, because it's a disrespect to those who work so hard to race.

I've said this often in my life: If something looks easy, try it. Maybe it is easy…but until you've done it, you don't really know, do you?

In addition to our involvement at Boone, Speedway Motors is a corporate sponsor of IMCA. I envision us being involved well into the future.

We do this because it's smart business; but we also do it because I have a powerful desire to see racing flourish long after I've passed on the baton to the next runner.

I guess it's all about that passion I keep talking about. The best way I know to cultivate such passion is to do things that keep the racing industry and the performance industry strong.

Way back in 1961 I was offering parts and kits and all kinds of things to both the racing community and the hot rod hobbyist. Why? Because it helped people get involved in our sport, our hobby. Yes, it was profitable, but more importantly it made it easier for guys to participate, and they stuck around. If they stuck around, the sport—and our business—was better for it.

I guess that's part of why I get so excited when I come to work each morning. It's more than simply business; by that I mean it's more than just counting dollars and cents and keeping score.

It makes me feel good that our business is helping somebody have fun. Helping them be successful at their hobby, whether it's oval racing or drag racing or street rods or vintage cars or whatever.

Listen, it's important to make the world of performance a pleasurable experience for people. If I have to learn to weld and grind and work all day to make one piece, maybe I'll lose interest. But if I can get that piece from someone like Speedway Motors, and they can share with me the knowledge on how to best use it, that's a good arrangement.

That's what makes the sport grow. Today it's so much easier to race, so much easier to restore and improve cars, because knowledge is within reach for so many people. I think that's a very good thing.

30

Signature Series

Writing this book has got me thinking about many different things, particularly some of the "big" questions about why a person would devote his entire life to cars and racing and performance.

Most of us are too busy to spend much time thinking about stuff like that, which is probably best. But I will admit that during the countless interviews and conversations that went into creating this book, there have been a couple of times where I've thought more deeply about the "big picture."

As you might guess, it's hard to find the right words to tell about your life, your experiences, and why you feel like you do and did what you did. It would be neat to find the right words to distill everything—all these 80 years—into a paragraph or two.

Then I got to thinking: If I wanted to really pin down something that best describes me, I'd get up from my desk and walk back through the long building that houses Speedway Motors. Past the huge order-processing operation we call "the battleship," and various order-processing and shipping operations.

Back in the far reaches of our building, I'd turn the corner and walk into a well-lit room. Sitting inside would be a bright red example of what Speedy Bill is all about.

It's an all-steel 1932 Ford roadster, a turnkey street rod that's arguably the finest "new" street rod ever produced (of course, this is proud papa speaking). That car probably sums up my passion and desire as well as any words I could ever come up with.

We call it our "Signature Series." That isn't just a slick marketing name, either. The fact is, it really is my signature. That car is *me*.

To begin telling you about the Signature Series '32, I have to introduce you to Dick Beith.

Dick and I met in the early 1960s and immediately became good friends. Our backgrounds were similar, as Dick was also educated as a schoolteacher in industrial arts. He went on to create the first five-spoke racing wheel in his high school industrial arts class where he taught.

Pretty soon Dick founded ET Wheels, becoming a major force in almost every type of performance wheel market. By the early 1970s Dick sold the company and went Indy car racing, running an Offy-powered Eagle with Bill Simpson driving. The team was called American Kids Racing.

Although Dick lived on the West Coast, we stayed in close contact. After he parked the Indy car he stayed active in many things, including running a car at Bonneville.

Like many of my friends, Dick and I connected because we are car guys. He is a good observer of all things automotive, and I enjoy getting his take on our industry. He's a smart guy with a keen eye.

One day about 10 years ago we got on the topic of Cobra reproductions. Even though Carroll Shelby — creator of the original Cobra — is a good friend, I was never active with Cobra cars.

But, boy, you couldn't help but notice how many people were manufacturing Cobra replicas! In Nebraska alone there were three or four companies building Cobras. It never ceased to amaze me how many people were active in that niche.

With that many players, quality was all over the place. I had studied several of these offerings at various car shows, and frankly the workmanship wasn't all that great.

"Have you seen this Cobra that is being imported from South Africa?" Dick asked. "You would be impressed at their quality, I'll tell you."

By pure chance — fate, maybe? — there was one of the South Africa imports in the Ford booth at the next SEMA show. I looked it over carefully, and said to myself, "Wow! This is really something!"

I can still recognize quality, craftsmanship, design, fit and finish, all the things that make a piece good or bad. And this example was all good, in every category. I saw Dick later at the show, and told him I was impressed by that particular example.

"You ought to get in touch with the guy in South Africa who is building those things," he said.

"How am I going to do that?" I said. "Fly down there on a whim?"

Early years...

*High school,
and I still like
pinstripes!*

*Graduation from
Nebraska Wesleyan
University*

On a trip to the Indianapolis 500, my dad and I visited the Chicago Museum of Science and Industry in 1949

Speedy's first car: a 1917 Model T pickup, and I'm all of 15 years old

Ready to race, 1949

My pals were dreaming and building too

Now this is a STOCK car!

My '32 Packard tow vehicle

*Joyce and I,
around
1951*

One of my last outings as a driver before I hung up my helmet for good

Our first Speedway Motors location at 2232 "O" Street

The '40 Ford is still one of the most popular hot rods of all time

An early 4x car with some winning hardware

An early '50s drag race in Lincoln...how can you lose if you built both cars?

Winning at Capitol Beach with Lloyd Beckman in 1953

Young Carson with our car in 1956, which was numbered 99 to "skirt" the rules and run as an Iowa car in the Iowa State Championship with Tiny Lund at the wheel

Relaxing at home in 1955 with my father, while son Carson sits in his pedal car

Tuning up the Hemi with Bobby McKee (L)

Tiny Lund and Bobby McKee ready to hit the road to NASCAR in 1956

Tiny Lund was a great friend, and one helluva racer

Our fiberglass bodies were a breakthrough in hot rodding

One of my early drivers was IMCA flagman Woody Brinkman (R), who later became the owner of IMCA

Joyce and I worked a LOT of car shows in the early years

Ah, the "sedan"...Lloyd Beckman and I were in Victory Lane often with this car

Gene Barnett

Lloyd Beckman was the best "short track" racer I ever had in my cars

In 1961 Lloyd won the Spencer, Iowa 5-State Championship. In 1962 Gordon Woolley won the championship again in the same 4x

Gene Barnett

Some of the crew in the early '60s: (L-R) John Marsh, Bob Anderson, Marty Bassett, Jim Fulton, Jerry Jensen, Johnny Young, Speedy Bill, and Larry Kruse

Gene Barnett

*Lloyd Beckman in the
4x chases Kenny Gritz
at Midwest Speedway
in 1965*

Gene Barnett

*The Speedway
Motors display
at an early
1960s auto show*

*Bob Coulter on the
IMCA trail, 1965*

Our state-of-the-art towing outfit at Midwest Speedway in 1965

Jerry "Butch" Weld

With a Speedway Motors T-bucket in the late '60s. That's "Yogi" Jerry Jensen (L) and Marty Bassett (R), Speedy Bill is the wheelman

Don Brown, the
"Prince of Darkness"

Leroy Byers

Grady Wade in
the 4x at
Belleville, 1967

The Speedway Motors
counter, mid-1960s

A promo for our Cool Man Glass Tint. Cool, man!

With Joe Hrudka of Mr. Gasket in 1967

Speedway Motors at 1719 N Street

Joe Saldana at Topeka, 1967

Leroy Byers

Keith Hightshoe at Eagle, 1968

My first outing after my death-defying incident in 1968, and my good friend Lloyd Beckman helps me get around at the Nebraska State Fair

It doesn't get much better than this...Jan Opperman at Topeka, 1969

Beetle Bailey

Ken Simon

Opperman wins at Knoxville, 1969

I didn't just SELL performance tools...I USED performance tools that we built

Don Maxwell is pictured here in 1971 at Erie, Colorado, just before he came to work for me

Leroy Byers

Bob Mays Collection

Jan Opperman wins the '74 Winternationals at Tampa

Midwest Speedway champs in 1975: Gary Swenson (left), Ray Lee Goodwin, and Speedy Bill

Terre Haute Action Track, 1976: Jan Opperman wins in the Speedway Motors car, changing sprint car racing forever. Here, Jan rides the rim outside of Tom Bigelow

Lots of happy faces in Victory Lane at Terre Haute...we beat ALL the big dogs on this day!

John Mahoney

Teaming up with Doug Wolfgang in early 1978 began our lifelong friendship...plus we won hundreds of races!

Hours before we won the Knoxville Nationals in 1978. I look confident!

Shane Carson wins in the 4x at Sedalia in 1979

Ken Simon

End of the line: Ron Shuman in the 4x in 1980, my final year as a car owner

Win or lose on Friday, Saturday, or Sunday night, Joyce and I were back in the office on Monday morning, helping our customers build cool cars like the very trick Parts Showcase roadster at left.

One of the most interesting and improbable cars in automotive history, the Dale. I'm thanking Dean Moon for helping get the car back to Lincoln

The fabulous Buccialli automobile, which also resides in our museum today

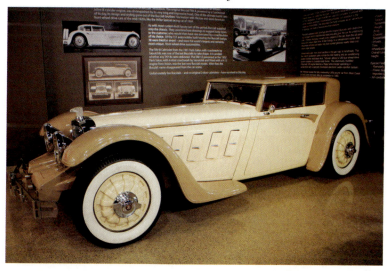

Carson (second from R) and Don Droud Jr. after a win in the Speedway Motors "house car" in the early 1980s

Jason and I set up the Speedway Motors display at the NSRA street rod nationals in the early 1980s

A new kind of 4x: Robby Unser wheels the American IndyCar Series machine. This was a serious effort for Carson and Jason during this period

Jason during his career in the American IndyCar Series

With their AIS championship hardware in 1989 is (L-R) son Carson Smith, Robby Unser, son Jason Smith, and Bobby Unser

With Doug Wolfgang in 1995

Ah, lifelong friends. I'm pictured here with Els Lohn (L) of EELCO and Angelo Giampetroni of Gratiot Auto

This is when I'm most comfortable: hanging around a neat hot rod, sharing the "world according to Bill!"

*On a chilly day at Pikes Peak in 1993...Carson (L) with one of his
radical hill-climbers, with (L-R) Clay, Jason, Joyce and me setting
records that still stand*

With Big Daddy Don Garlits on the Bonneville Salt Flats

Speedway Motors, today

With my co-author in Indianapolis in 2008

This Total Performance machine is a great example of some of the advancements in the rodding world...what a cool piece!

Here's my baby...the Speedway Motors Signature Series '32 Ford. I believe this represents the finest "new" street rod ever produced

When my friend Jim Voyles saw the very first Signature Series '32 when it was unveiled, within 15 minutes he was our first customer! Thanks, Jim!

Chris Economaki of National Speed Sport News wrote, "If Ford needs examples, Bill Smith's fabulous Speedway Motors museum in Lincoln, NE is the place to look."

Today, the Speedway Motors counter is as busy as ever

Kevin Lee, editor of Rod & Custom magazine, presented me with a Lifetime Achievement Award a few years ago. It was kind of ironic for a guy who once pored over the pages of magazines and dreamed!

In 2007 Nebraska governor Dave Heineman presented me with the NebraskaLand Foundation's Trailblazer Award. I was a proud Nebraska boy at this moment!

Sharing my thoughts with event announcer Toby Kruse at the Speedway Motors IMCA SuperNationals in Boone, Iowa

Dave Argabright

Talking it over with event promoter--and longtime friend--Bob Lawton at Boone

Dave Argabright

I'm as busy as ever, and enjoying working trade shows, car shows, attending races, and most of all spending time talking to friends and customers!

Dave Argabright

Joyce and I with Clay, Carson, Craig and
Jason...we're awfully proud of our boys!

57 years together, and we're not done yet...still with the pedal down!

Dave Argabright

"No, they've got a distributor in Columbus, Ohio," he explained.

I thought it over for a moment.

"Can you find out who is making the cars in South Africa?"

He said he could, and after that I kind of forgot about the topic for a while.

However, I was intrigued by the South African product, but I'm not sure exactly why. I didn't have any specific project in mind; but in the back of my mind I had the sprouts of an idea brewing, and I wasn't sure how to implement it.

Instead of a Cobra, what if somebody could build a "replica" of a street rod but with top-quality components and expert fit and finish?

I knew I would need some help with the development of such a project, in terms of manufacturing expertise. It's one thing to build various performance components like we do now, but when you start talking about creating an automobile from scratch, you've entered a new dimension.

In due course Dick tracked down some information for me. The man in South Africa who did the Cobra work was Jim Price, and the company was called Super Performance.

I made a blind phone call, without writing him in advance. Jim got on the phone, and we talked.

"I really like the quality of your stuff," I said. "Would you be interested in building something along the lines of a street rod?"

He hardly knew what a street rod was. He seemed warm to the idea, and we finished our cordial conversation with a promise to talk some more down the road.

Six months went by and Jim investigated the street rod market a little bit. He called me back, and this time he was much more enthusiastic.

"That would really be something," he said of a potential product. "Let me fly up there and we'll talk."

He showed up in Lincoln on July 4, 2000, and we hit it off perfectly. He was very much an Englishman from South Africa, and maybe it was because my ancestors on both my mother and dad's side were English helped me feel instantly comfortable with Jim. We really clicked.

Everything he said, everything we talked about, there was no bullshit, no stretching the truth, no exaggerating, no nothing. Everything was right, and we saw eye to eye on nearly everything. It was one of those "made in Heaven" friendships.

We struck a deal to build some cars together. Jim had somehow acquired a bunch of stamping equipment from General Motors, and had it shipped to South Africa. Now, these were serious pieces of equipment; some of the presses were over three stories tall, and they are sunk one story into the ground so they don't shake the whole city when they operate.

We talked about what type of car we wanted to build.

"Well, everybody is building a '32 Ford roadster in fiberglass," I suggested. "Let's build a steel car."

"That's right on," he said. "That's what I want to do."

When I say "build a car," that's literally what I meant.

Notice I didn't say "kit." Everybody has built kits, for years. Hell, we were building "Kookie T-bucket" kits in the early 1950s and '60s, based on the popularity of a '23 T-bucket on the television show "77 Sunset Strip" and driven by a character named Kookie.

For the Signature Series, I thought this thing out very carefully. I wanted the car to be as turnkey as possible, yet leave the buyer some leeway in critical areas.

So I decided to build the complete car ready to roll, minus engine and transmission. And I mean "ready to roll." Wiring, plumbing, interior, steering, suspension...you just drop in your choice of engine and transmission and you're ready to take a ride.

In my eyes, this was critical. This would give a guy the best of all worlds: A beautiful, complete car, yet with his choice of power. You can put the finishing touches on the car as your own "signature," just like I would want if I were buying such a car.

Some guys would want to use a Ford engine. Other guys want a Chevy. One guy might want a 500-ci fire-breather, but another guy wants a nice little 302 for easy cruises to the street rod meets.

You want a 4-speed; I might want an automatic. Or 5-speed. Or 6-speed. Or an old M-22 rock crusher that sings to you when you cruise.

Your car. Your choice. Just like it ought to be.

I began the rigorous process of designing the car and all the components. It was a big undertaking, a significant amount of work. I had not been involved in anything along this scale, and it was exciting. But a lot of work, too.

The design work was a key part of the project. Jim and his staff didn't know these cars in the detail I did, and I knew how important the little details were. I poured every piece of knowledge from my lifetime involvement in cars into this process. Yes, every nut and bolt! Little things like where you mount the headlights, where do you mount the radiator, things like that. How do the radius rods go, and how far?

Every piece was orchestrated from scratch; it wasn't just copied. This was truly going to be an original car, based on the '32 Ford.

From all of this, Jim and his guys at Super Performance went to work. They developed the intricate tooling that would create the body and trim pieces, to exacting, rigorous specifications.

They then focused on the assembly, and the finish work. All along the way Jim was terrific to work with; we were of like minds here, because we both poured our heart and soul out in the quest of building the perfect street rod.

A year and a half later, my first one arrived. Boy, it was as perfect as it could be…what a wonderful feeling! You talk about having babies…and they were pretty, too!

When I opened the back of the shipping container and rolled that baby out, I almost wet down both legs, because it was really something. The attention to detail, and everything was done right…nothing compromised, nothing screwed up.

To get it perfect on the first try like we did, that was sensational. It was far beyond anything anybody has ever tried in our industry, I think.

You can probably tell, I'm still jazzed about this car, and this project. See, if you do this thing with cars long enough, you understand that rarely does something actually live up to expectations, and measure up to what you hoped for. Well, this one did. You grow cynical that it probably won't happen, and when you *do* get it right the "Wow!" factor is off the charts.

Most of this, I think, is because as a car guy you realize how hard it is to get things right, especially on the first try.

Throughout my lifetime of race cars and street rods and whatever, each time I built an engine or a car—anything, for that matter—as soon as I got it finished I would immediately say, "The next one I build, I'll change this, this, and this…"

It's always going to be better on the next round.

And that's always been the problem in the production end of everything we made: We were focused on making it better every time, not on the easiest way to produce it.

For example, when we were building sprint cars in the 1970s, we were focused on making them better. We were trying to build a perfect product, only we could never get it perfect because we were constantly changing the production process to accommodate all our "improvements."

We got knocked off so easily it was almost funny, because somebody came along who could built it much quicker, cheaper, easier, faster, and they beat us in price (not quality, by the way).

Sometimes it isn't just how "good" something is; it's about other things such as availability and value.

The Signature Series '32 has been one of the most reaffirming things I've ever experienced. Everybody I've showed it to has experienced the "Wow!" factor. And everybody who has the resources to buy this car, who knows good from bad and right from wrong, has bought this car.

For example, my good friend Jim Voyles bought car No. 1 at the Indianapolis Hotrod & Restoration Trade Show at our unveiling. Jim bought it 20 minutes after seeing it for the first time. Now, here is a guy with an IQ of 175-plus, and has been around all kinds of race cars and hot rods, a guy who clearly has a background in this sort of thing. Jim is married to Joan, the daughter of 1950 Indianapolis 500 winner Johnnie Parsons.

Ken Schrader also bought one, almost immediately. Everybody who has bought one just fell in love with it, just like I did the moment I opened that very first shipping container.

If you're a car guy, you understand.

It's that feeling of wanting something so badly; you'd trade almost anything in your life for it. Simply because it gives you such a great feeling. The intangible.

Now, the hard question: Has the project been a success from a business standpoint?

Oh, probably not. For many reasons, including my difficult geographic location. I don't have 10 million people at my doorstep like they do in southern California. It's harder for me to get the car in front of the right people.

If I lived in southern California I would drive that car around all day with a sign on it, and would probably sell a bunch of 'em.

Dealers? I could have gone that route, but I didn't. That sort of thing has to be orchestrated and managed, and who is going to do that properly? I could do it myself, but that's another job for Bill to do, and I don't need any other jobs.

I know in my heart I have the ability to make the car more successful. I would gladly take that challenge, but priorities figure into all this, and I can't justify taking time from managing my company to focus on one single project, no matter how emotionally appealing it is.

As an aside, I have done similar projects before. Some years ago we built a slightly scaled-down replica of a Mercedes SL convertible that was so "right," the mechanics at the Mercedes garage literally mistook it for one of their cars.

I did the Shay Model A project, and the '32 Ford lowboy project. The '32 lowboy was the only car to be on the cover of *Hot Rod Magazine* twice; once as an unassembled kit, and again as an assembled car.

These were things I built in my mind long before a weld was ever struck. Not on a sketchpad, or in a blueprint, but in my mind.

So you're probably wondering: Would I undertake the Signature Series again, 10 years later?

Probably so, because I'm a car guy.

I don't think my financial guys would say it's a good idea, and I doubt my sons would say it's a good idea.

However, the sense of accomplishment I got from building the Signature Series has been incredible. Knowing we built a car that was literally perfect right out of the box, that gives me tremendous pride.

The "proof is in the pudding," and in this case the pudding turned out perfectly right. The best pudding anyone could have imagined.

Business is business, but there is still room for some artistic expression. In the world of Speedy Bill, anyway. We didn't make a lot of money with that car, but we created a helluva car.

And, if you're a car guy, doesn't that count for something? Hell, a car guy will tell you it counts for *everything*.

That car makes a statement, and in essence it is saying: This is what Speedy Bill Smith is about. Getting it right because of the beauty of a hot rod, street rod, '32 Ford. The beauty of a car being a part of you, and you want it as perfect as it can be, both aesthetically and mechanically.

Plus, that car is a testament to my tenacity, if nothing else. People told me I was crazy to want to manufacture an all-steel '32 from scratch, but we did it. And we did it *right!*

31

On The Horizon

As I travel around the country to races and street rod shows and various functions, I get this question a lot:

"Hey, Speedy, what's going to happen in the future in our industry? Are we going to be okay?"

I don't have a crystal ball; if I did, I sure would've made a lot fewer mistakes over the past 60 years! However, I do try to listen and study and learn, and I constantly think about things in the context of the "big picture."

Like anybody, I want the things I love to be successful. Hey, if you've got this far in this book, you already know two things: I love racing, and I love everything related to automotive performance. I love cars; street rods or hot rods or whatever you want to call 'em, in almost any form. Ultramodern or retro rods, everyday cruisers or exotic machines, sprint cars or stock cars or Indy cars or modifieds or whatever.

I *love* these things, almost like I love my own family. Love them in a way that only a fellow "car guy" could understand. I'm not embarrassed or ashamed to say how much cars and racing mean to me. It's my passion and I wouldn't want it any other way.

The world has changed so much in my lifetime I can't even begin to express it. Obviously, if you're more than 30 years old, you understand. Even at age 30 you've seen tremendous change from when you were, say, 15. So imagine the change witnessed by an 80-year-old guy like me.

Endless change. Constant and tremendous change.

So what changes are coming? Nobody knows for sure, but I believe one thing in my heart: The performance industry is not going to die.

If gas went to $8 per gallon, people would still find a way to race and mess with cars. If the government banned all forms of automotive expression, you'd see all the car guys retreat into the shadows, and they would secretly still do their thing. They would because they can't help it: They're addicted, and cars are their fix.

About the only way our industry would totally, completely go away is if the U.S. lost all our freedoms, and our civilization disappeared. And I really don't see that happening anytime soon.

I am an eyewitness to the growth of automotive performance from literally nothing to a multi-billion dollar industry, over a span of more than 60 years.

Am I surprised that our fascination with the automobile has lasted this long? No, because it's a very powerful emotion. Just like me playing with toy cars in my sandbox at age five, or creating my own wooden cart with a Maytag washing machine motor. That tiny little impulse in my brain led to an interest that fueled my life. Look around in the pit area at the race track, or at the street rod show, or among muscle car guys talking about their rides at the Saturday night drive in: Those guys have a huge, powerful passion for cars, and performance.

You're not going to simply "outgrow" such a thing. Hell, I've got plenty of friends in their 70s and 80s and they're just about as consumed now as they were when they were a kid. It never went away, and it never does go away.

That's why I'm so optimistic. Sure, we've got some challenges facing us, but the ace up our sleeve is the total passion so many people have for our sport, whether you're talking racing or the performance hobby.

I recently saw on television a program that was created in 1936 about the soapbox derby. Boy, was it ever great! It told about the young lads of the day, and how they got into building their own downhill soapbox derby cars.

Those boys had that quotient in their being, that spark that got them fired up about their project. If you have that spark, it's almost always a natural progression to lead you to bigger and faster things.

I can't take a needle and draw a pint of my blood and inject it into somebody else and transfer that spark to them. It doesn't work like that. However, if you've got that spark in one form, it often translates into a similar form.

For example, many of my friends from racing—Jackie Howerton, Lee Osborne, Ken Schrader and Johnny Rutherford come to mind—are into street rods these days. The list goes on and on; it's a natural progression in the world of wheels. They're using their creative talents, and their passion for cars, only they're applying them in a different way.

So I'm not a bit surprised that our industry has sustained itself for so many years.

All of this is, for better or worse, a form of artistic expression. No two people are going to create something exactly alike, just like no two paintings are alike. No two hot rods are exactly alike, either. Which is good.

Go to a National Street Rod Association meet in Louisville, Ky., and you're likely to find a cozy little group of 12,000 of your closest friends. The concept is exactly like when I was 16 years old, eager to see what other guys were doing with their cars. Baby moon hubcaps? Neat. Smitty mufflers? Even neater. More horsepower? Neater still.

It's probably going to be like this until we are all cruising around in space ships. And then, naturally, guys will make their spaceships look different and faster and cooler than the other guy.

Not long ago we saw gasoline at nearly $3.50 per gallon, and people are talking about alternative forms of energy such as hydrogen fuel cells. Don't panic; they've been trying alternative energy forms in automobiles for quite some time, but the internal combustion engine has been an unbeatable form so far. I've got several electric cars in my museum from many years ago; some alternatives will prove viable, others will not.

The beat goes on.

A few years ago, this story was related to me, and I got a tremendous kick out of it.

In 1958 a young street rodder from Ceresco, Neb. traveled the 15 miles to Speedway Motors to buy parts for his '36 Ford coupe. Doug Swanson was 12 years old at the time, and his older brother "Stub" had brought him to town.

Doug related to me how he and his younger brother came to Lincoln each Saturday morning for swimming lessons at the YMCA located just down the street from my shop. They would sneak away from the "Y" early, run to Speedway, and then get back to the "Y" before their parents arrived to pick them up. Kids never change, it seems.

Through the years, the boys could hardly wait for Saturday and the trip to Lincoln—and Speedway. I was always trading, so I had a big selection of used goodies on display. This inventory changed constantly, and the Swanson boys were like many of my customers; they loved our "used" section.

Doug laughed as he recalled how his father and his uncle always had a fit when they discovered that the boys were hanging out at Bill Smith's hot rod shop.

That "car" thing...it's awfully addictive, isn't it?

Fast forward to today: 2009 was a special year for celebrating over in Ceresco. Swanson Ford celebrated 100 years of success, and they received great honors and tribute from Ford Motor Company as the fifth-oldest family dealership in the U.S. The same family, the same building, in the same town. Wonderful!

Doug and Elaine run the dealership; "Stub" and Diane have the body shop. Younger brother Gary is a railroader, but he was an early Speedway Motors counter man.

The Swanson family are real "car guys" who share with me a love of Ford, Model T's, and racing. They are exactly why I love this industry, and why I feel it's got a great future. The passion we have for our hobby is as strong as ever.

There will always be trends in the automotive performance world. Right now, for example, the trend is toward nostalgia. There's lots of activity in flathead Ford engines, and the six-cylinder Chevrolet engine has seen a resurgence. Older pickups are now popular again.

There is renewed interest in the things guys saw in their teens, things they couldn't afford at the time. Now they have some time and money, so they're buying and recreating the things that excited them as a younger person. This will continue, I hope, because at Speedway Motors we address many of those customer needs.

We've also seen a big resurgence in muscle cars, although the recent price escalation has taken many models beyond the range of the everyday person to afford. However, on the cover of a popular car magazine the other day I saw a big headline: "Rides You Can Still Afford!" The magazine listed several lesser-known muscle cars that are still very affordable.

So people are still very much interested in buying and building and creating to satisfy their passion for cars.

Remember, this is our hobby. It isn't curing cancer, or seeking world peace. The guy who owns a bass boat isn't going to throw it away, because that's his passion, and he's going to stick with it even though the bass might not be biting for a period of time.

When I opened my speed shop in 1952, I was in my early 20s. As I looked across the counter at my customer, he was typically a young guy, close to my age. You didn't see anybody in their 40s or 50s or 60s involved with hot rods and speed equipment.

As those young guys from 1952 grew up and grew older, many stayed with the hobby, and now we've seen them progress through an entire lifetime.

But what of today's young boys and young men? Are they going to be as interested in street rods, performance equipment, and auto racing?

How we get that 15-year-old kid interested is our greatest challenge. Everybody is trying to do this, and not just the performance industry. McDonald's tries to attract their future buyer of Big Macs by putting playgrounds and so forth in their restaurants.

But how do you attract the young street rodder, other than their dad being a street rodder himself?

It's part of our evolution, but it's also a big challenge. The generation gaps today are huge, and I mean *huge*. With our changing technology, media, culture, and so forth, the ideas and thoughts of a 15-year-old kid and someone 25, 45, 65 years old is enormous.

The difference between my dad and me was not that great; but the difference between my sons and me is great. They are very computer savvy, and they know so much more about how to use electronic tools. Welding techniques, painting techniques, machining techniques, lasers; everything today is done differently than how I was taught.

Almost everything technical I was taught 60 years ago is irrelevant today. We have discovered better ways to do nearly everything, and technology has moved so quickly in recent years I find myself amazed. All of this factors into the issue of younger people discovering our sport.

One element that *does* concern me is that many young men today were brought up on computer games. This is a no-work environment; just flick your fingers, and things happen. Young people are like anybody else: They take the path of least resistance.

To attract them is going to take many different things.

But remember something: Relatively speaking, hardcore automotive enthusiasts have always been a small percentage of our population. That's good news; we don't need to recruit *all* the young guys today, just a small percentage, like it's always been.

And I think we'll do it. The automotive and racing hobbies are so wonderful, there will be a certain percentage of younger people who will naturally stumble into it.

We just need to make sure we keep our sport interesting, and affordable, for the next generation. Don't get so caught up in "the way it used to be" that we dig in our heels and refuse to change with the times.

Although I love auto racing with a deep passion, I do think the sport has some challenges ahead, mainly because we lost sight of some fundamental things a few years ago.

Something I have been talking about for quite some time is that we need to begin explaining our sport better through the media. The vast majority of people who don't follow racing don't know anything about it, or they have false ideas about what they *think* it is all about.

If we told the story of what we do to the mainstream — I mean what our sport is truly all about — I think more people would be drawn to the sport.

For example, look at high school basketball or football. It isn't about money, or glitz, or glamour; it's about competition, at the local level. That competition gets entire towns fired up, because they want to beat their rival. They *care* about what happens at that Friday-night game.

If we would project the same sort of story, I think people would respond. If we could capture the essence of our competition, and our intensity, it would create a natural curiosity among people who don't know much about our sport.

"Last week Joe Jones beat his arch rival Mike Smith on the last lap, and this week...it's revenge, baby!" Build the rivalries, just like they are built between rival teams in other sports. Where the match, the game, the race, they really mean something.

Put a bounty on your top driver, and make him come from the back of the pack with a $500 bonus on the line. He's a wanted man! Guess what? People are going to come to the races that night because they are curious what might happen.

At least *some* of them will. They might be thinking, "Well, I was going to the movies or the picnic or even just sit home and watch TV, but...boy, I'd sure like to see what's going to happen to the guy with the bounty on his head. Can he win again? I don't want to miss this...let's go to the races."

Drag racing used to be very good at this, particularly with the match races it promoted. Shirley Muldowney versus Don

Garlits; there was something at stake, something bigger than just a race. They promoted it as an intense competition that meant something.

Racing was very, very dangerous throughout my lifetime. Today it is much less dangerous, which of course is a good thing because we don't want people getting hurt.

However, we've also lost some of the allure, the sensation of speed and the element of danger.

The cars go 225 mph at Indianapolis, but so what? When you get into an airplane and fly to California, you go 500 mph. Big deal. And you get off the plane with no sensation of speed at all. Speed is relative to the surroundings, and people understand that today.

The sizzle on the steak is creating the competition within the race. I've said this for a long time: We've taken the racing out of the sport. We need to let 'em race. In the World of Outlaws sprint cars, for example, when the fast guy starts on the front he can often wave goodbye to the field. With the equipment they have today, there is very little chance anyone can catch him or pass him, particularly on a bigger track.

One of the greatest things I ever witnessed was when my driver Lloyd Beckman won every feature race for over a year and a half in my '32 modified sedan. It was sensational, because they started Lloyd at the back every week. Starting 24th in a 24-car field for 25 laps...*that's* what created excitement.

"Can Lloyd win again this week? Say, he might get beat, and I don't want to miss it!" The big crowds proved people were hungering to see it happen. Some wanted to see him win, but more wanted to see him get beat. Either way, there was excitement. I still have old-time racing fans approach me and relive the Beckman/4x days. They never forget!

But how do we create such a racing experience today? They've tried to tweak the specs, but they've created cars that have a difficult time passing each other.

For example, the cars of my generation could really race with each other. These old eyes saw it firsthand, believe me. But look at today's cars: They have 10 times the amount of footprint on the race track as the cars I grew up with. Instead of tweaking things, they should look at the obvious.

Take away some tire. Take away some aero. Make the cars wiggle, make them difficult, make them hard to drive. Then watch them pass each other. That's what will get people fired up about tonight's race.

One of the problems plaguing our sport is not a new one. There are many smart people who have studied various problems in racing, but almost all of them have come at the problem with a personal agenda, or some financial incentive. It's human nature; people want to take care of themselves. Greed is the prevailing factor, almost always.

The tire companies are not going to solve the issue of too much traction. The engine companies are not going to solve the problem of engines costing too much. The shock companies are not going to solve the problem of the cars being too good, too hooked up. Not going to happen, not now, not ever.

Somebody has to step up and lead. If they don't, the sport is really going to be challenged.

Yet, I'm optimistic about our industry, and our sport. I still believe we have some really good days ahead of us.

One big change I've seen in my lifetime is public perception. When I got involved with cars as a teenage kid, we all hung out at gas stations and got dirty working under a car. People called us "greasers" and we were looked down upon.

You don't have that today. Both racing and the performance industry have been accepted socially by the mainstream, and that can only help. No longer does a mother quickly shun her kid away from a good-looking car because she fears he will become a "greaser."

In fact, parents spend money to send their kids to college to study automotive technology, and even racing technology! That's a far cry from the attitudes of earlier years.

I'm bullish on street rods and racing. Yes, we've got some work to do, but the foundation is very, very strong.

That's been a great part of my life. It's been wonderful to watch our sport grow, to be embraced by so many in the mainstream, to be an accepted part of society today.

In a way, that's the ultimate. To see something you love with all your heart, grow and become stronger and healthier.

I've seen a lot of great, wonderful things in these 80 years. But maybe that fact—that the love for automobiles and racing is as strong as ever—is the best one of all.

32

Legacy

It's a busy morning here at Speedway Motors, and I'm sitting in my office, surrounded by evidence of what seems like a thousand different projects. Paperwork, publications, things to review and proof, financial documents, letters and e-mails from friends and associates, and feedback from customers regarding recent orders.

I couple of months ago I celebrated my 80th birthday. I would guess that most 80 year olds aren't in the office every day, working 60-hour weeks. But work is all I've known—for better or worse—so it still seems natural to stay busy.

I have reached a point where I think more and more about my lifetime, the things I experienced, the people and situations I encountered, and what it all means. I'm not a guy who thinks really deeply about "the meaning of life" or that sort of thing, but living a long, eventful life kind of inspires you to think a little bit about the impact your life might have had on others.

I suppose that's really the reason I wrote this book. Oh, it's an ego trip, of course, to talk about all the things you've done, to tell your stories. And I do have a pretty healthy ego; that's good, in my opinion, because ego helps you get fired up and makes you want to succeed and accomplish things.

The most important message that I hope comes out is this: To get from Point A to Point B in life, and to accomplish things, requires a super desire and effort and a tremendous focus on whatever it is you're after. Just like my dad always told me: "Keep your eye on the ball." At 80 years old I still believe that's one of the most important life lessons I've ever heard. (In fact, I'm convinced that it's more important *today* than ever before, because there are so many distractions.)

See, that's just it. I was very fortunate to have so many good people helping me along the way, with good advice and guidance and inspiration. My dad, Milo Caslasky, Wally Smith, Hynie Hompes, Howard Johansen, and countless others. They were awfully good to me; I've tried hard down through the years to be equally good to anyone who asked for my help. I owed them that much, in order to pay back the many good things people had done for me.

This book is like one final extension of that. It's kind of like writing a note and sticking it in the bottle, then throwing it into the ocean. Maybe it will reach somebody else and give them inspiration or guidance or encouragement or whatever, long after I'm gone.

More than anything else, I want to get this message across: There are no "gimmes" in life. Even if somebody left you the farm, you'd better quickly figure out that it's going to take a lot of effort to keep it going, to hold onto it.

In my opinion, this isn't been taught to the younger people of today. We're sparing them from some awfully important life lessons. In fact, I think we're telling them it's going to be *easier* than it really is. We're not being honest about the sacrifice and effort it takes to be successful.

So if anybody — especially a young person — can get one thing out of all the crazy stories in this book, that's the key point: You are 100-percent responsible for making something of yourself.

Not your mom, not your dad, not your teachers, not your friends, not your boss at work, not your spouse, not the government.

You. It's all on you.

It's been that way for a long, long time. They've changed this ol' world a lot through the past hundred or so years, but they can't change that reality. If you want success, you've got to focus and work and go out and get it.

You.

If you haven't already figured this out, I'm a guy who is fired up about life. Every day when I wake up, I look forward to the day. I've still got that powerful spark of life, that desire to experience all the things this world offers.

Within the last year I had triple-bypass heart surgery and later suffered with pneumonia. In fact, on Christmas Day I was stuck in bed with pneumonia, the first time I've ever been down with something like that. I hated it; I wanted to get back to work, back into the world, back to places like the Chili Bowl where I would see all my friends.

A couple of times in my life they came very close to pulling the sheet over me and walking away. But each time — and when I've endured other less critical health challenges — there was a powerful spark within me that kept me going.

When the Grim Reaper was standing in the doorway looking at me, something inside me said, "No, I'm not gonna go with you just yet, because there are a lot of things I still want to see and do."

And I still feel that way. I love life; I love my family, my friends, my work. I still love watching race cars do their thing. I love looking over a nice street rod and talking with the owner, him telling me how he built his car and all the neat things he did to it.

The spark of life is something you have to nurture, I think. If you stick it in the dark closet, you'll probably die. It won't get the sunlight and water it needs to survive. You have to feed your spark, with stuff like optimism and hope and good things.

In my case, I really am excited about the future. Yes, there will be challenges, but boy, it's going to be an interesting time. I want to see as much of it as possible. There will be *huge* opportunities there, and new things we haven't even conceived in our minds yet. Isn't that interesting? I think so.

One of the things I've struggled to balance — probably just like all other human beings — is the fact that while lots of good things happen in our lives, lots of bad things happen as well.

On the plus side, I've had a great life. Joyce is the ideal wife and partner, and she's the best friend I've ever had. My four sons are good men and not only do I love them like a dad, but I like them, too. I like being around them, and we work well together.

I was blessed with a lot of business success, and my cars won a helluva bunch of races. No kidding, a lot of good things happened to me.

On the flip side, I don't know that I can adequately describe what a struggle my health has been at various times in my life. I had a ton of "sheet time," leading to many dark and difficult days.

And I can't describe the pain I endured in those early years when I lost so many friends in a race car. That was an awful, awful time in that respect. You make friends with someone, enjoy their company, and then see them get killed right before your eyes. I don't care if your ass is made of leather, experiences like that leave a mark on you.

I suspect some people might look at me from a distance and say, "Well, Smith, he's got it made. Made all that money with the race car, the speed shop, so he's got it pretty easy."

Boy, is that wrong. For every success I had, there was a setback. For every "lucky" break, something went wrong.

Listen, if what I've experienced is an "easy" life, I'm not brave enough to try a "hard" life! It's kind of like that old saying: The harder I work, the luckier I get.

And that's where tenacity comes in. I might not be anything else, but I'm a tenacious bastard. My competitive spirit channeled into a form where I figured that even if the other guy had more money/skill/luck, I could outwork him and outlast him.

My fear of failure was mighty. *Mighty!* I feared failure more than death. That kind of fear can be a pretty good motivator, but it also makes for some miserable soul-searching times.

I vividly remember a period in October of 1953, when I was at a crossroads with my business. The racing season was over, the fair circuit had come and gone, the kids had gone back to school, and winter was coming. Everybody had spent all their "hobby" money for the year, and it seemed like nobody had one extra penny to let go of.

For a period of almost four weeks, not one person walked into my store. Not one. Now, those are tough days, standing there looking at the front door and hoping it will open, trying to think of anything I could do to get people to come in.

I remember getting into my car and driving for 40 miles, depressed, confused, scared, upset. The leaves were falling, and I drove along to clear my mind, to try and make sense of what was happening.

"What in the hell am I doing?" I remember thinking. "Am I on the right path or the wrong path? Should I go back and lock my front door and quit, or should I keep going?"

Yeah, ol' Smith had it pretty easy.

I'm confident as hell — some would even say I'm cocky — but I'm human. I've second-guessed myself nearly every day for 60 years.

But my tenacity served me well. Even in tough times — and frankly I love tough times for this reason — you can outwork the other guy, and you can probably make it. My tenacity, and my fear of failure, kept me and my business alive.

A couple of months ago a pleasant young man from Chicago called me. He explained he worked for one of the big conglomerates in our business, and asked if Speedway Motors was for sale.

"We've examined your business," he said, "and we think it would be a wonderful acquisition for our company."

He asked me what I thought. Instead of just saying, "No, I'm busy, forget it," I listened patiently to his ideas. You can always learn from such a conversation, and it's a chance to hear about how the world is turning these days. So we had talked for about 20 minutes and it was interesting.

At the end, though, I explained to the young man that Speedway Motors wasn't for sale.

Would we ever sell the company? I suppose anything is possible, and in another time...you never know. But it would be terribly difficult to sell something you've invested your heart and soul into for almost 60 years. Plus, it isn't just about me and Joyce; we have our sons and their families to think about, and so much more: our dedicated employees and their families, our suppliers, our partners, and our friends and acquaintances.

Business isn't always a black-and-white decision. There is a lot of emotion tied to the idea of selling something you've been a part of for so long.

But who knows? We go through cycles, like every company, and with most cycles we raise the bar on everything each year. We've kept our trends going up, but I've also been careful not to grow too quickly. One brick at a time, not 10 bricks at a time; and don't put the roof on until you've got the walls not just up, but nice and sturdy.

Anybody who has done anything at all in life probably thinks about his legacy. That's only natural. And I guess doing this book has made me think about my legacy more than I thought about it before.

Not everybody gets to live for 80 years, so I've done okay in terms of longevity. Then again, lots of people live far longer; I'm a long way, I hope, from them closing the lid on me.

I suppose the museum is the number-one component of my legacy, because it's a tangible thing. You can walk inside and directly see the results of some of my work. And Speedway Motors, as well; on any work day you can walk through and see a bunch of hardworking people taking orders, filling orders, shipping orders, and making customers happy. That's a tangible thing that I set in motion in 1952.

The other parts of a legacy are not so tangible.

I've had countless friends, and hope I've been as good a friend to them as they were to me.

I loved racing, and it gave me years and years of pleasure. I hope I gave back as much as I got.

I loved cars and performance, and it enhanced my life more than I could ever explain. Cars and racing...that *was* my life. From day one I felt an obligation to make the hobby as strong and as good as it could be; I hope I've done that.

Naturally, I hope I've been okay as a dad and as a grandfather. Probably a better grandfather; I was gone almost all the time when our boys were young, chasing that damned race car. Lucky for me Joyce and our parents were there to pick up the slack.

It's pretty unlikely I've been as good a husband as Joyce has been a wife. I mean, how could I measure up to what she's meant to me? Every step, every minute, every day, she's been right there with me. Even as tenacious as I am, I doubt I could have reached this point without her. Hell, even if I made it this far, it wouldn't have been *near* as much fun without her.

Most of all, I appreciate *you*. If you're reading this book, you've at least shown an interest in my life, and probably been a customer, an employee, a business associate, a friend, or just a fan of racing and rods. Maybe I even raced against you!

Either way, I appreciate that so many people have been good to me along the way.

When I travel around the country and visit car shows or races or conventions, people tell me they appreciate my efforts in racing or street rods or whatever. Gee, that's the most wonderful thing a guy could hear. You can't buy that; you have to earn it.

When someone says things like that, it's the greatest affirmation that maybe I've done something right in my life.

So we'll wrap this thing up with a word of thanks, and encouragement.

Thanks for reading. Thanks for sharing our passion for race cars and hot rods and life.

It's a great world out there, full of challenges and opportunities and a tremendous experience. Whatever your path, I hope you're a success, and I hope you're happy.

Oh, and don't be a stranger. Come to Nebraska and see us, and visit our museum. We'd like that, very much.

That's pretty much it. That's the way I see it. That's *the world according to Speedy Bill!*

Index

Kunzman, Lee *238*

Lake Powell *220*
Lakeside, Kan. *234*
Landis Field *70*
Larson, John *22, 256*
Larson, Roger *235*
Las Vegas Convention Center *261*
Las Vegas, Nev. *82, 230, 251*
Lawrence, Richard *126*
Lawton, Bob *140, 313*
Leavitt, Eddie *178, 225*
Lee, Tommy *216*
Leep, Harold *186*
Leikam, Leona *218, 219*
Leikam, Pete *165, 218–221*
LeMay, Gen. Curtis *41*
Levernz, John *167*
Levi Straus Clothing Comp. *306*
Lincoln Air Base *54, 100*
Lincoln Airfield *41*
Lincoln, Calif. *250*
Lincoln, Don *142*
Lincoln engine *136*
Lincoln High School *43, 149*
Lincoln Telephone and Telegraph Co. 27
Little 500 *140, 182–185*
Lohn, Els *264*
Long Beach, Calif. *140*
Los Angeles, Calif. *144, 269, 296, 298*
Louis XV art *299*
Louisville, Ky. *328*
Lund, Tiny *60, 86, 94, 111–120*
Lundberg, Bob *73, 86, 90, 91, 93, 94, 190*

M&H tire *183*
M-22 rock crusher transmission *322*
Magnaflux *20, 217*
magnesium wheels *128, 138*
Manning, Peyton *145*
Manzanita Speedway *173, 225*
Marsh, John *79, 140, 256*
Martin, Dick *229*
Masters Classic *144*
Mattingly, Rev. *47*
Maxwell, Don *22, 176, 210, 211, 212–216, 224, 227*
Maxwell, Sandy *212*
Maytag Corporation *306*
McCullough go kart engine *107*
McCullough supercharger *106, 116*
McDonald's restaurants *330*
McElreath, Jim *208*

McKee, Bobby *111, 115–118*
McSpadden, Lealand *229*
mechanical brakes *105*
mechanical rabbits *142, 217*
Mechanix Illustrated magazine *36*
Meguiar, Barry *284*
Mercedes SL *325*
Mercury Cougar *179*
Messer, Dick *284*
Methodist Hospital *161, 208*
midget racing *67*
Midwest Auto Supply *262*
Midwest Speedway *144, 164, 170, 218*
Milford, Neb. *105*
Milford Trade School *79, 256*
Miller, Ak *41*
Miller and Paine *54*
Miller, Harry *293*
Milwaukee, Wisc. *110, 115*
Minneapolis, Minn. *152*
Minyard, Hal *183*
Mirage Lake *41*
Misle family *192*
Mississippi River *148, 200*
Missouri River *111, 137, 189*
Missouri Synod Lutheran *47*
Model T *59*
modified racing *127, 140*
Mondelo, Joe *264*
Montgomery Ward *63*
Moon, Dean *264, 270, 297*
moonshine *99*
Moore, Jerry J. *299–301*
Motor Trend magazine *266*
Moyer, Bill *141*
Mr. Gasket *264, 269, 272*
Mr. Gasket shifter *273*
Mr. Phone *153*
Mr. Roadster *260*
Muhammad Ali *113, 122*
Muldowney, Shirley *331*
Muroc Lake *41*
muscle cars *266, 329*
Museum of Science and Industry *46*

N Street *147*
Nagasaki *41*
Nance, LaVern *212*
NASCAR *89, 90, 94, 114, 114–120, 117, 118, 119, 124, 135, 221, 226*
Nash Motor Comp. *266*
Nashville, Tenn. *215*
National Dragster magazine *267*
National Speed Sport News *24, 117, 132*

"Speedy" Bill Smith and Speedway Motors Achievements

2009 NSRA Best New Product Award
Goodguys Best New Product Award
Robert E. Petersen Lifetime Achievement Award
2008 Hot Rod Industry Alliance Business of the Year
National Rod & Custom Car Hall of Fame Lifetime Achievement Award
2007 Rod & Custom Magazine Lifetime Achievement Award
Big Car Racing Association Hall of Fame
NebraskaLand Foundation Trailblazer Award
2006 Hot Rod Industry Alliance Hall of Fame
NSRA Best New Product Award
USAC Distinguished Service and Contribution Award
Nebraska Wesleyan University Alumni Achievement Award
Lincoln High School Distinguished Alumni Award
2005 Model T Ford Club of America Speedster and Racer Hall of Fame
2004 Honoree at NHRA Hot Rod Reunion
2003 Grand Marshall, Cornhusker Vintage Nationals
2001 Grand Marshall, Goodguys Street Rod Nationals
Ernst & Young Entrepreneur of the Year
2000 National Sprint Car Hall of Fame
NSRA Lifetime Achievement Award
Commercial Rehabilitation Award
Diamond Benefactor Award, Cedars Home for Children
1999 Belleville High Banks Hall of Fame
Grand Marshall, Belleville Midget Nationals
Inducted into the Nebraska Great Navy
Behlen Building of the Year Award
Community Improvement Award
President's Award, Near South Neighborhood Association
1998 Top 100 Hot Rodders, Hot Rod Magazine
Nebraska Auto Racing Hall of Fame
Grand Marshall, KKOA Nationals
Community Improvement Award
President's Award, Southwest Business Association
1997 Community Improvement Award
1996 Classic Car Hall of Fame, Auburn, Ind.
1995 Stroker McGurk Award
Key to the City, Lincoln, Neb.
Builder's Award, Downtown Development Association
1994 Community Improvement Award
1993 Cornerstone Award from City of Lincoln
1992 Performance Pro Award, Argus Publications
1991 Community Improvement Award
NSRA Man of the Year
1986 Pioneer Award, Performance Warehouse Association
1984 SEMA Hall of Fame

Also by Dave Argabright

Still Wide Open
with Brad Doty

American Scene
a collection

Hewitt's Law
with Jack Hewitt

EARL!
with Earl Baltes

Let 'Em All Go!
with Chris Economaki

Lone Wolf
with Doug Wolfgang

Reorder information:
American Scene Press
P.O. Box 11578
Indianapolis, IN 46201-0578
(317) 631-0437
www.americanscenepress.com
www.daveargabright.com

Speedway Motors
P.O. Box 81906
Lincoln, NE 68502
(800) 979-0122
(800) 736-3733 fax
www.speedwaymotors.com